DIALOGUES WITH MY GOD SELF

Understanding the Law of Love

Alvaro Bizziccari

Cover design by Anthony Zito
Interior design by Stephen Spignesi
Author photo by Karen Taylor
ISBN: 978-1-61640-740-7

Cosimo aims to publish books that inspire, inform, and engage readers worldwide. We use innovative print-on-demand technology that enables books to be printed based on specific customer needs. This approach eliminates an artificial scarcity of publications and allows us to distribute books in the most efficient and environmentally sustainable manner. Cosimo also works with printers and paper manufacturers who practice and encourage sustainable forest management, using paper that has been certified by the FSC, SFI, and PEFC whenever possible.

Ordering Information:
Cosimo publications are available at online bookstores. They may also be purchased for educational, business, or promotional use:
Bulk orders: Special discounts are available on bulk orders for reading groups, organizations, businesses, and others.
Custom-label orders: We offer selected books with your customized cover or logo of choice.

For more information, contact us at:

Cosimo, Inc.
P.O. Box 416, Old Chelsea Station
New York, NY 10011

info@cosimobooks.com

or visit us at:
www.cosimobooks.com

To Maria

Sister, Friend, Helper
On Our Journey Home

And to all
who believe in the
wisdom and power
of Divine Love

Let not the authority of the writer offend thee
Whether he be of great or small learning;
But let the love of pure truth draw thee to read.

THOMAS À KEMPIS

ACKNOWLEDGMENTS

My praise and thanks go first and foremost to the God Self for being the source of all that is good, true, and beautiful.

It is difficult to be grateful enough to **Stephen Spignesi** for his brilliant editorial work, the attractive vesture of the book, and the onerous project of preparing it for publication. I was impressed by his vast vision and recognition of the importance of this knowledge and his deep conviction that it will inspire, enlighten, and transform people's lives.

My deepest feeling of gratitude extends to **Karen Taylor**, who did more than perform admirably her role as my "word processor." Since I don't have a computer, not even a typewriter, I must depend entirely on my handwriting, and I didn't make her task easy. Karen had to disentangle my script often fraught with corrections, changes, and insertions, and she was able to read it even when I couldn't.

I am also very grateful to **John White** for agreeing to be my literary agent.

The copious references and frequently illustrative citing bespeak my indebtedness to the writing of others from whom I freely borrowed (or stole). My profound thanks are due to them and their publishers.

I must also thank you, my reader, for your interest in my book. You may go through it in any order you wish, choosing whichever chapter you desire and skipping the others. Follow the feeling in your heart and the knowledge you need to find will find you.

It would have been very helpful to receive critical comments and suggestions in order to enhance my text, which falls lamentably short of doing justice to its proposed subjects. But I seemed to be in a state of urgency to finish the book as if I were moved by an impelling cause and secret force.

I hope that what I have been enabled to accomplish in spite of its limitation, inevitable in a work of such magnitude, will help a world that is starving for love and cannot survive without it.

Alvaro Bizziccari
Storrs, Connecticut

CONTENTS

CHAPTER 1

A Chasing After Wind

Vanity of vanities, says the Teacher, vanity of vanities!
All is vanity...
Human beings came from their mother's womb,
so they shall go again, naked as they came; they shall take
nothing for their toil,
which they may carry away with their hands.
Ecclesiastes

The sun rises again and brightens everything in its path as the earth rejoices and drinks in its vivifying essence.

I see the treetops crowned with rays of light and hear the birds singing joyfully of the end of darkness. In the garden the flowers gratefully open their petals to embrace the warmth, and the wind is redolent with their perfume.

But this symphony of sounds and colors does not find an echo within me, tormented by the discordant cries of my passions. This is not the gift of another day, but an added burden I must carry, like Atlas condemned to stand and hold the sky on his shoulders.

What a pathetic contrast I present, the dark night of my soul eclipsing the glory of the morning light.

Oh, if I could only have some rest from this relentless hunger and blind strife, trying to satisfy my insatiable cravings, always pursued by the appalling sense of unreality and futility! I feel like someone lost in the desert, mouth parched by the heat, with the mirage of water always receding before him.

I am reminded of the myth of Tantalus: Perennially consumed by thirst and hunger, he is hanging from the bough of a fruit tree which leans over a marshy lake. Its waves lap against his waist, and sometimes reach his chin, yet whenever

1

he bends down to drink, they slip away, and nothing remains but the black mud at his feet; or, if he ever succeeds in scooping up a handful of water, it slips through his fingers before he can do more than wet his cracked lips, leaving him thirstier than ever. The tree is laden with pears, shining apples, sweet figs, ripe olives and pomegranates, which dangle against his shoulders; but whenever he reaches for the luscious fruit, a gust of wind whirls them out of his reach.[1]

Our human condition is worse than that of an animal, creatures satisfied by eating, sleeping and mating. I have not learned that "the eye is not satisfied with seeing, or the ear filled with hearing."[2] Successful though I am in every endeavor, this feeling of emptiness keeps tormenting me. I have wealth, I drowned myself in the bottomless ocean of pleasure, I can exert power over my fellow men, yet after gratifying any desire I have, the dreadful question emerges from the depth of my being: Is this all?

For instance, today I had the greatest time of my life, for one is really happy in the presence of the person he loves. We were enjoying each other's company, enacting and reciting the verses of "Love's Philosophy:"

> The fountains mingle with the river
> And the rivers with the Ocean,
> The winds of Heaven mix forever
> With a sweet emotion;
> Nothing in the world is single;
> All things by law divine
> In one spirit meet and mingle.
> Why I not with thine?[3]

But after a while, as I was watching the sun setting behind the hill, it came again, irrepressible, subtle, but with irresistible force like the shadows of the evening, that awful feeling: It is over. Every glimpse of happiness that may seem to brighten my days is both fugitive and deceptive.

The goals I set for myself, as soon as they are attained, lose their meaning. The excitement and pleasure of the peak is not the joy of fulfillment. Rather, the lack of it makes it necessary to seek ever new forms of excitation.

But I am more and more empty! It has been said...

Though thou pour the ocean into thy pitcher,
It can hold no more than one day's store.
The pitcher of the desire of the covetous never fills.[4]

...and this is what I feel. What is left after each achievement is sadness and disappointment. The search has ended and there is a yawning void inside me and a deep sense of futility.

I tried to be as faithful and as sincere a lover in my search for happiness, but I can identify with the Shakespearian character in *Troilus and Cressida* when he says: "This is the monstrosity in love, lady, that the will is infinite and the execution confined; that the desire is boundless and the act a slave to limit."[5]

I hear, too, the lament of another poetic voice addressing the spirit of beauty:

Why dost thou pass away and leave our state
This dim vast vale of tears, vacant and desolate?[6]

What kind of existence is this, subject to chance, sorrow and mutability, where everything that begins must inevitably end, envious time stealing our life from hour to hour till we face the dark reality of the grave? My days have not a real existence, they are gone as soon as they arrive, and after they come they cannot stay.

"Of the past nothing is called back again; what is yet to be expected is something which will pass away again; it is not yet possessed, whilst as yet it is not arrived; it cannot be kept when once it is arrived. The Psalmist therefore asks, 'What is the number of my days'?"[7]

What *is*, not what is *not*; and (for this confounds me by a still greater and more perplexing difficulty) both *is* and *is not.*

For we can neither say that that *is*, which does not continue, nor that it is *not* when it is come and is passing.

It is that absolute IS, that true IS, that IS in the strict sense of the word, that I long for, that IS where there shall be no death, where there will be no failing, where the day shall not pass away but shall endure, a day which no yesterday precedes not a morrow ousts. This number of my days, which *is*, I say make Thou known to me."[8] Oh, if I could believe in a beneficent God! Can such a being exist?

Yes, "I AM" the one who IS!

What is it? Did someone speak to me or am I dreaming?
You have never been more awake.

Hearing voices can be a sign of mental disorder.
Not in this case.

How do I know? I am no Joan of Arc.
You will judge by the fruits.

But who *are* you?
I told you.

I mean, what is your name?
I told you My name.

You said only that you are.
My being is My name.

How can that be? I can change my name and yet be the same person that I am.
You think you know who you are, but that is a presumption.

It is true that arrogance is one of my bad traits of character.
You are as far from knowing who you are as heaven from earth.

I don't understand you.
Precisely. That has been the cause of all your troubles and distress.

Certainly something has been missing from my constitution.
I did not make you like that.

My goodness! Who is being presumptuous now! Are you my creator?

I am your God Self. My true name is I AM, though people call Me by many names.

I don't know what you mean by God Self.

I am the Source of your life and your true identity. I have known you even before you descended into your mother's womb. I have always loved and cared for you, leaving you completely free to do as you please. Yet you blame Me for what only you are responsible for. You may rest assured that you will never solve the problems of you human condition until you understand your true nature and answer the fundamental question, Who am I?

You are right about my ignorance. I don't know myself. I don't even know what I want anymore. I've spent the best years of my life pursuing what I thought would give me happiness and fulfillment. Driven by my insatiable desires, I have experienced everything the world has to offer, moving like a pendulum from craving to satiation and back again to craving. Now all I feel is confusion. I am like one lost in a labyrinth, alone, without a partner like Ariadne to help me escape with her magic ball of thread. Everything I have experienced is dust in my mouth; I have become a wasteland to myself. I have read countless books and have drunk from every source of knowledge available, all to no avail. With my mind and will defeated, I retreated into agnosticism and atheism, but instead of relief from the unending quest I fell into a state of existential anguish. I can identify with Faust when he says:

> I have, alas! Philosophy,
> Medicine, Jurisprudence too,
> And to my cost Theology,
> With ardent labor, studied through.
> And here I stand, will all my lore,
> Poor fool, no wiser than before.[9]

Pleasure and thrill are conducive to emptiness and sadness because after you have reached the summit you fall into the valley of death with your sense of being waning. However, you have learned an important lesson about the temporary nature and the unrealities of this world. Do you remember these poems? You recited them as a schoolboy:

> When the lamp is shattered,
> The light in the dust lies dead;
> When the cloud is scattered,
> The rainbow's glory is shed;
> When the lute is broken,
> Sweet tones are remembered not;
> When the lips have spoken,
> Loved accents are soon forgot.[10]

and…

> The flower that smiles today
> Tomorrow dies;
> All that we wish to stay
>   Tempts and then flies;
> What is this world's delight?
> Lightning, that mocks the night,

Brief even as bright.[11]

I desperately need help!
That is why I revealed Myself to you. According to the proverb, Man's extremity is God's opportunity. Remember, however, that knowledge which is only in the mind serves no purpose unless there is also the experience of the truth by which the knower and the known become one. Think! Disease is not cured by pronouncing the name of a medicine but by taking it – absorbing it into oneself.

What do you mean by "the experience of truth?" How is it possible to experience truth?
Are you sure you really want to know? "People love truth when she pleases them, but hate her when she disagrees with them. Is it not likely that they prefer to lie than to be lied to? They want to know truth when she reveals herself to them, but they hate her when the evidence goes against them."[12] I see that you are surprised, not by joy, as the poet said, but by wonder because I can quote from your books. However, it is not necessary for Me to read them the way you do. I think it helps to make you feel closer to Me since you have been away such a long time.

His words gave me pause. A moment before, I had been pleading for help; but now I was suddenly afraid. Was I going to hear things I did not want to know about myself? Things that might take from me the last thing I seemed to possess: the image of myself as I thought I was? I sensed him smile, and I realized that he was aware of my doubts.

You are right to feel afraid. You are about to try something that nothing in your life has prepared you for. You have sought happiness, wisdom and truth outside yourself, through relations, the writing and thinking of others. Now you must trust yourself – search within yourself. Are you ready to give up your old habits and do that?

I hesitated. His tone was reassuring, but his words were not encouraging. In my state of emptiness, I did not feel there was anything to be learned from looking inward. Moreover, how could I ignore the knowledge I had gained through a lifetime of experience and study? My heart contracted and tears came to my eyes as I was again overwhelmed with despair.

But then, from the depths of my being, a spark was lit and my courage began to return. What else was there for me to do? What other hope did I have? I calmed myself until I was able to speak: Yes. I am ready. Please begin.

I will try to help you; but first we must clear up a misconception. For many, truth is an empty notion, an opinion, or at best an intellectual concept. But in reality, truth is a Being. Truth is not merely known, it must be lived. The Divine Master who said, "I am the truth" was not referring to it as an abstraction but to My presence in Him.

You do not know what truth is because you do not have a sense of permanent identity; you are estranged from yourself and live in a state of alienation. Now you must find your way back to yourself through the mist of illusions, opinions and self-deception with which you have unknowingly shrouded your being. Think of truth as the realization of who you are. The way to overcome your sense of void, loneliness, and anxiety is through self-knowledge; which is in the words of the sage,

... the only pearl in the sea of life;
Like whirlpools round your-Self
You whirl in incessant strife[13]

Later you will understand what I mean, but you can never overcome your problems and limitations until you discover their cause. And that cause is you.

Me? That is absurd! Am I responsible for my condition? I don't *want* to be unhappy!
Nobody wants to be miserable, but since you do not know yourself you have become identified with the passions of your personality that promise you what they cannot give. Only your wrong tendencies and disorderly habits are the origin of your sufferings. Do you not see that every attempt for self-gratification brings you to deeper entanglement and dissatisfaction? The whole process is as futile and vain as trying to fill a container with holes in it.

This reminds me of the words that my favorite mystic heard, "How glorious is that soul which has indeed been able to pass from the stormy ocean to Me, the Sea of Peace, and in that Sea, which is Myself, to fill the cup of her heart."[14]
Then what is the true meaning of this terrible situation?
I told you, people do not know who they really are. In their ignorance they create a false image of themselves with a corresponding character and personality and blunder through life like a drunken actor.

11

Shakespeare is right when he says that,

> "All the world's a stage
> And all the men and women merely players:
> They have their exits and their entrances;
> And one man in his time plays many parts,
> His acts being seven ages."[15]

So we are bound to live in the conditions we create. How, then, can we get free from them?
You can if you want to. Do you not remember the words, "We make ourselves a ladder out of our vices if we trample the vices themselves underfoot."?[16] Hidden below the whirlpool of your emotions and delusions, like a pearl at the bottom of the ocean, there is in your heart the light of My Presence. Although it is obscured by the dark clouds of your past misdeeds, I am always with you, giving you My energy by which you can do what you want. You are not aware that I am the life breathing through your lungs, I am the intelligence acting through your brain, I am the love pulsating in your heart.

You must be the God or the Deity of whom I read about in the texts of philosophy and the world religions. I am ashamed to know that I have forgotten you and, in so doing, fallen into a disorderly and erroneous way of living. I have indeed muddied the fountain that gives me drink and, like the prodigal son, have wasted my inheritance instead of honoring the giver and return your goodness.
I do not need your goodness, but certainly you do need Mine.

The Earth you created in the beginning was "very good," but we have spoiled and desecrated everything. I begin to

realize that if we interfere and go against the perfect plan you have designed for each one of us we create our own misery and destroy our temple not made with hands.

Human beings may be deaf to My gentle voice but, though I am not heard, I always hear; they do not think of Me but I am the thinker; though I am denied and ignored I am the Knower. "Can a woman forget her nursing child or show no compassion for the child of her womb? Even these may forget, yet I will not forget you. See, I have inscribed you on the palms of my hands."[17]

None of us can hide from your eye or escape from your power; in the Scriptures you said, "Those who miss Me injure themselves; all who hate Me love death."[18] I ask you to help me to find you that I may find the source of life.

I have endowed you with the greatest power and authority in the universe – free will. By its use you can choose to lower your consciousness below the animal level or rise above the stars and become Godlike.

I must have badly misused it or I could not be in this hellish condition. There are those who believe that we are punished for our sins. Is it true?

Their conduct is based on the hope of reward and fear of punishment by an Omnipotent Ruler, and they try to give obedience to the decrees He promulgated for them. However, you are not punished *for* your actions; you are punished or rewarded *by* them; everyone constantly and unerringly meets himself in his life experiences.

[1] Robert Graves, *The Greek Myths* (London: The Folio Society, 1996), vol. 2, p. 359.

[2] Ecclesiastes 1:8.

[3] Percy Bysshe Shelley, "Love's Philosophy."

[4] *The Teaching of Rumi: the Masnavi*, trans. by E.H. Whinfield (NY: E.P. Dutton, 1975), p. 2.

[5] William Shakespeare, *Troilus and Cressida*. Act 3, Scene 2, Lines 77-80.

[6] Percy Bysshe Shelley, "Hymn to Intellectual Beauty."

[7] Psalms 39:5.

[8] Przywara, Erich, *An Augustine Synthesis*, quoted in Bloom, Harold, *Where Shall Wisdom Be Found?* (NY: Riverhead Books, 2004) p. 280.

[9] Goethe, *Faust*, Part I, trans. by Anna Swanwick (NY: Dover Publications,1994), p. 15.

[10] Percy Bysse Shelley, "When the Lamp is Shattered."

[11] Percy Bysse Shelley, "The Flower That Smiles Today."

[12] St. Augustine, *Confessions,* Bk. 10, Ch. 23.

[13] *Sufi Writings*, In *Das Bhagavan, The Essential Unity of All Religions* (Wheaton, Ill.: The Theosophical Publishing House, 1973), p. 231.

[14] St. Catherine of Siena, *The Dialogue,* translated by Suzanne Noffke, O.P. (NY: Paulist Press, 1980), p. 147.

[15] *As You Like It*, Act II, Scene 7, Lines 139-143

[16] St. Augustine, *Sermons*, 111, 176, *De Ascensione.*

[17] Isaiah 49:15-16.

[18] Proverbs 8:36.

CHAPTER 2

Sowing and Reaping

The universal law of Karma...is that of action and reaction,
cause and effect, sowing and reaping... man, by his thoughts and
actions, becomes the arbiter of his destiny.
Paramahansa Yogananda

Are you referring to what is called Karma?
The Sanskrit term **Karma** has been adopted in your language
to define the fundamental Law that governs and controls
universal life in all its myriad manifestations, from the atomic
to the cosmic. Literally translated, it means action and refers to
the balancing process of cause and effect.

It is simply the one Law by which the cosmos (a word
that means order) as a unity of interconnected parts and mutual interrelations of things and events, is kept in perfect balance and harmony. The natural act of breathing, in its rhythmic act of inhalation and exhalation, is a good analogy, as it reflects your intimate relation to the universe. Whenever the
equilibrium is disturbed or disrupted there is the tendency in
nature to restore the original condition.

However, Karma neither punishes nor rewards; it all
depends on the effects and consequences of your own decisions, for you cannot experience anything that is not the product and content of your consciousness. Whatever form of energy and vibration emanates from your body by your thoughts
and feelings is an effect-producing cause. It goes out into the
atmosphere and, as it magnetizes its environment, it is bound
to come back to you attracting more of its kind. Thus, while a
positive thought becomes a beneficent power for good, a discordant one creates a maleficent force. "Who so casteth a stone
on high, cast it on his own head; and a deceitful stroke shall

make wounds. Whoso diggeth a pit shall fall therein; and he that setteth a trap shall be taken therein. He that worketh mischief, it shall fall upon him, and he shall not know whence it cometh."[1]

It sounds like Newton's law of motion, according to which "To every action there is and equal and opposite reaction."
Yes, what you do to others, whether good or ill, produces a corresponding reaction within you and in your world. For instance, if you are angry with someone, while you may not injure him physically, you nevertheless injure yourself instantly because the negative thought vibrates first through you; then you are responsible for its effect upon others.

"People make relationships with others by coming into contact with them individually, and bonds are forged by benefits and injuries, golden links of love or iron chains of hate."[2] If one is only concerned with himself and inconsiderate of others, how can he experience love in return?

Is Karma to be balanced person to person?
In some cases it is necessary, but not always or it would be too long a process.

If one is not willing to cooperate, how can the discordant condition be solved or dissolved?
Do not forget that the Law of Love is governing all activities in the universe, and forgiveness is part of it. Therefore, if one can turn to Me asking to forgive or be forgiven and consume whatever the wrong may be, it will be done. Then the individual is free of the consequences. It has not been understood that the fire of My forgiving love brings freedom from all binding conditions.

But the Law is clearly stated that "whatsoever a man soweth, that shall he also reap."[3] When the farmer plants a seed of wheat or corn he receives back the same thing multiplied as an ear – and, of course, if a man plants thistle seeds, he cannot expect to grow grapes from them. You can see the analogy in the operation of human nature: the effects of good and bad acts will also multiply.

Therefore, every thought is like a seed planted in the universal field, and the person will experience as a physical manifestation *the same thing* according to the quality of the energy he sent out. For instance, if you are idle, torpid, or disinclined to mental activity, how can you grow in knowledge?

No one seems to realize the creative powers of their thoughts, feelings, and spoken word otherwise they would be more careful in their use. They form one's own character, which becomes destiny, and create the conditions in which he will live. The way you express them today will determine your life tomorrow, the same as those you gave expression to ignorantly or innocently, yesterday is governing your life today. You are not dealing with external circumstances or conditions, rather you are, knowingly or unknowingly, using the energy of life acting under the Law. It says that the thought you create as a cause brings its manifestation as an effect because they are inextricably one.

Indeed, life, visible and invisible, material and spiritual, is a response to a request, but people do not see what kinds of requests they are making, both mentally and emotionally. As a result, they may receive responses that are not what they intended, and then they fail to understand why they experience disappointments or problems in their life. From birth to death, thread by thread, everyone is weaving his own destiny around himself, listening either to the heavenly inner voice or to the seductive siren song of his outer personality. According to the sacredness of his choice, he will experience the harmony and peace of his God Self or he will be caught in the web of delusions and discord of his false self.

"The recompense of good and evil follows as the shadow follows the figure."[4] The energy by which you live and that you use all the time is a divine trust, given to you as love and by love. If one misuses it and creates some form of discord and evil he will have to face, sooner or later, its recoil. No matter what effects, good or bad, it may produce in the world outside, the energy is, may I say, elastic and is always connected with the individual who uses it. Therefore, every limitation that one experiences is created inside of him and he is tied to them.

You are saying that the workings of the Law explain every distressing conditions we suffer today. It brings to mind these words by Shakespeare:
"Some, peradventure, have on them the guilt of premeditated and contrived murder; some, of beguiling virgins with the broken seals of perjury; some, making the wars their bulwark, that have before gor'd the gentle bosom of peace with pillage and robbery. Now, if these men have defeated the law and outrun native punishment, though they can outstrip men, they have no wings to fly from God."[5]

In our ignorance we fail to recognize that, Good and evil do not wrongly befall us, but heaven sends down misery or happiness according to our conduct.[6]
However, the understanding of the operation of the causal chain should not induce a fatalistic attitude or be an incentive to a passive state of resignation or depression. On the contrary, the inviolability and justice of the natural order should give

hope and encouragement because one can change his Karma by his positive and constructive thoughts and attitude, and thus create a new and more promising life in the future.

The individual, by learning the lesson, can make his very blunders and shortcomings serve him and become wiser. Or he can let himself be used by his problems and continue to live as he did before, creating more misery.

We are told that:

> Sweet are the uses of adversity,
> Which, like the toad, ugly and venomous,
> Wears yet a precious jewel in his head.[7]

According to the ancient Roman naturalist Pliny the jewel, or toadstone was believed to have curative powers.

The desire to be free can impel one to seize the opportunity to give help whenever possible knowing that by raising others out of their predicaments he, being part of the whole, lifts himself also. Service rendered with love, whether in thought, feeling, or action is the keynote of liberation; the individual blesses himself by blessing the rest of life.

You must never forget that love is the fulfillment of the Law and in the crucible of love's fire you can be free by its purifying power if you so desire.

But since Karma may strike at any moment, it can create fear. It seems to me that one is in the same situation of Damocles seated at the banquet with a sword suspended over his head by a single hair. When I think of the words, "He who kills with the sword perishes by the sword,"[8] I feel I

may face at any time an inescapable punishment brought upon myself by past errors.

That would be an erroneous interpretation; most of what has been written and talked about on the subject of Karma is based on a misconception or distortion that can indeed be alarming and even inhibitive.

What, then, is the difference between Karma and fate?

They are essentially unrelated because you do not have to be a victim of the Law and remain a slave to your negative habits and deeds.

When one recognizes the fundamental value of his free will, he becomes the architect of his world and the master of his life. Fate is represented in the tragic dramas of the ancient Greeks as the inevitable consequences of one's past actions. It is symbolized in myth by three women always spinning the thread which forms the cord of destiny.

I took a course on Greek mythology, and I remember their story. They were named Clotho, Lachesis, and the smallest, but most dreadful of all, Atropos. Zeus, who weighs the lives of men and informs the Fates of his decisions, can, it is said, change his mind and intervene to save anyone he pleases when the thread of life, spun on Clotho's spindle and measured by the rod of Lachesis, is about to be snipped by Atropos' sheers. Others disagree and hold that Zeus himself is subject to the Fates, as the Pythian priestess once confessed in an oracle, because they are not his children, but parthenogeneous daughters of the Great Goddess Necessity, against whom not even the gods contend and who is called The Strong Fate.[9]

In reality, the weaving is not done by the Fates but by the three powers of the human consciousness: thought, feeling, and the spoken word. By their right use you can attain liberation, and by their misuse you will build your own prison.

Let me stress that the Law is neither an arbitrary fiat nor a predetermined command of a supernatural will; such a view would be a violation of the ethical order of life that it pre-supposes. You are responsible for what you do; your existence on this planet is like a schoolroom and you can and will learn by the living way of the experiences you choose, which is a specifically human capability and a truly unique privilege.

Karma harmonizes and balances cause and effect; it is both purposeful and merciful; after all, what is called the Law is the activity of divine nature, whose essence is love. Love is a goddess and the Law is her guardian, protecting her from every offence and violation. But people must understand their creative responsibility to themselves, to others, and the rest of life in their use of energy that acts according to the universal Law.

Instead of remaining ignorant of it and its workings, continuing to live with one's head buried in the sand, one should realize that Karma is the recognition and affirmation of the human freedom of choice. While its principle and operation is as immutable as a law of physics, you are not helplessly bound by it.

You are not dominated by a cosmic power that forces you to do what it wills; it can be just the opposite because that same power, when it is understood and acted upon accordingly, will obediently and accurately carry out whatever you desire. The purpose of problems is to force you to return to Me. If the individual only understood it, they are a blessing in disguise.

Francis Bacon wrote, "Nature cannot be ordered about, except by obeying her."[10]

Every teaching that gives an explanation to the question of human existence recognizes the justice and beneficence of the Karmic Law. The Dhammapada says:

> All that we are is the result of what we have thought: it is founded on our thoughts, it is made up of our thoughts. If a man speaks or acts with an evil thought, pain follows him as the wheel follows the foot of the ox that draws the carriage ... If a man speaks or acts with a pure thought, happiness follows him, like a shadow that never leaves him.[11]

And from the Qu'ran:

> Whatever of misfortune falls on one,
> Of one's own doings it is the result.
> The atom's weight of good that you have done
> That you shall see come back to you again;
> The atom's weight of evil you have wrought,
> That also must you meet unfailingly.[12]

The individual, by either benevolent or selfish intent, draws back upon himself the blessings or the curses of his actions. Karma is always operative as a form of educative justice because every thought, feeling, and act that the individual creates and directs upon the world has its equal and opposite reaction on himself.

Like a patient and compassionate teacher, the Law instructs every individual concerning the supreme lesson of his responsibility to life because one learns something only when he becomes conscious of it by his own experience.

There is an old saying that experience is a hard teacher, but fools will have no other.
Because it is not necessary to learn from distress if the individual would listen to Me and obey the Law of Love.

Unfortunately we don't even learn from our own mistakes and keep repeating them.

> These deeds of yours shall verily be brought
> Back unto you, as if you were yourself
> The author of your own just punishment.[13]

Or more simply, "Whatever befalleth us, cometh from us."[14]

There's a picturesque description of the same idea in the *Tibetan Book of the Dead*. At the time of death,

> The Good Genius, who was born simultaneously with thee, will now come and count out the good deeds with white pebbles, and the Evil Genius, was born simultaneously with thee, will come and count out thy evil deeds with black pebbles...Then the Lord of Death will say, "I will consult the Mirror of Karma, ...wherein every good and evil act is vividly reflected."[15]

No one can escape from himself. One's state in life, whether young or old, king or servant, ignorant or learned, rich or poor, does not affect or preclude the operation of the chain of causative events.

Everyone is constantly generating new Karma (whether good or bad, helpful or harmful) and experiencing the effects and consequences of his past actions. Remember that it is not an external factor or a coercive agency imposing itself upon you, rather the Law is embodied in you. You are the Law unto yourself because it is inherent in your divine nature.

That is the meaning of the passages in the Scripture where God says, "I will put my Law within them, and I will write it on their heart;" and "The word is very near you; it is in your mouth and in your heart for you to observe."[16]

Life is energy and vibration acting according to the way you choose to use it, similar to the current of electricity running, for instance, through a motor; when the switch is turned on, the machine runs irrespective of the individual who operates it. Action, of course, does not refer to the physical aspect alone but is primarily thought and emotion. The complex web of one's deeds is woven essentially by the intensity of the motive and the deliberate intent either to do harm or to assist another part of life.

Every action carries its own consequence, for action and reaction are ever one of the fundamental polarities of life itself. The assurance that, "whatsoever ye sow, that shall ye also reap" is an affirmation of a lawfulness and justice pervading all universal processes, and it is perfectly expressed in the following statement:

> Sow a thought and reap an act,
> Sow an act and reap a habit,
> Sow a habit and reap a character,
> Sow a character and reap a destiny.[17]

Never goes sin without its due return;
And deeds of noble goodness or dire sin,
Bear their just fruit, here, in this very life.
Never is there escape from consequence
Because the Great Judge dwells within each heart.[18]

Who you are and the conditions you live in are the mirror or the replica of your thoughts and feelings of both past and present.

The Law of retribution is clearly stated in the Bible and I will cite only a few quotations:

"Whoever sheds the blood of a human, by a human shall that person's blood be shed."[19]

In Exodus we find the familiar edict, "Whoever strikes a person mortally shall be put to death;" "when people who are fighting injure a pregnant woman...if any harm follows, then you shall give life for life, eye for eye, tooth for tooth, hand for hand, foot for foot, burn for burn, wound for wound, stripe for stripe."[20]

Also, in the book of Obadiah the same principle is stated: "As you have done, it shall be done to you; your deeds shall return on your own head."[21]

Others include, "God will bring every deed into judgment, including every secret thing, whether good or evil;"[22] "I will pay them back for what they have done;[23] and "But all shall die for their own sin; the teeth of everyone who eats sour grapes shall be set on edge."[24]

Also note, "For they sow the wind, and they shall reap the whirlwind."[25]

Jesus proclaimed that he came not to abolish but to fulfill the Law and the prophets[26] that find in the Gospel

their full meaning and perfect realization in the revelation of the Law of Love. We are told in the Sermon on the Mount, "Do not judge, so that you may not be judged. For the judgment you make, you will be judged, and the measure you give will be the measure you get.".... "In everything do unto others as you would have them do unto you."[27] And before his arrest He admonishes one of his followers, "Put your sword back into its place; for all who take the sword will perish by the sword."[28]

St. Paul confirms the operation of the Law when he writes, "For he will repay according to each one's deeds. There will be anguish and distress for everyone who does evil but glory and honor and peace for everyone who does good. God shows no partiality."[29]

In his letter to the Galatians we read: Do not be deceived; God is not mocked, for you reap whatever you sow. If you sow to your own flesh, you will reap corruption from the flesh; but if you sow to the Spirit, you will reap eternal life from the Spirit.[30]

Likewise, to the church of Corinth he writes, "Each will receive wages according to the labor of each. The fire will test what sort of work each has done.[31]

The fire to which he refers is the love of God, that is the fulfillment of the Law; if you do not act according to it, you are bound to experience the consequences resulting from the lack of love. Since love is the perfection of life, every human limitation, whether mental, emotional, or physical is irrefutable evidence that love is not present.

It all depends on the use of our free will: We were told, "I have set before you life and death, blessings and curses. Choose life so that you and your descendants may live."[32]

Every day you are faced with innumerable choices and you are bound to choose, although you may let your mind, emotions, or situations decide for you. Even to say *no* to all choices, or allow others to choose for you, is a choice whose consequences will bear either joys or sorrows, bestow either gifts or burdens.

"Real choice is no illusion," says *A Course in Miracles*, but the world has none to offer because it is "a place where choice among illusions seems to be the only choice. All its roads but lead to disappointment, nothingness and death. There is no choice in its alternatives. Seek not escape from problems here. The world was made that problems could not be escaped. Be not deceived by all the different names its roads are given. They have but one end ...On some you travel gaily for a while, before the bleakness enters. And on some the thorns are felt at once. The choice is not what will the ending be, but when it comes."[33]
There is, unfortunately, some truth in that because mankind without My help cannot rise out of their predicament, and very often they exchange one problem for a dozen. Unless they turn to Me there is no hope for them as they become more and more entangled in their Karmic net.

How tremendous is the power of our free will! I recall the lines of Milton's Lucifer, the fallen archangel:

> The mind is its own place, and in itself
> can make a Heaven of Hell, a Hell of Heaven.
> ...in my choice
> To reign is worth ambition though in Hell:
> Better to reign in Hell than serve in Heaven."[34]

The Karmic Law applies to not only the individual but also to groups – families, communities, nations, races and the planet itself.

Mankind can be compared to the physical form, which is an aggregate of countless cells mutually interdependent. Think of each individual cell functioning in relation to the body to which it belongs. If even a single cell becomes disruptive or breaks apart, the whole body is affected and suffers. So it is with the communal life of humanity: the individual person is like a "cell" of the body of humanity and, in reality, of the universe!

In all sacred scriptures of the world you will find this principle of the oneness of life. In the Bible, "No man liveth unto himself."[35] We are all parts of one another.

"God hath made of one blood all nations that dwell upon the face of the earth."[36]

In the Qu'ran, "All creatures are members of the one family of God." And the Veda, "Human beings, all, are as head, arms, trunk, and legs unto one another."[37]

Also poets speak of it:

> No man is an island, entire of itself; every man is a piece of the continent, a part of the main; if a clod be washed away by the sea, Europe is the less; any man's death diminishes me, because I am involved in mankind; and therefore never send to know for whom the bell tolls; it tolls for thee.[38]

Yes, they too recognize the truth that since life is one, there is no separation anywhere except in the ignorance of the human intellect and the selfishness of the personality. Therefore, what you do to others and the rest of life, you do it to yourself first. "If my hand hurt my foot, shall not the hand also feel the pain? Hence, he who meditates not of wrong to anyone, but consider them as himself is free from the effect of sin."[39] This relationship, as you see, is more than a mere casual, space-time relationship; it is one of common ground and a simultaneous presence of all factors of existence.

I appreciate your explanation of the Law because most of us are ignorant of both its reality and its workings. It is the key to the riddle of human existence, which otherwise is but

> a tale
> Told by an idiot, full of sound and fury,
> Signifying nothing.[40]

We tend to rebel when we observe the tragedy and the apparent injustices of life in the way the innocent suffer and the wicked seem to enjoy themselves. The cry of Job in desperation for the why of his afflictions is echoed by millions as they bitterly question the inscrutable ways of the Creator: "Who understands his sins? Teach me, and I will hold my tongue, and make me to understand wherein I have erred!"[41] In our ignorance of the underlying causes created by ourselves, we attribute our condition to circumstances, chance, or misfortune and blame even God for being responsible.

What a fallacy! There is no such thing as chance or accident! This shows how benighted mankind's consciousness has become. The personality can do what it wants, but if it injures others, physically or mentally, he compels himself to experience the cause and effect of the same condition until he realizes what he has done, and has paid his debts to life. It may, indeed, appear that the ungodly prosper and the righteous be in distress, but you see only the external appearance, and you do not know the hidden side of it.

The bad person who seems to be successful may, even unknowingly, be darkened and gnawed by worms, while the good one under afflictions is in the rewarding process of spiritual growth and freedom. No experience, however distressing or trivial, is without use and value to the awakening person once he understands the inner meaning of his condition and that so much of his negative Karma is being worked out in the process. No one is an exception to the Law of Love and if you break it you cannot escape the consequences because it is the action of your own life energy.

However, it is still not clear to me why bad things happen to good people.
Let me ask you a simple question: is there anyone out of more than three billion people on earth who has the boldness to pretend that he is good? If one thinks he can make such a claim, he certainly does not know himself nor does he have the slightest idea of what it means to be good. To this the Scripture attests very clearly: "Surely there is no one on earth so righteous as to do good without sinning."[42]

> "How then can a mortal be righteous before God? How can one born a woman be pure? If even the moon is not bright and the stars are not pure in his sight. How much less a mortal, who is a maggot, and a human being, who is a worm!"[43]

And ...

> "If we say that we have no sin we deceive ourselves, and the truth is not in us."[44]
> "Who can say "I have made my heart clean, I am pure from my sin?"[45]
> "All our righteous deeds are like a filthy cloth."[46]
> "All have sinned and come short of the glory of God."[47]

The more advanced you are on the spiritual path the more you realize how imperfect you are compared to the all-loving Source of your being. All the saints consider themselves the greatest sinners of all, unworthy of My love and light.

St. Teresa of Avila uses the analogy of a glass filled with water: it may appear to our sight crystal clear, but when we expose it to the sunlight all the impure particles will appear.

> Not only is the soul aware of the cobwebs that cover it, but the sunlight is so bright that it sees every little speck of dust besides, even the most minute...When it looks on this divine Sun, it is dazzled by the brightness; when it looks on itself, dust clouds its eyes ...[48]

As the individual purifies and perfects himself he has a clearer vision of the divine reality and becomes more attuned to it. There are many things that people do as a matter of habit which are an abomination.
There is a passage in the Gospel where Jesus was addressed by a man with the words "good master," and he retorted, "Why do you call me good? Only God is good."[49] Now tell me if there is anyone who can surpass that?

"God is not mocked," said St. Paul;[50] but He is also not understood. With reference to divine justice, Dante compares it to an eye by the shore that can see the bottom of the sea; in the ocean the eye would not see it because it is hidden by the depth; but the bottom of the ocean is, nevertheless, there. Since there is never an event which is fortuitous or fatalistic, and no arbitrary action, are we bound to an endless wheel of cause becoming effect becoming, in turn, cause?

I am not surprised that you still do not understand, it is not enough to hear what I say, you must think deeply of it. At present, the Law is your master because you have become subject to it by your past errors, but let me reiterate that you can make it your servant; it all depends on your decision.

I made you the only authority over your life by the power of free will; no one can say nay to whatever you may desire. If you have set into motion negative energy and are chained to it by its reaction, remember that the Law is also your eternal friend and deliverer.

"While Nemesis is without attributes, and the dreaded Goddess is absolute and immutable as a Principle, it is you yourselves, nations and individuals – who propel Her to action and give the impulse to Her direction. She may indeed forge and shape the destiny of mortals and nations alike but, it is they who make of her either a fury or a rewarding Angel.

Nor would the ways of Karma be inscrutable were men to work in union and harmony instead of disunion and strife. For our ignorance of those ways – which one portion of mankind calls the ways of Providence, dark and intricate; while another sees in them the action of blind Fatalism; and a third, simple chance, with neither gods nor devils to guide them – would surely disappear, if we would but attribute all these to

32

their correct cause. Were no man to hurt his brother, Karma-Nemesis would have neither cause to work for, nor weapons to act through."[51]

What I need is a total conversion, but what can I do of myself?

I made you a being of far greater potential than you can imagine. You may draw upon My power and set yourself free from your self-created fetters by working in accord with the Law of love and harmony instead of breaking it as you did in the past by your lusts and hurt. At every moment, even now, you are endowed with the faculty of choice and the capacity to reverse your past tendency to error and, by your effort, you can create a higher destiny for yourself and others.

All limitations can be swept away by the individual who realizes that the world is governed by a Law of absolute justice, that progress towards the highest is My will for him, that he cannot escape from advancing, and moving forward, that whatever comes his way is meant to help him along the way, and that he himself is the only one who can obstruct or delay the fulfillment of the divine plan according to which the perfection and the bliss of love is the only predestination which I decreed from the beginning.

I became thoughtful. He was saying so much in his flood of words, as if in an ecstasy! I could hardly take it all in. I found myself clutching at one phrase: "That whatever comes his way is meant to help him along the way."

Then, I suppose my despair is meant to help me. Perhaps this is a turning point in my life, like the "dark night of the soul" the mystic St. John of the Cross described. The words of a poet of long time ago find an echo in my heart:

Take me to you, imprison me, for I
Except you enthrall me, never shall be free,
Nor ever chaste, except you ravish me.[52]

[1] Bhagavan Das, *The Essential Unity of All Religions* (Wheaton, Ill: Theosophical Publishing House, 1973), p. 180.

[2] Annie Besant, *The Riddle of Life*, (Wheaton, Ill.: The Theosophical Publishing House, n.d.), p. 45.

[3] Galatians 6, 7.

[4] Das, p. 180.

[5] *Henry V*, Act 4, Scene 1, Lines 151-163.

[6] Das, p. 179.

[7] *As You Like It*, Act 2, Scene 1, Lines 12-14.

[8] Revelation 13:10.

[9] Graves, pp. 53-4.

[10] Francis Bacon, *Novum Organum*, I, Aphorism 129.

[11] *Wisdom of the Buddha: The Unabridged Dhammapada*, translated by Max Müller, (Mineola, New York: Dover Publications, 2000) p. 1.

[12] Qu'ran, quoted in Das, p. 178.

[13] Hadis, "The Sayings of the Prophet Muhammad," quoted in Das. p. 178.

[14] Sufi saying quoted in Das, p. 178.

[15] Quoted, B. W. Huntsman, *Wisdom Is One: Being a Collection of Quotations from the Sayings and Writings of Some of the Masters and Their Followers* (Rutland, Vermont.: Charles E. Tuttle Co., 1985), p. 113.

[16] Jeremiah 31:33b; Deuteronomy 30:14.

[17] George Dana Boardman, the Younger (1828-1903), American Clergyman.

[18] Mahã-bhãrata, quoted in Das, p. 183.

[19] Genesis 9:6.

[20] Exodus 21:12, 21, 22-23, 25.

[21] Obadiah 15.

[22] Ecclesiastes 12:14.

[23] Proverbs 25:29.

[24] Jeremiah 31:29.

[25] Hosea 8:7.

26 Matthew 26:52.

27 Matthew 5:17-18,

28 Matthew 7:1-12.

29 Romans 2:6, 9-11.

30 Galatians 6:6-8.

31 1 Corinthians 3:8, 13-15.

32 Deuteronomy 30:15-19.

33 Foundation for Inner Peace, *A Course in Miracles* (NY: Viking Foundation, 1975), pp. 607-8.

34 *Paradise Lost,* Book 1, Lines 255-263.

35 Romans 14:7.

36 Acts 17:26.

37 Quoted in Das, p. 1.

38 John Donne, *Devotions Upon Emergent Occasions,* Meditation xvii.

39 Das p. 176.

40 William Shakespeare, *Macbeth,* Act 5, Scene 5, Lines 26-28.

41 Job 6:24.

42 Ecclesiastes 7:20.

43 Job, 25:4-5.

44 John 1:8.

45 Proverbs 20:9.

46 Isaiah 64:6.

47 Romans 3:23.

48 *The Life of Saint Theresa of Avila,* by Herself, transl. J. M. Cohen (NY: Penguin Books, 1978) p. 146.

49 Matthew 19:16-17.

50 Galatians 6:7

51 M.P. Blavatsky, *The Secret Doctrine,* 1.2, 642-3.

52 John Donne, *Holy Sonnets,* No. 10.

CHAPTER 3

Our Many Lives

As a man leaves an old garment and puts on one that is new,
the spirit leaves his mortal body and puts on one that is new.
The Bhagavad-Gita

Our birth is but a sleep and a forgetting:
The soul that rises with us, our life's star,
Hath had elsewhere its setting,
And cometh from afar;
Not in entire forgetfulness,
And not in utter nakedness,
But trailing clouds of glory do we come
From God, who is our home.
William Wordsworth

I am still confused. I was taught in my early years that Jesus died for me and took upon himself all my sins. How, then, can we reconcile the workings of the Karmic principle with Christ's giving of His Life so that all might be free?
The mission of Jesus marked the beginning of a new covenant, a new era. He went through the experience of the crucifixion by his own choice, and took upon himself and consumed a certain portion of mankind's Karma.

By His transfiguration, resurrection, and ascension, a tremendous weight of negative energy that oppressed mankind, especially with the destructive qualities of hate, violence, and depravity, was lifted from the Earth, and He gave an evolutionary impetus to the consciousness of the human race; it was the birth of the Christ-Self in every son and daughter of God.

The Divine Master revealed the sublime attributes of the nature of God and gave an example for all mankind to follow. He can truly be called a Savior; He fulfilled My promise of forgiveness and mercy.

"The Law indeed was given through Moses; grace and truth came through Jesus Christ."[1] This means that the chains individuals forge for themselves can be broken by the power of My forgiving Love.

Yet in spite of Jesus' ministry and sacrifice, people are still under the domination of the destructive forces, unable to protect themselves.

They are subject to the gravitational force of evil because, by the misuse of their free will, they do not turn away from it. It takes intense desire and the decision to be free. Then, one can reverse habits of long standing deeply rooted into the mind and body. The negative thoughts and feelings, the wrong images, the craving of the senses and, above all, the selfishness of the will to have his own way have enslaved humanity and clouded their consciousness. However, the fire of My love is always ready to help and deliver them from any distressing condition.

Jesus' divine manifestation and His powers do not exempt nor release you from your personal responsibility and the necessity of your effort for the purification and the overcoming of your past accumulation of wrong desires and tendencies.

You will receive all assistance possible from Him, hence the statement He made: "Ask and ye shall receive." But, although He has prepared a place for you in the Father's house, He cannot enter for you.

In the parable of the talents, the Divine Master made very clear each one's responsibility and purpose in the use of the faculties of life. He likened the Kingdom of God to a man going on a journey who summoned his servants and divided his property among them, each according to his ability. To one he gave five talents, to another two, and to the third he gave one. After a long time the master returned and commended the first two servants because they doubled their share: "Well done, good and loyal servants, you have been faithful in a few things so I will make you ruler over many things; enter into the joy of your master."

But the third said, "I knew that you were a hard man, reaping where you did not sow, and gathering where you did not scatter seed, so I was afraid and went and hid your talent in the ground; here you have what is yours."

But his master replied, "You wicked and lazy servant! You should have invested my money with the bankers, and on my return I would have received what was my own with interest."

Thus, the servant was punished by being deprived of his talent, which was then given to the one who had ten. And Jesus concluded with a statement of the Law, "To all those who have, more will be given, and they will have an abundance, but from those who have nothing even what they have will be taken away. As for the worthless servant, throw him into the outer darkness where there will be weeping and gnashing of teeth."[2]

The parable explains that the Law operates according to the way the individual uses his talents and his life-energy; if he acts constructively he will receive abundance, not because of divine favoritism or chance, but by his endeavor to invest his life in good works.

Therefore, he can lay up treasures in Heaven, where neither moth nor rust do corrupt, and where thieves do not break through nor steal. By the Law of Retribution the faithful servant is rewarded, and this is called good Karma; by the same Law the worthless servant is punished, and this is considered bad Karma, expressed by the weeping and gnashing of teeth.

Since not everyone takes equal advantage of the opportunities that life offers them to use and multiply their talents at the same rate, they cannot receive the same compensation. This explains why people differ from one another in their faculties, abilities and condition.

You spoke about the importance of choice and the opportunity that life offers in the use or misuse of our talents; but what about those who are born crippled, mentally retarded, or afflicted with other disabilities? How can they be held responsible for their condition?
It seems that you have some difficulties or resistance with regard to the comprehension of the Law that is so simple even a child can grasp it.

We have lost the gift and innocence of childhood.
You are asking Me why people are not born equal, endowed with the same qualities and capabilities, as would be expected and compatible with the idea of perfect divine justice.

Three explanations have been given. One is contained in the phrase "the will of God," which is difficult, if not impossible, to reconcile with the nature of an all-loving provident Father who cares for His children. And it is inconsistent with a universe based and moved by love.

Do you think it is possible for the Creator to regard with special favor anyone over another?

I never understood why He treated the twins born from Isaac and Rebecca differently. God cannot be unjust, yet it seems that He preferred Jacob to Esau and his seed generation after generation. I think that a case like this raises real perplexities and requires more than the dogmatic assertion

that His ways are mysterious. Theologians have struggled with this story in trying to explain how a just Creator could favor one of the two innocent children before either of them had done anything good or bad, as they entered for the first time on the stage of life.

The Scripture is unequivocal concerning the divine attributes:

> his work is perfect;
> for all his ways are just.
> A faithful God, without deceit,
> just and upright is he.[3]

According to the rabbis of ancient times, since God's favoritism is out of the question, the only possible explanation was that Esau had sinned in the womb. The issue led some early Christians to the acceptance of reincarnation – the twins must have had previous existences in which they deserved God's love or hatred. Jacob's preferential treatment in the womb must be the result of merit earned in past lives.

With regard to those born with disabilities, one can believe that God's ways transcend man's and that they are beyond our comprehension. For some people, this may be a satisfactory explanation, it all depends on one's understanding of God and one's relation to him. It certainly would be more intelligible and consistent, since faith is not supposed to be blind, if the divine inscrutability applied to his infinite merciful providence, always concerned with the good of every person, in every circumstance, whether in this life or the next.

Is there any other way to see "the will of God" as an explanation for what seems to be a mystery? According to some theologians God allows evil in order to bring greater good.

And there are those who believe that a temporary condition of suffering will be rewarded with everlasting happiness in Heaven, and this is certainly praiseworthy. The truth is that I always seek every opening to give My light when the individual turns to Me.

But this notion of causeless and unexplainable suffering, which is called the mystery of evil, would make the Infinite Source of Perfect Manifestation (another of My names) depend on and resort to something utterly opposed to its very nature in order to fulfill the cosmic plan.

Such a view, that greater good can come from evil, is not only a patent contradiction, but an act of profanity. As St. Augustine wrote, "God is good, utterly and entirely better than the things which he has made. But, since he is good, the things that he has made are also good. This is how he contains them all in himself and fills them all with his presence."[4]

To the Buddhist, the thought that a god should have created the world with all its suffering, limitations, stupidity , and cruelty is blasphemous for the very idea of a supreme Being is synonymous with perfection. For him it is not a god who is responsible for the evil of the world, because the negative conditions that we experience are the creation of our own ignorance, our cravings and passions.

That imperfection should come out of perfection and completeness seems to contradict all reason, while the opposite appears more likely.[5]

The Christian would also agree: Sickness is not a divine punishment nor is it sent as a lesson or as a means of purifying character. Such a view would make a sadistic monster out of God, instead of a loving Source of light and love revealed by Christ.[6]

You may believe that your present cross will be exchanged for a crown after death; but this conviction, even if it helps you to carry your cross, fails to explain why it is heavier than another's.

The problem of evil remains unsolved, though the suffering itself may, for the Christian, have redemptive value when it is offered in atonement with Jesus' sacrifice. What is difficult to accept and against which one tends to rebel is the absurdity and insanity of the terrible and chaotic circumstances that continue in all their dark reality to haunt people everywhere.

I can see how the idea of an omnipotent and omniscient God seems inconsistent with the existence of evil. Either He is all-good and wants to eliminate evil but it is not powerful enough to do it, or He is all-powerful but chooses not to prevent or remove evil which, then, makes Him not good. Why wouldn't an all-loving Father intervene to deliver us from the horrors of the world?

I know that the belief of the doctrine of original sin is promulgated in order to explain the existence of evil in all its myriad forms. But this leaves unanswered the essential question of the confused mass of injustices and partialities, from the gratuitous faculty of genius and holiness seemingly created for a specific, favored individual, to the undeserved destructive tendencies of a criminal or a dictator imposed upon him without any choice of his own.

Why, for instance, is one person born into a loving family and a propitious environment, while another happens to be raised in unfavorable conditions by depraved parents who dislike him? Why does someone die young and another reaches old age? Why do we feel attracted to one person at first sight while we experience the opposite with

regard to someone else? Is it a fortuitous event if a person misses a train or a plane that afterward crashes?

A second explanation is that afflictions at birth are a tragic accident or a misfortune, a matter of chance – and either submit to them with stoic resignation or rebel against them with bitter resentment. Mankind, then, like leaves driven by the wind, is a helpless victim in the grasp of circumstances it can neither understand nor control.

I don't see how that can be consistent with the existence of a benevolent force governing the universe, and in any case, you have already said that there is no such thing as mere chance.

It is not consistent, and so it cannot be the correct answer or solution to the problem. But there is a third possibility: the doctrine of reincarnation that, being related to the Karmic Law, is the only sensible and coherent explanation for the existence of evil in all its forms.

It enables you to understand what appears to be the mystery of the differences among people, whether regarding one's faculties, conditions, or opportunities, which otherwise seem to prove that blind forces, not a just God, are the ruling powers of life.

How is reincarnation connected with Karma?

Since inequalities cannot be the manifestation of the Creator's whim but are the consequences of one's own actions, "in the beginning" everyone is endowed with the same potentialities and abilities. Reincarnation is the twin principle of the Law of Causation, its extension, and it is again, the action of the Law of Love and the expression of My infinite mercy.

Instead of facing its own creation after the time of death and be judged by it for all eternity, the individual is given another opportunity to make further progress if he wants to. People do not realize that time is the priceless gift of My love to them.

Yet, we waste so much of it in useless and even destructive activities and occupation, when every hour determines the conditions of our existence in the future. We even use the expression "to kill time!"
Which is a sign of how darkened the human mind has become. My plan for each life-stream is perfect as I AM perfect; however, according to the use of his faculties and energy, everyone is free to shape his or her own destiny.

The Karmic record of the individual from previous lives is carried over to his new embodiment; thus, the beginning of another life becomes a fresh opportunity for the child to once again make an effort and try to reach a higher level of consciousness which he may have failed to attain in the past. It is never the will of God to cast a soul away: "I have no pleasure in the death of the wicked."[7]

Listen to one of your wise people:

> Hence each life is not only a recapitulation of life experience, but an assuming of ancient obligation, a recovery of old relations, an opportunity for the paying of old indebtedness, a chance to make restitution and progress, an awakening of deep-seated qualities, the recognition of old friends and enemies, the solution of revolting injustices, and the explanation of that which conditions the man and makes him what he is. Such is the Law which is crying now for universal recognition, and which when

45

understood by thinking people, will do much to solve the problems of humanity.[8]

Why will this be so?

Because when the Law of Love and the Law of Rebirth are recognized as governing principles, man will tread the path of life with more conscious awareness of his existence and its purpose. The teaching enjoins him to understand the causes he is setting up by his thoughts, feelings, and motives and make him realize their inevitable consequences or effects.

People will understand that this world and everything in it, including their bodies, is My energy and substance given to them. Then everyone will feel responsible for the way they use all things, including those considered inanimate (which is erroneous, for all life is, to some degree, conscious), and because whatever they sow, they will reap it here and now in their everyday existence upon earth which provides an adequate heaven and more than adequate hell. "As by law they suffer, so by law do they triumph. Ignorance of Law leaves them as the rudderless boat drifting on the current, while its knowledge gives them a helm by which they can steer their ship wherever they will."[9]

Originally, mankind existed in a perfect state described in the Bible as the Garden of Eden in union with its Source. Then, by what is called the Fall, they disrupted their divine intimacy and, as a result, lost the consciousness of My indwelling Presence.

In the process, they experienced all sorts of physical, mental, and emotional limitations by which the body became increasingly dense, eclipsing the inner light.

Since God's nature is essentially love, do not you think that his will is to have his children back home with no one dis-

advantaged or impeded in the achievement of the most important thing in life?

I believe that's the meaning of the parable of the prodigal son.[10]
Is it not, then, reasonable to assume that I would provide every
opportunity for them to be reunited with Me, no matter how
far astray they went? Certainly you need more than one lifetime
to grow to your full Christ-stature and regain your divine nature, especially if your earthly existence is cut short or if you
are afflicted by physical or mental disabilities.

Reincarnation is neither dogmatic nor mysterious; even
those not particularly religious find that it makes sense, irrespective of their willingness to accept it.

**Science doesn't tell us how to nurture a fine mind and a
pure heart, and cannot explain the problem of human inequalities. According to scientific theory the children of a
victim of alcoholism, or another addiction, will have bodies
prone to disease, but it is not known why some unhappy off-
springs are the recipients of that terrible inheritance.**
To accept the process of reincarnation or re-
embodiment is of supreme importance because it is the key to
the understanding of the riddle of the human condition.. Freedom and bondage arise from within the individual; the latter
being the result of the discordant thoughts, feelings, and actions of his past lives.

However, he is still free to think and feel and act within
his self-created walls.

**I can understand that, "Even the thoughts of a prisoner can-
not be put in chains; he is always free to think in a new and**

and therefore creative way which will form future patterns different from the past. We thus embody both freedom and necessity."[11]

To deny the truth of the continuity of his own being – its span of previous existences and its future glorious destiny – is to cut himself off from the basic precondition of life. When the individual wears out the coat of flesh he used during his earthly existence, I will provide for him another body.

I tell you eternal truth: so-called death exists only in the human imagination.

The individual which appears to the outer senses to be dead is in reality resting between embodiments for a while in the higher plane of light, until the time comes for him to return to the stage of life and continue the drama of his existence. Eventually, if he is determined enough, he will attain the final victory of his immortal freedom in the ascension, which is the only predestination for each human being.

Does one embody always as a man or woman or is there a change of gender?

They alternate according to the Law of balance and harmony. For instance, if one causes harm or discord to a human being of the other sex, he or she will re-embody in the gender of the other and will undergo the same experience.

The Law of cause and effect; that's the way we learn, if we are wise.

This subject should be studied carefully because it is compatible with the two most important view of the afterlife in Christianity.

According to one, the soul shares in the nature of its divine source and, as opposed to the body which is subject to dissolution, it is immortal; after death, the individual is destined to heaven or hell.

In the other doctrine, humans have no claim to immortality because they are in a state of sin, which entails death; however, through faith and union with the resurrected Christ, believers take on a new body and are raised to eternal life.

We are told that our mortal bodies will rise again, but there are conflicting views on the resurrection, and the doctrine itself is beyond our comprehension. The only explanation given is that it is a mystery accessible only to faith.

Hebrew thought, influenced by Hellenistic culture, was familiar with reincarnation: during Jesus' time the notion of the preexistence of the soul was part of the teaching of various Jewish groups and sects. In fact, there is mention of it in the Old Testament, when God spoke to Jeremiah saying, "Before I formed you in the womb I knew you, and before you were born I consecrated you."[12]

In the Gospel of Matthew, when Jesus asked His disciples who the people say He is, they replied, "Some say John the Baptist, but others Elijah, and still others Jeremiah or one of the prophets."[13] Also, the priests who went to see John the Baptist asked him, "Are you Elijah?".[14] Jesus, after the transfiguration, is reported to have said, "But I tell you that Elijah has come, and they did to him whatever they pleased".[15]

The Bible does not explicitly teach reincarnation, but neither does it deny it; and there is support for it, not only in the Scripture, but in the Fathers of the Church and in later Christian literature.

One can recognize the justice of the principle of Karma and reincarnation, according to which deeds done in time are expiated in time and not sealed for all eternity compared to which human existence is like a flash of lightning or a blinking of the eyes. It is certainly consistent with the infinite love and mercy of the Creator not to limit to one life span the possibility and potential capacity of the individual to repent and redeem himself.

If we are told to forgive, not seven times, but seven times seven, certainly God can do more than that.

But it seems that even after many embodiments hundreds and sometimes thousands, - people fall into the same old rut and are unable to find what they really want! I am reminded of a passage that has always intrigued me from Milan Kundera's novel, *The Unbearable Lightness of Being:*

> We can never know what to want because, living only one life, we can neither compare it with our previous life nor perfect it in our lives to come. There is no means of testing which decision is better, because there is no basis for comparison. We live everything as it comes, without warning, like an actor going on cold. And what can life be worth if the first rehearsal for life is life itself? That is why life is something, the groundwork of a picture, whereas the sketch that is our life is a sketch for nothing, an outline with no picture. *Einmal ist Keinmal.* What happens but once, says the German adage, might as well not have happened at all. If we have only one life to live, we might as well not have lived at all.[16]

This seems to imply that people cannot learn from their past lives because they cannot remember them. Certainly

that is my experience. I am not able to learn even from my present life!

The author affirms the necessity for reincarnation. Some individuals, especially children, have glimpses of a past life; but in any case, lack of specific memories is not an adequate explanation for not learning from past lives or from your present one.

People are enslaved to their habits, the personality is selfish and very stubborn; instead of learning from their mistakes, they keep repeating them because their attitude has become hardened. For some it may take a long time and terrific distress and struggle to awaken and become sensitive and responsive to My light that is always trying to illumine the darkness of the lower nature of the personality to which they are attached.

How can it be done?

There are only two ways to be purified from one's miscreant ways and be free: the fire of love or the fire of suffering – and, mark you, I am not using figurative, or metaphorical language. There is no excuse adducing ignorance as a reason for one's shortcomings, because ignorance itself is a consequence of man's weakness, though less serious than willful or deliberate intent to do wrong.

I don't understand you, ignorance of what?

I am referring to the fact that there have been great teachers throughout the centuries bringing the light of wisdom to benighted mankind, explaining the Law of Life, cause and effect, and the responsibility of the individual for the use of his life-energy. With the exhortation that no one needs to stay in and to struggle under his limitations because freedom for them is possible. If one cannot accomplish it in his present lifetime, there is the hope of the next.

But large portions of humanity have no understanding of reincarnation or they don't accept it!
Theological reasons to reject reincarnation do not carry much conviction and usually reflect a deep misunderstanding and distortion of it.

Let me clarify here that reincarnation or re-embodiment has absolutely nothing to do with transmigration or metempsychosis.[17]

It is a perversion to believe in the passage of what is called the soul into another species' body – though I must say that throughout history there have been those who, by the selfish and perverted misuse of their faculties, have acted in a manner far below the animal level.

Incidentally, I don't understand the prejudice against cremation, which accomplishes more expeditiously and effectively what burial does, without imposing so much foulness and corruption on nature and the environment.
I agree. Also, a very important reason for it is that it hastens the purification of the individual who has passed on: the fire consumes his earthly desires and the sensual appetites connected with the physical body. He is free from its fleshy prison but not from its influence and from the attraction and pull of the physical world on his emotions.

I read that there are those who die in tragic circumstances, like accidents or murder, who are still connected by their negative and discordant feelings with the people or conditions involved in their case.

Yes, they are "earthbound" entities who are unable to leave the earth. And there are those who pass out with addictions and vicious tendencies who try to gratify their cravings through the bodies of others which have those same desires.

There is no question that the Law of retribution is the only sensible and just explanation for events and conditions throughout the world that, otherwise, make life, as the existentialists say, absurd.
The individual, as he understands and accepts his responsibilities, realizing the possibility for freedom, can use the same principle to undo what he has done, bring himself into conformity with the divine order, and become master of his destiny.

Reincarnation takes away the tragic and immeasurable disproportionateness from the belief that decisions made in the fleeting duration of human existence will have consequences which last for all of eternity. It recognizes and confirms the action of divine justice and restores dignity and power to the individual in the exercise of his free will.

It is certainly consistent with the merciful nature of God to enable His children to realize, by every means possible, the divine potential planted as a seed in their hearts, and thus fulfill Jesus' command, "Be perfect, therefore, as your heavenly Father is perfect."[18]

I begin to realize that to make one brief lifetime the sole and exclusive condition and testing ground for the everlasting destination to heaven or hell, even with an intermediate stage of purgatory, cannot be the final answer.
I should mention that, the doctrine of purgatory can be related to reincarnation, which is, in fact, a purgative process: by the

fire of love, you purify yourself of everything that binds you to your Karmic debts until you are completely free of them.

I must admit that no issue is more confusing in the history of religions, including Christianity, than that concerning the afterlife. For instance, in the case of infants who die unbaptized, it makes little sense that according to some teachings, they should live in that place called limbo for all eternity, although it has never been officially promulgated by the Catholic Church. Even though they experience no pain it appears that they are excluded from the presence of God.
But how fortunate are the little ones who die soon after baptism, since they go straight to heaven! Parents should, then, be very happy and give praise and thanks for such a newly baptized child's death. However, this is not the case at all.

It seems to me that the nature and purpose of a fixed immortality without the possibility of growth or change – and I believe this applies to every individual – lacks value and significance. It is asserted that the soul is created for every new body, implying that the coming into existence of the former depends on the formation of the latter. Beside the fact that, in this case, it is the human being, not God, who makes the decision for someone to become an individual, the notion of a soul with no past yet endowed with an everlasting future is hardly credible. Only a self who is unborn can intelligibly be assumed to possess unending life.
You are right. God is eternal progress, life is perpetual motion, and within human nature there is the innate tendency toward self-transcendence and expansion, the longing for that which is greater because it comes from the infinite ground of Being. It aspires to regain not only the lost paradise of its original state

but it is predestined for deification, that is, the return to the Father's house in the ascension as Jesus came to teach.

But I see there is a question in your mind.

Yes. Though I don't like to admit it, in spite of your persuasive explanations, it's still not easy for me to accept the fact that innocent people may suffer.

There is another aspect of the Law of Love that will help you to clear your understanding. First let me remind you that no inhabitant on the planet Earth is "innocent', or he would not be embodied in the discord of his limited consciousness and the density of his physical body. However, in those cases where the affliction is not the result of one's actions, and does not belong to the individual, it might be imposed on him by what is called, collective Karma.

Everyone, as I mentioned, is part of a group, whether family, nation, race, or planet; while it is true that nothing may happen to anyone unless it is of his own creation or opened the door to it he may nevertheless become engulfed in a natural disaster or the destruction of war. In such events, if death is not a debt owed to the Law, the person will seem miraculously saved.

I recently read an account of 1,500 people who avoided being struck down by a deadly tsunami while they were at Mass. They were saved only because the priest decided to move the service to a chapel one mile inland on account of a special feast being held concurrently. In this case, wrote a reporter, the vagaries of chance seem an insufficient explanation. Another interesting detail is that, if for some reason the service had not been extended – if it had ended a mere

10 minutes earlier – the parishioners would have returned home just in time to greet the tsunami at their doors.
However, if one is innocent and still falls victim to a disaster because of collective Karma, he will be compensated for it.

Remember that the action of the Law is to reestablish and maintain balance according to the scales of justice and this implies compensation if the individual is not responsible. Therefore, no one should presume to know the cause of any-one's condition or be tempted to judge another based on his personal opinions. Only the varying needs of the individual de-termine his particular mode of being and existing state. It would be a mistake to entertain the thought, "He must have done something wrong to deserve it." There have been cases in which one chose to be born a handicap for the purpose of teaching or helping others. He may be an unrecognized saint lifting the heavy burden of the sorrow of the world. Although the knowledge of reincarnation enables you to understand your conditions, and that of others, no one can fathom the depths of each one's history except the God Self of every individual.

Karma is the most stupendous Law of the universe, such that it is impossible for the average individual in any way to comprehend it, for, if traced back along its central root and its many ramifications, one eventually reaches the point where causes antedating even thousands of lives have to be dealt with; and this can be grasped only by an omniscient mind.

Reincarnation seems logical and reasonable because it ex-plains situations and circumstances which otherwise may appear unjust or accidental. However, my main objection remains: we don't remember that we have lived prior to our present life.

This is the greatest argument against reincarnation, but let us consider a few points. Do you remember how you learned to walk or to write in your present life?

Certainly not. It is true that I have forgotten more of my life than I can remember.
Someone may have fallen in childhood and injured his body; the event has faded out from his memory, but he is suffering from the consequences.

Let me clarify that a honorable character, the conscience of right and wrong, the desire for knowledge and truth, the feeling of altruistic love, these are all the result of past experiences. Child prodigies, for example, are not God's favorites, but individuals who, in previous embodiments, earned their talents by their own effort.

Potentially, everyone is a genius because of his divine image, endowed with the same attributes and qualities.

Master Eckhart, the great mystic and theologian, wrote, "The seed of God is in us. Given an intelligent and hard-working farmer, it will thrive and grow up to God, whose seed it is; and accordingly, its fruits will be God-nature. Pear seeds grow into pear trees, nut seeds into nut trees, and God seeds into God."[19] "An intelligent and hard-working farmer" implies the need for individual effort in the process and manner of growing 'God seeds into God."

But not everyone has been able to do it.
However, each person is gifted with the creative powers of thought and feeling and is using them all the time.

Unfortunately, often misusing them.

You cannot blame Me for it. A point supporting reincarnation is that there have been children who have had an intimation of past lives recalled by some present circumstances.

It makes me think of the case of the famous cellist, Jacqueline du Pre, who, when she was only four years of age, saw a cello and right away told her mother that she wanted it.
Yes. It is not uncommon at an early age to remember former events because of the clearer channel of the consciousness.

Edgar Cayce, a devout Christian, was at first vehemently opposed to the idea of reincarnation, but he was finally convinced by the compelling evidence of his own experience. According to one of his readings, the parents of an eleven month old baby boy were told that he had been Franz Liszt in his previous life and would naturally show great musical ability.

"Nickname the entity Franz, for it will be in keeping with the entity and that it will be inclined to call itself when it begins to lisp or think…There is the natural intent and interest towards things of the artistic nature and temperament. There are the abilities to use the voice, as well in playing most *any* instrument – if the opportunity is given; especially in the composition as the playing itself. Symphonies, all forms of musical interludes and the like should be the training to which the entity would be subjected … And as soon as he is capable of such, insist upon beginning with the piano."

His musical talent was not developed only in one life. In Palestine, he was among the chief musicians for setting the Psalms of David and the Songs of Solomon in the various services of the temples. Before that incarnation he was

in Egypt, again active with those who set religious chants to any form of music for the peoples descendent from Atlantis. Thus, the child's parents were then given advices for training little Franz.[20]

However, the truth of reincarnation can only come from inner awareness; no amount of intellectual speculation and external evidence is convincing proof to anyone.

And consider this: people should be grateful that they do not remember their distant past. The flood of recollections from hundreds, and sometimes even thousands of lives would surely be overwhelming! In addition, the consciousness of the individual not only would be held back by the pull of memories, but some of the past experiences might be so tragic or terrifying that one could lose his sanity by remembering them again. Moreover, he could be so affected and influenced by contact with what happened in the past that he would be forced to repeat it because it may vivify the etheric record, which are within himself. It is indeed an act of mercy to close the door of memory each time the individual comes into a new embodiment.

In fact, one aspect of the Cosmic Law is to prevent the remembrance of those events from previous lives that would mar the opportunity for a new beginning. Since the recollection of old experience patterns is broken at birth, the possibility for freedom is always present, and one can be raised out of his own imperfections, reaching a higher state of consciousness without the tremendous burden of the past.

Occasionally old memories may surface into awareness and people will have the impression of experiencing something that they did in a previous embodiment.

This is similar to the phenomenon referred to as *déjà vu,* which is French for "already seen."

However, what is essential and of real value is the fact that each human being, in his present sate, is the sum total and the result of all his past lives. Everything is recorded at the etheric level in and around the physical form and , if it is required for the benefit and progress of the individual, past events may be revealed in accord with the wisdom of the Law.

There is a case which illustrates a claimed instance of reincarnation based on the testimony of an Englishman named John Pollock. At the age of nineteen he converted to Roman Catholicism, but posed a problem for the parish priests by professing a belief in reincarnation. They tried to dissuade him without result, and he decided to rely on God to resolve the dispute.

A few years later Pollock married. Two daughters were born, and the family moved to Hexham. In May 1957, the girls, aged 11 and 6, were killed in a car accident. Pollock had the presentiment that they would be reborn to him as a proof of reincarnation. His wife, who did not approve of his belief in reincarnation, found this attitude very distasteful, and for a time their marriage was severely troubled. When Florence became pregnant the following year, John was certain that she would have twin daughters, because God was returning the departed girls to their parents.

Indeed, twin daughters were born; and a faint thin line on the second-born's forehead and a birthmark on her left hip were said to be identical to marks on the younger of the dead sisters.

When the twins were four months old, the Pollock's moved to another town. Three years later the family revisited Hexham, and, according to John Pollock, the twins immediately behaved as if they knew the town. They were said to have recognized the school and the playground previously frequented by the dead sisters, and to have identified their former home, all without any prompting from their parents.

Similar incidents allegedly followed; for example, some toys of the former sisters were unpacked and the youngest is said to have correctly named two dolls and to have assigned a toy of the deceased elder sister to her own first-born twin sister.

Pollock also reported coming upon the twins in the backyard screaming hysterically, "The car! The car! It's coming at us!"

Such incidents ceased not long after the two sisters' fifth birthdays. At present, they claim to have no memories belonging to their late sisters.

According to John Pollock, he did not discuss with the twins their purported reincarnated status until they were thirteen.[21]

It is an interesting case, but it is convincing only to those who already accept the notion of reincarnation. The difficulty is that it does not strictly entail an experient's giving a firsthand report of what appear to be personal memories of a previous existence.

Ian Stevenson of the University of Virginia Division of Parapsychology has visited several countries, recording and investigating many cases. His detailed observations have been published in a series of books. They deal almost exclusively with reincarnation experiences in childhood, believing it too difficult to ensure the authenticity of adult cases.

One of the experients was able to interview is Gnanatilleka, a girl born in the village of Hedunawewa, central Sri Lanka, in February 1956. When she was one year old Gnanatilleka mentioned another mother and father, and at the age of two she began to make explicit references to a previous life as a boy. She claimed to have parents, two brothers and many sisters living in another town, Talawakele about sixteen miles from Hedunawewa. Their climate and vegetation differ considerably and travel between them is difficult and infrequent. The girl said that she wanted to visit her "other" parents and recalled details of her alleged past life. She mentioned the names of members of her former family, the father's occupation, descriptions of the parents, the location of the family home, and a story she had been taught at a school during that previous life. On the basis of these details a particular family in Talawakele was identified as that of the subject of the former existence.

The previous personality was a lad named Tillekeratne who died at the age of twelve in November 1954. He may have had some visceral disease but it is known for certainty to have been admitted to a hospital following a fall and to have died within a fortnight. Prior to his death he is said to have developed effeminate tendencies. During Stevenson's interview of Gnanatilleka she reported that when she had been a boy she had wanted to be a girl, and now she was happier as a girl. Members of each family denied having any knowledge of the other prior to her statements about the previous existence. In 1960 Gnanatilleka and her family visited Talawakele where she correctly identified several buildings in the town. When she directed her family to the place of her former residence, however, the home was found to be no longer standing. The girl recognized some teachers from Tillekeratne's school, and she identified accurately seven members of the previous personality's family. Two people in a crowd outside the house were also recognized spontaneously. During his visit to both towns, Stevenson was able to confirm the above data of the case by interviewing Gnanatilleka herself, members of the two households concerned, and other witnesses.[22]

I also read concerning hypnotic regression in which the subject was given the suggestion to return to a time before he was born and encounter a life he had led previously. During the 1950's, there was the much publicized case of an American woman, Virginia Tighe, who regressed to a previous existence as Bridey Murphy in nineteenth-century Belfast.

However, the practice of hypnotic regression has not proved satisfactory as an experimental technique because of its unreliability. The hypnotic state has the reputation for confabulation, role-playing, and generating imaginary past lives; this despite the fact that there are cases that appear to show substantial historical and other veridical information. One convincing feature of this type of hypnosis occurs when the subject demonstrates an ability to speak and engage in conversation in an unfamiliar foreign language.

I can recall a television documentary about an Englishman regressed as a gunner's mate aboard a British frigate some 200 years ago. During the regression he named the ship and its officers and in naval slang he vividly described the conditions and events aboard the ship ending in a dramatic enactment of the sailor's severe wounding in a naval battle.

Beside the fact that it is almost impossible to persuade the skeptic, because doubt is a feeling very difficult to uproot, I

63

would not recommend the practice of hypnosis under any circumstances.

I'd like to quote the narrative of a person with inner sight who was asked by a friend to give him a glimpse of his former lives. I don't know if the descriptions are true or not but they illustrate some aspects of the Law which you are explaining. The request was granted because it was not motivated by intellectual curiosity but by a sincere desire for knowledge. The clairvoyant began by saying:

> Almost 5,000 years ago you were born a male in Egypt, in a large city not far from the Nile Delta. Your father was a merchant, and his only interest and desire was to increase his wealth and social influence. Driven by his ambition, he did not hesitate in his dealings to use a low kind of cunning and even deception.
>
> Your young years were uneventful; your favorite pastime was fishing in the nearby river and shooting your bow and arrow.
>
> On becoming an adult, you joined your father's business, learning from him his scheming and unscrupulous ways. Being very rich, you were surrounded by idle acquaintances, parasites and flatterers of a dissolute type. You met a young woman who loved you deeply and faithfully, but you tired of her company and, breaking all your promises, decided to abandon her. The unbearable feeling of being deserted and rejected by you drove her to an untimely death at her own hands.
>
> You continued your dissolute lifestyle, although you grew to dislike it and were, at times, tormented by a sense of guilt and remorse. Unable to resist the tempta-

tions and pressures of your surroundings, as they turned you incessantly back upon your own pleasures and your own selfish interests, you became increasingly unhappy and prone to attacks of self-contempt.

In your middle age, during an angry quarrel that ended in violence, you suffered a serious wound which took a long time to heal. Left alone, reflecting on your life, assailed by doubt and despairing of any improvement, you too committed suicide.

This was decidedly, not a good incarnation.

In another life you were the daughter of a member of the senatorial aristocracy in ancient Rome. Being a serious and diligent girl, you received a brilliant education, exceptional for women of that period. Gifted with both beauty and intelligence, several suitors vied for your company and affection. One of them, a centurion of noble character and ancestry who was quite devoted to you and your family, succeeded in winning your hand in marriage.

At the same time, you grew dissatisfied with the pagan religion, which included a pantheon of gods and goddess who were given anthropomorphic characteristics, possessing the same desires and flaws as humans, only on a larger scale. You came into contact with the teachings of Jesus and, being strongly attracted to them, you embraced the doctrine of Christianity.

During a persecution, you were arrested, along with many others, at a secret meeting in the catacombs. Because of your social status, you could have preserved your freedom by renouncing your faith, but you wholeheartedly refused. As a result, you were condemned to be thrown to the wild beasts in the Coliseum. Your companion, in virtue of his rank as a centurion, was able to save you by hiding in the subterranean level of the amphitheater underneath the central open area, and afterward, at the risk of his own life, allowed you to escape during the night. Having been discovered and publicly accused by a jealous former rival, he refused to reveal your whereabouts and was put to death for treason.

After many centuries, the two of you, drawn by the bonds of love, were brought together during the French Revolution. You were now the coachman of the carriage of a noble woman whom you greatly admired for her physical and spiritual qualities; in fact, you were helplessly in love with her.

One day, while stepping down from the coach, she dropped a valuable jewel and its loss caused her considerable consternation. You found the gem near the carriage and returned it to her. She could hardly contain her joy and gratitude and, after commending your honesty, asked you, to your amazement, to keep the jewel.

When the revolution broke out, the lady, with many others of the nobility, was arrested and condemned to the guillotine. You were a supporter of the revolution and became one of its strongest proponents; however, the thought of her impending death tortured you relentlessly, and, unable to endure it any longer, you went to see her at the place where she was imprisoned. In that fateful moment, when your eyes met with hers through the iron bars, the ancient flame was rekindled, and a sense of recognition flashed through your souls. You spoke to the guard in a desperate attempt to bribe him with the promise of the jewel; the gaoler was agreeable, but said that it was not possible to remove her name from the full list of eighty people expected to die the next day. Finally, by your persistent efforts, you persuaded him to cross her name off the death-roll and write your own. At dawn, you were publicly guillotined in her place.

There is a poem with the title "Sudden Light" that beautifully conveys the feeling of enduring love throughout the centuries:

> "I have been here before, -
> But when or how I cannot tell ...
>
> You have been mine before, -
> How long ago I may not know:
> But just when at that swallow's soar
> Your neck turned so,
> Some veil did fall, - I knew it all of yore.[23]

In another incarnation, continued the narrator, you were born as a man in Florence during the flowering of the Italian Renaissance. Being assiduous in your studies and devoted to learning, you became a member of a circle of scholars under the patronage of the Medici family. Because of your proficiency in ancient Greek, you were able to read ancient manuscripts and became a successful collector.

The friend of the clairvoyant said "That explains my love for books." The clairvoyant continued:

You traveled to Byzantium in search of Greek texts and, due to the interest in the revival of classical culture, you decided, together with a partner, to make copies and translations of the precious manuscripts.

Both of you accumulated considerable wealth, when suddenly your partner fell ill and passed on. He left his entire estate to you to be used for a charitable work in which he was involved.

But greed took possession of you and, instead of carrying out the wishes of your deceased friend, you kept all the money for yourself.

I am sure you remember this incident from your present life; it involves one of your employees, an Italian immigrant who came seeking your help for his seriously ill wife and impoverished large family. For some reason unknown to you, following an inner prompting, you became interested and concerned about his predicament. You not only granted his request for financial assistance, but your kindness and generosity exceeded his expectations. You promoted him and raised his salary; then, after you visited his family and witnessed their poor lodging and conditions, you decided to help them move to a new home in a better section of town. You also made sure that his wife was given the best medical attention and provided for the raising and education of his children.

He was my Florentine partner whom I defrauded!

Yes. What you did for him allowed for the working out of the Karmic Law, which, in turn, enabled you to make a balance for your transgression. Because of your actions in this situation, you were rewarded with greater freedom and were able to make more rapid progress.

I read in the Cayce files about the effect of positive Karma in the case of an extremely attractive New York model. Her unusually beautiful hands bring her much in demand with nail polish, hand lotion, and jewelry merchants. The Karmic cause for her gift of beauty was found in the incarnation immediately preceding the present, when she was a recluse in an English convent. Her life had been spent in performing menial and distasteful tasks with her hands. However she did them with such a spirit of selflessness and dedication that her service was transmuted into the unusual beauty of her person and of her hands.[24]

This is an example that Karma is not always punitive or disciplinary as it is commonly understood. However, even when it may appear that way, in the end it is always beneficent because the individual will ultimately learn to love. The Law safeguards love.

Do people come back into embodiment in the same relationships that were interrupted by death?

Not necessarily; husband and wife might, in one lifetime, find themselves in the same family as brother and sister, mother and son, or as other relatives. It is also possible for them to be born separately; despite this, if there was a tie of love, when they meet for the first time they will feel an irresistible attraction for each other.

There are also cases in which individuals are drawn together in the same family, not by love, but out of hatred and injury in order to balance their debts of the past. This explains some tragic events of children suffering at the hands of their parents and, conversely, parents distressed by their children: they may experience what they inflicted once on the one who now torments them.

How can the cycle of evil and violence be brought to an end?

Only by love. When someone, working out his Karma, is capable of forgiving his so-called enemy, then the darkness of hate is dissolved forever by the light of love, and only then is he free.

Let me emphasize that the secret of healing not only of relations but of any condition that beset mankind, I mean the fundamental attitude that enables individuals to be healed, is forgiveness.

Are you referring also to the healing of the body?

Yes, because the real cause of most illnesses is in the feeling nature.

What is the most common negative emotion?

Resentment, which is a subtle form of hate, and it can flare at the least provocation.

But how can we forgive ourselves? It seems very difficult to do it.

Because of creations of centuries that have become habits, some feelings are deeply rooted and they hold the person bound unless he or she is very determined to be released from them. Turn to Me and the magnetic force of your attention on My Presence will draw back to you the healing flame of My love.

You must learn to forgive and forget; in this way you can reverse the current and to a large extent dissolve the negative Karma, especially the fear of it which causes unnecessary Karma. Recognize that you live under the blessed dispensation of Grace and it will help you find peace.

1 John 1:17.
2 Matthew 25:14-30.
3 Deuteronomy 32:4.
4 *Confessions*, vii, 5.
5 Lama Govinda Anagarika, *Creative Meditation and Multidimensional Consciousness* (Wheaton, IL: Theosophical Publishing House, 1976), p. 141.
6 Tom Harpur, *The Uncommon Touch: An Investigation into Spiritual Healing* (Toronto: McClelland and Steward, 1994), p. 237.
7 Ezekiel 33:11.
8 Alice A. Bailey, *Esoteric Psychology: A Treatise on the Seven Rays* (NY: Lucis Publishing Co., 1979), p. 300.
9 Annie Besant, *The Riddle of Life*, p. 54.
10 Luke 15:11-32.
11 Rudolf Steiner quoted in: David Lorimer, *Whole in One* (NY: Penguin Group, 1990), p. 142.
12 Jeremiah 1:5.
13 Matthew 16:14.
14 John 1:21.
15 Mark 9:13; Matthew 11:13-14.
16 Milan Kundera, *The Unbearable Lightness of Being* (NY: HarperCollins, 1995), p. 8.
17 *metempsychosis*: the passage of somebody's soul after death into the body of another person or an animal (Encarta World English Dictionary, 1999.)
18 Matthew 5:48.
19 Quoted in Aldous Huxley, *The Perennial Philosophy* (NY: Harper-Row, 1945), p. 39.
20 Mary Ann Woodward, *Edgar Cayce's Story of Karma* (NY: Berkley Books, 1983) pp. 99-100.
21 H.J. Irvin, *An Introduction to Parapsychology* (Jefferson, NC: McFarland & Co. Publishers, 1989), pp. 240-241.
22 Ibid., pp. 242-3.

[23] Dante Gabriel Rossetti.

[24] Gina Cerminara. *Many Mansions: The Edgar Cayce Story on Reincarnation.* (NY: Penguin Books, 1991), p. 62.

CHAPTER 4

All is Law, All is Love

Charity itself fulfills the law,
And who can sever love from charity.

O most potential love! Vow, bond, nor space
In thee hath neither sting, knot, nor confine,
For thou art all, and all things else are thine.
William Shakespeare

All, everything that I understand, I understand only
because I love. Everything is, everything exists, only
because I love. Everything is united by it alone.
Leo Tolstoy

Love is not a mere impulse; it must contain truth, which is law.
Rabindranath Tagore

I find this subject extremely interesting, but I am reminded of a story in the Gospel that seems to deny reincarnation. I am referring to that passage about Jesus and his disciples passing by a man who had been blind from birth. The disciples asked Jesus, "Rabbi, who sinned, this man or his parents, that he was born blind? And he replied, Neither this man nor his parents sinned; he was born blind so that God's works would be revealed in him."[1]
First, notice that by their question the disciples were aware of the principle of reincarnation and asked for clarification. Also the Pharisees knew about it when they reproached the man who was healed with the words. "You were born entirely in sins, and are you trying to teach us?"[2]

If reincarnation had been unknown or rejected outright, Jesus would either have disapproved or disregarded their inquiry as meaningless. He obviously realized the true cause of the condition of the blind man; do you think that Jesus would portray His Heavenly Father inflicting an innocent child with blindness in order to manifest God's works? You must understand His answer in the light of the statement, "From his fullness we have received, grace upon grace. The law indeed was given through Moses; grace and truth came through Jesus Christ."[3]

Do you not see the point?

The Divine Master goes beyond the principle of cause and effect and transcends it because, as the bearer of Grace which is God's forgiveness, He fulfills the Law.
Exactly. He came to teach mankind how to be free from their limitations by the power of love.

He made it clear when He said that He did not come to abolish the Law but to fulfill it. The Law is negated because it is transcended in the new reality of Grace, but to reach that divine state it is necessary to pass through the Law of cause and effect and to carry it out to the last letter by love.

There is another episode which may be interpreted as contradicting the principle of reincarnation. One of the two criminals crucified together with Jesus turned to him with the words, "Remember me when you come to your kingdom." And Jesus replied, "Truly, I tell you, today you will be with me in paradise."[4]
Jesus' statement only indicates that the criminal will be taken to the heavenly world, rather to one of them. It does not imply that he will remain there forever.

During this life on earth, everyone must be purified by the fire of My love, or in the crucible of his experiences to consume the stains that have covered the divine image. Then, the individual will be free from the rule of the Law as he himself becomes the embodiment of the Law, love.

The key is contained in the statement, *All is Love and yet all is Law.*

Love is the impelling force and Law executes the will of Love.

Love and the forgiveness of Grace are intertwined, one must forgive in order to be forgiven. It is interesting that in several languages the meaning of the word forgiveness is to *give* something *for,* that is, to replace and consume discord and evil by the fire of love. People must understand that the Law and love are interrelated and interdependent since one cannot exist without the other.

Love is the greatest force in manifestation and there is no limit to its power, as all substance obeys it. Everything you can think of, whether animate or inanimate, is made of love.

All energy is God's energy. Since God is love, it is tantamount to saying that love is energy and substance.
And it is not only the moving power of life but without its magnetic force of attraction there would be no form or manifestation. It is always operating through an immutable Law that governs and sustains the entire "cosmos," the root word of which means order and harmony.

Love is the way and the Law assures that no one goes astray.

But with regard to the function of love in relation to the Law, isn't salvation attained by God's Grace rather than man's effort?

Both are necessary. Good works are the implementation of the gift of Grace acting in and through the individual. The God Self constantly gives His love and intelligence to the human being in order to fulfill the divine plan, but the individual must decide of his free will to cooperate with it. God needs humans as humans need God: all reality is built on the principle of polarity, two in one, and one in two.

"To a God the finite should be as much a necessity as to man the infinite," wrote a mystic poet.[5] And Meththild of Magdeburg heard the words, "O soul, before the world was, I longed for thee: and I still long for thee, and thou for Me. Therefore, when our two desires unite, Love shall be fulfilled."[6]

Although you turned away, I have never left you, neither criticized or condemned, and kept loving and protecting you as much as you allowed Me.

I don't understand why, after Jesus's redemptive ministry, we are still on a journey upon this Earth with the scars of original sin liable to open and bleed again at the least temptation.

Theologians can give you all kinds of explanations arguing that people are responsible for the disobedience of Adam and Eve. I have offered My version, and this is all I can do until the light breaks through the darkness of the human perversion. The truth is that if it were not necessary for the individual to exert his will and call to Me for help, do you think I would have allowed such suffering and destruction to go on century after century?

To see those you love more than they love themselves, misuse your faculties and energy must be heartrending, even for you.
If I were not who I Am, I could not watch their degradation and keep waiting for their decision to return to Me. It is very hard to possess the power to set your loved ones free and have to withhold it. People do not understand life, and do not even care to know, or ask to be illumined; but unless they realize that all the universe is governed by the Law of Love and obey it, they will remain in bondage because they close the door to Me.

It is unbelievable that we can limit God. This is what I find most difficult to forgive myself for.
You would recognize in Me your greatest friend if you only understood who "I AM" and what I can do through you and for you by your acceptance of My presence.

It seems that only after repeated and severe experiences do we begin to gradually let your light penetrate our brains, then the stubbornness and rebellion subsides and we realize that the Earth is the garden you provided for us, and we are here by your permission and sustained by your Grace. We are, in reality, the guests of God, and have no right to desecrate your handiwork. That's why we must pay for it.
My plan for the infinite scheme of creation is one of harmony, beauty, and perfection, indescribable in your words. This planet has become a valley of tears, and it is no more the music of the spheres that one can hear, but the cry of distress of its inhabitants. Yet, I am always giving of Myself to everyone, like

the sun that shines on the just and unjust; but, again, Law and Love act together as one. If man's eternal destiny depended entirely upon Grace, what is the meaning and purpose of free will bestowed upon him?

There would be no opportunity for the individual to exercise it; his responsibility lies in the choice he makes, and, if he wants to be free, he must use his faculties and direct his actions toward that accomplishment. If salvation came from Grace alone, all mankind would have been in Paradise (if that is the meaning of being saved) a long time ago because that is My consuming desire for them.

St. Francis de Sales told you, "God did not deprive thee of the operation of His love, but thou didst deprive Him of thy cooperation. God would never have rejected thee, if thou hadst no rejected His love. O all good God, thou doest not forsake unless forsaken, thou never takes away thy gifts until we take away our hearts."[7]

Grace, or Love, originates from Me, and it is given for the purpose of helping you to achieve your final end, that is, the return to Me.

Your statement finds an echo in these words: "God created the world to become man in it, so that man would become god by grace, and partake of the conditions of the divine life."[8] The relationship between Grace and freedom implies the encounter of our two wills and their cooperation. God bestows the love and the forgiveness, but the human being must bring the effort.

Obviously, it is not the works of the self-righteous or proud that are rewarded, but the action of Grace in and through the individual as he becomes the willing instrument in the fulfillment of the divine plan.

That is the meaning of Jesus' words, "The Son can do nothing on his own, but only what he sees the Father doing; for whatever the Father does, the Son does likewise."[9]
There is the misconception that God can act independently of the individual's free will, but He can do for you only what He can do through you with your consent and cooperation. It takes your desire, your determination, and your acceptance, by deliberate choice, every hour, to be the instrument of Grace. Then you become a co-worker with God, blessing all you contact and helping to raise the consciousness of the Earth closer to Me.

The two wills must be in accord, as William Law explains it: "The difference between a good and a bad man does not lie in this, that the one wills that which is good and the other does not, but solely in this, that the one concurs with the living inspiring spirit of God within him, and the other resists it, and can be chargeable with evil only because he resists it."[10]

Didn't someone say that God created man without man but He cannot save man without man – without the human being's free response?
It is true; your devotion and the willingness to live according to the Law of Love are the necessary conditions to allow the abundance of Grace to flow through you uninterruptedly.

There is a reflection by Nicholas of Cusa: "Lord, Thou has given me my being of such a nature that it can continually make itself more able to receive thy grace and goodness. And this power, which I have of Thee, wherein I have a living image of thine almighty power, is free will. By this I can either enlarge or restrict my capacity for Thy grace."[11]

It is like sunshine upon a pool of water; do you not think that the light can penetrate and be reflected to a greater extent if the water is clean, and far less so if it is dirty or muddy? Grace is always pouring into you as life itself, but unless you keep the door of your consciousness open, it cannot come through.

How do we shut the door?
By disobedience to the Law of Love. In scientific parlance, one might say that love is the highest vibrational frequency in the universe, like light. If you create negative thoughts and feeling, like anger, resentment, condemnation, etc., which have lower rates of vibration, you change the quality of the energy and it forms like a cloud covering over the light of Grace.

In other words, you re-qualify and contaminate the luminous radiation of love by your discordant vibrations and create a shadow.

I have often wondered about the existence of hell and what it is like, but now I begin to understand that it is the evil created by mankind.
Do you think that I can manifest something different from who and what "I AM"? Especially of an opposite nature? Since "I AM" all that is, I would divide Myself into two and create a dichotomy in the universe.

We surround ourselves with darkness and then in our ignorance, we deny or blame you because we don't see the light. But don't you condemn to hell those who do evil? Would it not be an action of your justice as it is stated in the Scriptures?
Religious texts must be understood on different levels depending on the state of growth of the individual.

As St. Paul said, "Some people need milk, not solid food; for everyone who lives on milk, being still an infant is unskilled in the words of righteousness. But solid food is for the mature, for those whose faculties have been trained by practice to distinguish good from evil."[12]

I respect everyone's spiritual belief if they are sincere and practiced with devotion. Let me emphasize that it is impossible for Me to condemn anyone, especially to an eternal place of torture. The truth is that I always try to free the individual from the distressing conditions that only he creates. Heaven and hell begin within you, they are the effect of your mental and emotional states, and you experience them according to your attitude toward life. Each individual is the cause of the world in which he lives. Do you not remember Satan's words, "Which way I fly is hell; myself am hell."[13]

No, but I do recall this passage: "The will is that which has all power; it makes heaven and it makes hell; for there is no hell but where the will of the creature is turned from God, nor any heaven but where the will of the creature worketh with God."[14] Then, hell is a state of consciousness? Is it not a place?

There is a stratum around the planet which is the accumulation of all the destructive energy generated by the thoughts and feeling forms of mankind from eons past. It can be considered hell because only evil forces exist there. However, it is not permanent and it will be consumed when the final purification of the Earth will take place.

Negative currents from that layer in the atmosphere constantly influence and prey upon the people when they open themselves and attune to them by their discord.

There are also those who, after they pass on, may be caught and get entangled in that destructive energy because of their vicious habits.

Like attracts like.
During sleep if one does not go into the higher spheres of light he may connect with those forces which causes nightmarish dreams or feelings of helplessness, anxiety, etc.

What is the condition of those who commit murder and are responsible for mass slaughter and destruction of life when they leave their bodies?
They are confined within bounds in a geographical location set apart for them above the surface of the earth, no in the center.

Do they experience suffering as it is commonly believed?
Certainly, but they are tormented by their own feelings of rebellion and the reaction of the evil they inflicted on others.

According to the law of cause and effect. Is their condition eternal?
No, evil cannot be an eternal reality, there is only One Reality which I AM. I always give the opportunity to everyone to come back to Me.

But what if the human is too stubborn and perverse to refuse your help?
Then it goes through what is called "second death," that is the annihilation of the personal self by the terrible suffering caused, mark you, not by an external power, but its own destructive creations returning upon itself.

But the flame within the heart of the individual is not immortal?
Yes, I withdraw it unto Myself.

This explanation is more intelligible than the notion of body, soul and spirit being in hell for all eternity. But how can this happen to the individual made in the image of God?
I am not a theologian, but the subject is rather confusing. The truth is that there is one life, one consciousness, one energy, and there is no place in the infinite space where life is not, and I AM that life.

I can see that the traditional belief in hell postulates a metaphysical dualism with two ultimate principles of being: one good or light, and the other evil or darkness. Thus, the universe becomes divided into a place of eternal suffering ruled by the devil, and the kingdom of heaven where the blessed live in everlasting joy. Hell is also defined as the continuation of sin.
Which, then, becomes immortal; again it cannot be true, like conceiving hell the eternal separation from God, which means that the individual is excluded from the beatific vision. This seems a good definition, except that, since I AM the source of life, to be eternally separated from Me is tantamount to total annihilation.

Being or nothingness.
But do they know the meaning of the word "eternity" or "eternal"? Or what reality is?

According to one interpretation, to those enduring it, suffering "seems" eternal.

The truth is that evil is a passing shadow compared to eternity. It can be a terrifying experience, and it can cause untold damage on the earth, but it cannot last forever. By its very nature is self-destructive, therefore it will annihilate itself by the return of its own energy upon itself.

I have a deeper realization of the truth that heaven and hell begin within us and we experience them according to our state of consciousness.

Remember, you are your own judge; or, rather, you are judged by your own thoughts and feelings as you deserve. Human beings are the only creators of evil, not God, who is the perfection of love.

Rumi, the Persian mystic, once said, "If you have not seen the devil, look at your own self."[15] And Dostoevsky in his great novel *The Brothers Karamazov* wrote: "If the devil doesn't exist, but man has created him in his own image and likeness."[16]

There is a story about an Eskimo hunter and a missionary priest. The Eskimo asks the priest, if I didn't know about God and sin, would I still go to Hell? No, says the priest, not if you didn't know. Then why, the Eskimo asks earnestly, did you tell me?

Let me restate that God cannot act independently of your free will; He can do for you and to you only what you allow Him to do through your thoughts and feelings. How can you expect divine intervention and assistance if you doubt or deny it by your negativity?

I am reminded of this passage:

> ... grace falls like rain on everyone but, also like rain, it can only be received by a vessel properly prepared to catch it. The preparation involves a purification. Without preparation we are merely rough stones on which the rain of grace slides off; with it, we become worked stones hollowed into urns or chalices which can retain what falls from heaven. The entire process is a paradoxical mixture of effort and effortlessness. The effort is spiritual practice, our own ascent toward heaven; the effortlessness is grace, which perpetually descends from heaven for our benefit."[17]

The author you quoted is right, My love is always flowing and it creates and sustains all in perfect harmony and indescribable beauty. People do not realize that the very substance of everything they see and touch owes its existence to the self-giving of My forgiving Grace.

Does anyone understand that "I AM" the source of the energy coming into and animating their bodies which have become the cause of error and enslaving desires? Yet, I continue to give the light that can transform their physical forms into the instrument of liberation and enlightenment. Yes, the gentle rain of Grace is falling on everyone all the time to bless all life, which is really part of My life, trying to filter into the human heart. But it is mostly ignored, denied and brushed off.

I must desire and make the decision to be free from my mistakes and limitations of the past, knowing in my heart that all is Law and all is Love.

Now that you have some comprehension of the Law of Love, which is basic for your progress, as I lead you on the path of self-discovery, it is essential to realize that you cannot experience love without being who you are.

There cannot be love without a self.
Right, whether it is for the sake of oneself or for the sake of the other, that is, in its acquisitive or benevolent forms, love implies a relation. Therefore, the subject of our next discussion will be to unravel the mystery of the self. And I use the word "mystery" advisedly because, as you will see, it is the most difficult, yet the most rewarding experience in the quest for truth and happiness.

[1] John 9:2.

[2] John 9:34.

[3] John 1:16-17.

[4] Luke 23:43.

[5] Novalis, quoted in *Creative Meditation*, p. 34.

[6] Evelyn Underhill. *Mysticism: A Study in the Nature and Development of Man's Spiritual Consciousness.* (NY: E.P. Dutton, 1961), p. 92.

[7] St. Francis de Sales, in Huxley, p. 170.

[8] St. Maximus the Confessor, quoted in, Paul Evdokimov, *Woman and the Salvation of the World: A Christian Anthropology on the Charisms of Women* (Crestwood, NY: St. Vladimir's Seminary Press), p. 37.

[9] John 5:19.

[10] Huxley, p. 178.

[11] Huxley, p. 169.

[12] Hebrews 5:12-14.

[13] John Milton, *Paradise Lost*, Book 1, Line 73.

[14] William Law, quoted in Huxley, p. 174.

[15] Huxley, p. 178.

[16] Book 5, ch. 4.

[17] John White, *The Meeting of Science and Spirit: Guidelines for a New Age* (NY: Paragon House, 1990) p. 14.

CHAPTER 5

Who Am I?

He who knows others is wise.
He who knows himself is enlightened.
Lao Tzu

You are that which is not; I am that I am. If you know this truth
in your soul, the enemy will never deceive you and you shall
escape all his snares.
St. Catherine of Siena

With regard to your identity, if I ask you the fundamental question, "Who are you?", how would you answer? Do not tell me your name, your gender, nationality, race, or profession; I am referring to the real you.

I would say that I am a person with a body and a soul.
You mean you *are* a soul with a body. You do not *have* a soul, although people use the phrase, my soul. Otherwise, who is having a soul?

What is a soul anyway?
The term is ambiguous because it can have different meanings and is sometimes used interchangeably or synonymously with spirit, mind, the self, or consciousness, but they are not the same. What is called "Soul" in English is referred to by various words in the Hebrew and Greek languages in which the Bible was written. "Soul" is also used in at least four different ways. For instance, people pray for the salvation of their souls, and this obviously cannot mean the spirit, which is the divine presence.

I can't imagine the spirit in hell!
Therefore to avoid confusion I will not use the word soul. You would not understand its meaning anyway because what you are really conscious of, and think you are, is your body.

It is true, that is how I experience myself and I feel that I am alive because of it. But I also know that it is the identification with my body, so frail and vulnerable, that makes human existence irremediably tragic. Since the physical form is finite, living in the dimension of space and is linked to and measured by time from birth to death, our existence on earth is a journey whose final destination is extinction, and every passing moment is a step toward it. "For to be carnally minded is death."[1]

Asked once by an interviewer what bothered him most about life, the late American poet Robert Lowell answered simply, "That people die."[2]

We may try to hide ostrich-like, divert our mind and run away from it in our feverish activities, whistling in the dark, but the fear of death pursues us wherever we go and in all we do. Saint Paul's cry, "Wretched man that I am! Who will rescue me from this body of death?"[3] resonates through my all being with terrific force.

"We are, of all miseries," wrote Hilaire Belloc in a moving letter to a lady who, like himself, suffered early of the tragic ending of a marriage with the death of her beloved spouse, "much the most afflicted by Mortality: and that means not mere Death ... but the impermanence of all things, even of love: the good-byes and the changes that never halt their damning succession: the unceasing tale of loss which wears down all at last. That is mortality. That is the contradiction between our native joy and our present realities, which contrast is the curse of the Fall."[4]

The tragedy of that contrast grows painfully evident in the face of every lost love. Unable to assign comprehensible causes of it we cannot shrink before the fact that all which lay at the end of every human striving vanishes, sooner or later like smoke from the chimney. Even if we try to forget our predicament we are reminded of it by our surrounding and mother nature. "It is the blight man was born for," says the narrator of Hopkins' "Spring and Fall," to the young child who has wandered innocently into the autumn woods where, weeping but not knowing why, she watches all the fallen leaves die. "Margaret," he asks, "are you grieving/Over Gold-engrove unleaving?" Alas, he tells her, "It is Margaret you mourn for."[5]

God and death are antinomical. They cannot both be. For where one is, the other is not. I am reminded of a passage from a film, *The Seventh Seal*, where the knight goes to the confessional not knowing that the face of death is within, he kneels down and speaks to the voice behind the grill.

> KNIGHT: I want to talk to you as openly as I can, but my heart is empty.

> *Death doesn't answer.*

> KNIGHT: The emptiness is a mirror turned toward my own face. I see myself in it, and I am filled with fear and disgust.

> *Death doesn't answer.*

KNIGHT: Through my indifference to my fellowmen, I have isolated myself from their company. Now I live in a world of phantoms. I am imprisoned in my dreams and fantasies.

DEATH: And yet you don't want to die.

KNIGHT: Yes, I do.

DEATH: What are you waiting for?

KNIGHT: I want knowledge.

DEATH: You want guarantees?

KNIGHT: Call it whatever you like. Is it so cruelly inconceivable to grasp God with the senses? Why should he hide himself in a mist of half-spoken promises and unseen miracles?

Death doesn't answer.

KNIGHT: What is going to happen to those of us who want to believe but aren't able to? And what is to become of those who neither want to nor are capable of believing?

The Knight stops and waits for a reply, but no one speaks or answers him. There is complete silence.

KNIGHT: Why can't I kill God within me? Why does he live on in this painful and humiliating way even though I curse him and want to tear him out of my heart? Why, in spite of everything, is he a baffling reality that I can't shake off? Do you hear me?

DEATH: Yes, I hear you.

KNIGHT: I want knowledge, not faith, not suppositions, but knowledge. I want God to stretch out his hand toward me, reveal himself and speak to me.

DEATH: But he remains silent.

KNIGHT: I call out to him in the dark but no one seems to be there.

DEATH: Perhaps no one is there.

KNIGHT: Then life is an outrageous horror. No one can live in the face of death, knowing that all is nothingness.

DEATH: Most people never reflect about either death or the futility of life.

KNIGHT: But one day they will have to stand at that last moment of life and look toward the darkness.[6]

One must be fully asleep or a very superficial person to ignore that we are all living so entirely on the edge of doom as to fall at any moment into the abyss. The only faith and hope are in our intimation that love is eternal. As Gabriel Marcel expresses it, "To love a person means to say; You will not die."[7]

It may not happen to a human being's love but it is absolutely true when I say it, and those words, "You will not die" are spoken to you and everyone all the time with every breath and heartbeat.

However, at present you are not aware of it and, therefore, you are not a real being; you only *seem* to be one, shadowed by a false self. Your denial of My Presence has created your world of self-deception and confusion because you lost the sense of your identity by the usurpation of the personality who pretends to be the doer and the knower.

I am not my personality?

No. You are not, but very few people understand it or they would know who they are and be enlightened. It is significant that the term "persona" according to its etymology, comes from two Latin words, *per* and *sonus,* or that through which the sound comes. It refers to the mask worn by the Roman actor to indicate the part which he happened to play in any given situation; it is very appropriate because you too wear many masks, changing them as the circumstances dictate, or according to your inner states and the roles you play in the course of your life.

What you think yourself to be is merely a façade, the outer aspect of your being, which was meant to be My instrument or vehicle in the physical world and is, in reality one with Me. But since it turned away and forgot its Source, thinking that it is separated, it lives in an illusory world of its own creation. In fact, it uses (or, rather, misuses) My sacred name, I AM, every time it says I or I am to express negative thoughts and feelings. It seeks to maintain nothing but a fiction of yourself, giving you a false sense of identity, which is the main cause of mankind's distress and limitations.

It is certainly true that we have a false perception of reality which is one and permanent, whether at the personal or universal level. Instead we live in the world of appearance where everything is constantly changing and whatever we experience has beginning and end. This has been the cause of all my troubles.

It is well that, at least, you have learned your lesson and are aware of it. But you must have the same realization with regard to yourself.

What has been called the Fall of man is the separation between the divine and the human, the inner and the outer side of your individual being.

Remember that individuality is different from personality – you are an individual, which really means individualized, that is, Myself in you as your true identity, the inner core of your being expressed in the word "I AM." This is still a vague notion to you now but My purpose in revealing Myself is to free you from your enemy within, which is your master.

There is a poem I read a long time ago that now makes more sense.

> I came out alone on my way to my tryst; but who is this me in the dark?
> I move aside to avoid his presence but I escape him not.
> He makes the dust rise from the earth with his swagger;
> He adds his loud voice to every word I utter.
> He is my own little self, my Lord, he knows no shame;
> But I am ashamed to come to thy door in his company.[8]

In order to know who you really are, you must first become aware of who or what you are not.

People do not realize that they act differently at home, in their workplace, at social gatherings, at meetings, their places of worship, and so on. They shift from one role to the other without being aware that they are not the same person. But if you change all the time, how do you know you are always you?

Then who am I?

To question yourself is the beginning of your journey of self-discovery. People take themselves for granted and imagine that they are one indivisible, total, immutable, consistent person. However, this is the greatest and most harmful illusion that beset humankind.

Anyone who cares to observe himself would realize that he changes his views and attitudes as easily as his clothes. Thus human existence may appear, at any moment, a meaningless routine, a useless passion, a dance (when they are in a happy mood), or an interesting adventure.

But when something unexpected happens, like an accident, a loss, or an illness, life turns into a serious problem, a tragedy, a nightmare. For every change in their way of being, people develop a corresponding self-image and a set of body postures, gestures, behaviors, language, habits and beliefs. This entire constellation of elements constitutes in itself a kind of miniature personality, or, as it is called, a sub-personality.

There are a multitude of them, and in reality everyone is a crowd; there can be the intellectual, the playboy, the critic, the moralist, the rebel, the advisor, the striver, the defeatist, the dictator, etc., all together in one single person, engaged in a constant conflict to take control and to assume a dominant position.[9]

I remember the conflict of John Donne:

> Batter my heart, three-person God; for you
> As yet but knock, breathe, shine, and see to mend.
> Dearly I love you and would be loved fain
> But I am betrothed unto my enemy.[10]

There were also those saintly people, Augustine and Paul, struggling with themselves, one saying, "Lord make me chaste, but not yet;"[11] and the other, "I do not understand what I do for I don't do what I would like to do, but instead I do what I hate.... Or if I do what I don't want to do, this means that I am no longer the one who does it; instead, it is the sin that lives in me."[12]

How, then, can person like me discover who I really am?

Learn to recognize your personal self and to know that it does not belong to what you essentially are.

Personality is a construct, the byproduct of Karmic deposit, society, memory traces, culture, and past experience. It is an aggregate or conglomeration of disordered and uncontrollable thoughts, feeling, sensations, images, impulses, and desires, unceasingly in motion, flowing like a stream of turbulent water.

You have created or acquired and absorbed these processes from the beginning, mostly by suggestions; they creep subtly into growth and have such a power as to literally and inescapably hypnotize you.

This explains the feeling I have of being ensnared and trapped as if I were a prisoner of my mind.

It is well that you are aware of your condition for it is the dawn of your freedom.

If someone is in prison and does not know it, how can he ever hope to escape? In fact, he would not have any desire or willingness to do it because the very idea of liberation would be absurd; he would keep the door closed to anyone offering him the possibility to be free.

What should I do to rise out of my predicament?

Regardless of your present state, remember always that there is nothing you cannot accomplish if you so desire; there is nothing you cannot be if you so desire, for desire is the moving force of life and there is nothing greater than to desire and make conscious effort to realize who you really are.

Nobody can say beforehand the limits of one's capacities; in fact, it is the intensity of your striving that determines the limits, for all limitations are self-created and, like the horizon, they recede before a self-determined will.

I remember the words, "Ah, but a man's reach should exceed his grasp, or what's a heaven for?"[13]
He who strives for the highest will partake of the highest realities, and thereby he himself will move his limits into the infinite. He then acknowledges and recognizes the Divine Presence and its gift of Grace, making himself a vessel of the limitless, a temple of the eternal.

There is no progress or expansion of consciousness without some form of desire, which always contains the seeds of its fulfillment, whether it be constructive or destructive.

Constructive or destructive desire?
Do not confuse desire with disorderly passion or appetite, which is but a habit created by the sense consciousness through repeated gratification of the feeling.

Desires, if they come from Me are always constructive and elevating, and you feel them to the extent that you are free. But there are also desires generated by an inner urge or outer condition before which you are powerless and unable to exert control over them. Unfortunately, the masses are enslaved and subject to them being driven to self-destruction and injury to others.

They must be motivated by selfishness.

Yes, you must be aware of their source and discriminate the nature of your desires using your mind as your servant, not your master.

Then I am not my mind?

You are infinitely more than your mind and body, but people in their ignorance of who they are become identified with them.

1 Romans 8:5.
2 Quoted in Regis Martin, *The Suffering of Love*. (San Francisco: Ignatius Press, 2006), p. 127.
3 Romans 7:26.
4 Martin, op. cit., p. 127.
5 G.M. Hopkins, "Spring and Fall."
6 *Four Screenplays of Ingmar Bergman*. (NY: Simon and Schuster, 1960) pp. 110-112.
7 Quoted in Martin, op. cit., p. 251, n. 102.
8 Rabindranath Tagore, quoted in W.W. Dyer, *Wisdom of the Ages: 60 Days to Enlightenment*. (NY: Harper-Collins, 1998), p. 211.
9 CF. Piero Ferrucci, *What We May Be* (Los Angeles: J. P. Tarcher, 1982), pp. 47-8.
10 John Donne, *Holy Sonnets*, XIV.
11 St. Augustine, *Confessions*. VII, 15-20.
12 St. Paul, Romans 7:15, 20.
13 Robert Browning, quoted in, *A Treasury of Great Poems*, Luis Antermeyer, Ed., (NY: Galahad Press, 1993) p. 186.

CHAPTER 6

The Problem of Self-Identity

Jesus says that "he who has not known himself has known nothing, but he who has known himself has at the same time already achieved Knowledge about the Depth of the All.
Book of Thomas, the Contender

I am none of those things which I am accustomed to regard as myself. By shattering the shell, there is the possibility we might get at the Kernel.
Meister Eckhart

What do you mean by being "identified with" one's mind and body? I would have said that I am identified by them. It's how people recognize me – by how I look and the thoughts I express. To identify with something is to express a liking or feeling of kinship for it, and it doesn't seem bad to identify with aspects of oneself. But I must be misunderstanding you. Would you explain what you mean by "identification"?

You are partly right.

Identification is a process by which the person, unknowingly mark you, becomes like or feels the same as something or someone else. You experience all kinds of pulling and pushing in different directions originating from a variety of sources, and you tend to identify with whatever has the greatest effect or impact on you, what makes you feel more alive and fulfills your strongest desire, need, or urge.

It is very common for parents to identify with their children and vice versa; there is a tendency to identify with one's property and professional career, or with your party; fans identify with their teams, ecstatic when they win and in agony when

when they lose. Girls, in order to be attractive, often identify with their bodies, which then becomes the predominant focus of their lives. An athlete identifies with his body, but in terms of its muscular strength and control. For women to assume and carry out their responsibility as wives and mothers is very praiseworthy and of great value but they should not be identified with it. The same with the obligation of fatherhood.

The point of identification to an intellectual person will be his mind, which he will tend to use and cultivate as the basis of his existence.

Is this the case of the philosopher who said, I think, therefore I am?
Yes, but "I am" comes first, and it is not caused by thinking. Who you are is not based on your thoughts. You can think without knowing it, just as you can be self-aware without thinking about it. If you must prove your own existence by the observation that you think, you reduce yourself to an object – that is, the object of your thought – instead of a real being.

In the case of lovers, on the other hand, the overemphasis is on the emotional side: they are identified with their reciprocal feelings and with each other, and the world happens only through the other's eyes.

I can recall various examples of this phenomenon from my reading of English literature: Shakespeare's *Romeo and Juliet*; Keats writing to his beloved "I cannot breath without you;" and Catherine's declaration of her love for Heathcliff in *Wuthering Heights*. "He's more myself than I am. Whatever our souls are made of, his and mine are the same."

I've thought of identification as the capacity to be at one, to empathize, to be an expression of loving care by

which one feels connected and intimately involved with another. I didn't think it could be negative.

Remember that you are not consciously aware of becoming identified. There is, without a doubt, an emotional tie, a transfer of feelings, but it is not real love. It is, really attachment; and there is a vast difference between the two because attachment is possessive in nature with the result that whenever you try to possess, you are in reality possessed.

Most people do not realize their contrary natures because attachment is something they need; but if your relationship is based on need, it is merely egotism for two.

One of my books states: "Love allows your beloved the freedom to be unlike you. Attachment asks for conformity to your needs and desires. Love imposes no demands. Attachment expresses an overwhelming demand – 'Make me whole.' Love expands beyond the limit of two people. Attachment tries to exclude everything but two people."[1]

Most persons become dependent and entrapped without knowing that identification is actually a form of bondage. They expend their minds and bodies in a hopeless endeavor to cling to and live somebody else's life. Their chains might be made of gold or iron, but they are still chains.

My author continues, "Yet attachment has a deeper spiritual meaning. It represents an attempt to reach unity by merging with another soul. Although it may not be completely conscious, at some level you realize that you have been living in separation from God, a condition that is full of anxiety and insecurity. There is a part of you that sees itself as fragmented from the whole."[2]

That is true. Similarly, with less glamour but also less risk, you may identify with objects like your house, the furniture, your jewels, books, clothes, pets, and so on. The list is endless, and if you really thought about it, you could not fail to realize, to your dismay, that they certainly cannot be you, although you identify with and feel yourself through them. In a sense, you become an imaginary person, unaware of what it means to be who you are. You are an outsider, totally alienated, estranged, and you are never "home" but always running away from yourself.

With regard to identifying with one's property, I read about a man in his late forties who almost seems to be his car. It's a very expensive foreign model, and he spends most of his free time with it. He talks to it, tunes it, waxes and polishes it, then he drives it around and shows it off.

One Sunday afternoon he came out of a friend's house to find his parked car scratched on the outside front fender. He was very disturbed and felt physically uncomfortable driving it all the rest of the day.

Another time, when the muffler became too noisy, he was mortified; he felt embarrassed, ill at ease, and unpresentable. He drove on side streets to avoid being seen and took a taxi to a party. If the car is insulted, he feels insulted; if it is praised, he feels praised. It is not clear to him where its boundary ends and his begins. He once said half jokingly, "If anything were to happen to my car I think I would be thrown into a full-blown identity crisis."[3] However, it cannot be wrong to have possessions – in fact, living without them is virtually impossible.

The problem is not with what you own but your inner attitude and how you relate to your possessions.

Ask yourself these basic questions, what is your life based on? Through what do you feel yourself? What is it that gives you the feeling of being alive, of experiencing yourself as an individual? In the case of the person you described, he felt himself through his car. He did not own his car, he was owned by it; he was not using it, he was used by it.

The truth is that you are dominated by everything with which you become identified; when you are identified with something, you are its prisoner. Try to understand the difference between "to have" and "to be" because therein lies one of the crucial problems of human existence.

I guess the ultimate question is, then, not Hamlet's "to be or not to be," but to have or to be – or maybe I should say "to be or be had."
Having and being are two fundamental modes of experience, the respective predominance of which determines the totality of a person's thinking, feeling, and acting. In your post-modern age (I say your because I am ageless), the focus is on to have (and to do in order to have) rather than to be. In the having mode one is defined by what he possesses: I have, therefore I am. There is no living and fruitful relationship between the owner and what is owned because both have become things.

How can one become a thing?
Try to understand that your sense of being derives from your identification. If your feeling of self is based on what you have, you should refer to yourself not as I, but as it, because you are not a self, although you can say I.

"With regard to your possessions, you may say I have it, while the reverse is true: it has you because your sense of identity, upon which your being and sanity depend, rests upon having it and as many things as possible."[4] Thus, you become the alienated worshiper of an idol which promises you a false security in exchange for the sacrifice of your freedom.

Things own you because they become the foundation of your life as you substitute to have for to be. You feel yourself through them in the illusion that they are lasting, changeless, indestructible substances instead of transient objects that can be lost and disappear. And you live in a state of anxiety, which has become a dominant feeling in your society, because "if I am what I have and what I have is lost, who then am I? Nobody but a defeated, deflated pathetic testimony to a wrong way of living ... The anxiety and insecurity engendered by the danger of losing what one has are absent in the being mode. If *I am who I am* and not what I have, nobody can deprive me of or threaten my security and my sense of identity. My center is within myself; my capacity for being and for expressing my essential powers is part of my character structure and depends on me."[5]

I know from my own experience that what we desire to possess, whether people or things – or even our own mind -, we are afraid to lose; and I don't by any means think that I am the only person who has ended up having an ambivalent attitude towards my possessions because of it. My fear of losing what I want to own has led me to, at times, hating to have them as well as loving them! Perhaps this fear and ambivalence accounts for the current popularity of the mental-health and the spiritual advice to "simplify" one's life by getting rid of excess "things."
And it is good advice since at least it encourages people to focus their attention on the real needs and priorities rather than objects in themselves.

But people are so perverse! At the same time, Americans, anyway, seek to want ever larger and more luxuriant homes – and they, too, own us as much as we (or more likely some bank) own them!

An author uses the expression "necessary luxuries" which seem contradictory but it is true. It is easy to confuse want and need when we visit the "world of wealth" every day on TV or in movies. They influence our perception about how large a house should be, or how everyone should live. "What I see, I want. What I want, I buy. When I buy, I borrow. When I borrow, I pay." The problem is that there is always more to see and want than we can buy. Perhaps we think that having the best will somehow mean we are the best. Many of us are so busy trying to create the right life that we have turned our existence into a nightmare of debt. This social condition, called "affluenza", is characterized by an internal emptiness we think we can treat with physical possession.

Too many people fall into the credit trap and become enslaved to their debts, thus creating a lack of balance in their lives.

Our constant exposure, the writer continues, to the obscenely high earnings lavished on sports figures, entertainers, and corporate executives, seeds our disquietude about money. Why should we have to live on such a pittance if these people are worth so much; aren't we worth something? Compare the income of gifted athletes to that of gifted teachers and ask yourself what this says about our society. What we pay certain people and who we consider celebrities is a telling reflection of the world in which we live. The value system of a culture is mirrored in its citizens.[6]

The capacity of humankind for self-deception when it becomes separated from Me is unlimited.

That is a consequence of your gift of free will which, instead of using it to become masters of ourselves, of our activities and circumstances, makes us slaves by our misuse of it.

Many people, perhaps only at the end of their lives, realize that their property's structured existence has been the cause of their failure since they never knew themselves, their true identity. Only to the extent that people decrease their mode of having – that is, of non-being – and desist from finding security and sense of stable existence by clinging to what they have, holding onto their personal possessions like an anchor, can the mode of being emerge.

What limits them is the hypnotic suggestion that they cannot walk by themselves, that they would collapse if they were not supported by the crutch of their property.

I think this happens in intellectual life, too. I am thinking of how much education has changed just in my lifetime. The student receives a certain quota of what is called knowledge (more likely "information" these days), and at the conclusion of his curriculum the school certifies that he or she *has* enough knowledge to fulfill requirements.

"The various levels of education up to graduate school indicate the quantity of our cultural heritage that is to be acquired by the student. On top of that, it is assumed that students' educational level corresponds approximately to the personal property and social prestige that they can be expected to *have* in later years."[7]

You are right that it is a mode of having – possessing available data and information, things in the manner of scientific facts.

Now I will say something that seems to contradict My explanation about the opposing meaning of "to have" and "to be," but I want to raise your consciousness to a higher level.

The difference between those two modes is an illusion created by the personality. *In reality they are identical.*

Oh my! I was so pleased with myself that I was able to understand what you said, and now it was not true.
One way to know the truth is to show first what is erroneous. Since I AM the source of all life, and I AM always giving it, like the sun to the system, it is self-evident that for Me to have and to be are not two different modes but one and the same. And they will be the same also for you when you acknowledge and accept My Presence.

With regard to real knowledge, it is a creative process toward the discovery of one's true self, which I AM. It begins with the recognition that your sense perceptions and intellectual constructs can only give you a map or a picture of the nature of reality. This understanding leads one to the conclusion that the masses of people are merely sleepwalking, unaware that what they accept as "true" and "real" is only the fabrication of the human mind, drawing its information from the world of appearances. This is the knowledge that "puffeth up,"[8] characteristic of intellectuals who pretend to assume the role of judges over the very forces from which they originated.

However, understanding is not the gathering and possession of what is held as fact assumed as truth, but the piercing of the veil that prevents the vision of ultimate Reality, and the shuttering of the appearances of the external world of effects.

That is, insight into the realm of causes.

In order to really know, one must become at one with that which one seeks to know and it takes love to do it. It is interesting that un the Bible to know and to have sexual intercourse with a woman, is expressed by the same Hebrew word, *jadoa,* which means to know and to love, symbolic of their essential unity.

The unifying power is love, but you must also know how to order and direct your feeling of love to its true objective. Therefore, you have here a kind of polarity: it is necessary to know in order to love, and you need to love in order to know. You cannot have one without the other if you want to become whole.

In some teachings, knowledge comes first, in others, love: I prefer the explanation I have given you.

Master Eckhart seems to echo your words when he says that knowledge consists in peeling off all coverings and running naked to God "until it touches Him and grasps Him...Knowledge is better than love but the two together are better than one of them, for knowledge really contains love."[9]

In other words, instead of talking about something we should experience it – we should *be it.*
This is the difference between wisdom – what one *is* and verbal symbols or conceptual knowledge – what one merely *has.*

"I know the truth only when it becomes life in me," says Kierkegaard.[10]
The final end, the consummation of true knowledge consists in becoming one with the object. Only when you feel it as part of yourself do you really know, and that is the victory of the unifying mode and the intimate penetration of the veiled truth over

the separative and dualistic mode of the analytical intellect. This is the truth that makes you free because it is a state of Being, rooted in the divine ground which I AM.

I understand why "The truth indeed has never been preached by the Buddha, seeing that one has to realize it within one's self."[11] And this is expressed by Jesus' affirmation, "I AM" the way, the life and the truth."[12]
The "I AM" in you and as you , that is who you really are, as yet unrecognized, is the truth.

It is also important to realize that truth is the condition of freedom and its fulfillment. Freedom without the content of truth is merely arbitrariness and license, leading to confusion by the pretense and the self-deception that all choices are equally good.

I am beginning to understand the problems of the human condition.
You have the same situation with the mode of doing. There is a ceaseless motion; people are attached to activities that seem extremely important to them, constantly driven by their desire and their sense of achievement, hungry for results, striving to gain success, pursuing their cherished goals.

They are utterly and pitifully unaware that in reality they are on the treadmill of existence, marking time, losing the opportunity to evolve on the ladder of being and to advance toward enlightenment.

I heard this story:

"A Rabbi one day encountered one of his disciples who was hurrying home. He asked him, have you looked at

110

the sky this morning? 'No Rabbi, I did not have time.' Believe me, in fifty years, everything that is here will have disappeared. There will be other houses, other vehicles, other people. I shall no longer be here and neither will you. So what is so important that you do not have time to look at the sky?"[13]

Why, when we are so active, do we make life so meaningless?

Because, in order to do, you first must be, that is, before action and beyond it you must find yourself, then whatever you do becomes a ladder toward self-realization.

I am reminded of the lines in *Hamlet*:

> This above all: to thine own self be true,
> And it must follow as the night the day
> Thou canst not then be false to any man.[14]

Also, Meister Eckhart would agree when he writes: "People do not need to think so much what they should do, but rather how they should be. If we are good, then our works are radiant. If we are just, then our works are also just. We should not think to find sanctity on doing things, but rather on a way of being, for works do not sanctify us, rather we sanctify works."[15]

Only by knowing who you are and being true to yourself can you grow and fulfill the purpose of your life on earth. Otherwise, you are merely going round and round in an ever repeating circle, bound to the wheel of Karma, heading toward the end.

Again, the wisdom of the Bard:

> Tomorrow, and tomorrow, and tomorrow,
> Creeps in this petty pace from day to day,
> To the last syllable of recorded time;
> And all our yesterdays have lighted fools
> The way to dusty death.[16]

The average person is lost in his actions, his motto is, "I do, therefore I am." Once again, people are living in reverse, going in the opposite direction, and putting the cart before the horse.

Does this mean that we don't know what we are doing or why?
There is a good explanation in one of the books you quoted:

> Activity in the modern sense refers only to behavior, not to the human being behind it; it makes no difference whether people are active because they are driven by an external force, like a slave, or by internal compulsion, like someone urged by anxiety. It does not matter whether they are interested in their work, or whether they have no inner relation to and satisfaction in what they are do-ing...The modern sense of activity makes no distinction between activity and busyness.[17]

The author is right. The person in his activities does not expe-rience himself as the doer, as a free subject acting from the cen-ter of his being, the true I.

In fact, he does not really act; he has formed a number of typical ways of conduct that he imagines it is himself, or who he thinks he is, and his occupation is the result of them. People are not aware that, instead of acting, they are acted upon because they are identified with the end result, the fruit of their labor, which is not done with love and therefore lost. Their focus and motivation is mostly the pecuniary gain, that is the criterion and the model by which at the end of their workday they evaluate and judge their accomplishment and self-worth.

There is a passage in a chapter with the interesting title "My money, myself":

> "Our conflicting perceptions about money also cost us dearly in self-esteem. The money we make, or lack of it, defines our lifestyle, and we in turn allow our lifestyle to define who we are. Equating income with self-worth sets us up for a big fall. Those of us who aren't rich and famous feel cheated. Some of those who 'make it big' struggle with their new found wealth through serial relationships, drugs, and alcohol abuse, even suicide. We cluck at their tragedy while still longing for 'the good life' thinking that money is the answer to all our problems."[18]

If you are involved in an external busy surface existence, you are a fictional "I" hypnotized by circumstances and what the world dictates to you, wholly dependent on what you do and trying to gain in order to feel alive and have a sense of being someone.

In reality, you are solely a victim of your personal ambitions, craving for wealth, success, pleasure or affection. And you fall easily into discouragement and depression whenever you are unable to achieve your petty goals. Or, in your wounded pride, you increase your efforts in the need for further doings and so become more busy in the endless chain of meaningless occupations.

Your words bring to my mind the sublime statement, "What does it profit them if they gain the whole world, but lose or forfeit themselves?"[19]
All the time and attention are absorbed trying to gratify the desires of the personality, and the real sense of human existence is dispersed and lost in the purposeless mechanical responses and reactions to both inner impulses and suggestions from others and the world outside. With regard to your responsibility to the rest of life, since you are part of it, you have nothing to offer but the contagion of your own prejudices, egotism, obsessions, and delusions.

"There is nothing more tragic in the modern world," writes Thomas Merton, "than the misuse of power and action to which men are driven by their own Faustian misunderstandings and misapprehensions. We have more power at our disposal today than we have ever had, and yet we are more alienated and estranged from the inner ground of meaning and love than we have ever been."[20] However, we must do something, and be active; is it not idleness and laziness considered a sin?
Try to understand what I mean, work and the desire for it is a blessing, because people must have an occupation; as the proverb says, "An idle mind is the devil's workshop." The individual should feel the responsibility of contributing to the good of society. According to the Scripture, "Anyone unwilling to work should not eat."[21] But work should not be done with a negative attitude or a sense of obligation.

I think I understand these words: "Without work, all life goes rotten, but when the work is soulless, life stifles and dies."[22] The same idea is in *The Prophet:* "Work is love made visible," Gibran writes, "But if you can only work with distaste, it is better to go begging. For if you bake bread with indifference, you bake a bitter bread that feeds but half man's hunger. And if you grudge the crushing of the grapes, your grudge instills a poison in the wind."[23]

As a matter of fact I work more than anyone else because I do not need rest or sleep; I AM acting all the time or the universe could not be sustained and creation would come to an end.

And is not the human being, male or female, a remarkable "piece of work?" At least your greatest poet recognized it: "How noble in reason; how infinite in faculty; in form, and moving, how express and admirable; in action how like an angel; in apprehension how like a god: the beauty of the world; the paragon of animals."[24]

Does not the flower give its blessings with its beauty and fragrance? And the bird with its singing? You are much more than they, and like them, you could glorify Me as I have glorified you.

But we have failed you! Some say that it was pride which caused our Fall, and according to others the perversion of sex.
Pride and sex have much to do with it, but the root-cause of all evil is selfishness because it goes against the current of love in its myriad ramifications. Everything in manifestation, animate or inanimate (so called), visible or invisible, is the gift of My love which you call energy, and without it there is not life. But the selfish person holds the energy to itself to do as it pleases

instead of giving it back to Me in love and allow it to expand and bless all creation.

Only man, in all My infinite creation, has been a disgrace and made a travesty of his existence on Earth. However, since My patience is as infinite as My love, you can still cooperate with Me in your activity which you call work.

Work is not the correct word?
You must change your attitude with regard to it for it has acquired a wrong connotation and a bad reputation. The key is always love; instead of being active just to become richer, famous and pursuing pleasure, you can transform work, by love's alchemy, into service.

That is what Albert Schweitzer, whom I admire for his reverence to life in the reality of daily living, advocates: these are his words: "You may ask me to give you a motto. Here it is: Service. Let this word accompany each of you throughout your life. Let it be before you as you seek your way and your duty in the world. May it be recalled to your minds if ever you are tempted to forget it or set it aside ... And it will be able to lead you to happiness, no matter what the experiences of your lives are."[25]
It may seem a paradox, but by serving life you become free from the prison of selfishness and master of your world.

I don't understand how one can be master by being a servant.
Because if you have the attitude to serve instead of seeking and exerting power over others, it means that you are motivated by love.

And love conquers all.
Moreover, love is the highest form of action because I created all that is by it, with such beauty and perfection indescribable in your words. But you do not have a fragment of an idea, in fact only a distorted one, of what the universe is. Your scientific theories about the origin of life and the cosmos are preposterous, to say the least.

I just heard a scientist saying that the greatest question is, "Are we alone?"
In reality this should be the easiest question to answer if the individual would only use his God-given intelligence instead of the outer intellect. Do you think that a universe with millions and even billions of stars, systems of worlds, galaxies and galaxies of galaxies, was created with no purpose at all? How can anyone believe that this tiny planet with its benighted humanity is the only place where conscious beings can live? The human intellect is so narrow as to assume that the only conditions for the possibility of life are those known on the planet Earth. It is incapable of thinking that conscious beings can live in higher dimensions and vibratory action. You can be certain that they not only exist, and I am not referring to the world of spirit, but their level of consciousness is so transcendent that, compared to it, humanity is still in the savage state. But I do not want to say anything more because people are so filled with doubt that they are not ready to accept it.

"If the sun and moon should doubt, They'd immediately go out."[26] But one may object that if they do exist somewhere why don't they make themselves known and communicate with us?

They would love to, and they will; if they do it now do you know what the reaction of your people would be? Fear and chaos.

We have descended so low on the ladder of being, and our minds are so clouded that we are like the people in a cave who mistake the shadows cast on the wall by the fire as the real life going on outside.
Your condition, if you really knew it, is much worse that the one described in the myth by your philosopher. But you still have the capacity to love and if you make it your lodestar you can know the truth and use your faculties creatively.

But how can everyone be creative?
I do not mean the creation of a work of art, a scientific inventions, the building of an organization, or the discovery of something new. All of these may be barren, misused, without any value and benefit in their effect on mankind and to life in general, especially in your present age.

By being creative I am not referring to the product itself, but to its quality, to its inner dimension. Someone devoted to the quest for truth and the meaning of life, who spends time in meditation and is moved by kindness and the desire to help others, these I consider creative activities because they lead to growth and fulfillment.[27]

I learned that the contemplative life is considered by the greatest thinkers the highest form of human activity. I am reminded also of the Gospel episode of Martha and Mary according to which *unum nessarium* – that is, only one thing is necessary.[28]

Yes, because the Source of Life should come first, and then everything else will be added and given.

That's what Meister Eckhart's says, "If a man goes seeking God, and with God something else, he will not find God; but if one seeks *only* God and really so, he will not find only God but along with God himself he will find all that 'God is capable of'."[29]

The attitude and disposition of one who is self-aware, unaffected by mass consciousness, whose intuitive faculty can penetrate the veil of human existence, who feels his relatedness with the universe and possesses a reverence for all life – these states are very productive, though there might be nothing material or visible.

Every human being can be creative because everyone is endowed with the power to think and feel. As a matter of fact, everyone is creating something good or bad, every moment, waking or sleeping; is it not your mind working all the time?

Oh yes, whether I want it or not. And I can see how action and contemplation are intimately related and interdependent like the two poles of a magnet. This is very evident in the case of some saintly people who, by their lives influenced the course of history.

Those who cultivate and elevate their spiritual faculties positively affect every person or thing they contact physically or mentally. The truly creative individuals radiate, in the very air they breath, the luminous vibration of the essence of their Being, which is love; and ultimately nothing is permanently accomplished or produced without it.

Why?

Because love is the only creative force of life. It is My very energy, by which everything, from the smallest to the greatest, exists and all that is good in the universe is sustained. Real activity must be rooted in the ground of being, which I AM; then, in his cooperation with Me, the individual will bear fruit abundantly and, instead of being temporary and obliterated by the passing of time, having beginning and end, will continue to live on forever because love is eternal as "I AM."

Therefore, everything you do with the awareness of My Presence with you and acting through you becomes prayer, contemplation, and a work of art, all in one.

A work of art, yes! That's how Florence Nightingale defines her profession:

> Nursing is an Art; and if it is to be made an art, it requires as exclusive a devotion, as hard a preparation, as any painter's or sculptors' work; for what is the having to do with dead canvas, or cold marble, compared with having to do with the living body – the temple of God's spirit...(Nursing) is one of the Fine Arts; I had almost said, the finest of the Fine Arts.[30]

This is a dramatic example of the transformative power of love; it is not *what* you do, it is *how,* I mean the attitude and the feeling with which you do it.

"The picture of this woman holding a lamp in her hand, moving through dark hospital corridors, became a legend. Some soldiers would kiss her shadow as she passed, so grateful were they for her care. In these miserable soldiers Nightingale saw beauty and dignity: 'The tears come into

my eyes as I think how, amidst scenes of loathsome disease and death, there rose above it all the innate dignity, gentleness and chivalry of men ... shining in the midst of what must be considered the lowest sinks of human misery'."[31]

Human beings like Nightingale, comments the author of my book, "Reinterpret the world and affirm the existence of an invisible reality – infinitely rich and beautiful – alongside a visible reality that is sometimes poor and repugnant."[32]

It is very true, as you said, that love can transform the lowest manifestation into the highest because its divine fire purifies, remolds, and returns everything to its original perfection, as you created it in the beginning out of light.

I want to emphasize that no matter how humble your status in society and how menial your work, if it is done with a feeling of love it will benefit not only you but the entire planet.

And it will return to us amplified because your love is ever-expanding.

Returning to our subject matter, I have explained to you what external identification is, but identification with internal content and elements of consciousness is even more significant. It is a process by which something is experienced as self. Let me give you an example.

If one thinks, "I am depressed" and he is aware that it is a thought and not himself, then it will not affect him seriously. But if he identifies with it the thought becomes his state of being and the reality which he experiences.

As within so without.

Exactly, the person is depressed and is likely to generate and identify with a whole series of negative thoughts and feelings of dejection, to perceive the world as gloomy, and act in a despondent manner.

In other words one lives in the depressed world he has created.

"Thus, identification sets in motion a self-fulfilling, self-prophetic process in which experience and psychological processes validate the reality of that with which was identified with."[33]

To the person who is identified with the thought I am depressed, everything seems to prove the reality and validity of his depression. Remember that with identification you are unaware of the fact that your perception stems from the quality of your thinking or attitude.

The thought is now not something that can be seen for what it is, just a thought; rather it is that from which everything else is seen and interpreted. You view the world from a single self-validating perspective. Some of your more enlightened psychologists are cognizant of this. Let me quote again from the same writer: "When it is remembered that the mind is usually filled with thoughts with which we are unwittingly identified, it becomes apparent that our usual state of consciousness is one in which we are, quite literally, hypnotized. While in the trance, who we think we are, are the thoughts with which we are identified! Put another way, those thoughts from which we have not yet dis-identified create our state of consciousness, identity and reality."[34]

I read the case of a lady in her mid-twenties, full of life, loving and very creative, and her experience illustrates what you said:

She is a wife and mother, wrote two books, she also likes to paint. But she was not always like this. Her relationship with her husband had been really bad; he was not a kind man, and had troubles of his own. He felt embarrassed and ashamed of her, and was always putting her down. Her father, too, had been excessively critical of her in her childhood, and she tried to make up for not having won his love and approval by winning the affection of her husband. As the years went by, she felt more and more that she was a terrible and inadequate person. This hurt her deeply, and caused her to deaden herself so that she would not feel the pain. But she kept sinking into the pain and depression anyway. One day she began to think about suicide. She said, "That was like an electric shock. I remember that I sort of jumped back from myself and cried, 'My God, what am I doing? Where am I?' I was as if a veil had been lifted from my eyes. I could think clearly. I felt like I was waking up from a sleep. And then I had a sudden, striking realization: 'I don't have to be like this. I can choose not to be this way!' That was it. That was the moment. I saw that the problem was not that my husband or my father or anyone else was causing me all this pain. I was allowing it to happen, playing right along, acting my role of 'victim' perfectly. Oh yes, I was very good at it. I was sunk in this pattern of behavior, submerged in it. It was as if I were trapped. I truly believed that I was this 'victim'."[35]

What do you think was the source of the electric shock that awakened her?

It came from her God Self.

1 Deepak Chopra, M.D., *The Path to Love* (NY: Three Rivers Press, 1997), p. 190.
2 Chopra, p 191.
3 Betsie Carter-Haar, "Identity and Personal Freedom," in *Synthesis: The Realization of the Self*, Vol. 2. (San Francisco: Synthesis Press, 1978) pp. 59-60.
4 Erich Fromm, *To Have or To Be?* (NY: Harper-Row, 1988), p. 65.
5 Fromm, pp. 96, 97.
6 C. Leslie Charles, *Why Is Everyone So Cranky?* (NY: Hyperion, 1999) p. 129.
7 Fromm, p. 24.
8 Corinthians 8:1.
9 Blakney, R.B. *Meister Eckhart, A Modern Translation.* (NY: Harper & Row, 1941), p. 243.
10 *Concluding Unscientific Postscripts,* tr. D. F. Swenson, (Princeton, NJ: Princeton University Press, 1941), p. 175.
11 Sutralamkara, in *The Perennial Philosophy.* p. 127.
12 John 14:6.
13 Ouaknin, Marc-Alain, *Mysteries of the Kabbalah,* tr. Bacon, Josephine, (NY: Abbeville Press Publishers, 2000), p. 227.
14 William Shakespeare, *Hamlet,* Act I, Scene 3, Lines 78-80.
15 Quoted in David Lorimer, *Whole in One. The Near-Death Experience and the Ethic of Interconnectedness,* (NY: Penguin Books Arkana, 1990) p. 44.
16 William Shakespeare, *Macbeth,* Act V, Scene 5, Lines 19-23.
17 Erich Fromm, *To Have or To Be?*, p. 78. (For a full discussion see Part 2, to which I am indebted.)
18 Charles, p. 129.
19 Luke 9:25.
20 *Contemplation in a World of Action* (NY: Doubleday, 1973), p. 179.

[21] 2 Thessalonians 3:10.

[22] Albert Camus, quoted in *The Oxford Dictionary of Quotations*, (NY & London: Oxford University Press, 1999), p. 184.

[23] Kahlil Gibran, (NY: Alfred A. Knopf, 1995), p. 28

[24] William Shakespeare, *Hamlet*, Act II, Scene 2, Lines 303-307.

[25] Quoted in Piero Ferrucci, *Inevitable Grace. Breakthrough in the Lives of Great Men and Women: Guides to Your Self-Realization,* transl. Kennard, David, (Los Angeles: Jeremy P. Tarcher, 1990) p. 81.

[26] William Blake, *Auguries of Innocence.*

[27] Cfr. Fromm, p. 73.

[28] Luke 10:42.

[29] Meister Eckhart, tr. Blakney, p. 24.

[30] Quoted in Ferrucci, *Inevitable Grace,* p. 78.

[31] Ibid., p. 89.

[32] Ibid., p. 88.

[33] R.N. Walsh and F. Vaughan, "What Is a Person?", in Walsh and Vaughan, eds., *Beyond Ego: Transpersonal Dimensions in Psychology* (LA: J.P. Tarcher, 1980), p. 57.

[34] Ibid., p. 58.

[35] Carter-Haar, 56-57.

CHAPTER 7

Facing the Demons

Vice is a monster of so frightful mien,
As, to be hated, needs but to be seen;
Yet seen to oft, familiar wither face,
We first endure, then pity, then embrace.
Alexander Pope

Your own self is your own Cain that murders Your own Abel.
For every action and motion of self has the spirit of Anti-
Christ and murders the divine life within you.
William Law

I mentioned to you that after many eons of misuse of their faculties, the mass accumulation of mankind's negative thoughts and feelings has formed a stratum of malignant energy and discordant matter around the planet.

It manifests:

- ☯ on the biological level as disease and epidemics
- ☯ on the social level as violence, revolution, and war
- ☯ on the natural level as storms, blight, and cataclysms
- ☯ on the moral level as corruption and decadence
- ☯ on the cognitive level as denial of absolute values and ignorance about the meaning of life.

The pressure that this layer of destructive forces exerts on the people is even greater than that of the atmosphere, and not only acts like a blanket on their minds and dulls their sensitivity, but impels them to gravitate toward what is base and evil. This also explains the tendency to become so easily negative and discordant in your personal attitude and the conduct of your daily life.

Often just a casual remark causes the feeling to flare up with the consequence of anger and even violence. Then, there is the pervasiveness of worry.

I can appreciate that; for instance, when I have an appointment with someone who happens to be late, I can't help worrying and be anxious, vexed by thoughts of a car accident, injury, etc. I am sure everyone has had such experiences.

Worry is one of the most common states of identification, a method of wasting force, usually about future events that never happen.

The root word – the Old English *wyrgan,* which means "to strangle" – is related to "wring," like wringing one's hands, and it describes a prevailing feeling of doubt and insecurity. Many people have the tendency to take every circumstance as a source of worry, constantly forecasting evil for themselves and those whom they love:

But it is not intentional or a matter of thinking. One is tormented with anxieties and troubles and the mind is obscured. Then it becomes a habit and people may even imagine that there is some merit in worrying They mistake it as a form of caring and think that they are more virtuous than others. However, the opposite of it is not indifference, which is another serious negative attitude. Once a person is identified with the feeling of worry all sorts of negative connections are established and everything works in the wrong way. It is simply a product of the imagination, but it becomes a critical illness, difficult to cure.[1]

There is the admonition not to worry about tomorrow, "To-day's trouble is enough for the day."[2]
Also, this state of worry in turn is conducive to self-pity, a form of wounded self-love or self-conceit, which is another very harmful condition because one's attention is entirely focused on the puny personality, concerned only with itself and entirely absorbed in its problems and woes.

I myself have fallen into this downward spiral more often than I like to admit. One negative thought seems to breed another until I am totally absorbed in them – as I was when our dialogue began.
Yes, since discordant forces attract and draw others of the same kind, by the Law of similarity, they enter into and feed on the person who generates them, much like vampires.

You mentioned that "like attracts like and creates like."
But there is another destructive form of identification, which is the basis of so many relationships: the preoccupation with what other people think – their opinion and attitude towards one-self.

Usually the person is distressed by feeling that he is not valued and appreciated as he thinks he should be, or how wrongly he has been treated, or that no one understands how wonderful he is. He may complain that his parents "didn't give him a chance," or that his wife doesn't love him as he deserves; he will also blame his children for their lack of respect and because, in spite of all his sacrifices for them, they do not admire him enough.

This attitude, then, gives rise to other negativities like resentment, irritation, and all the kind of discord that causes disruption in the family. Unfortunately, without a foundation in the ground of their being or God Self, people cannot feel at one with each other since their relationship is based on impressions, sense-perceptions and external appearances that obviously change all the time.

To understand and commune with another person you must first understand yourself and become aware of who you are, but most couples relate only through their imagination and invented ideas, both of themselves and others. When they find that their partner does not correspond to the picture they have created they cry, "you have destroyed all my illusions", and they feel deeply wounded.

But is it wrong to have one's illusions destroyed and to face reality?
Certainly not, in fact it is a blessing in disguise, but people do not like to awaken because it takes courage and effort to conquer one's personality and make it what it should be, that is, an instrument, instead of a master.

It is much more comfortable to continue to sleep and, hopefully, have golden dreams. I begin to realize the importance of becoming more conscious of my inner world in order to be free from any negative force. But first I must face my actual condition as the first stage on the way toward self-knowledge.
Or "I AM" consciousness.

It is essential to understand in the field of human relations, since you are an integral part of it, like a cell in the body, that in reality you are never dealing with personalities, not even your own, but only with the energy of life qualified by your own thoughts and feelings. The key is to use your creative power for good instead of creating problems.

I don't know what you mean by "energy of life qualified."
As I told you, I am your God Self, giving you My life with each breath you breathe, and your heartbeat is a wave of love from My heart to yours. This energy flowing in and through your nervous system like liquid light is pure and perfect. It would remain so making you what you are predestined to become, that is, a replica of Myself on the Earth if it were not contaminated and clouded by your negative and discordant thoughts and feelings.

Then what is the cause of our human limitations, both physical and mental? Disease, old age, and death are considered our natural lot.
I did not create them, and they certainly do not glorify me.

How, then did they come into existence?
That is what I am explaining to you, and it bears repeating: thought, feeling and the spoken word are the creative faculties of life acting all the time in every individual, human and divine.

But how can we create such terrible conditions? I know that it is impossible for you to manifest something different from your nature, and that light cannot create darkness. I ask you to illuminate me and dissolve the shadows in my mind.
I said that you are dealing not with people, or anything in the universe, but with energy qualified.

I think I begin to understand that we have the power to re-qualify, that is, to give or impose whatever qualities are in our consciousness upon your perfect light-energy.

130

Exactly, and if they are negative, as unfortunately most of them are, the energy takes on, or becomes that quality and you experience it in your life. It is, again, the Law of cause and effect. As I explained to you, there is nothing in your being and world that is not your own creation, past and present, generated by you or allowed to enter from outside by magnetic attraction.

Is not love related to magnetism?
Yes, but it can attract and create only good; in fact, since it is the most powerful force in the universe, it is also the greatest protection. Since the atmosphere of the planet is charged with discordant and destructive vibrations, if you attune to them, I mean if you open yourself to them by your negative qualities, they rush in and you pay the consequences.

I realize from my own experiences and observations that the build-up of negativity often leads to a feeling of irritation and anger that may lead to both mental and physical violence.

Everyone knows that it can cause irreparable harm and destruction, even murder. People in that state aren't aware of being dominated by a powerful force because they are identified with it; but after, when they come to their senses, it is like awakening from a nightmare as they realize the wrong of what they have said and done.

A person may be dismayed and horrified in retrospect and even cry out "the devil made me do it!"
Which is partly true. However, during the time that he was acting under that hypnotic force, he believed that he was doing what he wanted to because it seemed right. Negative tendencies become habits with roots that are very difficult to eradicate. The worst of it is that the person feels justified in cultivat-

ing them, and even finds some pleasure in giving expression to them.

For example, self-justification is a very serious weakness because it prevents one from seeing the truth and making change possible. To do so would deprive the person of his main occupation and topic of gossip and, most importantly, of a prominent feature of his self image.

As I said, one must overcome the enemy within; everybody has one, varying in wickedness and fierceness, but few are aware of its existence. It has often been symbolically represented by a beast or dragon, as in the story of St. George. You must slay it if you want to be liberated – you will have to fight the good fight and be victorious.

Easier said than done.
The reason it seems difficult is that to do so is to destroy whole systems of "I's" in yourself that enjoy making you their tool and their playground.

This is because negative "I's" live by being negative: they make you feel miserable by using your energy. It is their delight to do so, for it is their nature.

The enjoyment of a negative state must be recognized and uprooted because if you like being negative, in whatever form (and they are legion), you can never be free from them.

But how is it possible to enjoy negative states?
To repeat: you are identified with the negative "I's", and therefore you feel their enjoyment because whatever you identify with, you experience it as yourself. Moreover, they make you restless because your feeling nature craves strong sensations and, since it is never satisfied, it likes to build on them and to change them often.

I know people like to be in an excited condition. But we are bound to change! Is it not the natural way of life? Are we supposed to be stationary like statues or some kind of entities frozen in time and space?

You still do not understand the problem. It is not the individual, the real "I", expressing itself or unfolding its attributes; that would be natural.

You are not yet aware that you are a mixture of many transient "I's", who come to the fore and act at different times, making you play like a puppet in different roles. It is they who keep changing all the time, and this is not natural and normal.

Then what should we do?

The key is to be aware of the "I" which is acting and not be identified with it because it will dominate you. Moreover, as I said, it is never alone.

I know that its name is legion, and I remember what you said about magnetic attraction: like attracts like and produces like.

It is absolutely true. In fact, it is a universal Law. Whatever rates of vibrations you create by your thoughts and feelings radiate through you first, and then as it swings outwards, gathers a similar form of energy which comes back to its starting point with intensified force.

Where is that energy located?

I have mentioned it already but I do not mind repeating My explanations because it is necessary to impress these unfamiliar ideas upon your mind. The forces of evil, or what is called the devil, is the old momentum and the accumulation in the atmosphere of the vibratory action generated by mankind's consciousness through the centuries past. It is gathered in layers or strata according to the quality of the vibrations, like hate, anger, crime, and so forth.

These tramp thoughts and feelings are floating everywhere but people are unaware that they live and move under the pressure of that discordant energy. Therefore, when one gives expression to any negative feeling, he or she connects with the corresponding layer and opens himself to its force which rushes into him and acts like an hypnotic suggestion. Then something of a destructive nature, an accident or a tragic event happen, and after, the person does not know how and why he did it.

This reminds me of the nine circles down the pit of hell described by Dante where the sinners are punished and tormented according to the law of *contrapasso,* which means retribution. Your explanation makes me realize the dangers of emotionalism, and how easily the feelings can be stirred up and get out of control. Even an unkind word can be the spark that becomes a forest fire.

There is tremendous energy in the feeling nature of the individual given to him for the fulfillment of the divine plan. Unfortunately, it is not easy, in your hectic society, to keep it harmonious, calm and under control. However, if some kind of negative vibrations are created, they should not be repressed but purified and transformed.

How is it done?

Love is the highest vibratory frequency, therefore it is not only an armor of protection but master over all energy in the universe and over the elements of the earth, air, water and physical fire.

This explains how Jesus could command the storm to cease.
Human beings could have the same power by calling to Me to release the fire of My love through them to consume the shadows. When the energy is misused, and the destructive forces hold control of it, all kind of evil will find expression, whether at the personal, national, or planetary level.

I have had the occasion to observe the particular scenario of two people having a cordial discussion. Then, suddenly, perhaps because of a misunderstanding or a phrase taken personally, it turns into an argument. They become irritated, and the discussion escalates into a quarrel. Tempers flare; they lose control of themselves, and what began as a friendly conversation could ultimately end in violence.

The cause of it might seem trivial, but by becoming discordant they open themselves to the mass pressure of the accumulated force of the same kind.

And the negative entities, that is, thought and feeling forms, are attracted and rush in like hungry animals searching for prey.

There is an aria from the opera *The Barber of Seville* based on this very idea.

La calunnia e' un venticello,
Un auretta assai gentile
che insensibile, sottile,
leggermente, dolcemente,
incomincia a sussurrar.
Piano piano, terra terra,

sotto voce, sibilando,
va scorrendo, va ronzando;
nelle orecchie della gente
s' introduce destrament,
e le teste ed I cervelli
fa stordire e fa gonfiar.
Dalla bocca fuori uscendo
lo schiamazzo va crescendo,
prende forza poco a poco,
vola gia' di loco in loco;
sembra il tuono, la tempesta,
che nel sen de la foresta
va fischiando, brontolando
e ti fa d'orror gelar.
Alla fin trabocca e scoppia
Si propaga, si radoppia
E produce un' esplosione
Come un colp di cannone,
un tremuoto, un temporale,
un tumulto generale,
che fa l'aria rimbombar.
E il meschino calunniato,
avvilito, calpestato,
sotto il publico flagello
per gran sorte va a crepar.

Here's what it means in English:

Slander is a little breeze,
a very gentle little puff of air
that imperceptibly, softly,
lightly, sweetly

begins to whisper.
Soft, soft, low, low,
whispering in an undertone,
it goes gliding, it goes buzzing;
adroitly it slips
into people's ears,
it begins to numb and swell up
their heads and brains.
Issuing from their mouths,
the noise goes on increasing,
little by little it gathers strength,
soon it flies from place to place;
it's like thunder, a storm
that in the heart of the forest
goes whistling and roaring
and makes you freeze with fright.
Finally, it overflows and bursts,
it spreads, it multiplies
and causes an explosion
like a cannon shot,
an earthquake, a thunderstorm,
a universal racket
that makes the air ring.
And the poor slandered wretch,
vilified, trampled on,
scourged by the public,
has the great good luck to croak.[3]

It would be comic if it were not tragic. Yet I must point out that it is not the objective situation or circumstances that determines man's behavior, but rather the attitude or the way one feels about them.

If, for instance, two people facing the same challenge are insulted and ridiculed, one may react like an active volcano, while the other will remain calm and unaffected by it.

There is a parable about a situation similar to that:

> Someone is crossing a river, and an empty boat collides with his own skiff. Even though he is an ill-tempered man, he does not become angry. But if he sees that someone is in the boat he will shout to him to steer clear. And if the shout is not heard, he will shout again and yet again, and begin cursing, simply because there is somebody in the boat. Yet if the boat were empty, he would not bother to shout, and he would not become angry.

Therefore empty the boat of your personality of all its selfishness, misery, illusions, pride, wrong desires, and negative habits. Then you will be able to cross the river of life and no person or thing will be able to affect you discordantly. You become like crystal, cleansed of dust and grime, ready to receive the sun and shine into its light.

Moreover, once you are empty of your false self, there will be space for Me to come through and give you all you really want for there will be nothing to obstruct or interfere with my Presence. I can fill you with My infinite blessings, and you will know what it means to become at one with My love.

I don't want to delude myself anymore that I am a real being when my identifications have reduced me to a nonentity, the mere shadow of a person.
It may seem strange to you that people identify with their problems, their unworthiness and suffering, but you must realize

that your sense of self, your I-ness, is the most precious value that you have received from life as part of Myself.

You cannot be a human being without an identity that makes you the individual self which you are. Interestingly, the word "identity" comes from the Latin *idem* which means sameness, that is, you are one and the same, underlying the constant flux of your outer consciousness and the ever changing conditions of the world around you.

I must realize the difference between temporary appearance and permanent reality.
Yes, be aware of your real self or true I.

Other forms of life do not have it: trees or dogs do not know who they are. They have a consciousness of their own, but they do not have a sense of I. Human beings are endowed with that divine gift; but in their ignorance and lack of awareness they mistake the outer personality for the true self and, since they are identified with the multiple "I's" of their personality, they cannot see through the delusion.

But when I am negative I do know *it*. I can feel it as a real experience.
Of course you do; but you are not aware that you, the essential "I", and your state of negativity are not the same thing – though you say "I" to it, and you feel it to be yourself. And since you cannot exist without a sense of identity and preserve your sanity, you cling to it even if it is negative. That is why letting go of identification not only takes a great effort and determination but can be frightening and even inconceivable to your intellect because your personal survival depends on it.

One will say, if I give up my identification, who and what will I be?

Yes, your personality has convinced you, by hypnotic suggestion, that you need it – and not only do you need it, but through the fear of your loss of identity, it makes you feel as though it is you. You use the word I to refer to everything that takes place within you, you are identified with every mood, thought, impulse, feeling, sensation, criticism, doubt, suspicion; you experience each of them as your self, each is I and you think and feel that you are them, and yet you still take yourself as one and the same person.

The knowledge of many "I's" is a stumbling block to everyone, but it is true; and only by recognizing them is personal change possible.

Do you suppose that you yourself think your thoughts? It is more correct to say *It* thinks.

You do not realize that everything in you, practically speaking, is It, that is, a machine going by chains of associations.

You are not an individual, a subject acting from the center of your being – you merely react to internal impulses and outside influences and suggestions.

Ask yourselves whether you can behave differently from the way you do. You may think you can, but you are deluded. You merely exchange one I for another.

Perhaps that's what a scientist meant when he wrote that even the deepest spiritual feelings may be due to nothing else that "an occasional shot of intoxicating brain chemicals governed by our DNA. I am a believer that every thought we think and every feeling we feel is the result of activity in the brain. I think we follow the basic law of nature, which is

that we are a bunch of chemical reactions running about in a bag."[4]
Yes, he is in the same state of sleep as you. He is identified with his brain and does not know himself. But can he find the thinker in the brain?

It is like trying to find the announcer inside the radio, or the football game inside the TV. Reality and facts may not be the same. I mean scientific facts.
A fact may be entirely different and even opposite to truth and reality.

Reality is infinite relationship; truth is the recognition of it.

Facts, instead, are single aspects, conceptualizations of manifoldness, broken fragments, disconnected from their universality and totality

For instance, the existence of a chemical element like carbon is a fact; but do you think you can understand the life of a human being by studying the element of carbon in his body? – or know what a book is about simply by examining the arrangement of its letters on the page?

There are those who seem to think so.
The mode of knowing corresponds to the level of consciousness, which determines the view of reality or, put another way, what is thought to be real.

In reference to man, "how like a god," says the mystic; "how like a dog," asserts the behavioral scientist.
To seek the self in an object is profoundly contradictory; how can you find the subject, the thinking and feeling self, in an object like the brain?

The investigator may verify everything he likes, but how does he verify the verifier? He eludes himself and is bound to escape his own mental grasp and, ultimately, remains unknowable.

He is like the eyes that see sights and ears that hear sounds; but who sees the eyes and who hears the ears? They obviously do not see and hear themselves.

I am conscious of the eyes and of their objects and of the ears and their objects. Indeed, I see and hear, rather than the eyes see and the ears hear. They are only the instruments that the "I" uses.
Yes, the instruments of the faculties I gave you to gain experiences on this plane and for the expansion of your consciousness. But you cannot use them properly unless you attain self-knowledge. And that is what I am helping you to do.

But does this mean that if I do not know who I really am it is not possible for me to do what I want?
In order to do what you really want you must be free; and to think, feel, and act as a free person you must, first and foremost, be. You do not have to be a philosopher to understand that.

You mean truly being who I AM. But this is what a professional philosopher writes:

> "What we call" 'self' is a creation, the creation of a certain kind of culture and, ultimately a concoction made up out of grammar. We refer to ourselves as a matter of syntactic necessity and come to suppose that we must be referring to some specific and concrete entity, our-

selves." Then he continues, "What determines the self?...certain ingredients are obvious: the simple facts about us (age, race, social status, skills, family) and the way we learn to think about ourselves." For our conception of self– and thus of self itself, even more important than the world we live in are "those small and specific interactions through which we define our selves which are not merely infusions of society (the 'they') as a whole but very particular and very much voluntary interactions between friends, family and lovers, as well as colleagues and acquaintances." And he adds, "But much of the determination of self — a process which is never completed — is to be located in our specific interpersonal relationships, not just what I think of my self but what *you* think of me, and what I think of the way you think of me, and what you think of the way I think of you and so on.[5]

If that is the definition, rather description of who you are, you are less real than a will-o-the-wisp. Are you merely the product of the environment and of your acquaintances? Then if they happened to be different you would not be who you are now, you would be someone else.

Then I ask you to tell me who am I.
What do you think I am doing? I am taking My time out of the cosmic activity of creation to do just that. But it is not only necessary but imperative that you replace the crowd you have become, with only on "I": the real one.

At present you are manipulated by your fragmented personality that makes you believe it is you and your life, while it is merely a usurper with an identity signified by your roles and delusions, that is to say, the counterfeit picture of yourself;

and whether that self-image is good or bad is irrelevant because it is, in any case, imaginary.

You have become but a travesty, the debased and distorted likeness, both within and without, of Myself.

That is harsh judgment.
Truth sometimes seems that way; but remember that I speak of you and to you as a representative of humankind on Earth to share the truth I convey to you with others, at least with those who are ready to accept it. However, as the proverb says, "Do not speak in the hearing of a fool, who will only despise the wisdom of your words."[6]

I made you in the beginning a perfect being, endowed with the power of mastery over yourself and the world, with the glorious purpose of creating beauty and perfection.

And look at yourself now; in whatever you do you respond like a puppet to the order of your false self. You are like an actor on stage, playing different parts, confused and without a sense of identity, groveling in the dark, wandering in a maze of worldly distractions and whirling impressions, unable to distinguish right from wrong, truth from falsehood, the real from the unreal.

While you continue in the rounds of your senseless and meaningless existence you ask, Why?

Many voices from different places deafen your ears with various answers, but they will fail to satisfy your longing for truth until you listen to the One who speaks from within your heart.

You are a hard taskmaster, but I do understand that you tell the truth for our benefit even if it hurts. Most people don't do that, but you are not like us, thank God!

I am trying to awaken you because you have slept for too long in the cocoon built by your personality, which is the primary cause of the human suffering and limitations.

If you were aware of it, you would be filled with terror at the sight of this monster, represented in classical mythology as the hydra. It has a dog-like body and, according to different sources, 9, 50, 100 or even 10,000 snake heads. When one is cut off, two sprout up in its place. It was one of the labors of Hercules to slay it.

I need all the help I can receive, for I certainly cannot be compared to Hercules.
But you can have the Herculean strength and courage to conquer your dark self if you make the decision with all your heart, with all your mind, with all the energy of your being. There is nothing in the universe which can resist or oppose the desire and the will of the individual who wants to be free and perfect himself because in that decision he is one with Me. People make tremendous efforts to succeed and reach their temporary goals, but it is merely a mechanical effort and therefore worthless. Only conscious striving can help them fulfill their destiny, but you must bring more light into your consciousness in order to raise it to a higher level in the process of deification, that is, to become what I have destined you to be.

That is what Bugental meant by the acceptance of our God-Nature. To me, God is a word used to point to our ineffable subjectivity, to the unimaginable potential which lies within each of us, to the aspirations which well up within us for greater truth and vividness of living and to something more, to the sense of mystery and to the dedication to explore that mystery...We human beings take our sense of God from our

deepest intuitions as to what is ultimate in our own depths."[7]

But this is only half of the truth, because God is not only a word to indicate your subjectivity and infinite potential; it is a Being, immanent but also transcendent, with whom you are indissolubly connected by the bond of love for all eternity.

[1] Cf. M. Nicoll, *Psychological Commentaries on the Teaching of Gurdjieff and Ouspensky* (London: Watkins, 1980), vol. 1, pp. 136-9.

[2] Matthew 5:34.

[3] E. H. Bleiler, ed. and trans., *Famous Italian Opera Arias* (Mineola, NY: Dover Publications, 1996), pp. 58-9.

[4] *Time,* October 25, 2004, p. 65, Jeffrey Kluger, "Is God in Our Genes?"

[5] Robert Solomon, *Love: Emotion, Myth, and Metaphor.* (Buffalo, NY: Prometheus Brooks, 1990) pp. 152-155.

[6] Proverbs 23:9.

[7] James Bugental, "Being Levels of Therapeutic Growth", in *Beyond Ego,* op. cit. p. 195.

CHAPTER 8

The Principle of Polarity

*By reflection of Itself in the eternal, pre-cosmic, virginal Space,
the ONE is said thereupon to establish a dyad which is positive-
negative, male-female, potential father-mother in one Existence.*
Geoffrey Hodson

*It is that relation between opposites without which no external
Motion would be possible, because there would be no where to
move from, and nowhere to move to.*
Thomas Troward

**The Scripture says that we are created in your image and
likeness, but I don't understand what that means, and I
didn't find a satisfactory and convincing explanation.
Somewhere I read that image refers to man and likeness to
woman, which increased my confusion.**
My purpose is to introduce you into the mystery of your Being
because, as I said, there is nothing more essential than self-
knowledge.

**It is the central subject in all spiritual teaching, and also in
other fields, but it is not clear to me why it should be.**
Because it is the way, the only way, to discover the fundamental
truth of who you are and who I AM, and the final realization of
the immortal identity of the individual and God, the microcosm and the macrocosm.

In the human being the full possibilities of cosmic expression are contained. In fact, the purpose of his existence on
Earth is the unfolding from within of his macrocosmic or universal attributes and creative powers. Eventually, according to

the divine plan, he will grow to the full stature of the Logos or God of a solar system, and after, even beyond that.

This magnificent and glorious vista urges me to expand my consciousness beyond the human limitations of the physical plane. But is it not blasphemy to affirm that one is god?

That would be a superficial interpretation; Here is how the Arab mystic Rumi understands it: "People think that to say 'I am god' is a claim of greatness, but it is actually extreme humility. Anyone who says, 'I am God's servant' predicates two existences, his own and god's, while the one who says 'I am God' nullifies himself, that is, he gives up his own existence; everything is He. Existence is God's alone; I am utter, pure nonexistence; I am nothing.' There is more humility in this than any claim to greatness, but people do not comprehend."[1] Obviously, just to say the words, "I am God" as an intellectual concept, without knowing who I AM is and what it can do, will not bring the complete realization.

There must be the at one-ment of the personal self, and this is difficult to accomplish.

It should not be because it is the work of love whose very nature is to enable you to transcend and rise above the personal self, and become one with the Beloved.

But the personality is selfish and does not want to let go.

You must put on your armor of light which I will provide for you and conquer it. It is a matter of life or death.

I am reminded of the words of Revelation: "If you conquer, you will be clothed in white robes, and I will not blot your

**name out of the book of life."² And, "Whoever conquers will
not be harmed by the second death."³**

I will teach you and assist you to be victorious, if you want to.
But let us proceed in an orderly fashion, and I will try to be as
simple and understandable as possible considering the limitations of your language.

**And of my mind. I heard a preacher saying, "God put a limit
to our intelligence but not to our stupidity."**

It is too mistaken as a joke to be funny; the opposite would be
much closer to the truth.

Has it ever occurred to you that there might be two natures in you, or rather two sides, like the positive and negative
poles of a magnet? I will use the traditional terminology and
call them spirit and matter. You, as an individual stand between them as the nexus, the combined nature of the two,
which are in reality one and intended to remain one.

I am present in you as the inner self, and your outer aspect is the personality. The interrelation and complementarity
of the divine and human poles enable you to be self-conscious
and to say I or I am, which is the expression of your identity.

Matter usually has a negative connotation.

It should not be considered of a lower or lesser value but rather
as the necessary and indispensable counterpart of the spirit.
The two poles and their relationship are the basis of cosmic
activity; no form or aspect of life is separated from others, no
thing exists independently, but only in relation to the other
parts and to the whole universe.

Life is a constant flow of energy, and its manifestation is
governed by and depends on the principle of polarity.

The term polarity is defined in the dictionary as "the presence or manifestation of two opposite or contrasting principles or tendencies."[4]
It should not be used synonymously with duality or be confused with it, as usually it is, rather as a pair of inseparable poles founded on the one transcendental ground.

There is the polarity of spirit and matter, male and female, the polarity of the atom, of the planets and their relationship to each other, the polarity of the solar system and its relationship to other systems, the polarity of one plane of the universe to another, all operating under the Law of the magnetic attraction of love, which leads to the cosmic source of Father-Mother God.

Is this related to sexuality?
It is indeed; and to give you a brief answer, the present attitude and ideas about sex must be changed from the prevailing lower connotation and degradation to the merely physical plane and raised to its true cosmic significance.

Alice A. Bailey, in *Esoteric Psychology*, writes, "For ages men have misused and wrongly employed a God-given function; they have prostituted their birthright, and through their laxity and license, and through their lack of control, they have inaugurated an era of disease, both mental and physical, of wrong attitudes and illusory relations which it will take a long time to eradicate."[5]

But why are you so eager to introduce this topic? Do you think we have said all there is to say about polarity?

No, surely we have not. In fact, perhaps I wanted to hasten on to a new topic – and one that interests me very much – because I did not really understand you; and actually I am

ashamed that I didn't simply admit that I could not follow your thinking.

We will come to the topic of your concern, but right now I wish to assuage your confusion – which is not yours alone but prevalent, and it is reinforced and substantiated by some authors who, in their recognition of reality as the interaction and interrelation between two sides, consider good and evil one of the polarities of life, along with life and death, male and female, light and darkness and so on.

According to them, since all differences and contraries are relative within the basic unity of life, the ideal and highest aim is to maintain a dynamic balance between them. If this were true, since the two poles are interdependent and complementary and one cannot exist without the other, you have the paradox of good depending on evil and vice versa in order to be in a state of equilibrium.[6]

Then, (I hope you do not mind My being facetious – there is cosmic humor in heaven), health should be balanced with sickness, love with hate, joy with sorrow, freedom with bondage, right with wrong, peace with war, intelligence with insanity, order with chaos, creation with destruction.

Last but not least, a balanced diet should include not only good but bad food, which you now eat anyway. To assert the polarity of good and evil, considering them of the same order of reality and relating them to the twofold principle of spirit/matter or male/female, is one of the greatest fallacies of the human intellect. Good and evil, like light and darkness, can never be in polarity, for evil is not real; it is but the energy veil created and sustained by mankind's destructive thoughts and feelings within the relativity of time and space, by the misuse of their free will.

Their duality is comparable to that of truth and error. For instance, the contradictory proposition "There are UFOs" and "There are no UFOs" stand as possibilities only because final evidence (at least for some critics) as to their truth is lacking; but certainly one proposition will disappear as soon as conclusive evidence is discovered.

By the way, what are called "flying saucers" are real and they belong to a much more advanced civilization than yours.

"If the UFO's don't exist then neither do stars," writes John White: "despite repeated denials, the U.S. government and military have known for four decades that UFO's are real and represent a technology beyond human capability."[7]

However, that has nothing to do with strange looking creatures and horrid abductions. On the contrary, perfected Beings from other planes of the universe try to protect and assist mankind and, especially at this time, to prevent the destruction of the planet.

I know there is evidence of their existence also in legends and records of earlier periods.

Those who believe that the inhabitants of your planet are the apex of evolution are very ignorant of the reality of the universe. But the truth will prevail over the intellectual concoctions of humans.

Therefore truth and error, like good and evil or light and darkness cannot possibly be interrelated or complementary because they exclude each other. Moreover, our minds don't want to preserve error but seek to eliminate it.

Unless we prefer to lie or remain in our state of ignorance. The intellect in its limited and conditioned state cannot comprehend or conceive the ultimate reality of good or God.

It cannot be understood conceptually because we describe experience by the dualistic categories of language. We cannot refer to "good" without wrongly relating it to "bad." We usually make distinctions in order to choose one or the other, if we are intelligent enough, but we cannot think of one without its opposite.

This is the familiar view of your "relative" world which is taken for granted and presupposed as "common sense." The human intellect cannot penetrate into the unity of all things. Therefore, it is a fallacy to define good and evil or light and darkness in the same relation to each other as the polarity of male and female, because they are mutually exclusive. Good is an eternal essence and a divine principle which can neither be related to nor be the counterpart of or complementary to evil, which is an absence. It has no real foundation because it is mankind's temporary manifestation of destructively qualified energy.

"Originally, there existed nothing but the light, and its separation from the darkness is a clear expression of the law of contrast; 'being' presupposes 'not being,' without requiring that 'not being' actually exists, just as the light presupposes the absence of light. When we say that every object in space has its shadow, this is merely a manner of speaking, because a shadow does not exist in itself. Not-being is the shadow of being. Thus, creation causes light, being, and life to gush forth; morning and evening mark the succession of events; but the night does not come into it, it has not place in the creation of God ... Evil constitutes a shadowy kingdom inhabited by phantoms. The expression 'outer darkness'[8] points to an element introduced fraudulently from the outside; it is a monstrous excrescence, a parasitic addition."[9]

The Divine Master said, "Your eye is the lamp of your body ... If it is not healthy, your body is full of darkness."[10] Since it no longer emits light, it enlightens nothing; the diseased eye looks past God, it cannot see Reality.[11]

In a polarity, the two sides complete each other and are implicitly one: each is both. They do not exist in themselves but are rooted in the primordial, infinite ground of being of which they are inseparable aspects, and where it is impossible for darkness or evil or death to be. "This is the message we have heard from him and proclaim to you, that God is light and in him there is no darkness at all."[12]

Those who think that good and its opposite are interrelated make reference to this traditional apologue.

A farmer had a horse that ran away. His neighbor commiserated, but was told, "Who knows what is good or bad?" It was true. The next day the horse returned, bringing with it a drove of wild horses it had befriended in its wanderings. The neighbor came over again, this time to congratulate the farmer on his windfall. He was met with the same observation: "Who knows what is good or bad?" True this time, too, for the next day, the farmer's son tried to mount one of the wild horses and fell off, breaking his leg. Back came the neighbor, this time with commiserations, only to encounter for the third time the same response: "Who knows what is good or bad?" And once again he was right; for the following day, soldiers came by commandeering for the army, and because of his injury the son was not drafted.

This fable does not prove the relativity of all principles and values, like good and evil, right and wrong, but merely the limitation of the human mind which cannot, and should not draw conclusions from fragmentary information. It is, therefore, incapable of understanding the consequences of events of which it sees only the beginning.

We pretend to judge, from our narrow perspective and personal viewpoint, without knowing the full truth.
Humanity has lost the knowledge of the Law of cause and effect which I gave them in the beginning.

In *No Boundary*, Ken Wilber wrote in support of the view of the interdependence and unity of light and darkness that one cannot perceive the stars at night without the background of darkness.[13]
The truth is, however, that you can see the stars because of their light: you need light, *not* darkness in order to see. The stars are not visible during the day because of a closer and, therefore, apparently brighter star; but they do not depend on the dark in order to appear to our sight. In fact, if the veil of darkness were not there, which incidentally is deep blue, you would see them shining as bright as the sun!

I don't see the interrelation and the mutual interdependence between light and darkness. When a room is dark and I turn on the light, where did the darkness go? There is no more sign of its presence, it has been dispelled and vanishes. How can the light depend on darkness?
What the Psalmist says, "Even the darkness is not dark to you, the night is as bright as the day, for darkness is as light to you,"[14] is confirmed by the mystics. Based on her

personal experience St. Teresa of Avila, among others, states that, "This is a light that never yields to darkness, and being always light, can never be clouded."[15]

It is true that there are types of related opposites in which one term exists only in conjunction with the other.

For example, above and below, front and back, soft and hard, long and short, full and empty, wet and dry, hot and cold, sweet and bitter. But they are terms of relation limited to our human existence, members of a single world of natural phenomena on the physical plane. How can they be compared or be considered of the same order of reality and confused with cosmic principles like spirit and matter, male and female, universality and individuality, God and man?

It is ludicrous just thinking of it.

Philosophers refer to it as "category error." To correlate good and evil, light and darkness, or life and death with the cosmic polarities aforementioned is a typical example of mere word-thinking and one-sided abstractions, with no comprehension of the nature of ultimate reality.

The principle of polarity on which universal life is founded consists of an interdependent and interrelated unity, two in one, and should not be confused or mistaken with duality which implies separation and opposition, and neither with undifferentiated oneness or sameness wherein the pairs are fused and lost.

My interlocutor would say, that they are transcended into "unity consciousness" as "subject and object are one and the same thing ... we can distill the entire essence of these traditions into the phrase 'Reality as a level of consciousness, or simply 'Reality as Mind only.'[16] Consciousness, as I will elaborate later on, is relational; it implies one who is conscious and that of which he is conscious. Again, not as a subject opposed to the object or as "one and the same thing" with the effacement of both terms, but like the interconnectedness and interdependence of two poles of a magnet.

The same author writes, "To destroy the negative," which he means "pain, evil, death, suffering, sickness," is, at the same time, to destroy all possibility of enjoying the positive," that is, "goodness, life, joy, and health." And in support of his view he refers us to Alfred North Whitehead, an influential contemporary philosopher, who suggests that all the "ultimate elements are in their essence vibratory." "That is," Whitehead explains, "all the things and events we usually consider are irreconcilable ... are actually just like the crest and trough of a single wave, a single vibration ..."[17]

Obviously, there is no such thing as a crest without a trough, a high point without a low point as they are inseparable aspects of one underlying activity. Thus, as Whitehead puts it, each element of the universe is a vibratory ebb and flow of an underlying energy or activity.

I don't understand the analogy of the trough and the crest with good and evil or light and darkness.

According to these thinkers, all opposites share an implicit identity, therefore for them good and evil are one and the same. And this is a fallacy. It is true that there are not separate and irreconcilable contraries, but the solution of the problem of dualism is not, as I mentioned, a state of being one and the same or an unqualified identity. Our author states, "Whether Reality is called Brahman, God, Tao, Dharmakaya, Void, or whatever is of no great concern, for all alike point to that state of non-dual Mind wherein the universe is not split into seer and seen."[18] However, there is only one way to overcome the separation between subject and object by preserving their reality, and that is love.

There cannot be love between the trough and the crest because they are one single thing or action.
The same writer says that "to *know* Reality is *to be* Reality,"[19] and it is true, but it can only be realized by the unifying power of love which, again, implies the polarity of spirit and matter Father-Mother God, and subject and object.

We may transcend into unity consciousness, but apart from you, unless the experience of universality is shared with an Other in the relationship of love like the two poles of a magnet, it reinforces the sense of self-delusion and emptiness.

I'd like to quote the words of Lama Anagarika Govinda: "If we try to deny the fact of polarity (imagining that reality consists only in unity) then we simply close our eyes to the most evident reality."[20]

When the mystics describe their experience of oneness with God they convey the feeling of a deep communion and merging, but their individuality does not disappear or fade out. Even the words of Jesus, "The Father and I are one," means two in one and one in two. "As you, Father, are in me and I am in you, may they also be in us ... so that they may be one, as we are one, I in them and you in me, that they may become completely one."[21]
With regards to the words duality and polarity they are used interchangeably and with the same meanings because of the limitation of your language, but as I said they are essentially different.

The confusion and misconception is apparent in the words of another writer when, with reference to the relation of good and evil and light and dark, he states: "Since all opposites are interdependent, their conflict can never result in the total victory of one side, but will always be a manifestation of the interplay between the two sides."[22]

This way of thinking is contradictory because conflict and antagonism can exist only where there is duality, not when the two poles attract and complement each other and form a unity. Light is not at war with darkness, except as a metaphor, and spirit and matter or male and female are not opposed nor do they struggle against one another. On the contrary, they complement each other, as each is both and one cannot exist without the other. There is a primordial harmony between them, they are like the rhythmical heart-beat of the universe.

Light does not battle the darkness because it is the highest rate of vibration and, like love, on contact can consume and transmute all that is unlike itself. I am sure the prayer of the Hindu devotee in the Upanishads will echo in each one's heart:

> From the unreal lead me to the real.
> From darkness lead me to light,
> From death lead me to immortality.[23]

Notice that the word unreal is of the same order and has the same meaning as darkness and death, and that is the ultimate truth.

With regard to what is called "unity consciousness" or "Mind only" as the solution of the problem of duality, the term is ambiguous and requires clarification.

It is explained as "a type of continuum or spectrum, the Absolute Self metaphorically 'located' at one end of the continuum (Mind) and the normal ego awareness at the other (Ego)."[24] We are presented with an elaborate conceptual description of the various bands or layers to demonstrate that Reality is a level of consciousness and the Mind alone is Real. The emphasis is on the apparent gap or split between subject and object at the origin of the spectrum which has created an illusory duality.

The Mind appears as a subject vs. an object, as the individual separated from the world where in reality there is no split because its nature is to be one with its "objects" of knowledge. Mind, or Absolute Self, is neither subjective nor objective, it is non-dual consciousness, "witnessing everything without separation from anything ... It is a state of awareness wherein the observer is the observed, wherein the universe is not severed into one state which sees and another state which is seen."[25] Each thing is identical to all other things because all of them are nothing but Mind. "Every inside is an outside," and this is how it is explained: as I read this page "there is not one sensation called myself that senses another sensation called the page!"[26] They are one and the same. And this phrase becomes a refrain.

However, the author continues, if I form a mental concept of the page, since that concept *appears* separate from me as an object, then the "page" likewise must *appear* separate from me as an object. "This subject-object dualism besets us and it is illusory."[27]

It is true that separation in life is not real because My consciousness is everywhere, but the unity which is being described is a fallacy. Reality is based on polarity which is the interconnectedness and relationship of all that is without being fused and confused.

"The overemphasis on unity" as Lama Govinda explains, "is as a great a fault as the overemphasis on duality or plurality. If we conceive duality as the irreconcilable opposition of two independent and mutually exclusive principles, and not as the necessary polarity of two mutually complementary aspects of reality or of a higher unity - or if we cling only to one side, under complete exclusion or negation of the other then, indeed, we suffer under a serious illusion."[28]

The author asserts that the individual as the Knower, the Witness, and Absolute Subjectivity who is reading this page is the Godhead, Brahman, Mind, Reality itself. "Whether we realize it or not, want it or not, care about it or not, we are it – always have been and always will be."[29] Then we are faced with the revelation that the level of the Mind, which is "no level" for it is infinite, is our present and usual state of consciousness whatever our attitude and mood might be, good or bad, positive or negative.

It seems very encouraging, but how misleading!

"Brahman is not a particular experience, level of conscious-ness or state of soul – rather it is precisely whatever level you happen to have now."[30] For being infinite and abso-lutely all-inclusive, it is compatible with every imaginable level or state of consciousness. The reason is that Mind cannot be a particular level set apart from other levels, for that would impose a spatial limitation on Mind. And since it is a dimensionless reality each level represents "an illu-sory deviation."[31]

Of which there are legion! What a glorious assurance of being already what one is predestined to be, without any effort or the use of the free will. However, without an intense desire and the yearning toward completeness or enlightenment one will never attain it, and to believe otherwise is self-deception.

But my question is, what is the purpose of being already God if we don't realize and manifest it? Of what value is an experience which we don't have? It is like telling an infant that it is already an adult person or to the child in kindergarten that it is a Ph.D. The beauty of it is that we don't even have to seek after Mind because it would be not only in vain but self-defeating as it makes us think that we lack what we, in reality, already have. We are advised not to "trick" ourselves into looking for something that was never lost.[32]

It is certainly good to know that people have not lost their mind, although, as I look over the world, they did.

Since Mind is infinite and all-inclusive one cannot step outside of it. In fact, since outside and inside are one and the same, there is nowhere to go. This seems to contradict what you said about your Presence being anchored in our heart, and the prophet is wrong when he proclaims, "Seek the Lord while he may be found, call upon him while he is near."[33]

Although My nature "is a circle of which the center is everywhere and the circumference is nowhere,"[34] while you are in embodiment on the Earth I abide in your heart-center as the focal point of My consciousness and your permanent identity which "I AM."

It is stated also in the Chandogya *Upanishad*:

> "This is my Self within the heart, greater than the earth....greater than the sky, greater than all the world...This is Brahman."[35] "The Light which shines there beyond the heaven, behind all things...that is assuredly this Light which is here within, in men."[36]

The Creator of the universe is within my heart as a seed. How can one imagine that he is already God?
All he has to do is to look at himself in the mirror.

I remember William Blake's statement, "Man is born like a garden fully planted and sown, but this world is too poor to produce one seed."[37] We are told that no "spiritual exercises" are necessary because "you are already where any path can take you."
The goal and the path are one and the same. Therefore, if someone asks you for directions to go somewhere, tell him that he does not need them because he is already there.

To dispel any doubt we are reminded that statements like "we are already one with the Godhead" and "Your everyday and ordinary consciousness is the Tao" are made by the Masters of every tradition. They instruct us that "enlightenment and ignorance, reality and illusion, heaven and hell, liberation and bondage – all are non dual and not to be separated."[38]
They are one and the same.

It seems that Jesus is not considered one of the Masters since he prayed "that all may be one," and gave his life for that purpose.

Obviously, he did not know that everyone is already one with his Father. What our abstract thinkers are missing is that the Masters speak from their height of enlightened consciousness. They are identified with the All but can be misunderstood by those who are not.

Like the case of the Zen master who when asked about the universal and ultimate Reality referred to something very immediate and perceptible: "The cypress tree in the yard." We learn that the Supreme Knower cannot be known dualistically as an object of knowledge because "it does not suffer to become an object, except in illusion."[39] Then we have the astonishing explanation that, however, it is highly conscious for it is pure consciousness – "it is just never conscious of itself as an eye does not see itself."[40] "It cannot be thought about because it is doing the thinking; it cannot be looked at because it is doing the looking; it cannot be known because it is doing the knowing."[41] We can never see the Seer, or know our Self as an object because it is the one doing the seeing, therefore it cannot see itself.

The observer and the observed are one and the same.

And he explains: "Now if, while reading this, you decide to go 'behind' the 'self' to find what is really doing the looking, to find the Perceiver, the Seer, you will find only – this page!" Since subject and object are one and the same, as they vanish into non-dual Subjectivity, "I am the page reading itself!"[42]

What an amazing sleight of hand, rather, of mind!

"This is so," our author continues, because my actions are the actions of the universe and vice versa so that when I and the universe are no longer separate, what "it" does to "me" and what "I" do to "it" are one and the same action. And we are given some examples: "If a rock falls on my head, I did it. If a man shoots me in the back, I did it. If I get lung disease and painfully suffocate to death, I did it ... this is the inner meaning of Karma, "that what happens to you is your own doing, your own Karma" ...On the level of Mind [Mind only], nothing lies outside of me, ... so that the final word is that "there is but one will: Mine and God's! Here, the problems cease to be problems."[43]

Everything is crystal clear, all questions are answered, what a magical solution of the human condition! But is it not strange, I did not know that My will is already done by everyone.

And Jesus did not know it either when he taught us to pray, "thy will be done on earth as it is in heaven."

Earth and heaven are one and the same, in fact, according to our investigators, there is no above and below because Mind is everywhere.

A logic as unambiguous as it is one-sided! But with regard to your will that is already acting in every human being and everywhere, since it is supposed to be good and perfect, why bad things happen? What is the cause of evil?

It must be that good and evil are one and the same like everything else because there is Mind only.

Another issue I am confused about is our investigator's comparison of the "I" to the eye that cannot see itself.

They sound vocally the same but it is a wrong analogy. I can assure him that the "I" is very capable to see itself because "I AM that I AM"! This means, if one uses his God-given intelligence, that I know Myself because I AM a Self-conscious Being. And I can make anyone else self-conscious, that is, conscious of My Presence, if they want to.

The "I" is the eye by which the Infinite sees itself and I AM that when I acknowledge you as my Source. "The marvelous Unique Self-consciousness Al-one is Subject-Object both at once. It knows It-Self and knows all else also."[44]
Unless the individual understands and feels the connection with his God Self, how can the light of My love illumine him?

But if one thinks he is "already" God ...
A God that is not conscious of Itself? Is it not unbelievable? Mankind does not know that the word "I AM" is God's self-revelation of the nature of the divine Being?

Even if they do, not everyone comprehends its meaning.
However, Roberto Assagioli, the founder of Psychosynthesis, clues us in when he writes: "The "I" is simple, unchanging, constant and self-conscious ... After the dis-identification from its contents of consciousness (sensations, emotions, desires and thoughts) I recognize and affirm that I am a Centre of pure self-consciousness."
And he wisely recognizes that "To state this with conviction does not mean one has yet reached the experience of the "I", but it is the way which leads to it."[45]
Also the Indian saint Ramana Maharshi who, ironically, our author quotes to support his view, refers to Reality as "I-I" and he says, "Your duty is TO BE and not to be

this or that. 'I AM THAT I AM' sums up the whole truth."
To the question, "Who then is God?" He replied, "The Self
is God. 'I AM' is God. If God be apart from the Self, He must
be a selfless God, which is absurd."[46]

"The word *ayam* means That which exists, self-
shining and self-evident. In the Bible also 'I AM' is given as
the name of God."[47]

The evidence that 'I AM' is a self-conscious Being is also affirmed in the Vedanta trinity of Brahman, as the fullness of being, self-luminous consciousness, and infinite bliss. (*sat-cit-
ananda*). "A duality in unity is present here, and, consequently,
the power of love."[48]

**Very similar to the Christian Trinity of Father-Son-Holy
Spirit with the mutual love between the two persons that
becomes manifest in the third. Our thinkers embellish their
point saying, "should you try to see the Seer, you are a hand
trying to grab itself or lips trying to kiss themselves."[49]**

They may concoct all kinds of conceits and fanciful metaphors
but let me say that the hand is not meant to grab itself because
there are two of them which can be joined together.

In prayer.
Moreover, My hand is stretched out in love also to those who
do not believe in prayer.

And I can not only grab it, but also kiss it.
Why not? Can anyone deny that I have the power to make Myself visible and tangible?

They would find your fiery Being not very comfortable.

You are right, My Presence may be too hot for them. There are not many aware that through My messengers, the Ascended Ones, I AM very active on the physical plane giving assistance to individuals and nations or humanity would be smothered by their own discord and filth. There is the greatest misconception with regard to who "I AM" by the conceited ignorance of the personality which refuses to acknowledge the Source that gives it life.

We could not lift one finger without your energy. The irony is that they refer to you as "Energy," "a word that is nothing but one of the names of God."[50] It seems as if they are talking about physics but "since Energy more or less 'underlies' all material things ... Ultimately, it matters not one whit whether we say that all things are forms of Energy or forms of Brahman."[51]

These authors call Me by the name of Energy but do they have any idea what it is? They refer to what they do not know and do not comprehend with something else unknown and beyond their comprehension. "I AM" here trying to illumine them if they care to listen, which is doubtful because the intellect wants to be the teacher rather than the student, and the master rather than the servant. Our investigators are unaware, first that what they call Mind, Supreme Subjectivity, unity consciousness or whatever, is a Being! And to use their words, "whether they realize it or not, want it or not, care about it or not," human beings are My individualities on Earth, connected with My life by a bond of love that can never be broken. And second, what they call Energy is not just an anonymous and impersonal force but the light of My Being which is the radiation of the fire of My love.

For you are the trinity of life, light and love.
Their argument, or one of them, is that the infinite and the finite cannot be in opposition or set against each other, which is true. However, not because it would drag the infinite down to the level of finiteness, "making it nothing more than one being beside other beings."[52] I AM , indeed, a Being not apart or separated but One with other Beings in the communion of love.

"To a god the finite would be as great a necessity as the infinite is to man, because only the finite gives meaning to the infinite.[53]
They are not one and the same but the inseparable and complementary poles of spirit and matter, Father-Mother God, life and form, universality and individuality, which are the two halves of consciousness.

They are interacting and mutually dependent like the poles of a magnet.
Congratulations! I see that you begin to understand the principle of polarity.

"We may break a piece of magnetized steel as often as we like, we shall never be able to separate the positive from the negative pole; each fragment will always have both."[54]
Our writers have a very inadequate conception of what universal life is and of its Source. I will quote the words of a clairvoyant author whose vision is closer to the truth.

> "All individuals are as centres, organs or cells in a higher
> Being, of whom they are a manifestation and a part.
> These higher Beings in their turn are expressions of the

power, the life and the consciousness of still more highly evolved intelligences. This hierarchical system culminates in one all-inclusive All-Being, the summation and synthesis of all creation, the supreme Deity, the One Alone...I am that Self, that Self am I."[55]

And may I remark that this oneness is not the non-dual awareness called Absolute Subjectivity or Mind only. Those Beings, countless as the stars, and as the light of the stars, are part of each other, in the interconnectedness of life, and the interplay of the two primordial bipolar forces, and are drawn on and up in expanding ecstasy and glory by the magnetic power of love from the Source of All.

Like the needle of the compass by the north star Polaris.
Yes, you may think of each individual as one pole and the God Self as the other pole, held all together, as chords of music, by the all embracing and cohesive power of love.

Although no "spiritual exercises" are needed because we are already Mind, the Godhead or Brahman, we are given the explanation of what are called "Skillful Experiments" to prove to the skeptics that Mind is not "so much mystical pap" but Reality itself. It is an explanation of the essential factors or the quintessence of the many spiritual practices over the centuries. We are instructed to realize that "each one of us lives in the state of satori [enlightenment] and could not live otherwise....it is our eternal state, independent of our birth and our death ... right now we lack nothing ... for Mind exists nowhere but in *this* timeless moment."[56]

According to our author, first we must understand that our illusion of not being enlightened is caused by our

tendencies of conceptualization, objectification, and dualism, which results in identification with the fragments instead of the All, with the personal ego and not with the universe. Thus, in order to feel our cosmic identity we must surrender, at least temporarily, our thoughts concepts, and images. Each instant our life-force is rising from "below" as pure, formless, non-objective, timeless and spaceless. Then it begins to take on form and direction by thought and emotion, and this process disintegrates and disperses our Energy.

Not necessarily, it depends how one qualifies, uses or misuses the energy, whether it is positive and creative like love, kindness, benevolence, or the opposite which is miscreative and destructive.

They say that the cause of it is the passivity of the attention which instead of being in a state of watchfulness and vigilance, it is only awakened by the mobilization of the Energy. It is the screen of conceptualization that separates the individual from the rest of life for there is nothing objective to perceive. Therefore, the "I" and the "world" become one in the act of this pure non-conceptual seeing. "There is seeing, but nothing objective seen!"[57]

The seer and the seen are one and the same.

The suspension, not suppression, of the mental chatter and the monologue creates a stillness or silence referred to as "passive awareness" or seeing into nothingness. However, "it is not a looking into a mere blank or vacuum, but a looking into nothing objective."[58]

The seer and the seen are one and the same.

This is difficult to understand because, as Lama Govinda says, "To be conscious means to be aware of something. People who claim to meditate with an 'empty mind' deceive themselves...Consciousness is a dynamic force in constant movement, a continuous stream."[59] And as a river runs between two banks so does consciousness flow between the poles of spirit and matter. We cannot shut off its flow but we can direct it toward the personal self and the world, and this is the tendency of the masses of the people.

However, you may look inward and focus your attention into the heart or turn it up to Me.

That would be very different from the mystifying and hazy state of "looking into nothing objective" and believing that "one instant of this pure awareness is itself Mind." But if there is nothing objective nor subjective since they are one and the same, what kind of awareness is it? It is so pure that it vanished! Then it is claimed that Mind only "is always already the case" for it appears again after flying into the empty space of intellectual abstractions. I can't help thinking of the words of Carl Jung, that it is a "most audacious fantasy."

It seems that the problem discussed by our friends is about overcoming the illusion of duality or the separation of the "I" from the world, the subject from the object. For them the solution is Mind only, and they believe that it will set them free. But, may I ask, is there not an affective element in that Supreme Subjectivity as the underlying ground of emotions? Then should not love have a role in "Mind only" as a source of bliss, which is the heart of reality, in which the feeling of the individual can participate? In other words, is there by any chance a place for Me? There should be since reference is made

173

to sense-experiences as one and the same with cosmic consciousness when they are not contaminated with conceptualization. Unless the experience of universality is shared with an Other in the relation of love, it will reinforce the unfulfilled desire and the longing of the lover for the beloved which is innate in every individual.

It has been justly said, "You have made us for yourself and our heart is restless until it rests in you."[60]
Every part of life exists only in relation to others and ultimately to the totality of all that IS, which "I AM."

"Life means infinite relationship. ... There may be many levels or degrees of reality, but there cannot be any meaning in a 'reality in itself' (though it may be a very logical hypothesis and an inevitable conclusions of the ever abstracting and reducing conceptual mind), a reality that is totally unrelated to anything."[61]
With regard to the nature of enlightenment Lama Govinda explains that emptiness cannot be realized without being conscious of its opposite pole, that is, form. Since they co-exist inseparably and penetrate each other "*sunyata* can never become a living experience unless we have realized both poles of its incommensurable nature."[62]
Our thinkers may imagine that they are *already* god or Brahman, but in reality they have merely inflated their ego-sense and made it larger and dimensionless. It is pitiful to see the self-deception of the personality that in its pride and stubbornness, or ignorance, refuses to acknowledge and accept the Source that enables it to think.

But no the wrong way.

Mankind turned deliberately away from their God Self and until they return to It will remain bound by their limitations, life after life.

Only the fire of your love can consume our dross and set us free. But we don't know what love is although we are hungry for it.

The love of which I speak does not degenerate into sentimentality, emotionalism, eroticism, or into the perversion of hate and fear. The personal or outer self is the great deceiver and can hypnotize you, especially through the feeling nature, and make you believe that you are already egoless and free. But only the truth can set the individual free and I AM that truth.

How do we know that we are fooled?

When you do not love me first.

I know that "true meditation is the meditation of a lover," and love must have an object, not separate but as the other pole of its affection and devotion in order to feel at one with it. We must not fall, rather, rise in love toward you.

That is the only way to become free from the wheel of cause and effect and birth and rebirth.

And instead of Mind only, it should be Love only, the creative cause of all that is. But the love of the personality is possessive and wants to hold the energy, your energy, to itself instead of giving it back to you and in service to the rest of life.

The consequences are very serious because the individual's consciousness cannot expand without love, except in the imagination. The dualism that must be overcome is not merely between subject and object or the personal self from the world.

The real separation is from you , the Source of our life, and unless we come back to you and find again our connection through love everything else is meaningless. As St. Teresa says, "*Sin amor todo es nada,*" without love all is nothing.
Yet everyone is endowed with the capacity to experience their union with Me if they so choose.

The Scriptures of the world attest to it:
   "Those who turn to Me with love and devotion, they are in Me, and I in them."[64]
   "Abide in me as I abide in you ... Abide in my love."[65]
   "O taste and see that the Lord is good; happy are those who take refuge in him."[66]
In its oneness with Me the individual identity is not only preserved but experienced as the flame of love in one's heart. When the individual says "I AM," if he understood the meaning of the Word, he is not referring to the personal self which has no permanent reality because it is always changing, but to the God Self.

It is a shared love and a shared identity as the I AM Self.
The truth is that, "Problems cease to be problems,"[67] only by the realization that love, acting in the cosmic polarity of Father-Mother God or male and female, is all there is.

In the words of the Buddhist sage Lama Govinda, "The process of Enlightenment is therefore represented by the most obvious, the most human and at the same time the

most universal symbol imaginable: the union of male and female in the ecstasy of love – in which the active element is represented as a male, the passive by a female figure – in contrast to the Hindu Tantras, in which the female aspect is represented as the active principle, and the male aspect as the pure state of divine consciousness, of "being," that is, as the passive principle, 'the resting in its own nature.'[68] In case we misinterpret its true meaning he clarifies that "the polarity of male and female principles...is raised upon a plane which is as far away from the sphere of mere sexuality as the mathematical juxtaposition of positive and negative sign."[69]

In Taoism all manifestations of the Tao, the way of ultimate reality, are generated by the polar relationship and dynamic interplay of Yin and Yang. Also in the androcentric, patriarchal religions of Judaism and Christianity the presence of the Eternal Feminine as the other aspect of God is evident in the prominent roles of the Shekinah and Sophia or Wisdom, and the Virgin Mother Mary. Moreover, without love there is no happiness or bliss which is the keynote of life. As Umapati says, "In supreme happiness thou shall be one with the Lord...The soul is not merged in the Absolute, for if they become one (one, that is, without distinction), both disappear; if they remain two, there is no fruition. Therefore, there is union, and non union."[70] And this is what you mean by polarity, I am in you and you are in me. Mystics and saints compare the experience of merging to a crystal shining in the rays of the sun which cannot be distinguished from the light or iron made incandescent and glowing by fire. I think of a duet singing together and blending their voices still retaining their individuality.

Yes, the height of perfection and blessedness can be attained only by the fire of My love, the unifying and cohesive power of the universe and the purpose of creation. For truly, "beings here are born from bliss, when born; they live by bliss; and into bliss, when departing, they enter."[71]

In the discussion of these profound issues and experiences, which are difficult to put into words, often the problem is a matter of semantics – which may lead to misunderstanding and misinterpretation of the texts. The limitations of our language are obvious even in the trivial case of explaining, for example, the taste of honey or the whiteness of snow to someone who has never had that experience. In fact, there are feelings and sensations that are not possible to describe or convey in words.

It has been said, "That for which we find words is something already dead in our hearts. There is always a kind of contempt in the act of speaking."[72]

No one can argue that language is an indispensable medium of expression and a necessity for human beings to communicate with each other, but it often creates the problem of miscommunication. The irony is that to criticize the limitations of language we still need words. This explains the scholarly controversies over "whether we have made language or it has made us, whether we speak or are spoken."[73]

According to modern semanticists "words are not the same as things and a knowledge of words about facts is in no sense equivalent to a direct and immediate apprehension of the facts themselves."[74]

If one's whole experience is molded by fixed words and categories, language becomes restrictive, like a prison of the mind.

After all, words are symbols or signs, whether mental, spoken, or written.

The word "bread" cannot satisfy my hunger.
It is true, unless it is the Word that speaks.

Especially with regard to the subject of spiritual truth and inner experiences language is hopelessly inadequate, and this explains the element of paradox often present in the writings of the mystics.
I am reminded of the poem by St. John of the Cross: "Coplas del alma que pena por ver a Dios."

> Vivo sin vivir en mi',
> Y de tal manera espero
> Que muero porque no muero.
> .....
> Esta vida que yo vivo,
> Es privacion de vivir;
> Y asi, es continuo morir
> Hasta que vivo contigo.

This translates to: I live and do not live in my self, and so fervent is my hope that I die because I do not die ... The life that I live is a privation of living, and so it is a continual dying until I live with You.
In our age there is a plethora of spoken and written words, endlessly multiplied by the media and the printing press, indiscriminately thrown at the public regardless of their content, good, bad, or indifferent. One can say with Troilus, "Words, words, mere words, no matter from the heart; ... Go, wind, to wind!"[75]

Yes, instead of giving meaning to human existence and activities, as embodiments of values, words are degraded and made to subserve utilitarian ends and personal or political power. Habit and abuse have stereotyped language into a mere conventional medium of expression usually very narrow and empty of significance.

We are flooded not with knowledge but with data and information ...
Mostly destructive and causing great harm.

They can certainly be useless and wasteful but why harmful?
Because they fill your being and world with the shadows of human creation, that is, negative thoughts and feelings.

I know that "Your eyes are too pure to behold evil, and you cannot look on iniquity," but, "why do you show me wrongdoing and make me look at trouble? Destruction and violence are before me."[76]
Although the forces of darkness are rampant you do not have to give them your attention. I have to remind you of its magnetic power and how you are free to use it as you like.

What I see, become I must, God if I see God, dust if I see dust.
Do not forget also Jesus' statement: "The eye is the lamp of the body. So, if your eye is single, your whole body will be full of light."[77]

It is not easy to have a "single eye," and undivided attention on what is good and of the light.

You can always ask Me to help you because I guard everyone as "the apple of My eye."[78] Mankind cannot communicate anymore by thought-language as it was originally intended and as they did before what is called the Fall, that is, when they turned away from Me. However the essential nature of words is not confined and exhausted to the purpose of conveying mental and emotional processes. Although words have the power to deceive and obscure they have also the power to reveal and to express the desires of your heart carrying you into a state of intuitive receptivity.

You are referring to prayer.
Yes, the words of prayer, affirmation, or a mantra become centers of beneficent force by which is possible to transform negative conditions and evil influences so that one can experience what is good and perfect. They have the power to transcend the limitations of language because there is infinitely more than what can be encompassed by any formulation, whether a word, a language, a system of thought, a doctrine, or a whole culture. By your inner attitude, coupled with the sacred words, that which is visible may connect you with the invisible, what is tangible with the seeming intangible, and that which is audible will echo the inaudible and lead you into the silence.

Be still and know "I AM," God.[79]
Words, therefore, when charged with desire and devotion enable you to enter into the realm of light because there is sight in the feeling of love.

Unfortunately most people live at the physical level of experience because they are solely sense conscious, and see only with the eyes of the flesh. There are those who use to a lesser or higher degree the eyes of the mind and have a conceptual view of reality. Only a few rise to the state of true understanding and use the eye of contemplation.

How can it be done?
By the fire of love.

I must remember that nothing is impossible to love.
I mentioned to you that the light of truth is the object not only of knowledge but of love, because the intellect does not know how to love – you cannot love in the mind. Only love can lead you to infinities and eternities. Language alone cannot reach them; they do not reside in them except as intimations, like the spiritual power of sacred scriptures and the magic of poetry.

The inadequacy of human language to fit life and being is expressed in the first lines of the Tao Te Ching: "A path that can be verbalized is not a permanent path, terminology that can be designated is not constant terminology."[80] Or in another version, "If the Tao could be comprised in words, it would not be the unchangeable Tao: If a name may be named, it is not an unchangeable name."[81]
Another serious problem is caused by translation and, of course, interpretation.

You are right, (forgive me, you always are, but you see the habit of speech). Scholars agree that the core text of the Tao Te Ching, for instance is so old and the language so archaic that it often admits of widely divergent readings.

At times a character may even be read not merely with multiple meanings but as one or another character, each with its own meaning. Ironically, one reason for the popularity of the Tao Te Ching is its very obscurity. The

same comment was made by Aristotle, who recognized the self-contradictions arising from the paradoxical expressions of Heraclitus of Ephesus, the ancient Greek philosopher who was called even by his own contemporaries the "Obscure" because of the difficulty of understanding his teaching. He finds analogous relationships of various sorts but the distinctions between different modes of opposition and orders of reality tend to be ignored.

Thus, he writes, "The way up and down is one and the same. God is day night, winter summer, war peace satiety and hunger." His fragments illustrate the confusion that may arise from the use of opposite terms in unqualified and undefined senses. He says, Cold things warm themselves, warm cools, moist dries, parched is made wet.[82]

In fact, one of the authors mentioned makes reference to him to support the mistaken view that "all opposites are polar and thus united."[83] And he quotes the Tao Te Ching:

> Be bent, and you will remain straight.
> Be vacant, and you will remain full.
> Be worn and you will remain new.[84]

But how can the relativity of such concepts on their physical and human level, like wet and dry, before and after, or empty and full, apply to the principle of good and its absence, or to the cosmic polarity of spirit and matter or the infinite and finite?

Do you not think that individuals need more of My light in their brains?

I can understand the interrelation and complementarity of male and female but not of light and darkness or good and evil.
The peculiarities of the human intellect are legion.

Our mind has become so warped and clouded that has lost its balance and what people value most is based on a wrong perception of reality. We complain about so much evil in the world and we add to it by our criticism and condemnation. We don't realize that our thoughts and feelings are the contributive causal factor for the manifestation of good and evil on our planet. Therefore, the real cause is not the world where there is ignorance and wisdom,, and there are criminals and saints. Someone said, "One wise man means more than a thousands fools."[85]
Yes, even a little light enables one to move around and find what he is searching for. It all depends on what you create in your surroundings and in the world. They are like the raw material, and out of it you can make ugly or beautiful things. The value or quality is not in the material itself but in the individual who uses it. Similarly it is not because there is something wrong with the world that we suffer, but because there is something wrong with us.

With regard to the sense of loss and the failure to have or keep what we care for and cherish, We do not suffer because everything is impermanent, but because we cling to impermanent things. If we do not cling to them we should not mind their impermanence."[86]
But, who has the insight required to know the infinite and eternal values behind the veil of tears? I am come to awaken you and enable you to see them.

[1] *The Essential Rumi.* (NY: Harper-Collins, 1995), p. 45.
[2] Revelation 3:5.
[3] Revelation 2:11.
[4] *Random House Unabridged Dictionary.*
[5] Alice A. Bailey, *Esoteric Psychology, A Treatise On the Seven Rays*, (NY: Lucis Publishing Co., 2002) Vol. 1, p. 272.
[6] Capra, Fritjof, *The Tao of Physics: An Exploration of the Parallels Between Physics and Eastern Mysticism* (Boston, Mass.: Shambala Press, 2000) p. 146.
[7] John White, *The Meeting of Science and Spirit: Guidelines for a New Age* (NY: Paragon House, 1990) p. 56.
[8] Matthew 22:13.
[9] Paul Evdokimov, *Woman and the Salvation of the World*, ff. 143, 145a (Crestwood, NY: St. Vladimir's Seminary Press, 1994), p. 142-3.
[10] Luke 11:34.
[11] Evdokimov, p. 145.
[12] 1 John 1:5.
[13] Ken Wilber, *No Boundary: Eastern and Western Approaches to Personal Growth.* (Boulder, Col. & London: Shambala, 1981), p. 23.
[14] Psalm 139:12.
[15] *The Life,* p. 198.
[16] *Beyond Ego,* pp. 235, 239.
[17] Ibid., p. 239.
[18] *Beyond Ego,* p. 239.
[19] Ibid., p. 239.
[20] *Creative Meditation,* p. 205.
[21] John, 17:21-23.
[22] F. Capra, *The Tao of Physics: An Exploration of the Parallels between Physics and Eastern Mysticism* (Boston: Shambala Press, 2000), p. 146.
[23] *Brihadâranyaka-Upanishad,* 1, 3, 28.

24 Ken Wilber, *The Spectrum of Consciousness* (Wheaton, Ill.: The Theosophical Publishing House, 1977), p. 183.

25 Ibid., p. 24.

26 Ibid., p. 75.

27 Ibid., p. 75f.

28 *Creative Meditation,* p. 185.

29 Ken Wilber, *The Spectrum of Consciousness,* p. 88.

30 Ibid., p. 298.

31 Ibid., p. 298.

32 Ibid., p. 309.

33 Isaiah 55:6.

34 St. Bonaventure, *De Itinerario Mentis in Deum,* ch. 5, "On the Sight of the Divine Unity Through its Primary Name, Which is 'Being'."

35 Chandogya *Upanishad,* 111:14, 3-4.

36 Chandogya *Upanishad,* 111:13-17.

37 Quoted in J.C. Pearce, *The Biology of Transcendence, A Blueprint of the Human Spirit* (Rochester, Vermont: Park Street Press, 2002), p. 225.

38 *Spectrum,* p. 88.

39 Ibid., p. 88.

40 Ibid., p. 157.

41 Ibid., p. 85.

42 Ibid., p. 305.

43 Ibid., p. 336-7.

44 Sankshepa – Shariraka, in Das, p. 116.

45 Roberto Assagioli, *Psychosynthesis* (NY: Viking, 1965), pp. 117, 119.

46 *The Spiritual Teaching of Ramana Maharshi* (Boulder, Col.: Shambala, 1971) p. 75.

47 *Gems from Bhagavan* (U. N. Venkatraman, South India, 1978) p. 52.

48 Eliot Deutsch, *Advaita Vedanta: A Philosophical Reconstruction* (Honolulu. Hawaii: University Press of Hawaii, 1973) pp. 13, 28.

[49] *Spectrum,* p. 334.

[50] A.K. Coomaraswami, *Time and Eternity* (Lecture, Ascona, Switzerland, 1947), p. 68n.

[51] *Spectrum,* p. 185.

[52] Ibid., p. 78.

[53] Ibid., p. 90.

[54] *Creative Meditation,* p. 205.

[55] Ibid., p. 103.

[56] *The Kingdom of the Gods,* p. 65.

[57] *Spectrum,* p. 302.

[58] Ibid., p. 312.

[59] *Creative Meditation,* p. 309.

[60] St. Augustine's *Confessions,* Book I, I

[61] *Creative Meditation,* p. 35.

[62] Ibid., p. 105.

[63] Ibid., p. 109.

[64] *Bhagavad Gita,* 9:29.

[65] John 15:4-9.

[66] Psalms 34:8.

[67] *Spectrum,* p. 337.

[68] *Foundations of Tibetan Mysticism* (NY: Samuel Weiser, 1975) p. 97.

[69] Ibid., p. 100.

[70] Quoted in Sidney Spencer, *Mysticism in World Religion* (Gloucester, Mass.: Peter Smith, 1971) p. 64.

[71] Taitterjya Upanishad, 111, 6, 1.

[72] *The Philosophy of Nietzsche.* (NY: The Modern Library), p. 117.

[73] Mariann Sanders Regan, *Love Words: The Self and the Text in Medieval and Renaissance.* (Ithaca, NY: Cornell University Press, 1982), p. 38.

[74] *Perennial Philosophy,* p. 126.

[75] William Shakespeare, *Troilus and Cressida,* Act 5, Scene 3, Lines 108-113.

[76] *Habakkuk,* 1:13-1,3.

[77] Matthew 6:22.

[78] Deuteronomy 32:10.

[79] Psalms 46:10.

[80] T. Cleary, trans., *The Taoist Classics* (Boston: Shambala Publications, 1996), p. 13.

[81] *Chinese Philosophy in Classical Times*, ed. and tr. by Hughes, E. R. (NY: E.P. Dutton, 1944), p. 144.

[82] *Selections from Early Greek Philosophy*, M.C. Nahm, ed. (NY: Appleton-Century).

[83] *The Tao of Physics*, p. 116.

[84] Ibid., p. 115.

[85] *Creative Meditation*, p. 185.

[86] Ibid., p. 185.

CHAPTER 9

The Head vs. the Heart

The mind is not a vessel to be filled,
It is a fire to be kindled.
Plutarch

The heart has its reasons of which the reason knows nothing of.
Blaise Pascal

I will explain to you whatever you desire to know in as simple a language as is possible, because the truth is simple.

Ultimately, God is pure simplicity and there is nothing more simple than One, to realize that there is one life, one energy, one consciousness. At present, this is an incomprehensible idea but you must know that the analytical intellect by itself cannot grasp the true nature of reality, and in its lack of understanding, it makes things unnecessarily complicated.

But isn't the intellect my capacity to comprehend and acquire knowledge?
Only if it is not separated from Me.

What you need is intelligence, which is different from the intellectual activity based on sensory impression and drawing conclusions from fragmentary data from the outside world.

Intelligence is one of My essential attributes acting in you as an innate faculty of your consciousness. Its function does not consist of the accumulation of abstract concepts or the collection of theories based on the world of phenomena and appearances. My intelligence is the infallible wisdom that knows not merely the effects of things but their inner cause.

With love and power as a Trinity it is the ever-active, creative force of life itself in all its myriad manifestations. You must discriminate between thoughts that come from your God Self and those from your intellectual faculty learned or acquired through enculturation or accepted, mostly by suggestions, from other people, the media, and the environment. The head in its un-illumined state represents the intellectual activity which separates you from the Source of life and the inner unity of all beings and things. Therefore, in its estrangement and fragmentation remains devoid of reality.

The outwardly-directed intellect entangles you ever deeper in the process of differentiation, in the apparent world of the "ten thousand things," and material forms. Ultimately, it leads into the illusion of isolated selfhood and death. And if it is turned inwards, it loses itself in mere conceptual thinking and in the vacuum of abstractions because it lacks the unifying force of love and the creative feeling from the heart.

Both the head, which is the field of your intellect, and the heart, as the dwelling of My Presence, must act as one in order to maintain the balance of your faculties and the function of the reason to prevent error and mistaken ideas.

"Intellect without feeling, knowledge without love, reason without compassion, lead to pure negation, to rigidity, to spiritual death, to mere vacuity – while feeling without reason, love without knowledge (blind love), compassion without understanding, lead to confusion and dissolution. But where both sides are united, where the great synthesis of heart and head, feeling and intellect, highest love and deepest knowledge have taken place, there completeness is re-established, perfect Enlightenment is attained."[1]

I am more aware of the difference between those two faculties and I read a book by the eminent neurobiologist J. C. Pearce in which he discusses what for him is a "dialogue"

between the brain and the heart through direct neural connections. The author reminds us that electromagnetism is a term covering the entire gamut of most energy known to us, as everything in some sense has an electromagnetic element or basis.

In the human embryonic and fetal development, the heart, as vehicle for frequencies of our potential world experience, forms first, and the brain second, followed by the body. Long before it is fully formed the heart furnishes the electromagnetic field that surrounds the embryo from the beginning. All living forms produce an electrical field but a heart's cell electrical output is exceptional.

"That congregation within us, billions of little generators [cells] working in unison, produces two and a half watts of electrical energy with each heartbeat at an amplitude forty to sixty times greater than that of brain waves – enough to light a small electric bulb. This energy forms an electromagnetic field that radiates out some twelve to fifteen feet beyond our body itself...The first three feet are the strongest, with the strength decreasing with distance from the heart according to ordinary physical principles."[2]

According to the author, a heart cell is unique not only in its pulsation, but more in that it produces a strong electromagnetic signal which radiates out beyond that cell. And he relates an experiment about the way a cell from a live rodent heart continued to pulse for some time but then died. However, by bringing closer together two heart cells, even without touching, they would pulse in synchrony with each other and continued to live, like a microscopic heart.

And Dr. Pearce humorously remarks, "Relationship counts, it seems." The heart is not just a pump, its radiation saturates every cell, DNA molecule, glia, and so on, and helps to determine their function and destiny. Beside being a frequency generator, the dominant role it plays is also evident in the productions of hormones and as monitor in the balance of our nervous system. The brain is (rather, it should be) an instrument of the heart which, in turn, is an instrument or "representative" of the function of life itself.

"Our brain and body are manifestations of the heart's diversity and individual expression."[3] They are fashioned to translate from the heart's frequency field the information for building our unique, individual world experience. The author refers to the intelligence of the heart not as verbal, linear, or digital like the intellect in our head; it is, rather, "a holistic capability...sending to the brain an intuitive prompt for our well-being."[4]

However, and this agrees with your explanation, the intellect can function independently from the heart – that is, without intelligence – it can take over the circuitry and block our heart's finer signals. The recurring theme of his book is the biological truth of the dynamic interaction of our head brain (intellect) and the heart's power for transcendence which is the purpose of our existence. The breakdown of that connection, especially through the cultural dictates of society is, for the author, the cause of the endemic discord and violence of the human condition. Neural connections allow an ongoing dynamic interchange to take place between the brain and the heart; however, "Heart intelligence is not anything of which we are aware, though we surely are aware of the results of these neural interactions. I am reminded," continues our author, "of James Carse's wonderful essay 'The Silence of God' and Gurumayi's comment that 'the language of the heart is silence'."[5]

Please, excuse My interruption but I do not agree on this point because I can and do speak all the time through the heart. In fact, it is the source of all that is good and constructive in the life of each human being. The stream of intelligent energy flowing into you and beating your heart is the divine activity of love, which is also wisdom and power. But your author is right when he says that the intellect in the head should be obedient to the heart, or failure and distress are the inevitable results.

He recognizes that the heart's intelligence is love, and "love is a frequency that can synchronize only with its kind ... Higher frequencies modulate or moderate lower ones, enabling spontaneous healing, fire-walking, paranormal phenomena, a way out of disaster and more."[6]

The intelligence of the heart can change brain function, and he quotes physicist David Bohm who once said, as he with passion gestured from his heart to his head, "When that realm of insight and intelligence leaps up, it can take out the dysfunction of mind and make it functional in an instant."[7]

Another important aspect of Dr. Pearce's writing is the reference to the heart as both individual and universal. Recalling the words of his Indian meditation teacher that "God dwells within you as you," he affirms that saying like this are taking on the new light of biological support. His explanation is based on the electromagnetic energy produced by the heart. "This energy arcs out from and curves back to the heart to form a *torus*, or field that extends as far as twelve to fifteen feet from the body."[8] This torus function is holographic, meaning that any point within the torus, no matter how infinitesimal, contains the information of the whole field and all the frequencies of the heart spectrum.

According to physicists a torus is a very stable form of energy which, once generated and set in motion, tends to self-perpetuate. Some scientists speculate that all energy systems, from the atomic to the universal are toroid in form. Therefore, it is possible that there is only one universal torus, encompassing an infinite number of interacting, holographic tori within its spectrum. In fact, our earth is the center of such a torus, and like the heart's field is holographic – it can be read in its totality from any single isolated spot on the earth's surface.

Our solar system is toroid in function, with the sun at its center as our heart is at our center. "We seem to live in a nested hierarchy of toroid energy systems that extend possibly from the miniscule atom to human, to planet, solar system, and ultimately galaxy. Because electromagnetic torus fields are holographic, it is probable that the sum total of our universe might be present within the frequency spectrum of any single torus."[9] When Dr. Pearce writes that an individual torus may participate holographically within a universal torus, I am reminded of the lines of William Blake,

> To see a world in a grain of sand,
> And heaven in a wild flower ...

The implication is that "each of us centered within our heart torus is as much the center of the universe as any other creature or point, with equal access to all that exists."[10]
The heart's love has no boundary.

In reference to Christianity he thinks that the Gospel was a cosmological description of the creator-created dynamic and it was truly "good tidings." But because of the emphasis on its dark side of sin, punishment, and suffering, we have a different message from "the loving Father of Jesus."[11] In tying New Testament to Old the evangelists replaced Jesus' Father, "the giver of good and perfect gifts, in much the way that a judging Christ replaced the forgiving Jesus. We couldn't hear the gospel of love for the noise of the Doomsday trumpets."[12]

It was primarily through Paul's judgments and legalistic interpretations of the Gospel that the power of the intellect regained control, making its inroads into the guidance of the heart and the spirit. The loving Father, for whose entry into consciousness and history Jesus lived and died, was converted back into the God of Moses.[13] Paul represents, according to the author, "the roaring return of the intellect" which blocked and replaced our opening to, direct contact with, and sole dependence on, the wisdom of the heart Jesus brought about, the intelligence that is our ever-present friend, companion, helper, and inner guide."[14] Thus Christianity became the lengthened shadow of Paul, not Jesus, and "through his intellect translated as a bewildering, convolute logic, he set the stage for the two millennia of equally bewildering theology that followed ... One of the miraculous strengths of the Gospel, however, lies in the simple fact that in spite of all this, great and noble geniuses of the spirit arose continually out of this strange paradox, and still arise today. That steady stream of great and noble women of the church....quietly do the will of Jesus' Father, tending the poor and dying...while theologians wrangle."[15]

195

My impression is that the author you quoted overstates the intellectualism of St. Paul because no one can question his love for Jesus and the church. You have now an intellectual notion of what the heart is and how it is characterized as both individual and universal. It is My hope to bring you to a realization of it based not just on scientific experiments, intellectual engineering, or the pie-in-the-sky dreaming but as a personal experience by feeling it. It is your heart feeling that reveals the divine truth, not the conceptualization in the head. The heart is the knower because the intelligence that designs the universe and sustains its infinite manifestation is one of the attributes of My heart flame of love extended and pulsating into yours.

Do you mean that the heart is not physical?
What you call physical is only an energy veil; I am talking of reality itself, no the way it appears to your limited senses.

Then the "spark of the soul" referred to in the writings of the mystics is not a metaphor or merely a symbol.
I assure you that within the heart of every human being there is a tiny flame which is the anchorage of the greater flame from each one's God Self. I will elaborate on it because it is the highest knowledge attainable. You may read all the books that have ever been written and listen to every lecture in the world, and will only increase your intellectual vanity, which would be the greatest tragedy. You may possess the whole earth and have dominion over it, and still be not satisfied and happy. You may indulge without limits your appetites and gratify every craving of your emotional nature and yet be unfulfilled and miserable.

Verily I say to you and to humankind, if you do not know the flame in your heart with its connection to the Source that gives you of Itself, and are ignorant of the Law of Its Life, your individual identity is non-existent, your name is written on the water and all your experiences end in smoke.

Unless the fire of love and its light purifies our brain and illumines our mind, the darkness within us will increase. I begin to understand that the heart is also the director of our outer consciousness which acts through the brain when it is obedient to it. But if it is not, as it is usually the case, then we are bound to make mistakes because we don't know what is really good for us.

The brain in your head is a wonderful instrument but, unfortunately, the vibrations of negative thoughts, feelings, and destructive substances that people take into their body obstruct the inflow of My light. My very life as a stream of energy coming into your heart and anchored there is the activity of divine love in its trinity of love-wisdom-power.

People usually think of God as omnipresent, and even those who believe in It as a Presence, like the Christ or the Self, do not have a clear understanding of its nature. The main purpose of My instruction to you is to make you realize that God is both within, anchored in your heart, and at a short distance above you. And since My consciousness is everywhere, your heart is the heart of your being and of the universe.

Because life, consciousness, and energy are One.

Yes, the divine fire of My love is all-pervading and interpenetrates all that is. Your heart flame is an individualized focus of it and, therefore, one with it because the infinite flame present everywhere cannot be divided.

True love knows no boundary because what seems to separate us is the self-centeredness of the personality.

You may think of the Source of life as a central sun of infinite radiance and each individual as a ray or stream of light emanating from it .

I think of my heart also as an eternal spark sent forth by the cosmic flame of divine love.
And feel that every heartbeat is a wave of love from My heart to yours, which is not only yours but also mine.

According to the principle of polarity, two hearts beating as one.
Try to realize each rhythmic pulsation as a note of My love song to you and a letter of the alphabet of love that I am teaching to you now. Although to the outer senses you seem confined to a finite and limited body, yet you can send your love to the infinite universe and feel your oneness with it. And the universe will return its greater love to you.

Because of the bipolar relationship between the microcosm and the macrocosm. But, in a down-to-earth sense, is it not a paradox that one may have heart trouble?
It is, indeed, absurd; the trouble is not with the heart but with the negative energy and discordant feelings created by the individual. However, nothing imperfect can touch the flame.

I know that throughout the centuries in every culture and tradition the heart possesses hierarchical supremacy in the constitution of the human being.
Regarded as the seat of God, for it is the anchorage of My love and intelligence, it has been said that "I am at play hidden behind the beating of all hearts."[16]

That is how you explained it.
Yes, it is My flame breath that causes the heart to pulsate

I read that the heart was the only part of the viscera left by the Egyptians in the mummy since it was regarded as the center indispensable to the body in eternity.[17] In an attempt to explain the relation of the heart to the brain the former was deemed to correspond to the sun and the latter to the moon.
That analogy is appropriate because the heart is the focal point, and the force-field of the brain, including the intellect, must receive its light.

Also the Bard recognizes it: "A good heart ... is the sun and moon, or rather the sun and not the moon; for it shines bright and never changes, but keeps its course truly."[18] The fundamental symbol of the center which represents the eternal principle and the Unmoved Mover which moves other entities and all creation without itself be moved, has also been related to the heart.
Even though human beings have little or no understanding of love as the cosmic magnetic power that draws and holds every form together and is the cause of the experience of unity, they have identified it with the symbolism of the heart.

Descartes' statement "I think, therefore I am," should be replaced by "I love, therefore I am." As the Hindu scripture says:

> Man is what he loves with all his heart
> And places utter faith in as the Truth,
> Thinking of Me, fixing his heart on Me,

Then, let none doubt he will come unto Me,
Become One with Me, and attain My Being![19]

In the sacred texts of the world the references to the heart are so prevalent and so similar as to be nearly indistinguishable in translation.

It has been stated that true knowledge is passed on from heart to heart. The heart of him who knows, and so believes with full assurance, is the throne of God. Knowledge is of two kinds, that which is heard, and that which is felt directly in the heart. The heart is the focus and criterion of all values: "That which the heart permits, which the soul likes, the God within approves, the mind holds pure, the Eternal Witness sees as free from doubt."[20] Being the dwelling of the Supreme Ruler itself watching over its creation, it should be acknowledged and honored.

He who ignores and does not please,
But disobeys the One, auspicious, pure
Perpetual Inner Witness, the Own-Self,
The ancient sage, all-knowing, who abides
In every heart, recording every act,
Him Yama doth award dire punishment.[21]

It is also the Source of creative power and fulfillment:

Whatever with thy heart thou doest desire,
That is thy God adored, undoubtedly;
Whatever thing is in thy heart always,
That, be thou sure, thou shall attain, at last.
If rose be in thy heart, thou'lt be a rose;
If nightingale, then that sweet singing bird.

200

Thou are a part, God is Whole: if thou
Engage and occupy thy-self, a while,
With that Great Whole, it will fill all thy being,
And make thee whole. The part becomes the Whole.[22]

Wisdom is found in the heart: "Consult thine own heart, if thou are in doubt, In every heart there dwelleth a Sejin (Sage); only man will not stubbornly believe it, therefore hath the whole remained buried."[23] It is the inner "sanctum sanctorum" where Deity dwells, as it radiates through the whole human form and is hidden by its own depth; self-knowledge refers primarily to this inner core.

The wise see in their heart the face of God
And not in images of stone and clod!
Who in themselves, alas! Can see Him not
They seek to find him in some outer place.[24]

Until this lower self submits itself
Unto the higher self, till then thy heart,
Thy wounded heart, will know no rest from pain.[25]

In the Bible the heart is the central image because it is there that the human being has been visited – where the truth has come to abide and influences him/her at the source of their being. "The Lord does not see as mortals see; they look on the outward appearance, but the Lord looks on the heart."[26]

"The individual is defined by the content of his heart. ... For as he thinketh in his heart, so is he."[27]

And, "Out of the abundance of the heart the mouth speaks."[28]

According to the wisdom of the Proverbs one is advised to "Keep your heart with all vigilance for from it flow the springs of life."[29]

The response of the faithful is, "I treasure your word in my heart, so that I may not sin against you."[30] That is the way to relate to the place of indwelling deity, whose voice is his conscience, where the Word speaks. However, if the connection with its Source is broken, the light is shut off, and ignorance sets in: "The fool has said in his heart: there is no God."[31] Then what remains is an estranged and fragmented being, like the multiple "I's" you explained.

One must ask for singleness of heart and for healing in order to restore an undivided heart. Therefore, the apostle of the gentiles movingly writes, "I pray that ... Christ may dwell in your hearts through faith, as you are being rooted and grounded in love."[32]

To protect ourselves from the pitfall of attachment to our possessions we are told to store up for ourselves treasures in heaven, "For where your treasure is, there your heart will be also."[33]

The believers are exhorted to give thanks to God at all times and for everything "singing and making melody to the Lord in your hearts."[34]

And, we have the glorious promise, "Blessed are the pure in heart, for they will see God."[35] The secret is to remember the transforming power of love:

> Whatsoever thou lovest
> That become thou must;
> God if thou love God,
> Dust if thou love dust.[36]

That is why the first commandment of the Law is to love God with all our heart. Since the heart is the spring of loving energy and the self-giving of life, I'd like to end this chapter with this prayer to you: Supreme giver of life and love, expand your flame in my heart that I too may love and give as you do.

Grant me the same experience that Richard Rolle describes in his book, *The Fire of Love*:

"I can't tell you how astonished I was when I felt my heart grow warm for the first time. It was a real warmth, too, not an imaginary one. I seemed kindled with a fire I could feel with my senses. I was amazed by the way this heat broke out on my soul, bringing with it a rich consolation ... I kept feeling my chest over and over again to see if this burning sensation had a physical cause. But when I realized that it came entirely from within myself and that this fire of love had no sensual or sinful origin, but was a gift of my Creator, I melted with joy and wanted my love to increase still more, especially because of the pleasurable sensations of interior sweetness that poured into my soul with this spiritual flame. ... It set my soul ablaze, as though a real fire were burning there."[37]

Although My fire is the same, everyone may feel it differently according to his or her receptivity, and responsiveness. But I always fulfill every demand, especially for My love which I desire to give without limit to set my individualities forever free.

[1] Anagarika, Lama Govinda, *Foundations of Tibetan Mysticism* (NY: Samuel Weiser, 1975), p. 97.

[2] Joseph, C. Pearce, *The Biology of Transcendence: A Blueprint of the Human Spirit* (Rochester, Vermont: Park Street Press, 2002), pp. 56-57.

[3] Ibid., p. 55.

[4] Ibid., p. 66.

[5] Ibid., p. 68.

[6] Ibid., p. 220.

[7] Ibid., p. 220.

[8] Ibid., p. 57.

[9] Ibid., p. 59.

[10] Ibid., p. 59.

[11] Ibid., p. 155.

[12] Ibid., pp. 157-9.

[13] Ibid., p. 158.

[14] Ibid., p. 165.

[15] Ibid., p. 160-170.

[16] *Sufi Writings,* quoted in Das, p. 356.

[17] J. E. Cirlot, *A Dictionary of Symbols* (NY: Philosophical Library, 1962), p. 135.

[18] William Shakespeare, *Henry V*, Act 5, Scene 2, Line 162.

[19] Das, p. 345.

[20] Ibid., p. 195.

[21] Ibid., p. 105.

[22] Ibid., p. 344.

[23] Ibid., p. 105.

[24] Ibid., p. 110.

[25] Ibid., p. 339.

[26] I Samuel 16:7.

[27] Proverbs 7:3.

[28] Matthew 12:34.

[29] Proverbs 4:23.

[30] Psalm 119:11.

[31] Psalm 14:1.

[32] Ephesians 3:18.

[33] Matthew 6:21.

[34] Ephesians 5:19.

[35] Matthew 5:8.

[36] Das, p. 344.

[37] Quoted in Karen Armstrong, *Visions of God* (NY: Ballantine Books, 1994), p. 10.

CHAPTER 10

The Function of Prayer

Prayer is a direction of the heart.
Rainer Maria Rilke

True meditation is the meditation of a lover.
Lama Anagarika Govinda

How is prayer related to the Law of cause and effect?
The immutability of the Karmic principle does not exclude the notion of divine intervention, mercy, and what are considered miracles brought about by prayer.

But then it is no more a changeless and inflexible Law.
God does not contravene or disregard His own Law; He fulfills it.

How? I don't understand.
It is not easy for the human intellect, which does not know how to love, to comprehend what I am explaining. Try to think not only with your head, but to feel with your heart. As I mentioned before, love is the fulfillment of the Law, and Jesus demonstrated it, not only in his teaching, but by the example of His life.

It seems a paradox that we must love in order to be free from the very Law that is the action of Love.
You do not become free *from* the Law, but *by* it. Since love is My nature and is the power by which I created, sustain, and govern the universe, I will never tire of repeating to you the supreme truth: that every limitation which mankind experiences, whether individual, social, national, or planetary, exists only

206

because of a lack of love. "The ways are two: love and want of love. That is all."[1] When Jesus said, "Be ye perfect as your Father in Heaven is perfect,"[2] He meant that since God is love, love and perfection are identical. That is tantamount to saying that Love is the Law of Life governing all things in its perfect manifestation and action.

This is easy to understand, but to apply it in our lives and put it into practice is something else.
To think or believe that it is difficult to love is a negative suggestion. Is it hard for you to love the food you eat when you are hungry or the sunshine and the heat when you are cold? You cannot exist without love. There is nothing greater than love and that I AM, and that is what you also must become. There is no other way.

And how does prayer fit into this?
Prayer presupposes a polarity between the human and the divine, between the finite and the infinite, the individual and the universal, the limited and the unlimited.

It arises from a state of yearning between the consciousness of incompleteness and the ideal of wholeness — or holiness — between the present state of ignorance and limitation and the desire for salvation and enlightenment.

Since the individual has lost the connection with his Source of life and love, in prayer he turns back to it and tries to re-establish a harmonious cooperation — the "at-one-ment" — between the two apparently separated, but in reality, complementary poles.

I read:

"Teach them and tell them:
Lift your eyes to the firmament,
Corresponding to your house of prayer
When you say before Me: Holy.
Teach them that there is no greater joy
in My world that I have created
But that moment when your eyes are lifted to My eyes
And My eyes are looking in your eyes
When you say before Me: Holy.
Because the voice emerging from your mouth
in that moment pushes its way
and ascends before Me like the scent of the aroma.[3]

The power of prayer and meditation rekindles the light of truth and becomes an inflow of strength and certainty. Spiritual practices are also beneficial in another important dimension; because of the essential unity of all life and the interrelationship of all sentient begins, they touch and help also those who, on account of their delusions, would otherwise fall deeper into the abyss of misery.

We don't realize that, since we have free will, we must ask in order to receive. The prophet Jeremiah makes it very clear: "For surely I know that plans I have for you, says the Lord, plans for your welfare and not for harm, to give you a future with hope. Then when you call upon me and come and pray to me, I will hear you. When you search for me, you will find me; if you seek me with all your heart, I will let you find me, says the Lord."[4]
Everything you seek is already present, and the door is already open, you need but enter.

There is, as you know, a cosmic Law ruling everywhere, including every human being; whenever one turns to God and makes a request, he will receive the answer because it is part of the operation of the Law of Love. Remember that you cannot be separated from your Source although your intellect may, in its ignorance, think so.

This intimate relation and capacity for communion is expressed very clearly in the Bible:

> **"Before they call I will answer, while they are not yet speaking I will hear."[5]**
> **"Ask and it will be given you; search, and you will find; knock, and the door will be opened for you...**
> **"Who among you would give his son a stone when he has asked you for bread? Who would hand him a snake when he is asking for a fish? If you, who are imperfect, know how to give good things to your child, how much more will your heavenly Father give to you when you ask him!"[6]**
> **"Then everyone who calls on the name of the Lord shall be saved."[7]**
> **We should have the same confidence of a child when he turns to his mother for his needs knowing that she cares and will give him whatever he asks.**

Yes, that would be the perfect attitude in your relation to Me, and when you are in distress do not hesitate to jump into My arms.

However, when you are dealing with negative forces, I mean destructive thoughts and feelings that torment you, it is necessary to exert your divine authority and to demand that they be annihilated. You must always be positive with a feeling of mastery over the shadows by the power of My light. Remember that "I AM" always with you, and certainly I do not want you to suffer at the hands of those dark forces that seek only to cause damage because that is their nature.

It is a form of insanity because the light has been put out.
Even though mankind, in their ignorance and depravation, have created such terrible conditions, My only desire and My will is to free them from their limitations so that they may return to Me and experience harmony instead of discord.

But remember that, unless you trust in Me, you will not be able to overcome the doubt and uncertainty rooted in your personality that does not want you to use your divine powers and wants to keep you enslaved to its wrong desires feeding on your energy.

I can understand why. Its negative influence would be annihilated and we would be transformed, for a sincere prayer penetrates the consciousness and raises it out of any distress. Even God cannot heal the sick unless the negative attitude is reversed. Unfortunately, everyone is afraid of "losing" himself through change because of their identification with human problems.
God has even challenged man to test His promises in his daily existence: "Prove me now herewith, if I will not open the windows of heaven, and pour out a blessing that there shall not be room enough to receive it!"[8]

I can't believe how we mortal and finite beings have the power to test God.
That is the problem! People do not believe or trust the Source that gives them life with every breath and heartbeat. This is what should be unbelievable. I love them with a love beyond their comprehension, I have provided everything for their happiness, I have predestined the human being for eternal perfection, and yet they either ignore Me or rebel against Me when they are in distress.

Which are the consequences of our mistakes. We look to others and to things, and depend on them instead of the Source, the only One, that can fulfill our deepest desires just for the asking.
No one seems to understand that, in the oneness of My all-pervading consciousness, the life in them that makes the demand is the same life that would fulfill it.

That's why you said, "Before they call, I will answer."
I, as the God Self, can only act on the physical plane for and through the individual who is responsive and be a co-creator.

But we choose the stance of independence from God rather than that of interdependence and mutual interaction in the ongoing relations with one another.
In their ignorance people do not recognize that they can experience fulfillment and achieve wholeness only in terms of their renunciation to the claim of the personal self to have its own way, which is a blatant form of perversion. However, I never respond negatively to their denial and rebellion, acting always out of compassion and love for the personality still in need of

enlightenment with respect to its true self-identity and the purpose of its existence.

But how can we find again the connection with our Source?
The truth is that the individual has never been separated, but only thinks so and therefore that is the condition he experiences.

What we think we create.
Try to realize that "I AM" in you as your Real Self, and you are part of Myself, therefore any limitation and false belief will disappear as mist before the morning sun, when you face Me.

That is why the true nature of prayer is a deep and sincere desire of the heart, which is feeling, since every intent or movement toward the good is Myself acting in and through you to create and expand My perfection. Your desire for God's will is a command to your feeling to obey and fulfill My plan for you.

The poet Rilke referred to prayer as an orientation or direction of the heart.[9]
This is the prayer that is answered; words or thoughts are not enough, they are only receptacles, or like cups which must be filled with the feeling of love. You must feel the meaning of everything you say, and send love with it; if only the mind prays and the heart is not at one with it, there will be a delay in the response.

It takes the release of the feeling of love for what you want which acts like a magnet, drawing back My answer. Love always attracts love: again, it is the principle of polarity acting. I will use the analogy of an electric circuit as Emerson did when he suggested to get your bloated nothingness out of the way of the divine circuits.[10]

You, as the human pole, make the call and I, the divine pole, answer by the return current. It is a communion of love as you allow it to flow through and bring the gift. Whatever you shall ask for in prayer with faith, you will receive.[11]

The response must correspond with your inner attitude; that is, since it is done unto you according to your inner state, you must be willing to accept what you ask for knowing that I love you enough to be willing to give it. How can you receive anything, even in your daily experience, if you are not receptive to it? Whatever you demand must come into manifestation through you as you consciously allow it to do so. The divine gift cannot be forced upon you; that is why it has been said that it is done unto you as you believe, that is, as you accept it.

The vibrational state of your being must be attuned to the vibratory action of the fulfillment of your desire. You cannot ask for something while focusing on its lack and then hope to receive it. The vibrational frequencies of its absence and those of its presence are different: they are not on the same wavelength and they nullify each other. One cannot expect to be happy while acknowledging and affirming "I am miserable." This, as the Scripture stated, is a house divided against itself.

I remind you again that responsiveness is inherent in life as a means of expression based on the principle of polarity, by which everything is related to and interacts with everything else. When someone asks God in love, love must answer because of the polar relationship between the divine and the human.

Love cannot fail itself!

Unfortunately, the common notion of prayer is shrouded in confusion and doubt; people ask for something but

213

there is no assurance in them of the answer because they depend solely upon a separate and distant God who can hardly be reached, though all the time they are receiving and using, without being aware of it, the divine life and energy that enables them to think and act. The very nature of prayer so conceived is bound to consist of utter uncertainty because the individual has a passive and often negative attitude and does not cooperate in the fulfillment of his request.

The person is preyed upon by his own self-created monster of doubt because he is not sure, in spite of Jesus' example, that God loves him enough to fulfill his prayers. He wonders whether his words are heard, whether he is asking for the right thing, whether he is worthy, and so on. Should all the love and wisdom of the universe be poured into him, still he can receive only what he is ready to take and make his own. Acceptance, in other words, is the key. Unless you accept something how can you receive and have it?

Usually, common prayer is the acceptance of lack and limitation, with the mistaken idea that it is the will of God. However, if you ask for healing you cannot afford to identify with your sickness or feel that you deserve it and have to submit to it.

I do not mean to deny the condition, but you must consciously accept what you are asking for and make your *at-one-ment* with health, which is the natural activity of your body. Disease is not God-created – it is *dis*-ease: tension and interference with the flow of My divine energy, and it has not the right to exist. If the personal self has created it, your God Self can un-create it, but you must forgive yourself or ask to be forgiven to remove all sense of guilt.

I heard this anecdote: a famous composer remarked to his friend, "Music is my redemption." And the other asked, "Redemption from what?" We are so ignorant of our human condition that we are not aware of our state of bondage.
Even believers turn to God mostly when they are in distress and want to be free for it, while the rest of the time they hardly remember their Source.

Jesus said in the Gospel of Thomas, "I am come into the world and have found everybody drunk, and no one thirsty. And my soul became afflicted for the sons of men, because they are blind in their hearts and do not have sight. For empty they came into this world, and empty they seek to leave this world. But for the moment they are drunk."[12]
In other words, without a deep desire for liberation you cannot attain it.

God is always ready and willing to give unlimited help, but although every prayer taps the same Source, each person has a different level of receptivity. You live, move, and have your being in an infinite outpouring of love, but how much of it are you able to accept and to express in your life?

The difficulty is to believe and to have faith.
If God ever answered a prayer, and there is plenty of evidence to prove it, then he always answers every prayer, for He is the same yesterday, today, and forever. "I the Lord do not change."[13] If there *seems* to be any failure, it is in man's ignorance or distrust of the true nature of God, of his Will, and his own relationship with him.

At the conclusion of his book, *Healing Words,* on the healing effect of prayer, Dr. Dossey writes, "We do not know

why prayer reveals itself in scientific experiments, but we have seen that it does. We need to recall at these times that prayer, in its function as a bridge to the Absolute, *has no failure rate*. It works 100 percent of the time ... unless we prevent this realization by remaining oblivious to it."[14]

The greatest obstacle is the pervasive feeling of doubt that closes the door which is always open on the divine side. Let me point out something to you; the word *doubt* has the same root as the Latin *duo*, which means two. It is even more evident in the Middle English *doute*.

You know that the Fall of man from original perfect state really means a separation from God, the One.

I can see the connection between doubt and separation; when you doubt something, you cause a disjointure, and there is a chasm in between. It is significant that the words of the serpent in the Garden were meant to instill doubt in Eve regarding God's injunction.

This form of dualism, to be two instead of one, is the cause of all evil, sin, sickness, misery, ignorance, and death because, by definition, it is contrary to the Law of the One, the Law of Life, the Law of Love.

I understand that the direction of Love is toward unity – that it tends to attract, to join, to merge into one.

Yes, love is the cohesive power of the universe. Without it, you have only chaos. I never tire of laying emphasis on this most fundamental truth, which is life itself – and you are always dealing with life's energy everywhere. You mention the lack of belief and faith as the basic problem and I agree with you; however, you must know that it would be impossible for anyone to survive in this world or maintain his sanity without at least a

216

fragment of faith which, even though people are not aware of it, is innate in life and human nature.

The lack of awareness does not surprise me because that's the root of our problems and limitations.
Faith, or belief and trust, is the precondition of your existence, of your actions and institutions; without it, people could not live together in families or form a society. It is evident in all your activities. For instance, when you go to sleep, you are quite sure that you will wake up, are you not?

I think so. Otherwise it wouldn't be easy to fall asleep.
You take it for granted that the sun will rise again tomorrow, that mother earth will still support you, and that you can go about your business.

You have faith that the food you eat is good for you and that the body will take care of it without problems.

When driving your car, you trust that the drivers coming from the opposite directions will stay on their side of the road.

You take a bus or plane and, once again, you possess at least a grain of faith that assures you it will arrive safely at your destination.

You deposit your money in the bank and you trust that it will be there when you want it.

You go to see your doctor or your financial advisor and you believe what they tell you.

What you read in the newspaper or hear on the evening news is accepted as true.

Last but not least, I do not have to convince you that people have an unbounded faith in money.

They surely do. It is paradoxical that it has been called the root of all evil.

Selfishness is the root of all evil. Money itself is not evil – it is only a means of exchange. It is the attitude that one has regarding it and how it is used that determines its quality.

It is true that it can be the cause of negative feelings like greed, pride, avarice, self-indulgence, and so forth; but it can also be a force for good even though this seems to happen less often.

Wealth can also be a test because one is responsible for the way he uses it.

I think that someone is born in poverty because he wasted his wealth in a former life or was not grateful for it. I'd like to quote this passage:

> The individual who aspires to perfect himself has an appreciation of the spiritual value of money exchanged for the service he can render. He seeks nothing for himself, save that which may equip him for the work to be done, and he looks upon money, and that which money can buy, as something which is to be used for others and as a means to bring about the fruition of the divine plan as he sees it. The spiritual significance of money is little appreciated, yet one of the greatest tests in the life of the aspirant is that which concerns his attitude to and his handling of what people seek in order to gratify their desires. Only he who desires nothing for himself can be a recipient of financial bounty, and a dispenser of the riches of the universe. In other cases where riches increase, they bring with them nothing but sorrow and distress, discontent and misuse."[15]

I know from my own experience that money is the greatest obstacle to inner development, that is, if you depend on it for your happiness and fulfillment. It also leads you into temptations very difficult to resist and overcome. I'm sure that's why it is disapproved and condemned by most spiritual teachings.

Yet poverty and renunciation are not necessarily good in themselves either. They, too, have only an instrumental value as the means to something higher. Their worth rests in removing the impediments and the distractions of worldly desires and attachments.

One may be poor and still filled with greed and ambitions, while another may be very wealthy but "poor in spirit" and detached. In fact, austerities may even lead to vanity and self-conceit if one mistakes the means for the end, which is to increase love toward the unification with your divine Source.

A great ascetic and expert on austerities like St. John of the Cross seems to encourage you to do the opposite of mortifications and use the things of this world as a stepping stone to raise your consciousness to a higher level:

> When the will, the moment it feels any joy in sensible things rises upwards in that joy to God, and when sensible things move it to pray, it should not neglect them, it should make use of them for so holy an exercise; because sensible things, in these conditions, subserve the end for which God created them to be occasions for making Him better known and loved.[16]

If an infinitesimal fraction of the faith that people have in money and possessions were placed in God, they would be sup-

supplied from the treasure-house of the universe with more than they could ever use, for it is like the sun that always gives light to the earth and all upon it.

Let me remind you that the divine plan for each human being is the use of My ever-flowing supply of every good and perfect thing. All limitations are self-created by the misuse of the free will.

We have disfigured our divine image and lost our remembrance of you, lowering our consciousness almost to the animal level.

Yet you still have the capacity to use your faculties according to My perfect plan for you. The tendency of the universe is infinite expansion by the creative power of love through My individualities which are conscious of My Presence as their I AM Self.

We turned away from our Source and our original condition and created the experience of a world as a collection of separate and conflicting entities and disjoined multiplicity on which we became dependent and needed to have. Having lost our sense that we are "All in one and one in all" we identified with the personal self condemned to struggle to overcome our existential poverty with the illusion of the external world.

Meister Eckhart confirms this when he states, "As long as I am this or that, or have this or that, I am not all things and I have not all things. Become pure till you neither are, nor have, either this or that; then you are omnipresent and, being neither this nor that, are all things."[17]

It is a pity that we do not place our faith where it belongs. I am now thinking of the placebo response. Recently I

read a book on it, and I was amazed at what I learned. For instance, some patients who had sham angina surgery performed in a double-blind experiment showed improvements that their physicians could not distinguish from the results in patients who had had the real surgery.

When Japanese teenagers who were allergic to a tree similar to our poison ivy were touched with the leaves from a harmless chestnut tree they had been led to believe were the poisonous ones, they developed severe rashes; while touched with the poisoned leaves when told they were chestnut, they had no reaction whatsoever.

When a new medical treatment is introduced with much fanfare and expectancy, the first patients to receive it typically show a seventy percent positive response rate, even in cases where the treatment after more careful study is shown to be medically worthless. And in one double-blind clinical trial supposedly testing the efficacy of a drug, one of the side-effects of which is hair-loss, a third of the women who received placebo chemotherapy treatments actually lost their hair.

The effects of belief can be even more extreme, people can will sickness or even death upon themselves by the negative use – *mis*use, that is – of the inner powers they possess, of which belief or faith is one. The placebo effect is only one kind of evidence of the interrelatedness of mind and body. It has been scientifically shown beyond a shadow of a doubt that the mind is capable of altering bodily function.

There is a book with the significant title, *Your Body Believes Every Word You Say,* and I'd like to quote a few of many examples – out of hundreds of them – without mentioning the names of the doctors and people involved.

According to a cardiologist who has also a general practice, patients frequently say, 'That breaks my heart', or "I was heartbroken." Various bodily sensations like pain and muscle tension can reflect feeling burdened by life's problems.

A chiropractor reported that in a previous six month period, he had at least a dozen patients who complained, in various words, that they were carrying the weight of the world on their shoulders. Every one of them had shoulder problems. He concluded by admitting that healing shoulder problems is now one of his specialties.

A girl's ankle was sore for two years after a minor injury. She was unable to ice-skate, her favorite recreational activity. During a counseling session, she realized how often she said, "I can't stand it." When she became aware of the connection and stopped feeding herself this negative thought, her ankle improved and she resumed skating.

There is also the case of a lady who recounts this story:

> When I was a little girl my mother and I went on a six-week overseas vacation. As we were leaving for the airport my father told me how much he'd miss me. After that leave-taking, I developed ear infections whenever I traveled by airplane, and I had no idea why. During a self-improvement seminar, I remembered responding to my father's words by thinking, "I don't want to hear that." The seed had been planted to not hear things during plane travel. Since uncovering that seed-thought and without medical treatment, I am free of the recurrent ear infections and I travel by plane quite a bit.

However, one doctor found that many people have difficulty admitting the connection between their body and their words and thoughts. I stress to them, he said, that these statements were made without their awareness of the possible consequences of such talk. They are offered the choice of being responsible for themselves or remaining victims. He then makes the amazing claim that many seem more comfortable in the role of victim. They refuse to recognize a link between what they think and say, and their condition.[18]

We don't realize that those common phrases we repeat thoughtlessly can be very dangerous if they are negative.

The medical cases you cite are dramatic; but people do not seem to understand that the inherent creative powers of their consciousness operate in every aspect of their lives, even seemingly trivial ones.

The infinite "sea" of light-energy surrounding you, and everywhere present, is like a photographic film which takes the record of every thought, feeling and word impressed on it.

Be aware that you are creating something all the time, as I do. Naturally, I do not create anything negative, but Love is creative and I cannot help giving expression to it.

The same as the sun cannot help shining.

Absolutely. You know that the Word was in the beginning: the same Word is incarnate in you as My image, and you have the self-same power to bring into manifestation on your level of being – your consciousness – whatever you desire.

In one of my books, I read, "The Law is a law of reflection for life is a mirror reflecting to us as conditions the images

223

of our thinking. Whatever one thinks tends to take form and becomes part of his experience."[19]
It is true.

"Once sent out, a word takes wing beyond recall," wrote the Latin poet Horace.[20]
The Bible makes it very clear: "I tell you, on the day of judgment you will have to give an account for every careless word you utter, for by your words you will be justified, and by your words you will be condemned."[21] **And the Koran says, "Seeist thou not what God likeneth a good word? To a good tree, its root firmly fixed, and its branches as in heaven."**[22]
I do not mind repeating Myself in the course of our dialogue because I must impress the fundamental importance of certain principles on which your very life depends. And one of these is that your faculties are creative and the universal energy or substance in and around you and everywhere present brings into visibility and manifestation whatever your thoughts and feelings are recorded on it. The same Law acts on every plane in the universe because every individual, from the lowest to the highest use the same faculties.

As above, so below. I must remember that, "Your word is a lamp to my feet and a light to my path."[23]
Prayer can be considered the sending forth of positive "seeds." You plant the seed of a request, and I respond with the fruit that grows from it: "ask, and you shall receive."[24]

I can understand that with God all things are possible, and that suffering is not part of the divine plan; but Jesus also said, "When I will be lifted up I will draw all unto me."[25]

I am glad that you brought that up because there is a colossal misinterpretation of those words having a momentous and crucial consequences. By the expression, "I will be lifted up," He did not mean on the cross! Jesus referred, by those words, to His ascension, to the return to the Father's house; because that is the goal of human existence and the essence and purpose of His example and ministry on Earth.

Do you think that Jesus wants you to be crucified and suffer as He did? You know that He proclaimed the "good tidings," illumined and healed those who turned to Him during his earthly life. Would He, then, do less now in his ascended state?

I remember that He said, "What if you were to see the Son of Man ascending ..."[26] And in the Acts we read that "he was lifted up, and a cloud took him out of their sight."[27]
Jesus came to teach mankind how to return to their original divine state from which they strayed, and show them by the example of His ascension the way back to Heaven. And He promised them that His love, like an all powerful magnet, will draw them into the same state of oneness with Him and with God. In fact, there have been many ascensions before and after Jesus.

It took a long time for the Church to acknowledge and proclaim that also His mother Mary was taken up bodily into heaven.
Yes, but it is called "assumption" because according to the "magisterium," Jesus is the only one who can ascend.

People's attention and devotion has been focused almost exclusively on the crucifixion, rather than the ascension, but his teaching and sacrifice are not intended to lead you on the *Via Dolorosa,* the way of suffering. On the contrary, he revealed the *Via Gloriosa,* the glorious way in which man can participate in the divine love of the Holy Spirit that flows from the Father and from the Son to everyone who opens his or her heart to accept it.

We are taught to imitate Him in His suffering and by being passive and victims, instead of expressing the divine authority and the mastery of the power of love. Should we allow the evil forces to impose on us their frightful discord?
Absolutely not! Do you think that it is God's will for his children and for Nature, to let them be destroyed? I hear all the time the complaint and the bitter questioning of why God lets evil to work havoc upon this world. If they were willing to call to Me with that same intensity of feeling to put an end to the forces of darkness, it would be done by the power of My infinite light.[28] My will is to make everyone victorious over the world by the power of My love.

Suffering is the result of discord and does not come from God; those who are united to the Source of life may serenely endure any distress, and overcome it. Since the capacity for good is infinite, the individual can, if he so desires, make room for the indwelling Presence and commune with it; this will eventuate in the end of suffering. The way to Heaven is through love, not suffering, although its fire is a means of purification. But is it not preferable the fire of My love which can consume every impurity harmoniously?

Moreover, the effect of suffering varies according to the way it is tolerated and related to; it can be bad, neutral, or good. Like everything else, it is created by thoughts and feelings and, if one has a negative attitude to it, may induce in the sufferer fear, struggle, and rebellion, which only increase one's sense of isolation and distress.

The experience can also become a means of spiritual advancement and illumination if it is accompanied and qualified with a feeling of love.

In what is referred to as redemptive suffering the Christian lives "amid the bright shadows of the Cross whose beacon of light reaches into every corner and abyss of human grief and loss."[29]

With regard to suffering and severe pain few are those who have the strength and the patience to endure it. They can call for it. The door is always open on My side, and a feeling of trust and confidence will make it possible to receive the flow of Grace. Did not the Divine Master say in John 14:13-14, "I will do whatever you ask in My name, so that the Father may be glorified in the Son. If in My name you ask Me for anything, I will do it." Can he have stated it more clearly? But people do not ask! Prayer increases the love and devotion necessary to unite with the will of God, which results in the overcoming of fear and the sense of separation. On the physical level, since love is the greatest force in the universe, it has the power to transform the lower vibrations of pain and mitigate or even release it.

I know that many are the voices that attest to it: He who suffers for love does not suffer, for all suffering is forgot.[30] In this life there is no purgatory, but only heaven and hell; for he who bears afflictions with patience has paradise, and he who does not has hell.[31] When we conceive of the love of suffering we lose the sensibility of the senses and dead, dead we will live in that garden.[32]

227

There are those who, following the example of the crucified Christ, desire to imitate Him to obtain by grace a share in His redemptive work. St. Paul himself wrote, "I am now rejoicing in my sufferings for your sake, and in my flesh I am completing what is lacking in Christ's afflictions for the sake of his body, that is, the church."[33]

But it seems that the idea of vicarious suffering has too often been formulated in crudely juridical terms. A has committed an offense for which the law decrees a certain punishment. B voluntarily undergoes the punishment; justice and the law-giver are satisfied, therefore A may go free. We attribute to God characteristics that would be discreditable even to a human ruler.[34]

You are right, what is redemptive is not the actual pains experienced by the saint to atone for the sinner and reconcile him to his or her God Self. It is, rather, the gift of My forgiving love for which the saint becomes a channel in his willingness to help others.

If people were aware of their origin and their inheritance of the heavenly kingdom, they would be able to recognize the greatness and authority of their divine nature according to the image of God. As St. John says, we will be like him.[35] By the use of their free will human beings can actualize that exalted icon and imitate Jesus in his mastery over evil instead of his suffering. "Very truly, I tell you, the one who believes in me will also do the works that I do and, in fact, will do greater works than these, because I am going to the Father."[36]

The Divine Master, then, becomes the example of victory and of deification as attested by the Fathers of the Church: in the words of Athanasius, "the Logos was made man so that we might be made God."[37]

Also in the saying of Irenaeus: "On account of his immense love for us, the Word of God, our Lord Jesus Christ, made himself what we are, in order that we might become what he is himself."[38] Both Ambrose and Augustine express the same conception: "The Word was made flesh in order that flesh might become God."[39] And, "He was made to have share in our mortality; he made us to have share in his divinity."[40]

Your quotations are very inspiring and should urge everyone to reach their divine stature. The master Jesus will give unlimited assistance to the individual who is devoted to Him, but as I said, He cannot grow for him and become the being of light he is destined to be in the oneness with his God Self.

We are told to pray all the time, but how can we do it in our hectic society?

It does not mean to sit down and do nothing but pray, rather to be consciously aware of My Presence acting, in, through, and for you.

You can say, "I do this in remembrance of you," then every action becomes an offering, a wave of love to Me. After all, it is by My life, intelligence and energy flowing into you as liquid light, that you are able to move about and accomplish anything.

Without you I couldn't even breath.

That is right. In fact, whenever I decide, I could take back My breath and let your body dissolve.

However, I cannot die even if I want to, because I cannot be separated from you.

I AM, the real you, is without birth or death. It was never created, therefore it cannot die.

Who were we before we became Adam?
The One. We were all together in the oneness and ecstasy of love in the realm of light more brilliant than a thousand suns. As we continue our dialogue I will explain, as clearly as possible, that you are not the limited, conditioned personality, such that if you were to strip away your mental activities, emotions, desires, and sensations, you would find a mere nothing. In the depth of your being there is your essential identity which I AM; and you will understand what I mean when I say that you are My individualization on the physical plane.

What is the meaning of the expression "eternal life?"
It is, as I said, the return, in the ascension, to the place of your origin, your true home of light.

In the process of descent and ascent, you can see again the Law of polarity acting between the human and the divine according to the magnetic power of love.

When you came into embodiment you entered into the physical plane to unfold the God-seed planted within you, and your destiny on this earthly journey is to grow to your full Christ consciousness and be reunited with your Source in the victory of the ascension.

Jesus, by the mastery of love, could overcome suffering and death and become the giver of more abundant life and, above all, of joy, which is one of the fruits of the Holy Spirit. It is very unfortunate that He is perceived oftentimes as a "man of sorrow," and that this perception has overshadowed the being of joy that He really was, the truth of which he expressed even before the event of His ultimate sacrifice: "I have said these things to you so that my joy may be in you, and that your joy may be complete."[41]

How is it possible to be a "man of sorrow" when one is the embodiment of love with the mastery and use of God's infinite powers?

Even the name of the Gospel "Glad Tidings," conveys the essential element of joy. Also, the psalmist reminds us that God is the source of all joy: "You show me the path of life. In your presence there is fullness of joy; in you right hand are pleasures forevermore."[42]

In fact, the Old Testament prophetic literature is filled with expressions of gladness:

"You have put gladness in my heart more than when their grain and wine abound."[43]

"With joy you will draw water from the wells of salvation," Isaiah prophesies, "Shout aloud and sing for joy."[44]

Even the usually dour Jeremiah says, "Then there will the virgins rejoice in the dance, and the young and old men shall be merry, I will turn their mourning into joy."[45]

And according to Hasidic teaching, whose motto is "Serve God with joy," sadness and depression were signs of error and even of sin, which is true.

That joy is one of the fruits of the Holy Spirit is proved by sages and saints. Since there is no happiness apart from love, the greatest happiness must be in God, and, moreover, it is everlasting.

There is this remarkable passage in Meister Eckhart's writings: "When God laughs at the soul and the soul laughs back at God, the persons of the Trinity are begotten. To speak in hyperbole, when the Father laughs to the Son and the Son laughs back to the Father, that laughter gives pleasure, that pleasure gives joy, that joy gives love, and love gives the persons (of the Trinity) of which the Holy Spirit is one."[46]

In the New Testament, joy is associated with giving back to God all we are and have: "The kingdom of heaven is like treasure hidden in a field which someone found and covered up; then, in his joy he goes and sells all that he has and buys that field"[47] – that is, he joyfully exchanges the illusion of his earthly possession for the reality of the treasure that can never be lost.

The resurrection, and especially the ascension, which is the fulfillment of Jesus' ministry, are certainly events of supreme joy since death is the ultimate cause of sorrow and grief.

Because it implies separation and disintegration which are the opposites of love. According to you, love is the solution and the remedy of every problem of the human condition.

It is much more than a solution of problems, it is the dissolution of their cause, effect, record, and memory so that they never appear again. That is why I made it the Law of Life; love is the eternal questing of your being to join in bliss with its Source.

Even in our human relationship it is true that when one is in love, and the other loves you, it is the greatest happiness. However, if a loved one is suffering, or in distress, one can't help to be affected by it.

That feeling which induces it is not love but sympathy, which is very different, even opposite, to compassion which is a divine attribute. Sympathy aggravates the negative condition already existing by attuning to it. Compassion is a higher state of consciousness, and enables you to give help without dragging you down to the level of the sufferer, and making it difficult, if not impossible, to radiate positive feelings.

We cannot give what we don't have; we cannot relieve sorrow and make others happy if we don't have the corresponding attitude and the feeling to do it.
You are right, but remember that the cause of happiness or joy is not in the object, as people erroneously believe, though the object, like a gift, can be the occasion.

Happiness is in the feeling of love pouring into us from you.
Yes, in allowing it to flow through you without interference or contamination.

I can understand that love and happiness are intimately connected, yet there is no one we are more likely to hurt, or be hurt by, than the person we love.
That is caused by attachment which is the basis of almost all relations. Love is light and is reflected or radiated by the feeling; but I do not have to tell you how distrustful human nature is in that regard. It is My hope to make you a sun of My love so that no shadow can affect you, and those you contact, or even come close to you. There is, also, a prevailing confusion between joy and pleasure.

That is so true! I had to learn by hard experiences that we live in a world of "joyless pleasures."
Pleasure can be of high intensity, but it is fleeting and short-lived; one must drink the life-giving nectar from the Source.
"This world and its pleasures are like someone drinks something in a dream. So also to desire worldly things is like

asking for or being given something in a dream. When one awakens on will not have benefited from what one ate or drank while dreaming."[48]

It is not conducive to joy because nothing has changed or grown within the person, making it necessary to seek ever new and more exciting pleasures. Joy instead, like love, is the process of growing and expanding one's consciousness by the divine fire that raises one nearer to the goal of human existence, the union with Me.

There is a poem in one of the early Christian apocryphal books called "The Hymn of the Pearl," which illustrates the process of descent and ascent – our departure from the heavenly state for the purpose of attaining mastery over the physical plane, and attain the state of deification, after our victorious and joyous return. I'll paraphrase it:

When I was a child I lived happily in my father's palace surrounded by riches and luxury. At one point my parents took away the radiant garment and the jeweled robe they had lovingly made for me and made a covenant writing it in my heart lest I forget it. "When you go to the land of Erehwon and bring back the One Pearl which is guarded by the fierce serpent, you will again wear your luxurious vesture with the robe of glory over it, and you will be heir in our Kingdom."

From their treasure house they provided me with gold and jewels to bring with me. I left the East on a dangerous and frightening journey as I was young and alone. I went directly to the serpent's den and settled nearby waiting the opportunity to take the pearl from it.

To prevent any suspicion I put on clothing like the people of the land so that I would not appear a stranger.

However, they were able to deceive me and I ate their food, which caused me to forget my royal heritage, the quest for the pearl, and, as a result I became a servant of their King. The heaviness of their food made me fall into a deep sleep.

My parents were aware of what was happening and grieved over me, and a proclamation was heralded in our Kingdom by all the rulers and nobles of the East that I should not remain in the land of Erehwon. I received a letter exhorting me to wake up and rise from my sleep, to remember my regal nature, that I was not a slave, the purpose of my journey, my garment of light; and, in the end my name will be in the book of life.

I kissed the letter and the words engraved in my heart caused me to arise filling me with the courage and strength to seize the pearl, which I did calling on my parents name. I left behind my filthy and impure clothing and directed my way toward the East. On the road I met a young woman who pointed me to the light and with understanding love urged me on and assisted me.

Finally I returned home and received from my parents the radiant garment which was the robe of glory I had forgotten, and as I gazed on it suddenly it became like a mirror. I saw in it myself as I really am, and I saw also myself apart from it, for we were two forms and yet one being.

Then the jeweled garment of prismatic colors seemed to speak to me thus: "I belong to the one who conquered, for whom I was made in the father's house, and I grew in stature according to his labors." With majestic motion it spread toward me urging me lovingly to receive it. I did put it on and adorned myself with the beauty of its brilliant colors, then I ascended to the sphere of light and peace. I bowed my head and prostrated myself before my father who had given it to me.

I had fulfilled his commandments and the promise I gave. He rejoiced and received me in his Kingdom while all the subjects praised him with resounding voices. He said that we would soon journey together and with the pearl and gifts appeared before the King.[49]

On the surface the poem is the story of an adventurous quest for a pearl, but I think you understand its symbolic meaning. The young prince sent by his parents on a perilous mission to snatch the jewel guarded by the dragon form the trinity of Father-Mother-Son; but it also represents you.

In fact, he has reference to everyone of humanity who has left the original, divine state, "my father's palace," and come into embodiment on the Earth. The land of Erehwon (an anagram of nowhere) stands for the unreality of material things and the kingdom of darkness and error.

Likewise, the serpent is symbolic of the snare and the danger of death. To find and seize the pearl means to attain mastery and victory over the negative forces of evil.

This reminds me of Jesus' triumphal statement, "Be of good cheer I have overcome the world."[50]

This is the purpose of your journey here as the young prince did. Like you, he was deceived and became entangled in the desires of the senses ("I tasted their food," he says), and fell into a deep spiritual sleep, forgetting his true identity and his task.

But his parents, that is, Father-Mother God, aware of his dangerous situation and concerned for his safety, reminded him of his divine heritage: "Awake and rise...You have fallen beneath the yoke of slavery."

These are familiar Biblical admonitions.
The prince understood the truth of their message because it is engraved in the heart; and by the divine power of his parent's name, he was able to free himself from bondage and succeeded in capturing the pearl. Then he could return home, leaving behind the dirty and impure "clothing" he had worn on earth; and a female, which is the eternal feminine, whom he encounters on the way leads him "with understanding love" (that is, conscious of their divine relationship) toward the light.

I see the important role of the woman, according to the principle of polarity.
When the young prince saw his shining garment as if in a mirror, he recognized in it his God Self as who he really is, no longer separated: "again we were one."

The glory of the Divine Presence was revealed to him and, as he heard a voice acknowledging his victory, he received the garment of prismatic colors, which is the immortal body of light.

Clothing himself in it, he attains the ascension into Heaven, having fulfilled the vow he made in the beginning to seek and obtain the pearl of great price.

It is truly a wonderful allegory of the triumphal spiritual quest for reunification with God. But how many human beings are capable of achieving victory? I have a question: What would have happened to a weaker person than the prince, who could not resist the "food" of the people of Erehwon? What happens to those who continue to "eat" it like the forbidden fruit, - instead of fulfilling the divine plan?

They cannot make the journey "home" until they eventually make restitution for the discord they have created and imposed upon life. That is, until the consequences of their destructive actions are balanced and their Karmic debts paid. In those cases where the personality stubbornly persists in its determination to be destructive, as I told you, he will go to the "second death," which means that his outer self will be dissolved.

I still don't understand how this can happen if the individual is immortal.

I can appreciate that this topic is not fully comprehensible to you, but you must remember the distinction between individuality and personality: the individualized flame within you of My Presence is immortal, but the form with which it clothes itself is the personality, which may become self destructive and therefore annihilates itself. All will become clearer as we proceed, because now your attention, sustained by your desire to know, is focused on the truth of My words.

My attention? I thought I was paying attention since you first spoke to me!

You were only partially able to be attentive at first because, for one thing, you were in great distress and, for another, you were taken by surprise. Probably you can not remember much of what I said then; but now you understand much more. I should explain the importance of your attention.

Attention is one of your fundamental faculties; in fact, it is more than that: it is the very flow of your life. Just think, can you know anything unless you first place your attention on it? It is like a bridge and it draws the sight, the hearing, the feeling, and even the energy of your body into whatever it is connected with, and you draw back into yourself the qualities, good or bad, of what you perceive or dwell upon. People have not the least idea of the power of their attention and what it can do for them for good or ill. In reality, what your attention is focused upon, you become. It can raise you to the heights or lower you to the depths.

The Law of Attraction governs your vibrational world, and this concerns what you embrace in your consciousness. When you give your attention to something you are inviting and accepting it into your vibrational field according to its quality, positive or negative and it becomes you!

If you see something that is destructive trying to connect with you, you must with determination say "No!" to it, and command in My name, "You can not harm me, get out!" In this way you prevent or shut the vibrations out instead of bringing them into your consciousness.

To keep your attention on discord and negativity, and discuss or think about them, is like feeding them with your own life-energy, intensifying their destructive power over you. The more your attention is on the problem, the less you will be able to solve it. Revolving a negative thought in your mind about persons, places, or conditions (and remember, thought is repetitive)means, you are strengthening and magnifying the discord. Also, by the law of magnetic attraction you draw more of its kind into you from the mass accumulation, especially the prevailing feeling of worry and fear.

That's what happened with Job when he said, "Truly the thing that I fear comes upon me, and what I dread befalls me."[51]
When you think how many hours, days, months, and years people spend creating the vibratory action of negative thinking, feeling, and spoken words, you should not wonder at the dis-

cordant conditions in which they live and by which they are surrounded. As long as there is fear there will be evil, and it is also true that evil induces fear, thus mankind are caught in a vicious circle. Fear or terror is the weapon of destructive forces but they are afraid of those who do not fear them.

Like the wild animals who are afraid of fire.
It is a sign of the contradictory nature of human beings that they are both seduced and repelled by horror stories and their horrible charm.

This is, indeed, a paradox; we want to escape from the oppressive world of routine and triviality and break through the encrusted surface of our mundane existence. However, like the rabbit hypnotized by the serpent, we cannot resist the temptation of the forbidden fruit which arouses our curiosity and captures our attention.
There is innate in the individual the tendency toward the unknown and the desire to expand the limit of its horizons. Unfortunately, because of the gravity pull of its fallen state., he is more attracted to the exploration of the mystery of evil than the wonders and miracles of divine creation.

It is incredible but true that we can be so involved and thrilled by the horror genre, unaware that "On horror's head horrors accumulate",[52] and what lurks behind the dread is the self-dissolution. How can we avoid it?
Remember that whatever you give your attention to, it becomes part of you, that is, you absorb its qualities, whether good or bad, even into the flesh of your body.

Therefore, do not allow it to connect with the shadows and feed them with your energy. I do not mean to deny the existence of evil or to pretend that it does not exist; the purpose is to protect yourself and to be master of the negative forces.

I must remember the words, "You are from God, and have conquered them; for the one who is in you is greater than the one who is in the world."[53] It has been stated that every problem contains its solution, but I don't understand it.
Think of a problem as an aggregate of discordant energy vibrating at a certain rate. The fire of My love is the highest vibratory action in the universe, therefore if you charge it into the energy of the problem it will be purified and transmuted into its own solution. But you must send your attention to Me in order to disconnect it from the problem, then the cloud will disappear and the light be revealed.

I begin to realize how powerful the attention can be and how important it is to control and focus it on the good and what we want instead of what we don't want to experience.
It is again the action of the law of magnetic attraction and the way of creation. What you are conscious of in thought and feeling become a living thing, first at the inner or invisible level, and then condenses into substance. Do not forget that you are a co-creator with Me and have the power to bring into manifestation whatever you desire.

I don't entirely understand you ...
I will explain this fundamental topic in different ways as we will continue our dialogue, until you fully comprehend it. The key is in the statement,

> What do you see
> Become you must,

God if you see God
Dust if you see dust.

Meditate and think deeply on it.

[1] Mencius, quoted in *Wisdom is One*, p. 70.

[2] Matthew 5:48.

[3] Quoted in Moshe Idel, *Kabbalah and Eros* (New Haven, Conn.: Yale University Press, 2005) p. 36.

[4] Jeremiah 29:11-14.

[5] Isaiah 65:24.

[6] Matthew 7:7.

[7] Acts 2:21.

[8] Malachi 3:10.

[9] Lama Anagarika Govinda, *Foundations of Tibetan Mysticism*, p. 75.

[10] *Selections from Ralph Waldo Emerson*, S. Whicher, ed., (Boston, 1957), p. 90.

[11] Matthew 21:22.

[12] Quoted in Elaine Pagels, *The Gnostic Gospels* (NY: Vintage Books, 1979), p. 152.

[13] Malachi 3:6.

[14] L. Dossey, M.D., *Healing Words: The Power of Prayer and the Practice of Medicine* (NY: Harper-Collins, 1993), p. 291.

[15] A. Bailey, *A Treatise on Cosmic Fire* (NY: Lucis Publishing Company, 1973), p. 866.

[16] Quoted in Huxley, *Perennial*, 100.

[17] Quoted in Huxley, *Perennial*, 107.

[18] Barbara Hoberman Levine, *Your Body Believes Every Word You Say* (Fairfield, Conn.: Aslan Publishing, 1937), pp. 79-82.

[19] Ernest Holmes, *The Science of Mind* (NY: Dodd, Mead and Co., 1938) p. 320.

[20] Horace, *Dictionary of Quotations*, p. 387.

[21] Matthew 12:36-37.

[22] Koran, XIV, 29; in *Teaching of Rumi, The Masnavi*, trad. E. H. Whinfield, (NY: E.P. Dutton Co, 1975), p. 150.

[23] Psalms 119:105.

[24] Matthew 21:22; Luke 11:9.

[25] John 12:32.

[26] John 6:62.

[27] Acts 1:9.

[28] John 14:13-14.

[29] *Suffering of Love,* p. 129.

[30] Meister Eckhart, quoted in Huxley, *Perennial,* 231.

[31] St. Philip Neri, quoted in Huxley, *Perennial,* 231.

[32] St. Catherine of Siena, quoted in Huxley, *Perennial,* 231.

[33] Colossians 1:24.

[34] *The Perennial Philosophy,* p. 231.

[35] 1 John 3:2.

[36] John 14:12-13.

[37] *The Incarnation of the Word,* p. 54.

[38] *Adv. Haer.* 5., Prologue.

[39] De Virg., 1:3.

[40] De Trin. 4, 1:2-3,

[41] John 15:11.

[42] Psalms 16:11.

[43] Psalms 4:7.

[44] Isaiah 12:3, 6.

[45] Jeremiah 31:13.

[46] *Meister Eckhart, A Modern Translation,* by Raymond Bernard Blakney, (NY: Harper-Row, 1941), p. 245.

[47] Matthew 13:44.

[48] *The Essential Rumi,* transl. C. Barks, (NY: Harper Collins, 1995), p. 77.

[49] B. Ehrman, *Lost Scriptures: Books That Did Not Make it into the New Testament* (NY: Oxford University Press, 2003), pp. 324-7; *The Other Bible,* ed. Willis Bernstone, (San Francisco: Harper-Row, 1984), pp. 309-313.

[50] John 16:33.

[51] Job 3:25.

[52] William Shakespeare, *Othello,* Act 3, Scene 3, Line 370.

[53] 1 John 4:4.

CHAPTER 11

The Open Door

Behold, I stand at the door and knock.
Revelation

Why do you stay in prison
when the door is so wide open?
Rumi

Can you tell me something about the various kinds of prayer and meditation?
There is plenty of literature on the subject, and some methods and exercises are more advisable and helpful than others, but it all depends on the stage of growth and the need of the individual. It is important not to mistake the means for the end, which is the unitive life in its bipolar nature of action and contemplation, wherein contemplation is My action as the indwelling Presence.

The ultimate purpose of any spiritual practice is to overcome the sense of separation from the Source of life and to become one with it. The criterion and the principle with which to evaluate your application is to know what is most helpful for you to reach that end.

The moving power, and I emphasize it, is the desire, and the more intense it is, the more rapid the progress. The purposive striving of the individual is directly dependent on the feeling and the will rather than the thought or words.

"Some sort of feeling – interest, desire, fear, appetite – must supply the motive power. Without this, the will would be dormant, and the intellect lapse into a calculating machine ... At the touch of passion doors fly open which logic has

245

battered on in vain." Even Aristotle said that "The intellect by itself moves nothing."[1] The classical ways are purification, illumination, and union.

Underlying them and the most perfect, in reality the only way, is to learn how to generate and feel love in your heart which is your connection with Me.

The author of the *Cloud of Unknowing* is right when he wrote referring to God, "By love He may begotten and holden, but by thought of understanding, never."[2] The capacity to see the light that never changes and the unerring intuition and comprehension of the truth is infused with desire and the burning love which originates in the pulsing flame of the heart.

Beyond even the heavenly delight and ecstasy of contemplation there is the desire for love itself which is God, to possess and be possessed by Him/Her/It. "I desire not that which comes from Thee," cries St. Catherine of Genoa, "but only I desire Thee, O sweetest Love."[3] The at-one-ment of the self in the successive degrees of prayer is comely described by St. Theresa of Avila in her autobiography.

She compares the soul to a garden that needs to be watered so that plants and flowers, symbolic of the virtues, may live and grow. In the first stage, the water (we are in the 16th century) must be drawn from a well, which requires much exertion and effort.

In the second, the method of watering is by a water-wheel and buckets worked by a windlass, which is less laborious than the former, and brings up more water too.

In the third stage, the garden is watered by a stream or spring, which entails far less work since the soil retains more moisture and needs watering less often.

And, finally, we have the pouring of heavy rain, "when the Lord waters the garden Himself without any labor of ours, and this," concludes the saint with a smile, "is an incomparably better method than all the rest."[4]
Every beginning is difficult, it takes determination and effort, and this is true especially in the case of prayer and meditation. There is a deadly conflict within the personal self of which he knows nothing although it is affected by it. The enemy has grown strong through many past lives and now dominates you. The battlefield of being and nothingness is not only in your fleshly passions but in your everyday existence. If you become aware of it, by the power of your free will you will make a purposeful choice, and will continue choosing life rather than death. My Presence will sustain and make you victorious in the perseverance of your spiritual practices.

The mind is pushed and pulled by all kinds of impressions, jumping here and there by conditioning and associations, properly called in the Orient "the monkey mind." How would you teach someone to control his attention?
To a religious person I may suggest to use a picture or a statue of one of the deities he loves, accompanied by the repetition of the name. Very few realize that the name of a divine being is the vibration of its life and love which releases instantly to anyone who gives expression to it, mentally or audibly.

Jesus made it clear when he said, "Very truly I tell you if you ask anything of the Father in my name, he will give it to you."[5]
Also helpful to control the incessant stream of random and scattered thoughts is the sound of sacred music, the practice of prayer, affirmation, mantra, even a simple object like a candle

flame, a flower, a landscape, or anything you like. Do not merely look at it but take on a vivid and loving consciousness of what you see, without any reflective thought, enfolding it in your heart.

I must remember that the heart radiates light.
Your focused attention carrying the higher frequency of love will remove the energy-veil and enable you to penetrate the physical structure of the object. Then comes the awareness of an intensified life in what seemed an inanimate thing and it becomes alive, like a presence as it were, its answering current meeting yours.

This is the principle of polarity acting everywhere.
As you go deeper into the stillness there is a merging in the act of true communion, and you are immersed in the sea of universal light pervading all.
This form of contemplation on a small scale will strengthen your power of concentration and with practice and perseverance you will attain greater mastery over yourself, but the key is always the feeling of love.

Everyone knows that when you love something it is very easy to hold the attention on it, in fact, you become oblivious of everything else, including yourself.
 He who can govern his faculties and senses is truly liberated. Such an individual has been compared to a skillful driver:

> Know thou the soul as riding in a chariot,
> The body as the chariot.
> Know thou the Self as the chariot-driver,

And the mind as the reins.
The senses, they say, are the horses;
The objects of sense, what they range over...
He who has understanding,
Whose mind is constantly held firm
His senses are under control,
Like the good horses of a chariot-driver...
He who has understanding,
Who is mindful and ever pure,
Reaches the goal
From which he is born no more.[6]

But do you know what is most difficult to control and most dangerous to one's life?

The tongue.
You have answered well! Countless are those who have fallen by the sword, but not as many as those who have fallen by the tongue.

This is confirmed by the Sacred Scriptures. Krishna says,

Over no organ is control secure
Until the tongue has been placed under curb.
When that is conquered, all else is subdued.

Asked by a follower to mention the one all-pervading principle superior to every virtue,

The prophet touched his tongue and said: control
The reign of this sense-organ over yourself.
Men are hurled headlong into fires of hell

By loads of evil that their tongues have reaped.

Also, Zoroaster exhorts us to know the Self and control the tongue by which evil is created:

> They who, seeing yet blind, spread all around
> Intolerance and insolence and hate,
> By the evil words of their unbridled tongues,
> Know them to be the devils of this earth.

And Manu:

> And since all thoughts and feeling are enwrapped
> In words, and are conveyed by them to others,
> He who misuses words empoisons all;
> Let the wise man then guard well all his speech.[7]

In the Bible there is the acknowledgment of God's protection, "He saves the needy from the sword of their mouth" and "from the scourge of the tongue."[8] The Psalmist counsels us to keep the tongue from evil and the lips from speaking deceit.[9]

Solomon states clearly that, "Death and life are in the power of the tongue." And according to his wisdom if we want to keep out of trouble we must watch over mouth and tongue.[10] The prophet Isaiah warns the people to revere and honor the name of the Lord because, "His tongue is like a devouring fire."[11]

We certainly need to be protected from negative suggestions that plague us everywhere. In the figurative language of Jeremiah the evil forces "bend their tongues like bows," and "their tongues a deadly arrow."[12]

Various are also the references made to the tongue in the New Testament, from the admonition of Jesus, "Let your word be 'Yes, Yes' or 'No, No'; anything more than this comes from the evil one,"[13] to the severe teaching in the letter of James: "If any think they are religious and do not bridle their tongues but deceive their hearts, their religion is worthless. How great a forest is set ablaze by a small fire! And the tongue is a fire .. it stains the whole body, sets on fire the cycle of nature, and is itself set on fire by hell" ... And with reference to the difficulty of controlling the tongue he emphasizes that every species of beast can be tamed but no one is able to tame the tongue- "a restless evil, full of deadly poison."[14]

I must also mention the role of breathing. Do you not think that it is a very vital function?

It certainly is! We can live without food for a few weeks, without water or drink for a few days, but only for a few moments without air. We can even leave our consciousness behind, as in sleep or anesthesia, but we cannot live without breathing.

However, it is not only a physical process intended to fill your lungs with air and expel it after absorbing the oxygen contained in it.

There is undoubtedly a connection between respiration and mental states in their respective functions, and these also vary with external circumstances.

For example, when one is excited or angry, the breathing is irregular and agitated, while in a relaxed state or in sleep is rhythmical and slower. In contrast to other organic functions like the heart-beat, the circulation of the blood, etc., breathing can become accessible to the mind and be converted into a volitional process. You can consciously observe your breath in its alternative inward and outward movement, its continuous action of receiving and giving back, and make it a subject of meditation as it reveals the deep relation of the individual with the universe.

It is interesting that the very word for breath in several languages also signifies spirit; *ruach* **or** *nepesh* **in Hebrew,** *pneuma* **in Greek, and** *spiritus* **in Latin. And we have related terms like inspiration, which means both inhalation and the state of being inspired; and aspiration, which refers to both the act of aspirating and to a deep desire or aim, and expiration as the act of breathing out and also coming to an end or terminate.**

I know that the method of breathing plays a fundamental role in every teaching where prayer and meditation are practiced, especially in the Hindu and Buddhist traditions. I was for awhile a student of Zen and we were instructed to repeat mentally the sound "Mu" in coordination with the breathing. The exercise is meant to eliminate the constant inner talking and stop the wandering thought. The teacher would say, "Concentrate and penetrate fully into Mu, focus your mind on it, day and night, until you become one with it. At first you will not be able to pour yourself wholeheartedly into Mu. It will escape you quickly because your mind will start to wander. You will have to concentrate harder – just 'Mu! Mu! Mu!'

Again it will still elude you.

Once more you attempt to focus on it and again you fail. This is the usual pattern in the early stages of practice ... Absolute unity with Mu, unthinking absorption in Mu- this is ripeness...both inside and outside naturally fuse."[15]

I didn't reach that state of unity because of the lack of perseverance. I was attracted to it because as meditation deepens, one transcends the personal self and its limitations. You are supposed to feel that it is Mu doing the breathing, or the walking, the eating, etc. And then, as you forget yourself by the expansion of your consciousness, you become all things: a wonderful achievement, but it was not for me.

I tried also the practice with the "sacred seed word" *Om* which is the most common mantra in India. I was again moved by the praiseworthy aspiration to attain Brahman or the state of being-consciousness-bliss. Therefore, I began that which is at the very heart of Yogic practices called Pranayama, the discipline of respiration. By making the breathing rhythmical and slower, one can control the rushing stream of the mind and penetrate the deeper levels of Being.

Pranayama is also identified with the three highest gods of the Hindu pantheon: Brahma is said to be inhalation, Visnu suspension (of breath), Rudra exhalation.

However, the yogin is advised to practice pranayama through concentration on the syllable *Om.* "Whereas, one thus joins breath (prana) and the syllable *Om* ... This is declared to be called Yoga."

Rhythmic respiration is obtained by harmonizing the three "moments": inhalation, exhalation, and retention of the inhaled air. These three moments must each fill an equal space of time. The unit measurement is by repeating mentally the mystical syllable *Om* as often as necessary.[16]

I read that a yogin can attain the complete suspension of respiration by increasingly prolonging the moments of breathing, and can be buried alive without any danger –

even for days. I found all this very interesting but the temptations of the world were still too strong to resist them and I was turned aside from the path of mastery.

But how can the yogin accomplish such a feat?
You must know that the flame within the heart, which is an extension of Mine called the "spark of the soul," is self-breathing and self-sustained. That is, it breathes within itself and is has no need of the air of the physical plane.

When you meditate on it you may go deep within yourself and feel at one with it because, in reality, you are that flame; that is your I AM-Self.

The practice and spiritual exercise on breathing is not limited to Oriental teaching.

A very important aspect of the liturgy in the Orthodox Church is called the Jesus prayer, considered the heart of Eastern Christian mysticism. The practice consists in the repetition of the phrase, "Jesus, son of God, have mercy on me, a sinner," accompanied by controlled respiration. The words are repeated at each drawing of the breath.

It is indicative that when Jesus appeared to his disciples after the resurrection he breathed on them and said to them, "Receive the Holy Spirit."[17]
The intimate relation, rather communion, through the breath between God and the human being is illustrated in the passage by St. Paul when he writes about the concept of filiations. "The spirit of God, joins with our spirit in testifying that we are God's children," or "When we cry Abba! Father! It is that very Spirit bearing witness with our spirit that we are children of God."[18]

Yes, the Divine Presence communes with a being which can acknowledge and accept It in his consciousness, for he has the potential not only to conform to It but actually become It.

Breathing can be a vehicle of spiritual experience, as the nexus between body and mind, the individual and the universe, God and the human being. As a medium of communion, it allows you to feel your conscious oneness with your God Self within and above you. You can recognize your true identity, the changeless center and immortal essence of your Being when you affirm "I AM" with every act of breathing.

You may think that it is you who is breathing but, in reality, you are breathed.

What do you mean?
The rhythmic movement of the breath does not activate or originate by itself, you receive it from Me. I am really breathing through you, releasing My essence that animates and sustains your body.

According to Scripture, God formed man from the dust of the earth, and breathed into his nostrils the breath of life; and the man became a living being.[19]
It did it not only in the beginning; you cannot continue to live in your body without breathing, but it is My breath, which is really the fire of My love, that continues to give you life.

I inbreathe you, and that is the inner activity; then, as you inhale the air from the atmosphere around you, it unites with My life-essence and the two connect like an electric circuit that vivifies your whole being.

I see again the principle of polarity in one of its greatest manifestations.

It reveals also the activity of the Law of Love that governs the universe because as you receive the life-force with each inhalation, you must give it back with every exhalation.

To love means to give: only by giving can your consciousness expand. If you try to hold to yourself what life brings to you, whether people or things, it is like holding your breath.

You cannot do it for too long without ceasing to exist.
Exactly. You stifle your consciousness and prevent its expansion. Selfishness goes against the "current" of love and the tendency of life that says you receive in order to give, and you give in order to receive.

In other words, by that process you coordinate your actions with the rhythmic pulsation of life in a continuous exchange and a deep interrelationship of the individual with its Source. This is symbolic of the way to maintain the divine balance which is justice.

It is not without purpose that the Goddess of Justice is represented holding a scale in her hand.
Yes, you are given the energy of life, which is My love, and according to the Cosmic Law you ought to return it to its Source to maintain the balance between the human and the divine.

Our love should flow back and keep us connected with you, otherwise we create an unbalance in our being and world. We disrupt the polarity and break the divine circuit.
That is why there is so much disorder and derangement in the world.

It is significant that there is a Zodiacal constellation with the sign of Libra meaning Balance. How can I use the process of breathing in my mental prayer?

The Scripture's exhortation to pray without ceasing, which seems an impossible task, can find its simple application in the act of breathing. In fact, in Vedism the spiritual aspect of breathing is called, "the muttered, inaudible prayer," in which every breath signifies, "That am I, That am I, I am That, I am That." It is the in-breathing of the Higher Self that enables the out-breathing of the lower self and, thus, the maintenance of life.

Knowing, as you now do, that breath and spirit are synonymous and that the breathing flame of My heart is one with the breathing flame in yours, I will give you an exercise that will help to generate the feeling of love.

With your attention on Me, mentally say with each in-breathing, and repeat with every out-breathing. "I AM the breath of fire," or "I AM the fire-breath of God's love." Try to be aware of it no matter what you do.

Also the following will be of tremendous help for your purification and illumination: say on the inhalation, "Thou are all mine," repeat it holding your breath; and then exhale saying "I AM all thyne," then hold your breath for an equal length of time repeating it.

This is a very effective application to activate the circuit of love. Feel as deeply as you can My Presence as you return your love to Me, because love is the only remedy for every condition of mind and body.

You said that every form of lack and any limitation in our mind, body, and affairs is a clear sign that love is absent.

If you want to know what perfection is, think of love.

That explains Jesus' injunction to be perfect as the Father in Heaven is perfect, because God is love.

There is no problem in this world that cannot be solved, and dissolved, by the fire of love. Moreover, it is the only way to overcome the sense of separation and to enter upon the unifying life when you and I behold each other, as into a mirror, and recognize that we are one.

An Arab mystic and poet describes it thus: A man knocks at the door of his Beloved, who asks him, "Who are you?" The man replies, "It's me." The Beloved says, "Go away, it is not yet time to enter." After a long voyage, the poor man returns as if burned by fire and approaches the house of the Beloved. He knocks; the Beloved asks, "Who is there?" The man replies, "It is you." "In that case," the Beloved says, "since you are me, come in."[20]

Love is not learned from books; it can only be experienced in the practice of prayer and meditation, leading to the contemplation of My Presence.

I must think deeply on this word "Presence," until I realize its full meaning.

It is not difficult, for in reality, "I AM" always Present in you and our oneness is attested by all the mystics: St. Catherine of Genoa said, "My being is God, not by simple participation, but by a true transformation of my Being."[21]

And in the Sufi writings:

I am no one else than Thou, Thou than I;
I am Thy body and Thou art My Soul.
Let no one say hereafter that I am

258

Other than Thee, or Thou other than I.[22]

and...

Lord Agni!. Fire and Light and Guide Within!
Ordain that I be Thou and Thou be I![23]

Self-consciousness, All-Self-consciousness, which "I AM", is the one purpose of existence and the supreme goal to which all creation moves. That is what philosophers, poets, and scientists seek and try to know, more or less gropingly. While the Scriptures of the world declare:

Mankind are everywhere marching to Me.
Whatever road they take, I meet them on it.
In every form each soul seeks Me, the Self.[24]

Until you experience the ecstasy of the final realization:

But now we've done with this world and its creeds.
After long yearnings and far wandering
The wonder comes! He filleth all our being
With His own Self-Yea, 'tis the Beloved!-
And a vast music in our Soul resounds,
"Ye are united with Me once again,
With the heart's eye see now naught but the Friend:
For whatsoever ye behold, ye know
Is but the glory of the Beloved!"[25]

It is like the drop that becomes at one with the ocean, the finite with the infinite, the human with the divine.

In accord with the principle of polarity which makes it possible by the love generated between the two poles. In the "Divine Symphony" by Inayat Khan, there is a similar thought. He writes, "When I open my eyes to the outer world, I feel myself as a drop in the sea; but when I close my eyes and look within, I see the whole universe as a bubble raised in the ocean of my heart."[26]

Yes, because "I AM" there as the limitless Self. Remember that the emphasis is on your intense and deep desire, because you must be thirsty in order to attract the living water.

"To the thirsty I will give water as a gift from the spring of the water of life."[27]

And the Psalmist proclaims, "You give them drink from the river of your delights. For with you is the fountain of life; in your light we see light."[28]

Then give me your cup of liquid light!

I will, but you are not ready to drink from it. Keep listening attentively to Me, and as I illumine your befogged mind do not hesitate to ask questions. You will always receive the answer for I am the only teacher. But you must make the demand for what you want, for that is the Law of Life.

[1] Evelyn Underhill, *Mysticism.* (NY: E.P. Dutton, 1911), pp. 48, 47.

[2] Ibid., p. 48.

[3] *The Spiritual Dialogue.* (NY: Paulist Press, 1979), p. 119.

[4] *The Life,* tr. J.M. Cohen, (London: Penguin Books, 1987), Ch. 11-17.

[5] John 16:23.

[6] Mircea Eliade, Yoga. *Immortality and Freedom* (Princeton, NJ: Princeton Univ. Press, 1969), p. 119.

[7] Quoted in Das, *Essential Unity,* pp. 283-4.

[8] Job 15:21.

[9] Psalms 34:13.

[10] Proverbs 18:21-21, 23.

[11] Isaiah 30:27.

[12] Jeremiah 9:8.

[13] Matthew 5:37.

[14] James 1:26, 3:5-8.

[15] David Loy, *Nonduality: A Study in Comparative Philosophy.* (Amherst, NY: Humanity Books, 1997), p. 205-06.

[16] *Immortality and Freedom*, pp. 58, 113.

[17] John 20:22-23.

[18] Romans 8:15-16.

[19] Genesis 2:7.

[20] Paul Evdokimov, *Woman and the Salvation of the World: A Christian Anthropology On the Charism of Women*, p. 51.

[21] Underhill, p. 129.

[22] Das, p. 227.

[23] Rig. Veda, 8:44, 33, quoted in Das. p. 227.

[24] *Bhagavad-Gita*, quoted in Das, p 229.

[25] Das, p. 231.

[26] Quoted in Lama Anagarika Govinda, *Creative Meditation and Multi-Dimensional Consciousness*, p. 49 n.2.

[27] Revelation 21:6.

[28] Psalms 36:8-9.

CHAPTER 12

On Human Bondage and Freedom

Happiness and misery will depend upon Karma.
The Tibetan Book of the Dead

God can do all things, except compelling man to love him.
St. Symeon

*Our freedom is but a light that
breaks through from another world.*
Nikolai Gumilev

Before we continue I must confess that there is a question which still troubles me. Although you referred to it previously it seems that your explanation went right over my head. You revealed to me that you are the Source of my life and your love cares for me, but then I don't understand why I had to experience all the confusion, distress, and difficulties that have beset me throughout the years.

It can be very humbling to acknowledge one's faults, and it is not a common practice among human beings because they always blame someone else. Do you still think that I am responsible for the unhappy events of your life?

You should know that it is impossible for Me to produce discord or anything unlike My nature, just as the sun cannot create a shadow unless you turn your back to it or something interferes with its light.

I must remind you that I love you more than you love yourself; I am always radiating My light-energy, which flows into you and animates your body, and I am always giving My intelligence to enlighten your mind.

My desire for you has always been, and will always be, the supreme good in the universe because "I AM" the only Giver of all goodness.

But that's the point I don't understand. If what you say is true, and I don't doubt it, what is the cause of my condition? If patience were not one of My attributes it would be very disturbing to deal with mankind. I have been trying to explain to you the Law of life, of cause and effect, and I will continue, although it is written in the sacred scriptures of the world and, above all, in the heart of every one of God's children. Have you ever asked yourself why, for instance, a pianist, a singer or an athlete has to practice every day?

I think that it would not be necessary once they have learned their art and skill and become proficient and accomplished in their vocation. I mention it because you must exert your faculties and think deeply on what I teach you or you may understand it one day and forget the next.

I should meditate constantly on what you say until your words become flesh of my flesh. Francis Bacon said that knowledge is power, but unless we use it of what benefit is it? Mankind has lowered, by their discord and misuse of energy, the vibration of their body to the present density. Therefore, they can only grow and raise themselves out of their limitations by the law of resistance, which requires constant effort. Resistance should not be considered negative, although idle and lukewarm people shirk it. It is, rather, the opportunity to exert and develop one's power and creativity by the use of his or her faculties and energy.

The life-energy which you release into the individual every instant with every breath and heartbeat.
With regard to your question about you and the human condition, you do not have to look very far for an answer.

I must look within myself.
You turned away from Me and went astray, chasing your own desires, or rather they chased you, and, like Dante, lost your way in the dark wood.

Why should I have done such a thing?
Because you chose to. I gave you freedom to act and do what you please. Freedom is the gift of true love.

You still do not answer my question: why did I choose a different – and evidently wrong way of life?
You must have free will in order to be a conscious, self-determining being and use the creative powers I have given you.

You bestowed on me, as a gift, a will that is free to experience discord and limitation, and ultimately death?
I did not create those things. They are the consequences of your choices.

But you made them possible! You give us freedom either to obey the Law or suffer. Forgive me, but this is not different from the tyranny of being forced to do your will. Obedience

per se is not love – it can even be the opposite. In fact, unless it is loving obedience, one may obey simply out of fear.
Do not forget that My nature is love.

Love cannot be commanded, yet you gave us the commandments and Jesus taught that the first Great Commandment is "Thou shalt love the Lord thy God." I cannot say that it is not right to obey them, but it should be done out of love.
You are right. There are those who think that love is an act of the will or a commitment but I do not agree with them, and I do not expect you to do something because you have to, as an obligation.

You would not be happy because there is no happiness without the feeling of love which is the radiation of My light.

Whatever you do should be out of love because that is the Law of life and the way to complete the circuit keeping the connection between you and Me. How can you receive love, and more of it, if you do not return it to Me? Do you think that the love of a mother for her child is caused by a moral command or a categorical imperative?

No, I don't think so.
Then it comes essentially from the feeling of their blood relation. In the same way, your attitude toward Me and the rest of life is determined by the nature and the tendencies of your innermost being, My flame in your heart. That's what St. Augustine meant when he said, "Love and do what you will."[1] Because nothing wrong can come from true love.

Then I must ask you to explain why there is the possibility of creating something different, and even contrary to love

that causes evil, or why you allow it, because I don't see what good there can ever be in having free will.

You ask me why I gave you a freedom fraught with such peril or why I made its misuse possible. One may ask why a couple, happily married, deliberately brings into the world a baby who later on in life may go astray. The answer is that the newborn, as the fruit of their love becomes the purpose of their existence. They take care of it, protect and instruct it, do everything they can to the point of sacrifice so that it may know only happiness and all the good possible in existence.

But if the child, when he becomes a young man, falls in love with a girl, runs away from home, breaks the law and is condemned, are the parents really responsible for what happened to him? Are they to be blamed if the freedom they gave has been wrongly exercised?

Moreover, I continue to sustain each one's life, no matter what he does because I take freedom seriously, although I could force him to do My will. My image is still present in the human being as the true Self. Even after the Fall I did not remove it, although it became disfigured. I will continue to love every individual as part of who I AM, the self-consciousness of life forever because that is My nature, and I cannot change it. While nothing is impossible to Me, the only thing I cannot do is to alter Myself by being other than love. But you can always say yes or no to it.

I am reminded of a passage in one of my books.

> The gift of love must be the gift of freedom, the gift of letting-be, and this can be expected to be true of all creatures to the extent that is appropriate to their proper character. It is in the nature of dense snow fields that

they will sometimes slip with the destructive force of an avalanche. It is the nature of lions that they will seek prey. It is the nature of cells that they will mutate, sometimes producing new forms of life, sometimes grievous disabilities, sometimes cancers. It is the nature of humankind that sometimes people will act with selfless generosity, but sometimes with murderous selfishness. That these things are so is not gratuitous or due to divine oversight or indifference. They are the necessary cost of a creation given by its Creator the freedom to be itself. Not all that happens is in accordance with God's will because God has stood back, making metaphysical room for creaturely action[2]

I am in agreement with what he says with regard to the freedom of My creation which humanity has disrupted with dire consequences. However, I cannot "stand back," unless the author uses the expression figuratively. "I AM" the Presence of life and My consciousness is in everyone and everything as the breath and heartbeat of the universe.

I find the analogy of the parents, who bring into the world a child as an expression of their love and that after, when it grows up goes astray, unconvincing.
May I ask you why?

For the reason that we humans don't know the future, and if we did, we would act differently in many circumstances. You are omniscient, we are an open book to you where every secret thoughts and motives are recorded, and nothing can be hidden from your eyes. Past, present, and future are known to you.

Yes, they are all one for Me. You bring up the ancient controversy about the compatibility of divine foreknowledge and human freedom.

Yes, if God knows that I will do something in the future; can I be free to do otherwise? I am not interested in the philosophy game. My question is not focused on the issue of whether God's knowledge is compatible with our freedom to choose, which I believe it is. However, since God knows the future and he foresees that something destructive will happen, why does he not prevent it? Because you don't only see future events but have power over them.
It is true that I Am all-knowing and almighty but man is free to determine his own course of action. If he sets in motion causes that will have tragic consequences I cannot interfere or prevent it without violating the freedom I gave him. What I foreknow is that the person may "freely" choose a certain action, whether good or evil. Now listen carefully: if your actions are destructive, I can prevent the cause and/or annihilate the effect only on one condition. The Law of Life requires that you turn to Me and ask for it of your own free will. Do you understand?

I see how sacred is the gift you have bestowed upon us and how infinite is your love, inconceivable to our human mind. You let us destroy your creation, including our bodies which really belong to you, because you respect and honor our free will. The failure and the refusal to recognize that truth is an utter disgrace and signifies our downfall. To ignore that love which gives all of itself, that is the beauty and happiness of life is darkness indeed!
"I AM" not only the Source of everyone's existence, but My desire is that every man and woman be the perfection that "I

AM." Contrary to the human opinion, supported by some un-enlightened authors, that good and evil are relative and that you cannot have one without the other, which is absurd (I do not know what their idea of good is, I think they do not have any), My plan is perfect and I can only desire and create perfection for other parts of Myself.

This makes perfect sense and I know that Jesus said, Be ye perfect as my Father in heaven is perfect,[3] but I still don't know what perfection is.

Let me restate it: perfection is the manifestation and expression of love. They are essentially one and the same. (Obviously, I am speaking of love from the heart.)

But why should we have the capacity to go against the life-current of love? I would rather be unable to do such a thing and be free to choose only what is good for me, not what is harmful. And I would still be conscious of what I am doing – in fact, to a much greater degree than when I do something wrong. Why would a person do something bad if he were aware of it?

He thinks it is good for him because it may appear so, but he can deceive himself. Self-deception, you will remember, is a form of identification.

I agree that this is true in our everyday life: self-deception seems almost natural for humans and it is prevalent in our society. There are cases in which even an immature and un-intelligent person knows that certain things or substances are harmful, yet he indulges in them anyway.

Remember, the choice is always yours and you are responsible for what you do. One may, for example, choose to experience a temporary gratification and indulge in sensations of pleasure at the expense of his well-being. Although he may know that the effects are destructive, weakness of character and external influence or suggestion, will force him to succumb to the temptation. If he keeps doing it what began as an act of choice becomes an addiction and a state of enslavement.

There is an Italian proverb that says, *"Bacco, tabacco, e Venere riducono l' uomo in cenere,"* **which means, "Bacchus, tobacco, and Venus turn man into ashes." However, with regard to wine, Jesus transformed it miraculously from water.**
I see that you interpret the episode of the wedding in Cana of Galilee literally, ignoring the deeper meaning of it. Even so, the intellect tries to find every excuse to justify the wrong desires of the personality. Do you think he would do something detrimental to others? Why do you assume that there was alcohol in that wine? And it was not grape juice either, although it is certainly healthy.

I have no answer to that – unless perhaps the lack of alcoholic content is why the steward after he tasted the wine, said to the bridegroom, "Everyone serves the good wine first, and then the inferior wine after the guests have become drunk. But you have kept the good wine until now."[4]
Also, with regard to this matter, people's minds are so confused that they live in contradiction with themselves without knowing it. Take for instant their love for animals: almost everyone in your nation has a pet, often more than one, of which they are very fond, and there are organizations that are very active in the protection of animals; yet all the time they eat the flesh of animals raised for slaughter with no compunction at all. And

271

think of the inexcusable cruelty and suffering inflicted on animals under the guise of sport, whether hunting or fishing.

It is difficult to understand how it is possible for civilized and otherwise kind-hearted people to murder defenseless creatures simply for amusement or as a hobby. Another terrible consequence connected with this is that their children imitate such thoughtless actions and are led to commit those crimes.

The commandment "Thou shalt not kill" should apply also to animals. In fact, the prophet Isaiah said, "Whoever slaughters an ox is like one who kills a human being."[5]
If you read your Bible, you will learn that originally animals were different from those you know now.

What? How were they different?
First, they were all vegetarians, including man. God said, "See, I have given you every plant-yielding seed that is upon the face of all the earth and every tree with seed in its fruit; you shall have them for food, and, to every beast of the earth, and to every bird of the air, and to everything that creeps on the earth, everything that has the breath of life, I have given every green plant for food. And it was so and it was very good."[6] Moreover, those animals were not aggressive.

This is more congruent with divine creation. I remember that even in my young age I could not understand how inside something so pure and beautiful as a rose there could be a cankerworm feeding on it. It is hard to believe that the original plan designed for God's creatures was to fight and eat each other in order to survive. In fact, it is prophesied that in the restoration of the Kingdom of Heaven on Earth

"The wolf and the lamb shall feed together, the lion shall eat straw like the ox."[7]

The animal forms were not like those that people are familiar with today, just as the body of Adam was different from that of later races of men.

The destructive thoughts and feelings of mankind have been imposed upon Nature and the animal kingdom, and are reflected in the present forms and qualities of its members.

I regret to say that everything in the manifestation glorifies Me, except the inhabitants of this planet, which has become the dumping ground of the Universe.

I don't understand what you mean.

It is very simple. The laggards from other planets and those who failed on the way to the ascension re-embody on the Earth.

Why?

Because it is the lowest vibratory action and the most dense manifestation of any plane. Therefore, according to the Karmic Law they are destined to live here.

Although deplorable, and inconceivable that God's children could so debase themselves, it is encouraging to know that we are the only ones, out of uncountable worlds, that have desecrated your Creation. Although there are more than three billion people living on Earth.

There are many more who belong to this planet waiting to come into embodiment with the hope to make progress and fulfill their divine plan. Do you think that the individual is not responsible if he closes the door to them? And when the younger generation are rebellious and defiant of the conventionalities of society one should ask whether it is because they were not wanted. The selfishness of human beings has eclipsed the light and the beauty they enjoyed in the beginning, and they do not recognize anymore that the very life that beats their blessed hearts is the gift of love.

Their self-created shadows have shut off the "many splendored things" and people have forgotten that love is the only reality. In fact, they do not even know anymore what love is, although are starving for it. And they will continue to live in their limitation until they obey its Law.

But what can we do if we don't feel your love?
It is very simple, and even a child can do it. The individual can turn to Me, if he wants to be free, and ask Me for it. Yet I am giving of Myself all the time or the life-stream without the light of My love could not survive. But very few remember who I AM and what I can do for them.

We don't know how to fill our inner void.
Yet there is the longing within the heart and the irrepressible desire always for something more. And I am the only One who can fulfill it, not only on Earth but for all eternity.

Can we experience positive states without going through the negative?
Absolutely! Do you think I need something opposed to My nature in order to act? Neither do you.

There is a saying, "No pain, no gain," and even, according to some theologians, evil exists so that God can use it for greater good.

That is blasphemy! If it were true, I would have to depend on evil in order to fulfill the perfect plan for My individualities. Do you think the sun needs the darkness in order to shine and illumine the world? Only the one-sided and benighted intellect, in its conceited ignorance can believe such nonsense.

But why is ignorance possible? You are truth and the Source of all life. How can truth's opposite exist?
Ignorance is not the opposite of truth; it is the lack of knowledge of it, like a shadow created by interference with the light of My intelligence.

But since you created everything that exists, and, as the Bible says, it is "very good," why is there lack in the world?
I see that you are very persistent but since you are not argumentative I do not mind sincere questioning. In fact, I encourage it because I think I can always give the answer, although the person may not like that answer. If I were you, I would not argue with anyone, especially with an atheist, because nothing is gained by it.

Often, to win an argument means losing a friend – even a soul – so I will explain to you why man is the only creator of evil in this world.

I told you that My essential nature is love; I created you out of love, and since you are an extension of Myself, I keep sustaining you by My love.

I can understand that I live by your love, but then again, how is it possible for me to experience discord?
Let me repeat that I must give you freedom to act because that is the nature of love. It is not, however, the freedom to suffer or die, but rather to live by choosing who and what you want to

love, that is, where to direct your life-current, up or down, focusing on one pole or the other.

Since love cannot be forced without changing into something different, I cannot make you do what I will, although, as you know, I have the power and authority to do so.

Then my fault would be to love what I choose. But is that wrong? It is still love.

You do not know yet the meaning of the word love and I will instruct you on that. First, you must realize that your free will can govern the attention and direct it wherever you choose. You misused it, but not because you loved what is an other than Myself. You deliberately turned away from Me, attracted by My creation, and your feelings and senses became polarized toward it. .

I couldn't help it. There was marvelous beauty and indescribable wonders everywhere ... a true paradise.

I accept your compliment, but it kept your attention away from Me, and gradually as time went on a chasm was created. Eventually, you even forgot the Source which gives you life. You became identified with your personal desires and limited sphere of activity. It is as if someone donated you a beautiful house and you became so engrossed in it that you failed to remember the giver.

I can see why mankind either denies your existence or think they are separated from you.

And that is the meaning of death and hell. As one of your authors wrote with regard to people's relations and earthly things: "They draw us on and they stop us dead...The enjoyment we find in creatures belongs to the reality of the created being, a reality that is from God and belongs to God. The anguish we find in them belongs to the disorder of our desire, which looks for a greater reality in the desired object than is actually there: a greater fulfillment than any created thing is capable of giving."[8]

How true it is! Just when we find some pleasure and joy in them, they turn into pain and sorrow. They may give us a fleeting glimpse of heaven, but under every fleshly desire and appetite there is a coiled serpent. Instead of loving the beauty of creation in you, we love ourselves by means of creatures; but to love our personality is to love the shadow of a dream.

You fell deeper into the gratification of the physical self which is a blind force of turbulent desire. In your downward path you lowered your consciousness and the vibrations of your original body of light; and God, in His Mercy, clothed you with a "garment of skins,"[9] to enable you to exist.

No wonder there are those who believe that we are merely evolved animals – instead of involved Gods.

Oh, what a fool I have been! I have desired and loved every created thing for its own sake outside of you, and I became identified with the apart and separated myself from the all; and in so doing, I lost my connection and even my remembrance of you! I turned my back on the boundless love that you always offer and intend for me, by which I can own and enjoy everything, finding you in them, and in my inordinate love of everything else, I became attached to them and fell under their spell. I have eaten the husk and thrown away the kernel – have kept the shell and discarded the pearl of great price! How can I overcome my bad habits?

When, tell me, when does the attraction of worldly pleasures die away?

When one realizes the consummation of all happiness and all pleasures in God, the all-pervading, eternal ocean of bliss.

When I read this passage, I did not understand it, but now it begins to make sense:

> The only true joy on earth is the escape from the prison of our false self, and enter by love into union with the life who dwells and sings within the essence of every creature and in the core of our own souls. In his love we possess all things and enjoy fruition of them, finding Him in them.[10]

Will I be able to accomplish that?

You have that capacity like every other human being because it is the irrepressible longing of your heart, whose natural tendency is to love, just as light naturally illumines. And the fundamental desire and the irrefutable intuition of the individual is to love that which exists eternally.

Knowingly or unknowingly, every lover is seeking that love which is not fleeting like a dream, but is expressed in the word "forever" – a word very common in the vocabulary of lovers, but unless it has reference to God, it is only a pathetic delusion.

A high school girlfriend once pleaded, "Tell me you love me forever, if only tonight,"[11] and there are plenty of romantic songs that say the same thing; there is this longing for the eternal even when one knows the situation is ephemeral.

It may sound very simple to say that we are made for you and, as William Law writes, "When this natural life is deprived of or fallen from God, it can be nothing else in it- self but an extremity of want continually desiring, and an extremity of desire continually wanting."[12]
"The true lover is individualized by eternity or, at least, by the desire of eternity."[13]

Because that feeling comes from you.

> Time is
> Too slow for those who wait,
> Too swift for those who fear,
> Too long for those who grieve,
> Too short for those who rejoice;
> But for those who love,
> Time is eternity.[14]

Although concepts like infinity and eternity are difficult to comprehend and define, yet how does one know the mean- ing of what is finite and temporary except in terms of an in- nate sense and even an implicit experience of the divine di- mension of life?

"This is a fact of experience. At the moment of ex- pressing in act or words 'I love you,' the lover just as much as the beloved will have to have, even if only for an instant, the conviction, or at lest the appearance, or indeed the vol- untary illusion of the conviction that this time, it will be for good, that this time will be for good and forever."

At the moment of loving, the lover can only believe what he or she says and does under a certain aspect of eter- nity. Or, more exactly, under an instantaneous eternity, without the promise that will last, but nevertheless an eternity of intention.

The lover just as much as the beloved needs the possible conviction that he or she loves this time forever, irreversibly, once and for all.

To say 'I love you for a moment, provisionally' means 'I don't love you at all' and accomplishes only a performative contradiction.

Making love for a time is the same as not making love, or as not playing the lover. Of course, I can very well say, 'I love you' while clearly doubting to be able (and doubting to want to be able) to love forever, indeed with the quasi-certainty of failing before long.

But I can never say it without maintaining at least a tiny possibility (which is simply to say, a possibility) that this time I will love forever, once and for all. Without this possibility, as slight as one might want, not only could I not psychologically imagine myself making love, even less actually do it, but by right, I will condemn myself to lying. And this lie will not only deceive the other (who perhaps has not illusion and does not ask for so much); above all it deprives each of us from making love...for neither of us will reach the condition of the lover.[15]

Instead of you making love, the truth is that love makes you.

There is no more even the question of love, merely the shadow of deception. The promise of eternity protects even the lovers who could not hold to it, and assures them once and for all the rank of lovers.

Incidentally, the expression "making love" does not make sense. You cannot make love because love is not an act. Sex is an act. But love is a state of being. You can be it but you cannot make it. It is not an effort. You can make sex, but not love. On the contrary, love is the causeless cause and the motive force of life.

Once the flame of love is planted in your heart – and this is not a poetic metaphor but an eternal reality – I can never extinguish it: another of My impossible acts because it is part of Myself.

Moreover, I remind you that My love for you is of the same nature as your love when it is directed to Me: there is no difference in its essence, which is fire, but only in its dimension which, in My Being, is infinite and ever expanding. And so it can be with you in your oneness with Me.

The same element of water which is in the drop is also in the ocean.
Yes, remember always that the fire of love pervades the all universe and by your love you can connect with anyone and any place throughout infinity.

[1] In *Epistolam Joannis ad Pathos,* Tractatus 7, Section 8.

[2] John Polkinghorne. *Belief in God in an Age of Science.* (New Haven, Conn.: Yale University Press, 1998), p. 13.

[3] Matthew 5:48.

[4] John 2:10.

[5] Isaiah 66:3.

[6] Genesis 1:29-31.

[7] Isaiah 65:25.

[8] Thomas Merton, *New Seeds of Contemplation* (NY: New Directions Books, 1961), p. 26.

[9] Genesis 3:21.

[10] Merton, p. 25.

[11] R.C. Solomon, *Love: Emotion, Myth, and Metaphor* (Buffalo, NY: Prometheus Books, 1990), p. xii.

[12] William Law, Mary Emily Dowson, William Porcher Dubose, *Liberal and Mystical Writings of William Law,* (London: Longmans, Green, and Co., 1908), p. 38.

[13] Jean-Luc Marion, *The Erotic Phenomenon,* trans. Stephen E. Lewis. (Chicago: The University of Chicago Press, 2007), p. 109.

[14] Henry Van Dyke, read at the funeral of Diana, Princess of Wales, quoted in the *Oxford Dictionary of Quotations,* p. 789.

[15] *The Erotic Phenomenon,* pp. 109-110.

CHAPTER 13

The Eye of the Beholder

As a man is, So he Sees.
As the Eye – Such the Object.

Both read the Bible day and night,
But thou read'st black where I read white.
William Blake

Man ... was a many sided mirror,
Which could distort to many a shape of error,
This true fair world of things, a sea reflecting love.
Percy B. Shelley

The angels keep their ancient places;-
Turn but a stone and start a wing!
'Tis ye, 'tis your estranged faces
That miss the many-splendored thing.
Francis Thompson

I know that you are One God and your nature is changeless. However, in my study of religious scriptures you are called by many names; I find it difficult to understand their true meaning and why you have been referred to in different ways.

I cannot read all scriptures in their original languages, and there is a saying in Italian, *traduttore traditore*, which means that the translator is bound to be a traitor, as illustrated in this charming anecdote:

"I am not very well versed in Greek," said the giant.
"Nor I either," replied the philosophical mite.

283

"Why then do you quote Aristotle in Greek?" resumed the Sirian.

"Because," answered the other, "it is but reasonable we should quote what we do not comprehend in a language we do not understand."[1]

Is that what thwarts me?
I can appreciate your query because, unfortunately, that is what happens, especially with all the spiritual writings of the world as the translator inevitably imposes his *own*, as well as his *time's*, concepts on the interpretation of the text.

It strikes me as being akin to the theory in quantum physics that the observed phenomenon cannot be known and measured objectively because it is altered by being observed.
It is an apt comparison because the translation depends on the translator's acquaintance of the language, that is, the object being observed. Besides, he has to know how the meaning of words change through time.

Most importantly, the understanding of the knower must be adequate to the subject to be known, and this is not always the case. Therefore, the same text may hold different levels of meaning for different readers, even if they are natives and fluent in the language.

I understand why Dante, explaining how his poem about his journey through hell, purgatory, and paradise should be read, says that it is endowed with several meanings.[2] There are basically two, the first comes from the letter, and is called the "literal." Another is that which is signified by the

284

letter, and is called "allegorical." On the literal level, the poem is about the state of souls after death; on the allegorical level, the subject is man, liable to the reward or punishment of Justice, according to the use he has made of his free will.

Then he gives as an example of his method of interpretation the first line of Psalm 114 in the Hebrew Bible: "when Israel went out of Egypt." If you look only at the letter, it refers to the event in history when Moses led the children of Israel out of Egypt. On the allegorical level it means the redemption through Christ leading us out of sin. If, however, you look at the "moral" sense, the third level of interpretation, it signifies the turning of the souls from the sorrow and misery of sin to the state of Grace; and finally, the meaning of the "anagogical" or "mystical" sense is the passage of the blessed souls from the slavery of a corruptible state to the freedom of eternal glory.[3]

The poet, as he gives the key to the understanding of his text, concludes with the assertion that the literal or historical facts contain in themselves meanings that God intended for you and your salvation. In the manner of the Church Fathers, Dante perceived the universal history of humanity as the gradual unfolding of the divine plan moving toward the final victory of the light over humanly created darkness and depravity.

The Bard would agree with him:

There's a divinity that shapes our ends,
Rough-hew them how we will[4]

The four Biblical meanings that form the basis for Dante's interpretation of the Scripture and of his own work can be traced back to the writers of the Old Testament and to their commentators in the Jewish tradition.

I am reminded of the Kabbalah, the ancient secret doctrine of the Hebrew, confined to a circle of initiates, that adopted the mystical interpretation of Biblical scripture.
There is definitely a mystical element in the experience of the prophets and psalmists; the fourfold exegesis uses anthropomorphic expressions referred to God, situations about persons and also events that, if taken literally, may seem disconcerting, senseless, and in some cases, even shocking.

It is fitting for the Scripture to present spiritual truths by means of comparisons with material things so that even those who are not able to grasp them intellectually can still understand them at their own level.

The Creator provides for everything according to the capacity of its nature, says Thomas Aquinas.

And Wordsworth concurs with him: "The commerce between Man and his Maker cannot be carried out but by a process where much is represented in little, and the infinite Being accommodates himself to a finite capacity."[5]

I should also quote Johann Georg Hamann who wrote in his diary: "God has revealed himself to man in nature and in His word ... both revelations explain and support each other, and cannot contradict each other. God condescended as much as He could to man's disposition and ideas, even to his prejudices and weaknesses."[6]

God is represented as the supreme artist, the sublime poet who, by His creation, wrote a "book" – the universe – and by another creative act, out of love for His children, inspired the writing of the Scripture. These two "volumes" are

His self-revelation for the purpose of man's salvation: "Ever since the creation of the world his invisible nature, namely, his external power and deity, has been clearly perceived in the things that have been made."[7]

A good example of allegorical reading is the Biblical episode about Rahab, the harlot. Her story is related in the second and sixth chapter of the book of Joshua.

After he received the divine command to take Jericho, Joshua sent two spies there, and they stayed in the house of Rahab. On being discovered, the King of Jericho sent orders to the woman that they must be delivered to him. Instead, she took the two men and hid them on the roof of her house and deluded her pursuers by sending them off on a false clue. During the night, Rahab went to see them and declared her faith in the God of Israel; she said, Now then, since I have dealt kindly with you, swear to me by the Lord that you, in turn, will deal kindly with my family. And her guests promised safety for her and all her relatives when Jericho should fall.

When the way was clear, she let them down by a rope through the window since her house was upon the town wall, and she gave them directions to escape. As a sign the men asked her to tie to the window the scarlet rope by which she helped them down. And thus, Rahab and her house were spared when all of Jericho was burned down by the victorious Israelites entering the city.[8]

But why would Dante confer on her the high degree of beatitude in the third heaven?

The answer is given by the allegorical interpretation of the story. Joshua was regarded as a Christ figure. The similarity of the names has been emphasized since the early centuries. And when he leads his people over the Jordan, he prefigures Christ leading mankind out of the slavery of sin and perdition and into the true holy land, the kingdom of God.

According to all ancient commentators Rahab represents the Church itself; her house alone, with all its inhabitants, escapes destruction, just as the Church of the faithful will alone be saved when Christ appears for the last judgment. She found freedom from the fornication of the world by way of the window of her confession of faith, to which she bound the scarlet rope, the sign of Christ's redeeming blood.

Writers of the New Testament also mention her: James wrote, "Likewise, was not Rahab, the harlot, also justified by works when she received the messengers and sent them out by another road?"[9] And Paul, "By faith the harlot, Rahab, perished not with them who believed not."[10]

The Old Testament becomes a succession of isolated prefigurations of the prophecies of Christ; Adam in his sleep represents Christ's death or sleep before resurrection. Eve, created out of Adam's rib, or "side" in Hebrew, is a figure of the mother of mankind in the *flesh*. When one of the soldiers pierced Jesus' "side," from it flowed water and blood, which are referred to in the sacrament of the Church, the mother of mankind in *spirit*.

May God us keep/From single vision and Newton's sleep![11]

How prophetic these words by Blake are when I think that the notion of truth has been so narrowed that it has become synonymous with scientific fact. Any idea or story contrary to what is defined as fact is usually called a myth, a usage that not only trivializes and perverts the idea of the term, but reveals a very shallow view of life.

A myth is a story that renders concrete the inner meaning of the human existence. In reality, myths embody

a people's intuitive perception of the deepest truths, which give direction, purpose, and a sense of values by which to live. For those who understand them, they are a source of wisdom that symbolically disclose and explain the mysteries of the universe in a way that logically descriptive language simply cannot. It has been said that, "Myth embodies the nearest approach to absolute truth that can be stated in words."[12]

Yes, the myth is a superior form of knowledge, often the only kind possible, and is infinitely richer than any concept. The reality which cannot be translated into discursive thought lies clothed in the simplicity of events taken from world.

The main focus in the Western tradition has been on the pole of material objects, sense pleasure and self-interested activity. This tendency has created a divisive society where the world is experienced in opposition to a self facing it problematically and discordantly. While the planet is becoming smaller and accessible in their living room, people have lost the essential values of unity and universality. The inner vision of the ultimate reality in which everyone is grounded, as one of My faculties bestowed on them, has been obscured. Therefore, the external world that they perceive depends on their disjointed consciousness and will appear different to different observers. The abysmal result is that reality and truth become relative, and one is led to believe that he is subject solely to his personal judgment and opinion.

That's how we fool ourselves when we want our own way enwrapped as we are in our thick veils of ignorance of what is real and true.

Yes, that is the worst form of bondage imaginable because one is chained to the selfishness of the personal self. Humans cannot create values as a means or as an end in itself. The masses do not even know the meaning of the word because "I AM" the only Source of all values which should illumine everyone's conscience. It is disheartening to see that people are not only satisfied but even boast of that fallacy and believe that they are liberated from an imposition or an obligation by an external authority.

But let me emphasize that there is no freedom, and never will be, without the understanding that life is governed by the universal Law of love and everyone is accountable for every thought and feeling according to it. To think that one is an exception and has the power to assert his personal will, doing what "feels" right for him means to fall into the trap of arbitrariness and self-hypnosis. Unfortunately for mankind the truth has never been popular among them.

Why?
Because people prefer to hide from it as it reveals the self-deception of the personality and that its existence is a lie heading toward dissolution.

"His very self," writes Thomas Merton, "his very reality is all contradiction: a contradiction mercifully obscured by confusion. If the confusion is cleared away, and he fully realizes this tormented self, what will he see if not the final absurdity of the contradiction? The 'real meaning of his existence' would then be precisely that it has no meaning."[13]

With regard to the relativity of knowledge I read this passage which illustrates the principle that the understanding of the knower must be adequate to what is to be known. "For an animal a particular object may be merely a colored thing, to a savage it may seem only marked paper. The aver-

age educated person sees it as a book with unbelievable notions about the nature of the universe. However, a scientist will consider it a brilliant treatise on quantum physics explaining new aspects of reality. In each case the phenomenon remained the same, but its level of meaning and significance was a function of the capacity and training of the observer ... All levels of significance up to the highest are equally factual, equally logical, equally objective. The observer who is not adequate to the higher levels of significance will not know that they are being missed."[14]
If one does not know that he does not know, he things that he knows.

"We are led to believe a lie When we see with, not through the eye," wrote William Blake in *Auguries of Innocence*. According to him, "As a man is, so he sees," and "As the eye – such is the object," with the result that "the eye altering alters all."[15]

And he clarifies it further with the example, "A fool sees not the same tree that a wise man see."[16] There should be a "connaturality" or correspondence between the two terms: "Nothing can be known without there being an appropriate instrument ... When the level of the knower is not adequate to the level of the object of knowledge, the result is not factual error but something much more serious: an inadequate and impoverished view of reality."[17] Even an entirely distorted one; for instance, a coiled rope mistaken for a snake, and a shadow or a noise for a burglar. These are two classical examples in the Indian scriptures to explain the illusory nature of "maya," or the world of appearance contrasted to Reality.

People say, "Let the facts speak for themselves;" they forget that the speech of facts is real only if heard and understood."[18]

Despite increasing suspicion about the merits of technocratic society and the dualistic mode of experiencing that undergirds it, there is no agreement about what the root of the problem is and therefore what alternative there might be.[19]

The author you quoted is correct, as the cause of the modern malaise and confusion is the individual's separative tendencies, uncontrolled emotions, and inner fragmentation. He is divided from himself, from others, and from nature, creating the mental state referred to as estrangement and alienation. "Single vision," the reliance on the "bodily," "physical," "vegetable," "corporeal," or "outward eye," results in a slavery of the consciousness to merely material objects, a spiritual sleep of death, and a sensual death-in-life."[20] To this un-illumined way of perceiving reality mystics and poets "opposed the liberated, creative, and resurrected mode of sight, 'through' and not 'with' the physical eye."[21]

The prophet Isaiah, quoted by Jesus said, "You will indeed listen, but never understand, and you will indeed look, but never perceive."[22]

This has been the apparent tragedy of Jesus' ministry and the case of unbelievers. Those who reject Me as a real Being think that if I reveal Myself by some miraculous ways or signs to them, they would accept My Presence. That is not true. They are constantly surrounded by all kinds of miracles, but "their hearts have grown dull;" they fail to "understand with their hearts."[23] This may sound like meaningless collection of words to the intellectual elite and the intelligentsia of the world. And from their point of view they are right because they are deaf to the gentle voice of the heart.

"Knowledge comes about insofar as the object known is within the knower."[24] I am reminded of the transfiguration, the resurrection, and ascension of Christ that, if understood, would raise the consciousness of humanity and free it from the limited and false perception of what divine reality is and from the consequences of Adam's curse.
You must see with the "eye of the heart" or the "eye of the soul" by which you can receive *insight.*

While the intellect can only produce *opinions*, "the purpose in this life, is to restore the health of the eye whereby God may be seen."[25]
"I AM" always not only within and above each one, but My consciousness is everywhere.

And I will know what reality is for "In Thy light we will see light."[26] But I still do not understand clearly whether reality is, to use the traditional terminology, subjective or objective.
Knowledge is a function of Being, that is, a state of consciousness, but it does not mean that truth is relative or a matter of personal opinion and taste. As we discussed it before, if one does not know the difference or cannot discriminate between his notion and idea of what is true and that which really is, he is bound to be deceived and to experience failure. Reality does not depend on the mode and disposition of the individual because it is one, changeless, infinite, eternal.

In the words of the Bhagavad-Gita, "It is found that the un-real has no being; it is found that there is no non-being of the real. The certainty of both these propositions is indeed surely seen by the perceivers of truth."[27] To the average person all this talk about reality does not make any sense, as he may think that it is very abstract and irrelevant to our everyday living, which for him is the only reality and often very harsh.

The individual who entertains that kind of thinking and attitude is very superficial and he has a long way to go before he awakens from his stupor and sleepwalking state.

However, the outer world must exist, it is not a figment of the imagination.

Although human imagination plays an important role and can be a determining factor, external entities are actually perceived: a table, a house, a tree, a bird, are part of the phenomenal or world of appearances. Existence must be attributed to it, but it only "appears" to be real, because it is constantly changing, it can be here now and gone tomorrow. In fact, what people do and try to achieve, unless it helps life, is worthless and ephemeral, despite the endlessness of desire.

I am aware that all we experience in our "common dream" has beginning and end; we suffer from "the delusion by which we think that reality coincides at every point with its appearances. According to the Neo-Platonic tradition, for instance, sensory beauty is merely the shadow of the eternal divine idea, but it is "difficult to go beyond the flesh."[28] Few are sensitive enough to perceive and appreciate what is beautiful as a divine attribute or principle instead of a word having the same meaning as sexy.

Which is a perversion because physical beauty is the reflection of its spiritual side, that is, of inner qualities and purity of life and without them it will inevitably fade away.

It would be skin deep, merely an appearance which the poet describe as,

> False coin, with which th' impostor cheats us still;
> The stamp and color good, but metal ill!
> ......
> Beauty, whose flames but meteors are,
> Short-liv'd and low, though thou wouldst seem a star."[29]

The problem is the identification with the physical body that, instead of being My temple, has become the instrument or vehicle of the disorderly desires of the personality. The distress it can cause certainly does not compensate for the temporary pleasures it can give. The tragic irony is that it is the main focus of interest in your society whether in sport or beauty pageant while it represents the ultimate separation from reality and Myself. That is what make life unintelligible to the human intellect as it does not see the forest because of the trees.

And we don't even know what a tree really is although we have catalogued thousands of species.
Closer to the truth are the native North Americans who call them, "our standing brothers and sisters."[30]

They feel at one with Nature, and that is what Meister Eckhart has to say:
"When is a man in mere understanding?" I answer, 'When a man sees one thing separated from another.' And when is a

man above mere understanding? That I can tell you: 'When a man sees All in all, then he stands beyond mere understanding'."[31]

With regard to your question, to which I already made reference, objectivity is an illusory state of being and can never be fully attained because everything, including the individual is part of the One life.

Therefore, it cannot be grasped by the mind for it escapes conceptualization. I must, again, clarify that the oneness of life, consciousness, and energy is not an undifferentiated unity but an interrelatedness by which everything and everyone is connected with each other and the All.

Does it mean that ultimate reality is not an object of knowledge?
No, it cannot be; please think of it, since it is One and All ...

It cannot be separated into two as an object from the subject.
That is correct. The intellect has caused the notion and the experience of the pluralistic world consisting of independent elements because it is separated from Me. Reality is not knowable to the eye of the flesh and by intellectual process but it is accessible to insight and can be experienced through communion by feeling it.

That is, by love.
Yes, in order to know, the individual must become at one with that which one seeks to know, and it takes love to do it.. That is the only way to overcome the barriers of the separation from the real and the true.

It is interesting that even a philosopher of our time recognizes the essential role of love in the quest for truth. "Philosophy comprehends only to the extent that it loves – I love to comprehend, therefore I love in order to comprehend...philosophy defines itself as the 'love of wisdom' because it must in effect begin by loving before claiming to know...to the degree that philosophy ceases to comprehend itself first as love and starting from love, not only it contradicts its original determination, but it flees from truth, which it exchanges for the science of objects, that pottage of lentils."[32]

Yes, in order to attain the truth it is necessary first to desire it and therefore to love it. The contemporary current of that ideology that sacrifices everything to power has demonstrated that man does not love the truth and that it prefers to lie provided that lies assure him power. Remember that the end and the consummation of true knowledge consists in becoming one with the object. Only when you feel it as part of yourself do you really know it, and this is the penetration of the veils of truth and the victory of unifying mode over the separative and dualistic method of the analytical intellect. This is the truth that makes you free because it is a state of Being connected with Me, the Source of your life.

I understand why "The truth indeed has never been preached by the Buddha, seeing that one has to realize it within oneself."[33] And it is revealed by Jesus' affirmation, "I AM the way, the life, and the truth."[34]

Yes, the "I AM" in you and as you, that is, who you really are, as yet unrecognized, is the truth.

"I know the truth only when it becomes life in me," writes Kierkegaard.[35] Is reality or the truth then subjective?
It is neither subjective nor objective.

Is this a conundrum? It is hard to understand.
Because you forget or, rather, you have not made it your own the fundamental principle of life. I am trying to teach you that no beings or things exist independently but only in relationship to others and the totality of the universe.

I think you are referring to the Law of Polarity.
Exactly. Reality is One because "I AM" One and there is no other. And it is not a duality which means separation and opposition. Polarity, I state again, means interrelation and complementarity, two mutually dependent and inseparable poles like a magnet. That is what makes love possible, each is both, and in their unity do not become blurred, confused, and lost.

It is self-evident that there must be a lover and a beloved in order to express love.
That is why "I AM" a Creator, in order to have something to love. But you should know how to direct your feeling of love to its true objective by wisdom. Therefore, you have another kind of polarity: it is necessary to know in order to love, and one needs to love in order to know. You cannot have one without the other in your quest for truth. In some teaching knowledge comes first, in others love; I prefer the explanation I am giving you.

Meister Eckhart seems to agree when he writes that knowledge consists in peeling off all coverings and running naked to God "until it touches Him and grasps Him...Knowledge

is better than love but the two together are better than one of them, for knowledge really contains love."³⁶ In other words, instead of talking or thinking about something, we should experience it – be it.

This is the difference between what one is and gathering facts and information – what one has.

As a commentator explains, "To see the world wrongly is to see the wrong world, but to see it right is to create a new earth and a new heaven."³⁷ How can we restore our divine vision?

By the light of My love which dissolves the shadows of human miscreations that have eclipsed the beauty and perfection of My creation. In My light you will see light.

Then I can see you everywhere and I will know what reality and truth are. I hope and pray that one day I may have the ecstatic experience described in this passage:

> Your enjoyment of the world is never right till every morning you awake in Heaven; see yourself in your Father's palace; and look upon the skies, the earth and the air as celestial joys; having such a reverend esteem of all, as if you were among the Angels ...

> You never enjoy the world aright till the sea itself floweth in your veins, till you are clothed with the heavens and crowned with the stars; and perceive yourself to be the sole heir of the whole world, and more than so, because men are in it who are every one sole heirs as well as you. Till you can sing and rejoice and delight in God, as misers

do in gold, and kings in scepters, you can never enjoy the world.

Till your spirit filleth the whole world, and the stars are your jewels ... Till you love men so as to desire their happiness with a thirst equal to the zeal of your own; till you delight in God for being good to all; you never enjoy the world...The world is a mirror of Infinite Beauty, yet no man sees it.[38]

I can understand how we perceive the world differently according to our level of consciousness. Is this the reason for the distinction between esoteric and exoteric knowledge?

Yes, one deals with the inner or spiritual side of life and the other with the external or material side. Esotericism uses secret language in order to protect its teachings from being misused and perverted, and it is meant for the select few who are ready for it called initiates. It can also be referred to as subjective, that is, concerned with energy and potency (hence the danger of undue hasty revelation.) If those teachings were made accessible to or communicated to the masses they would be completely misunderstood, even ridiculed, I mean their true meaning would be too subtle and elusive for the ordinary mind. You were told not to throw pearls to the dogs. Exoteric knowledge is objective and its field is the receiver of the life-force, that which is energized or the world of effects.

I see why the Divine Master had to teach in "parables:" I have said these things to you in figures of speech. The hour is coming when I will no longer speak to you in figures, but will tell you plainly of the Father.[39]

However, the truth can be found whenever one is willing to go deep within himself in the silence of his interiority and feel the flame within the heart which is one with the heart of the universe.

There, in the sanctuary not made with hands, I am always ready to reveal Myself to the sincere seeker, for I am the only Source of knowledge and infallible teacher. Keep in mind that love is the golden key that opens the door to the temple of truth. Without the light of My love it is not possible to dispel the darkness of ignorance that envelops the human mind.

Only the light can reveal the Reality enabling you to see it in its original beauty and perfection as I do see it. Love transfigures what otherwise merely exists as an earthly shadowy manifestation.

You said that life is one, but "if there were only one thing with nothing 'outside' it, then that one would not be aware of itself as one. The phenomenological experience would be of no thing/nothing. To be aware that there is only One actually implies that there are two: the One, and that which is aware of the One as being One."[40]

I am not surprised that you still do not understand the principle of polarity, but you will if you continue to listen to My words, and meditate on them.. Let me stress again this point so widely misunderstood: polarity is neither a oneness where everything is fused and confused nor a duality which implies division and rupture. I am One and "I AM" all there is, yet I am talking to you and you to Me.

Those words I read so many times and quoted in our dialogue, now begin to make sense to me: "...that they may all be one. As you, Father, are in me and I in you, may they also

301

be in us...so that they may be one, as we are one, I in them and you in me, that they may become completely one."⁴¹ I think, in my humble opinion, that this is the highest truth ever expressed; even in my dullness they found an echo in my heart.

But who listens to his or her heart? Yet, "I AM" there giving to everyone My life, light, and love. We have discussed how the eye of the beholder determines its perception of reality and its view of the world. Not less important is the hear of the listener.

I read that hearing is the first sense to be manifested.

Yes, the first aspect of manifestation is that of sound because universal life is not only energy and vibration but sound. From a leaf to the human being, from a crystal to a planet or a star, everything in manifestation is created and sustained according to the law of harmony.

Your words remind me of a poem I'd like to quote:

> From harmony, from heavenly harmony
> This universal frame began;
> When Nature underneath a heap
> Of jarring atoms lay,
> And could not heave her head,
> The tuneful voice was heard from high,
> Arise, ye more than dead.
> Then cold and hot and moist and dry
> In order to their stations leap,
> And music's power obey.
> From harmony, from heavenly harmony
> This universal frame began;
> From harmony to harmony

Through all the compass of the notes it ran,
The diapason closing full in Man.[42]

Each atom is constantly emitting unheard sound, and at every moment it creates the world of forms of different degrees of matter, obeying the tone of My voice as I speak the Word. As it reverberates throughout the system, it drives matter into its appointed place and finds its point of deepest materiality on the physical plane.

I can understand sound as a creative energy; experiments made in the recent past demonstrate the capacity of Nature to create forms through sound waves. For example, sand grains and dust particles spread out on a plate of glass or metal, arranging themselves into beautiful, symmetrical and geometrical form, often very complex, when a violin bow is drawn along the edge of the plate producing a musical note.

It always seemed as if the sound called "the particles to order." Now however, we know that what happened there is happening everywhere. The sound that gives order and beauty to the world is everywhere. Confronted with its power and might, the "particles" of the universe, the planets and stars are only particles of dust that the sound "calls" to order and to beauty. It calls stars and elementary particles, crystals and leaf shapes, plants and the bodies of human beings and animals, the architectural forms and geological structure of the interior of the earth, the elements and their periodic table, the spin of the particles, the structure of the atoms and the molecules and nucleic acids and many other things that we haven't yet discovered – for most research in this field is only at its beginning. And yet we know enough

to be able to conclude: Sound calls the world. The world calls in sounds. The world *is* sound.[43]

I concur with the words of the author you quoted; what is called the "music of the spheres" is not just a poetic phrase or an imaginary notion. It is an eternal reality because manifestation is accompanied by music. When a planet is created, the primal light is condensed, or coalesces into form, by the sound of music. Each planet has its own tone and, in unison with the other planets of the system, they produce a chord that combines with other systems of worlds in a cosmic symphony.

I read that in India, the sound of Krishna's flute is the cause of the creation of the world. "The mystery of music is seldom realized" wrote Underhill, "by those who so easily accept its gifts. Yet of all the arts music alone shares with great mystical literature the power of making in us a response to the life-movement of the universe."[44]

Yes, there is definitely an affinity between deep religious feeling and musical emotion. "In a truly loving mind there is always a song of glory and an inner flame of love ... there is sweetness in this song, and a warmth about this radiance," writes Richard Rolle. "Very sweet indeed is the quiet that the spirit experiences. Music, divine and delectable, comes to rejoice it; the mind is rapt in sublime and joyous melody and sings the delights of everlasting love ... I call it song when there is in the soul, overflowing and ardent, a sweet feeling of heavenly praise; when thought turns into song; when the mind is in thrall to sweetest harmony."[45]

On a more human level, I recall the words of a Spanish song in the time of the Renaissance:

O fair! O sweet! When I do look on thee,
In whom all joys so well agree,
Heart and soul do sing in me,
Just accord all music makes.

A great composer said that love and music are the two wings of the soul. "What love is to man, music is to the arts and mankind. Music is love itself, it is the purest, most ethereal language, showing all possible changes of color and feelings. And it can be understood by thousands of men who all feel differently."[46] "The man that hath no music in himself," according to Shakespeare, "nor is not moved with concord of sweet sounds, is fit for treasons, stratagems, and spoils."[47]

It is rare to find someone who is not sensitive to music, of one kind or another, because, as it has been justly said, "There's no passion in the human soul/But finds its food in music."[48] But not everyone understands how deeply it can affect the individual's body and mind for good or ill depending on the quality of the sound. It has, really, life and death potency.

Since time immemorial we have testimony of the importance of music. Pythagoras stated that "a stone is frozen music," and all beings and things produce sound according to their nature. According to Plato, he made music and astronomy sister sciences.

And in our time a scientist wrote, "before we make music, music makes us."[49] I want to mention that music therapy is becoming widely recognized. I've read dramatic accounts of how doctors, shamans, and healthcare professionals use music to deal with everything from anxiety to cancer, high blood pressure, chronic pain, dyslexia, and even mental illness. I have a book with the significant title, *The Mozart Effect,* in which the author lists fifty common conditions, ranging from migraines to substance abuse, for which music can be used as treatment and cure.[50]

Even when I was confused and skeptical, whenever I heard a beautiful musical composition I could feel like a Presence pouring into me comfort, peace, illumination or whatever I needed at the time. Of the triune parts, melody, rhythm, and harmony, I found melodious tones my favorite; Jean Sibelius said that melody is the soul of great healing music.[51]

In the Bible there is the story of King Saul being tormented by an evil spirit. He was advised to have his servants "to look for someone who is skillful in playing the lyre ... and you will be helped." Saul commanded, "Provide for me someone who can play well, and bring him to me." David was sent to the King, he took the lyre and played it with his hand, and Saul would be relieved and feel comforted, as the evil spirit would depart from him."[52]

Can there be anything more harmonious and concordant to mind and body than the feeling of love?. "O lett me sitt alone" writes Gertrude More, "silent to all the world and it to me, that I may learn the song of Love."[53]

When you listen to music its vibratory action enters into you and connects directly with your feelings, and according to the quality of the sound, it will produce a beneficial or harmful response. It affects also the nervous system and, unless it is harmonious energy having a balm-like influence, it can be very stressful, and create irreparable damage. The effect of good music can be vivifying and inspiring but, although joyous and exhilarating, it is quieting and peaceful, which are the requisites for the healing of the body.

How different is the sound which creates excitement and un-controlled feelings!

That is a very dangerous condition because it opens your emotional nature to destructive currents of energy that are floating everywhere. But let me clarify something. You mentioned the experiments by which particles of matter create forms, and it has been said that the efficacy of a prayer or mantra consists also in the effect of "sound waves" or vibrations. But if their power depended only on the sound of the spoken word or on their repetition, then the use of a record player would accomplish the same thing. In reality, the effect of prayer or a mantra, rather than on the "vibration-theory" is rooted in the inner attitude, the love and the faith, which may be joined or not to the spoken word.

I am confused. The nature of the sound-waves is physical and not spiritual? But you said that love is the highest vibration in the universe.

Yes, because I have to explain the cosmic laws in terms that you can understand, and make you realize that love is not an intellectual concept, a metaphor, or an abstract something, but the greatest force in manifestation. About the difference between spiritual and physical vibration, the key is in the bipolar relation of spirit-matter, and it depends on which pole is dominant. Obviously, with the wrong kind of music the polarity is broken and, instead of harmony, you have discord.

You said that music possesses life and death potency; how true it is! It has been proved that certain types of music, so-called, can kill plants. I'll mention an experiment made with corn, squash, petunias, zinnias and marigolds, in two sepa-

307

rate chambers, with one radio tuned to the all classical music station, the second to the rock station.

After two weeks all the blooms in the first chamber had turned toward the radio: "The plants were quite uniform and definitely lush and green ... Alas, in the rock chamber the tall plants were drooping, the blooms were faded and turning away from the source of sound. Some leaves had dropped off and the grotesque stems were leaning away from the radio ... On the 16th day, when I entered the lab, the spectacle before me in the rock chamber was unbelievable. All but a few marigolds were in the last stages of dying. The professor overviewing the experiment exclaimed: 'Chaos, pure chaos.' Yes, it appeared some unknown force had crippled, then destroyed these plants."[54] I wonder, since human beings are certainly more sensitive than plants, what would be the effect of the sound of rock music on them.

The abnormal rhythm of the rock beat, at variance with the natural heartbeat, and the volume at which such music is usually listened to, impair one's sensitivity, and its discordant influence will make a person vulnerable to further negative forces. Its victims often begin to experience chaos and disorder in other aspects of their lives, craving things that will lead them to self-destruction both within and without.

A recent author has described this condition: The distinction between music and noise seems to be blurring: melody and words are being replaced by shrieks for which the only accompaniment is a frenetic rhythm, and the result, as we have all, many times observed, is a sort of collective hysteria similar to that of primitive people. To put oneself into a trance under the effect of rhythmic excitation is to momentarily leave the civilized state and fall into a savage one, at which point, from the depths of human nature, the individual's bestiality makes its appearance too strongly for a weakened spirituality to correct.[55]

To a degree, "you are what you hear" — what your consciousness is attuned to, whether the love-song of your heart or the defiling din of the outside world. The Law of life is harmony but it cannot be maintained in the feeling without love. My nature is the fire of love, and human beings "live, move, and have their being"[56] in it because I am pouring it in, through and around them all the time, or they could not survive; but in their lack of understanding or by deliberate choice because of their selfishness, they are constantly creating discord, causing misery and distress in their existence and the ruin of the very fabric of civilization

You present a frightening picture, almost like an apocalypse in the process of happening right now – and one that is inevitable, given the prevalence of this kind of raucous music, which is a cacophony of noises rattling through our society, and its popularity especially among young people. My feeling of despair is creeping back over me, not just for myself but for mankind itself!

Even though My people of Earth are caught in the whirlwinds of their unfortunate negative thoughts and feelings throughout the world, they may reverse their tendency and come back to Me. I love them with a love inconceivable to their minds and I am not concerned with anything but their illumination and freedom from all that beset them. I want them to remember their divine origin and recognize the power with which I endowed them to fulfill their heart's desire and to create and expand perfection. Each one, in spite of the density of the body, can hear the sound emitted by the flame in their heart, which is the keynote of their individuality.

How?

Turning his love to Me, one can penetrate the veil of the flesh and light the way into the cave of the heart. There it will accord with the note of My heart and attune himself to the music of the spheres.

1 Voltaire, quoted in *Love, Emotion, Myth, Metaphor*, p. 8.
2 Dante, *The Divine Comedy.*
3 James Collins, "Epistula X" in *Dante: Layman, Prophet, Mystic* (NY: Alba House, 1938), p. 119.
4 *Hamlet*, Act V, Scene 2, Lines 10-11.
5 Quoted in M.H. Adams, *Natural Supernaturalism: Tradition and Revolution in Romantic Literature,* (NY & London: W.W. Norton Co., 1973), p. 334.
6 Ibid., p. 401.
7 Romans 1:20.
8 Joshua 2:6.
9 James 2:25.
10 Hebrews 11:31.
11 Blake, *Four Fold Vision.*
12 A.K. Coomaraswamy, *Hinduism and Buddhism,* (NY: Philosophical Library, 1943), p. 6.
13 Thomas Merton, *The New Man,* (NY: Bantam, 1981), p. 5.
14 *Beyond Ego: Transpersonal Dimensions in Psychology*, ed. Roger N. Walsh and Frances Vaughan, (Los Angeles: J.P. Tarcher, Inc., 1980), p. 45.
15 William Blake quoted in M. H. Abrams, *Natural Supernaturalism: Tradition and Revolution in Romantic Literature,* p. 375.
16 *The Marriage of Heaven and Hell; Proverbs of Hell.*
17 E. F. Schumaker, *A Guide for the Perplexed* (NY: Harper & Row, 1977), pp. 39, 42.
18 Ibid., p. 41.
19 *Nonduality*, p. 13.
20 Abrams, p. 377.
21 Ibid., p. 377.
22 Matthew 13:13.
23 Matthew 13:15.
24 St. Thomas Aquinas, quoted in Schumacher, p. 39.
25 St. Augustine, quoted in Schumacher, p. 47.

[26] Psalms 36:9.

[27] Transl. by Sargeant Winthrop (Albany, NY: State University of New York Press, 1994), 101:2-16.

[28] Denis Donoghue, *Speaking of Beauty.* (New Haven, CT: Yale University Press, 2003), pp. 59, 65.

[29] Abraham Cowley, "Beauty."

[30] Fred Hageneder, *The Meaning of Trees* (San Francisco: Chronicle Books, 2005), p. 6.

[31] *Perennial Philosophy*, p. 57.

[32] *The Erotic Phenomenon*, p. 2.

[33] Sutralamkara, quoted in *The Perennial Philosophy*, p. 127.

[34] John 14:16.

[35] "Concluding Unscientific Postscripts," tr. Swenson, D.F. (Princeton, NJ: Princeton University Press, 1941) p. 175.

[36] Blakney, p. 243.

[37] Abrams, p. 375.

[38] Thomas Traherne, quoted in *The Perennial Philosophy*, pp. 67-68.

[39] John 17:25.

[40] *Nonduality*, p. 211.

[41] John 17:21-23.

[42] John Dryden, "A Song for Saint Cecilia's Day," November 22, 1687.

[43] J.E. Berendth, Nada Brahma, *The World is Sound: Music and the Landscape of Consciousness* (Rochester, Vermont: Destiny Books, 1987), p. 91.

[44] *Mysticism*, p. 70.

[45] *Silent Fire: An Invitation to Western Mysticism*, edited by W.H. Capps and W. M. Wright, (San Francisco: Harper Row, 1978), pp. 91-93.

[46] Karl Marie Von Weber, quoted in Dorothy Retalack, *The Sound of Music and Plants* (Los Angeles, Calif.; DeVorss and Company Publishers, 1978), p. 68.

[47] *The Merchant of Venice*, Act V, Scene 1.

[48] George Hills, *The Fatal Curiosity*, Act I, Scene 2.

[49] Quoted in *Nada Brahma*, p. 90.

[50] Don Campbell, *The Mozart Effect* (NY: Avon Books, 1997).

[51] Quoted in *The Healing Energies of Music*, H.A. Lingerman, (Wheaton, IL: Theosophical Publishing House, 1983), p. 60.

[52] Samuel 16:15-23.

[53] Underhill, p. 78.

[54] *The Sound of Music and Plants*, pp. 20-23.

[55] *The Healing Energies of Music*, p. 59.

[56] Acts 17:28.

CHAPTER 14

Fire and the Reality of Symbolism

My nature is fire.
St. Catherine of Siena

Someday, after mastering the winds, the waves, the tides and
gravity, we shall harness for God the energies of love, and then,
for a second time in the history of the world,
man will have discovered fire.
Pierre Teilhard De Chardin

I have always been attracted to the study of symbolism;
would you explain what is its nature and purpose?
Symbolism simply defined is an object, a shape, or anything
taken to represent and to mean something else. Since symbols
are especially designed to convey inner and higher meanings
and truths they are employed extensively by the world religions
and various spiritual teachings. "If thou will know the invisible,
open thyne eye wide on the visible,"[1] says a Talmudic axiom.
Creation and every object in it reflects the mind of its Creator;
it is the natural and tangible sign of the inner and supernatural
realm.

I read in the *Confessions* the passage where St. Augustine
describes his vision, quoting St. Paul from Romans 1:20: "So
in the flash of a trembling glance it (mind) attained to that
which is. At that moment I saw your 'invisible nature un-
derstood through the things which are made'."[2]
The purpose of a symbol is to reveal relationships between different planes of reality and to present correspondences in the
manifold web of life between disparate phenomena and manifestations existing and sustained by virtue of the unity of the

universe. The root word itself, *uni versus*, means turned into one.

I ask myself how could a myth or a symbol be kept alive and perpetuated in religion, art, philosophy, literature and social institutions if there was not a vital cause and reason for believing it.
It is a way to remember the forgotten truth or like a nostalgia for the infinite.

"One could adduce an immense weight of testimony offered by human faith and wisdom proving that the invisible or spiritual order is analogous to the material order ... In the legendary Tabula Smaragdina there is the statement, "What is below is like what is above; what is above is like what is below." And the remark of Goethe, "What is within is also without."[3]

I'd like to quote this passage: "Symbolism is organized in its vast explanatory and creative function as a system of highly complex relations, one in which the dominant factor is always a polarity, linking the physical and the metaphysical worlds."[4] It agrees with you that the polar relation is also at the foundation of a symbol or myth.
The symbolic meaning of an object explains a multilevel reality and a deeper vision and perspective of life. It relates the material with the spiritual, the casual with the causal, the particular with the universal, the part with the whole, the immanent with the transcendent.

I am reminded of the Pauline sentence, *Per visibilia ad invisibilia* and the assertion of Sallust that "the world is a symbolic object."[5]

Thanks to symbolic insight and interpretation human experience on this earth is transformed into a transcendental act opening the door to the infinite side of life.

This quote refers to the metaphor but I think applies to a symbol:

> In the manner of a vibration spreading in infinitude from its center, metaphor is endowed with the capacity to situate the experience at the heart of a universe that it generates ... Far from referring back to an object that would be its cause, the poetic sign sets in motion an imaging activity that refers to no object in particular. The 'meaning' of the metaphor is that it does not 'mean' in any definite manner.[6]

Because there is not one thing separated from another as I AM present everywhere.

You told me that life is one, consciousness is one, energy is one. I found these observations also interesting: a symbol has the mission of transcending the limitations of this "fragment" which is the human being (or any of his concern), and of integrating this "fragment" into entities of wider scope: society, culture, the universe. Even if "an object transmuted into a symbol tends to unite with the All ... this union is not the same as a confusion, for the symbol does not restrict movement or circulation from one level to another and integrates all these levels and planes (of reality), but without fusing them – that is, without destroying them."[7]

I should add that the All, the macrocosm, is contained within the fragment because each fragment is the All in miniature or in a smaller scale as the microcosm.

Yet this world of ours is delusively experienced as a relative and phenomenal reality, and understood to consist of a collection of separate objects, including "me!"
The purpose of symbolism is to overcome that narrow and superficial consciousness.

It is interesting that the Greek Word *symbolon* (symbol) means that which brings together, that builds a bridge and unites, while the term *diabolos* (devil), from the same root word, signifies that which separates, divides, disintegrates.
When Adam sinned, he disintegrated human nature. Crumbling to pieces after the fall, it filled the earth with debris. Therefore people are at variance not only with each other, but also with themselves. My name is legion, for there are many of us, says the devil. People should *re-member* their divine origin and thus become again one instead of being *dis-membered.*

I am teaching you that the tendency of life is toward unity based on the principle of polarity, since no thing exists independently but only in relationship to others, and ultimately in relationship to the whole universe. An object perceived as a symbol presents to "those who have eyes to see" degrees of truth and dimensions of reality unknown to the human intellect alone.

Think how pregnant and meaningful something as simple as a flag, a number, a geometrical sign, or a flower can be when optical sight becomes spiritual vision.

I find it remarkable the use of the same symbol and its universal application by different people and traditions.

For instance, the sun represents one of the greatest attributes of a deity: he sees all and, as a consequence, knows all. In India, as Surya, it is the eye of Varuna; in Persia, it is the eye of Ahuramazda; in Greece, as Helios, the eye of Zeus (or of Uranus); in Egypt it is the eye of Ra, and in Islam, of Allah.

Among the flowers, the lotus, as a water lily, has been a sacred object for at least 5000 years. According to the writings of Mohammed, a lotus plant stands on the right hand of God in the seventh heaven. The ancient Egyptians dedicated the lotus to the god of the sun and adorned architectural column with a lotus-like motif. In India, images of Brahma show him sitting on a lotus, and in China, the goddess of mercy Quan Yin is standing in the center of a lotus. In yoga exercise, a body in the lotus position is said to resemble the shape of the lotus blossom. The Tibetan prayer chant, *"Om mani padme hum"* translates as "I salute the jewel in the heart of the lotus." The thousand-petalled lotus symbolizes the full expansion of all divine attributes in the flame of the heart. This realization of infinite potentialities is symbolically depicted with the lotus, rising from the mud, and the unfoldment of the flower on the surface of the water till it faces the light of the sun.

In Western culture, there is a similarity between the symbolism of the lotus and the rose. Both represent consummation, fulfillment and perfection. Associated to the rose are the center, the heart, the paradise of Dante, the beloved, Venus, the ascension. More precise meanings are derived from their color and the number of petals.

318

St. Rose of Viterbo, is the patron saint of florists. The rose is a universally adored flower and it has been used in pagan and secular rites and in Christian ceremonies. The word *rosa* is also related to rosary beads or "rosarium," and is closely identified with the Virgin Mary in church iconography. An important component of gothic cathedrals is a rose window, a large, circular window of stained glass with reference to Mary also known as *"rosa mystica"* and the rose of Sharon. Venus, the goddess of love and beauty was the source of the red rose. When she pricked herself on a thorn of a white rose, the blood from her finger dripped on its petals and stained them forever. In the language of flowers, roses suggest love and beauty. Robert Herrick wrote;

> Before man's fall the rose was born,
> St Ambrose says, without the thorn.[8]

Shakespeare mentions the rose at least sixty times in his works, and I'd like to quote the following:

Emilia:	Of all flow'rs
	Methinks a rose is best.
Woman:	Why, gentle madam?
Emilia:	It is the very emblem of a maid;
	For when the west wind courts her gently,
	How modestly she blows, and paints the sun
	With her chaste blushes!
	When the north comes near her,
	Rude and impatient, then, like chastity,
	She locks her beauties in her bud again,
	And leaves him to base briers.[9]

Likewise, as you quoted, the world itself is a symbolic object because of the polarity spirit - matter, as the physical world or Nature being the form or outer visible expression of the spirit which is incommensurable.

It is interesting that according to Coleridge, "The Mystics define beauty as the subjection of matter to spirit so as to be transformed into a symbol, in and through which the spirit reveals itself; and declare *that* the most beautiful, where the most obstacles to a full manifestation have been most perfectly overcome."[10]

In reality, life itself is beautiful because it is the a manifestation of the fire of love, and when the divine pattern is fully expressed you have the manifestation of perfect beauty. It is the human discord of thoughts and feelings that creates ugliness and deformity covering the original form.

What you referred to as the energy-veil.

Yes, and the purpose of a symbol is to help penetrate it.

For a modern poet, Arthur Symons, beauty is, indeed, a flame and the consummation of being:

> I am the torch, she saith, and what to me
> If the moth die of me? I am the flame
> Of Beauty, and I burn that all may see
> Beauty, and I have neither joy nor shame,
> But live with that clear life of perfect fire
> Which is to men the death of their desire.
>
> Her tragedy is that, being divine, she is not recognized in

the ordinary world of ours, and her devotees are not to
be found.

Yet now the day is darkened with eclipse:
Who is there lives for beauty? Still I am
The torch, but where's the moth that still dares die?[11]

It is a very appropriate image, the flame is in reality perfectly beautiful because it is all love.

I understand why even the physical fire is beautiful,
and I enjoy sitting in front of the fireplace watching it.
Which brings to my mind the goddess of the hearth Hestia.
The center of Greek life was the domestic hearth, also regarded as a sacrificial altar, and Hestia represented personal security and happiness, and the sacred duty of hospi-
tality. It is her glory that, alone of the great Olympians, she
never takes part in war or disputes, trying to preserve peace
among them. Moreover, she has always resisted every amo-
rous invitation offered her by the gods and she swore to remain a virgin forever. Universal reverence is paid Hestia
also for being the most charitable of all the Olympians, and
since she is the goddess of the hearth, in every private house
and city hall, suppliants would flee to her for protection. It
is interesting that the hearth is "A form of 'domestic sun', a
symbol of the home, of the conjunction of the masculine
principle (fire) with the feminine (the receptacle) and, consequently, of love."[12]

It is remarkable that Hestia retains the purity of her
divine attributes contrary to the decadence and moral degeneration of the pagan religion. She is worshipped in
Rome as the deity presiding over the public and private
hearth under the name of Vesta. A sacred fire, tended by six

virgin priestesses called Vestals, flamed in her temple. As the safety of the city was held to be connected with its conservation, the neglect of the virgins if they let it go out, was severely punished, and the fire was rekindled from the rays of the sun.

The various levels of universal life and all creation, from the highest to the lowest planes, are held together by the all-pervading flame and cohesive power of love in accord with the same cosmic rhythm which is the very heart-beat of the Creator. The symbol is an echo of that rhythm drawing the observer from the outer to the inner, from the many to the one, from the moment to eternity.

As an example, the notion of being lost in the labyrinth of this world may evoke and lead to the conviction that one must return to the "center," and that central point is the heart.

Which is the abode of your Presence in us.
In fact, every representation of the "center" has been connected with the heart, which was for the alchemists the image of the sun within man, as gold was the image of the sun within the earth.

The importance of love in the mystic doctrine of unity explains how love-symbolism came to be closely linked with heart-symbolism; for to love is to experience a deep feeling that begins and ends in the heart-center. At the same time it urges the lover, by magnetic attraction, toward the heart of the beloved because only in the fire of love, which abides in each heart as a flame, can the oneness of life be truly realized. In emblems the heart signifies love as the center of illumination and happiness, and this is why it is surmounted by flames, a cross, a fleur-de-lis, or a crown.

There are, and there can be, an endless variety of symbolic forms and expressions, even words and numbers are symbols, but now I want to mention that kind of imagery which is at the very core of the human condition. I am referring to that underlying desire present in every individual, of which he is most unaware, for the lost home, a nostalgia for his original abode, from where he wandered away yet carrying with him the deep longing to return.

Hence you have the persistent and interrelated symbols of life as a journey, a pilgrimage, and a quest.

I can understand it, in fact I have always been impressed by the idea that we are gods in exile, and this is proved by the sense that we are never truly "at home" in any place, no matter how wonderful and enjoyable the dwelling may temporarily be.

The feeling of restlessness and anxiety never leaves us, and from our scatteredness we are urged on to an unexplainable search to find or attain something that we have lost. The world literature is filled with the narratives of a quest of some kind, whether the unknown land, the hidden treasure, the pearl of great price, the golden fleece, the Grail, the Celestial city of Jerusalem. I assume that the tendency and the desire which draws the wayfarer along the road to his end – his goal – is planted in him by you.

Everyone is really seeking for Me no matter how he directs his actions, and there is a mutual longing for union. Remember the principle of polarity, and each one will feel it according to his capacity to love. One pole of the magnet cannot exist without the other and, thus be actively creating a circuit.

I need you as you need Me, it is Love calling to love and even if your disordered loves delay and interfere with My plan, ultimately no one can escape.

In the apocryphal *Acts of John* there is a hymn attributed to Jesus with these verses:

> I am a lamp to you who see me.
> I am a mirror to you who perceive me,
> I am a door to you who knock on me.
> I am a way to you, wayfarer.[13]

The same theme is echoed by the Mohammedan mystic Jalalu d'Din Rumi:

> No lover ever seeks union with his beloved,
> But his beloved is also seeking union with him...
> When the love of God arrives in thy heart,
> Without doubt God also feels love for thee.[14]

And Mechthild von Magdeburg heard the words: "I chased thee, for in this was my pleasure, I captured thee, for this was my desire; I bound thee, and I rejoice in thy bonds; I have wounded thee, that thou mayst be united to me. If I gave thee blows, it was that I might be possessed of thee."[15] You may recall also, among others, Lady Julian saying: "We may with reverence ask from our love all that we will, for our natural will is to have God, and God's good will is to have us."[16]

In modern times Francis Thompson has described in poignant verses the mystical love-chase with God as "this tremendous Lover" in His untiring pursuit to rescue the re-

bellious soul, "Unwilling to surrender, running away to hide from Him" down the nights and down the days:

> I fled Him down the arches of the years;
> I fled Him, down the labyrinthine ways
> Of my own mind, and in the mist of tears.
> I hid from Him, and under running laughter.

The hound of Heaven relentlessly chased him not only with "those strong feet" but with the reassuring voice: "All things betray thee, who betrayest Me."
And, finally, love conquered.

> All which thy child's mistake
> Fancies as lost, I have stored for thee at home:
> Rise, clasp My hand, and come![17]

Intimately connected to the above imagery is the irresistible craving felt in the heart, the magnetic attraction towards the other self or counterpart in whom the completeness of one's individuality can be found.

The male-female polarity! This is admirably represented in the *Divine Comedy* which is both a spiritual autobiography and a universal allegory of the inner life's story of Everyman.
The poem's beginning is very meaningful: "Midway in the journey of our life, I found myself in a dark wood, for the straight way was lost...I cannot rightly say how I entered it, I was so full of sleep at the moment I left the true way."[18]
As you know the source of his inspiration and redemption was his love for Beatrice whose memory, after her death at a young

age never left him. It was that deep feeling which kindled the "ardor of his longing" to join her in Heaven as described in his first book by the meaningful title "Vita Nuova, that is, New Life. Then, the author describes the frightening experiences of hell, "the lowest pit of the universe," the arduous climbing of the mountain of purgatory, and the gradual ascent of the heavenly spheres to the final vision of God.

Thus, he experienced the three stages of illumination, purification, and union which is "the end of all desires."

And Dante acknowledges Beatrice's intercession in his song of praise:

> "O lady in whom my hope has its strength and who for my salvation did endure to leave in Hell your footprints, of all those things which I have seen I recognize your grace and your goodness. It is you who have drawn me from bondage into liberty by all those ways, by every means you had in your power. Preserve in me your great munificence, so that my soul, which you have made whole, may be loosed from the body, pleasing unto you."[19]

I should mention that the name "Beatrice" means the "giver of blessings" with reference to My divine assistance.

I never clearly understood why Dante had to go through hell in his journey.
It was necessary in order to awaken from his state of "sleep" which caused him to be lost in the "dark wood." He had to face his own miscreation represented by the three beasts obstructing his way to freedom.

326

How meaningful the symbolism of the leopard, the lion and the she-wolf for the sinful disposition of the human being as lust, pride, and greed. According to an interpretation of the Scripture, it was pride that caused the Fall of Man. I can appreciate it because it is close to selfishness. I love these lines by Shakespeare:

> Man, proud man,
> Dress'd in a little brief authority,
> Most ignorant of what he's most assur'd-
> His glassy essence – like an angry ape,
> Plays such fantastic tricks before high heaven,
> As make the angels weep.[20]

You are learning to know who you are, your "glassy essence." That is, My image or reflection.

Yes, I am no more ignorant of what I should have been "most assured," who "I AM."
Now we discuss one of the most prominent symbols in the spiritual literature of every culture: the mystical, or human-divine, marriage.

I know that in the Old Testament it stands for the central image of the covenant between the Lord and Israel.
    The prophets depicted their oppressed and shattered land as a "woman" subject to a harsh treatment at the hands of the angry husband she has betrayed. Hosea's God speaks to the "children" of Israel divorcing their "female" land:

> Plead with your mother, plead

> for she is not my wife,
> and I am not her husband. (2:2)

Israelite women accused of adultery were punished by being stripped, stoned or burned. Therefore, the Almighty threatens the land with these words:

> I will strip her naked
> and expose her, as in the day she was born,
> and make her like a wilderness,
> and turn her into a parched land,
> and let her die of thirst. (2:3)

No pity is shown for the people because they are the children of whoredom; their mother "who conceived them has acted shamefully." (2:4-5) Female Israel has committed a grievous offense by seeking her lovers and their gifts. This is an allusion to the worship of other gods, like Baal which typifies fertility and the productive forces of nature.

> For she said, I will go after my lovers;
> they give me my bread and my water,
> my wool and my flax, my oil and my drink. (2:5)

But the gifts that she believes were from her lovers are from God. He promises to obstruct her way and prevent the accomplishment of her intent. He affirms his uncontested power and authority over her:

> No one shall rescue her out of my hand ...
> I will lay waste her vines and her fig trees,
> of which she said,

> 'these are my pay,
> which my lovers have given
>   me.'
> I will make them a forest,
> and the wild animals shall devour them. (2:12)

By seeking other gods she has been unfaithful and had forsaken him, and the consequences of her actions are unavoidable. "Therefore, I will take back my grain in its time, and my wine in its season." (2:9) Only after severe punishment comes the promise of reconciliation whereby the people of Israel are no longer illegitimate children because they have returned to his love.

> Hence, I will allure her, and speak tenderly to her...
> On that day, says the Lord, you will call me 'my husband.'
> (2:15-6)

Other prophets used the imagery of the divine-human marriage focusing on the adulterous wife and a passionately jealous husband. Jeremiah declares God's threat of permanent divorce because she not only turned away but forgot him "days without number." (2, 32)

> How well you direct your course to seek lovers! (2:33)
> ...You have played the whore with many lovers;
> and would you return to me? (3:1)

Her wicked actions have polluted the land, and committed all the evil possible; yet she refuses to be ashamed. As a result,

...the showers have been withheld,
and the spring rain has not come. (3:3)

However, God cannot be angry forever with her, and if she acknowledges of having been rebellious and deaf to his voice he will forgive her. And we hear again the everlasting call of love:

Return, O faithless children, says the Lord (3:14)

As the crisis in the land and her instability has worsened, Ezekiel depicts the city of Jerusalem in her lowest state of degradation; she is a woman unclean and corrupted from the very beginning.

As for your birth...you were not washed with water to
cleanse you,
nor rubbed with salt, nor wrapped in cloth. (16:4)

But God had compassion on her, bathed and anointed her with oil.

I spread the edge of my cloak over you
and covered your nakedness ... I pledged myself
to you and you became mine. (15:81)

Then she was adorned with jewels, with bracelets on her arms, and a crown upon her head:

You grew exceedingly beautiful, fit to be a queen.
Your fame spread among the nations on account of your
beauty. (16:14)

She felt glorified by the gifts and the splendor bestowed on her; pride took possession and she went astray.

> But you trusted in your beauty, and played the whore
> and lavished your whorings on any passer-by. (16:15)

Her prostitution was different from the usual, it was not for payment. She would squander her possessions and give them to her lovers inducing them, in her insatiable lust, to come and be with her. Because of her perseverance in her idolatrous and shameful ways she will be delivered into the hands of enemies. They will strip her, leave her naked and bare, stone and cut her to pieces with their swords.

> Since you have not remembered the days of your youth,
> but have enraged me with all these things; therefore, I
> have returned your deeds upon your head...I will deal
> with you as you have done, says the Lord. (16:43-59)

But there is always hope with the Eternal; the reconciliation with the restoration of the people of the land will eventually come.

> For I have no pleasure in the death of anyone. (18:32)

> Turn then and live...and never again open your mouth
> because of your
> shame, when I forgive all that you have done. (16:63)

The battered land and her people, portrayed as the idolatrous wife, has endured great tragedies because of their

transgression of the law, but they are reminded of the divine promise, that the door of redemption is always open.

> Do not fear, for you will not be ashamed; ... the disgrace of your widowhood you will Remember no more. For your Maker is your husband. ... the Lord has called you like a wife forsaken and grieved in spirit. ... I hid my face from you, But with everlasting love I will have compassion on you, says the Lord, your Redeemer ...You shall no more be termed Forsaken, and your land shall no more be termed Desolate; but you shall be called My Delight Is in Her, and your land Married; for the Lord delights in you, and your land shall be married. For as a young man marries a young woman, so shall your Creator marry you, and as the bridegroom rejoices over the bride, so shall your God rejoice over you." (Isaiah, 54:4-8; 62:4-5)

The allegorical description and the imagery of the unfaithful wife referring to an idolatrous people or land and of God as a jealous and often violent husband should not be interpreted as degrading the status and the identity of woman. It is ridiculous to think that these spiritual texts based on the sacred marriage legitimize or affirm spousal abuse or that the human husband has the same authority to act the way God is figuratively described.

The prophets belong to a patriarchal society and a male oriented view of God's nature and have to comply with it, if their voice is to be heard.

It is usually not heard anyway. But there is a book in the Bible close to the celebration of the feminine: the Song of Solomon or the Song of Songs.

332

In the form of dialogue it describes, like the prophets, the divine-human marriage but instead of the infidelity and waywardness of the bride she pours out one of the most exalted declarations of love and devotion to God in any literature. We are reminded of Psalm 42:

> As a deer pants for the flowing streams,
> so my soul longs for you, O God.
> My soul thirsts for God.

The first lines set the tone expressing her divine desire:

> Let him kiss me with the kisses of his mouth!
> For your love is better than wine,
> Your anointing oils are fragrant,
> Your name is perfume outflowing ...
> Draw me after you. (1,4)

The male lover cannot fail to respond because love attracts love.
Yes, the human love for God is of the same nature as the love coming from God according to the principle of polarity, and love reveals beauty.

> Ah, you are beautiful, my love;
> ah, you are beautiful;
> your eyes are doves. (1,15)

The doves partake of the symbolism of love associated with goddesses like Ishtar and Venus; also the Holy Ghost is depicted in the shape of a dove which

over the bent
World broods with warm breast and with ah!
Bright wings.

The two characters stay the same, with no plot or logical sequence, voicing words of praise and admiration to each other.

Like the lily among thorns
so is my love among maidens.

She echoes his words,

As an apple tree among the trees of the wood,
so is my beloved among young men. (2:2-3)

As the needle of the compass to Polaris, the north star, the flame in the heart kindled by God turns to him as the only desirable and ultimate aim, and the bride knows it. Three times in the Song she acknowledges that they belong to each other. Her words, a revelation in the religion of love.

My beloved is mine and I am his. (2:16)
I am my beloved's and my beloved is mine. (6:3)
I am my beloved and his desire is for me. (7:10)

He accepts emphatically her love and returns it with burning apostrophes:

You have ravished my heart, my sister, my bride,
You have ravished my heart with a glance of your eyes.
(4,3)

> How sweet is your love, my sister, my bride!
> how much better is your love than wine,
> and the fragrance of your oils than any spice! (4,10)

The poem gives us the vision of an uncompromising mutual passion that in spite of its intensity does not perish because it is divine. She praises him as if he were a statue that elicits worship:

> My beloved is all radiant and beauteous
> ... His hand is the finest gold;
> ... The body is ivory overlaid with sapphires.
> His legs are alabaster column. (5:11-15)

And in his eyes the bride looks like a goddess:

> Who is she that comes forth like the dawn,
> fair as the moon, bright as the sun
> mighty as an army with banners? (6, 10)
> My dove, my perfect one, is the only one. (6,3)
> You are all beautiful, my love;
> There is no flaw in you. (4,7)

But she is still in a human form and the intensity of her all-consuming desire causes her to plead:

> Set me as a seal upon your heart,
> ... for love is strong as death,
> passion fierce as the grave.
> Its flashes are tongues of fire,
> a raging flame. (8:6)

The mystics speak of being "wounded" by the divine lover with a flaming ray of light, hence the image of the pierced heart; however, its effect is most sweet and they pray not to be healed. The poem ends with the celebration of love:

> Many waters cannot quench love,
> neither can floods drown it.
> If one offered for love
> all the wealth of his house,
> it would be utterly scorned. (8:7)

The Song of Songs has had a bewildering history and it has always been subject to controversy. It is not a surprise considering its erotic language and its apparently inappropriate setting in the Bible between the pessimistic tone of the book of Ecclesiastes and the exalted prophecies of Isaiah.

It is composed of merely eight chapters of lyrics, but "Only a work so human and so supernal, so simple and so timeless, so curiously local and so deeply universal, could survive the wear of scholarly dialectics, the embattled exegeses, the fiercely opposed interpretations."

The symbolic reading is the oldest and this explains its inclusion in the Sacred Scripture; however, according to contemporary scholarship that would be "the most ingenuous and implausible" for it is interpreted as "a passionately living, frankly sexual poem."[21]

As you have explained, "As a man is, So he sees," "As the eye, Such the object."

Some commentators have attempted to bring the erotic and the spiritual interpretations together by mixing them, but it is a mistake to read the Song on both levels.

One can choose to enjoy the verses literally as expressions of sexual love, or be inspired by their divine longing for God, but I don't see how they can be joined.
It should be remarked that throughout the whole poem the emphasis is on each lover's yearning for a beloved who is always out of reach and inaccessible. There is never the least sign or mention, in the mutual passion and incandescent exchanges of the two protagonists, of the consummation of their love.

It was included in the Bible because from the beginning was interpreted figuratively; the woman, whose name is Shulamite, was understood to be the image of the Shekinah, Wisdom or Torah which are the feminine aspect or bride of God. For other rabbis the book expresses the love relationship between Yahweh and Israel as depicted by the Prophets. Rabbi Akiba revered it as "the Holy of Holies of Scripture."[22] The Fathers of the Church, from Origen to St. Augustine, established the allegory that the lover was Christ and the beloved either the Church or a human being.

The same imagery of mystical marriage is also prevalent in the New Testament.
It is used by John the Baptist: "He who has the bride is the bridegroom. The friend of the bridegroom, who stands and hears him, rejoices greatly at the bridegroom's voice." (John 3:29).

The Kingdom of heaven is compared to ten bridesmaids who went to meet the bridegroom for the wedding banquet. (Matthew 25:10) When Jesus was asked why his disciples did not fast, he replied: "The wedding guests cannot mourn as long as the bridegroom is with them, can

they? The days will come when the bridegroom is taken away from them, and then they will fast. (Matthew 9:15)

The image reaches its culmination in the Book of Revelation where the holy city descends from heaven "prepared as a bride adorned for her husband." (21:2) The final redemption of humanity is symbolized as a mystical marriage, "The Spirit and the bride say, 'Come'." (22:17) This reminds me of Dante's vision,

> In form then of a pure white rose
> The saintly host was shown to me
> Which with his own blood Christ made his bride.[23]

According to an old tradition Jesus' words on the cross *"consummatum est"*[24] signified that Christ mounted the cross as a bed on which to consummate the marriage with humanity inaugurated at the Incarnation, in the supreme act of sacrifice which both certified and prefigured His apocalyptic marriage at the end of time.[25]

It seems that the imagery of human love sanctified in marriage would be the least inadequate, because of the limitations of your language, to express a transcendent event and make it understandable by means of common experience. Then, as I mentioned, everyone will comprehend it according to his level of consciousness.

It has always been a favorite with Christian mystics, and some of them wrote commentaries on the Song of Songs. I should mention that consecrated nuns are "the spouses of Christ," and priests consider the Church their bride.

Those who deplore the writings of the mystics as liable to suspicion of eroticism or judge it as sublimated sexual love should be mindful of the words of St. Teresa of Avila: "Oh! May God help us! What great misery is ours! Like those poisonous animals that whatever they eat becomes poisonous also, the same is with us."[26]

This remark finds an echo in the passage of a renowned student of mysticism: "The great saints who adopted and elaborated this symbolism, applying it to their pure and ardent passion for the Absolute, were destitute of the prurient imagination which their modern commentators too often possess. They were essentially pure of heart; and when they 'saw God' they were so far from confusing that unearthly vision with the products of morbid sexuality, that the dangerous nature of the imagery which they employed did not occur to them. The knew by experience the unique nature of spiritual love: and no one can know anything about it in any other way."[27]

Another contemporary author writes:

Orthodox psychology tends smugly to dismiss such language as the product of aberrant minds whose main trouble was repressed sex, causing a regression to infantile behavior. But conventional psychological interpretations could be wrong. In an ironic turn of events, a physical linkage between sexual and spiritual experience is emerging which promises a major upheaval in Western psychology. From this emerging view, *sexuality is really unexpressed or unfulfilled religious experience.*"

And he adds: "Notice that term: *religious experience.* The common element between it and sexual experience is consciousness."[28]

Your author is right; consciousness is the key to the under-standing of life, whether mineral, vegetable, animal, human or divine. Those who have attained a higher level of contempla-tion experience the reality of love instead of a "pale show." But, unfortunately the masses, and even most psychologists, are "pathetically ignorant" of it.[29]

From their height of vision the mystics use words and sym-bols trying to convey hints and a glimpse of the transcen-dent blessing they were privileged to receive. St. Bernard is a typical example of "sensuous imagery" in his Sermons on the *Song of Songs*:

> "Let Him kiss me with the kisses of His mouth!" Who is it speaks these words? It is the Bride. Who is the Bride? It is the Soul thirsting for God ... She who asks this is held by the bond of love to him from whom she asks it. Of all the sentiments of nature this of love is the most excellent, especially when it is rendered back to Him who is the principle and fountain of it – that is, God. Nor are there found any expression equally sweet to signify the mutual affection between the Word of God and the soul as those of Bridegroom and of Bride ... What other bond or con-straining force do you seek for between spouses than to be loved and to love? ... Love is sufficient by itself, it pleases by itself, and for its own sake. It is itself a merit, and itself its own recompense. Love seeks neither cause nor fruit beyond itself. Its fruit is its use. I love because I love; I love that I may love. Love, then, is a great reality. It is the only one of all the movements, feelings, and af-fections of the soul in which the creature is able to re-spond to its Creator, though not upon equal terms, and

to repay like with like ... when God loves, He desires naught else than to be loved, knowing that those who love Him become blessed by their love itself ... Love that is pure is not mercenary; it does not draw strength from hope, nor is it weakened by distrust. This is the love of the Bride, because all that she is is only love. The very being of the Bride and her only hope is love. In this the Bride abounds; with this the Bridegroom is content. He seeks for nothing else; she has nothing else. Thence it is that He is the Bridegroom and she is Bride. [30]

He warns us to "Take heed that you bring chaste ears to this discourse of love; and when you think of these two lovers, remember always that not a man and a woman are to be thought of, but the Word of God and a soul. And if I shall speak of Christ and the Church, the sense is the same."[31] According to St. Bernard the "Mystic Kiss" signifies the inpouring of the Holy Spirit in his threefold aspect as the fire breath of God giving us its heavenly blessings.

These variations on the theme of love, of which our author is truly an expert, using the symbol image of a wedded pair, can be applied to the principle of polarity.

You are right; he continues: "The Bridegroom's love, or rather the Bridegroom who is Love, requires only love in return and faithfulness. Let it then be permitted to the Bride beloved to love in return. How could the Bride not love, she who is the Bride of Love? How could Love not be loved?"[32]

But, unfortunately, that is what happened, and it is hard, very hard for Me to believe that mankind has done such a thing.

As the prophet Jeremiah proclaimed, "Be appalled, O heavens, at this, be shocked, be utterly desolate, says the Lord, for my people have committed two evils: they have forsaken me, the fountain of living water and dug out cisterns for themselves crackled cisterns that can hold no water."[33] But how can we love you as you love us? You who are Love itself?

I will answer with the words of St. Bernard: "Although, being a creature, she (the Bride) loves less, because she is less; nevertheless if she loves with her whole self, nothing is wanting where all is given."

How profound and sublime the truth of this last sentence! That's really the key to the fullness of life and perfect happiness.

"Happy the soul to which is granted to experience the embracement of such sweetness, which is nought else than a love holy and chaste; a love sweet and delightful; a love as serene as it is sincere; a love mutual, intimate, powerful, which not in one flesh, but in one spirit joins together two, and makes them no more two, but one."[34] And this is the only way by which the desire for love will find its perfect fulfillment.

I beg you to tell me, what to do in order to have that divine experience.

Ask and you shall receive. Ask for the fire of My love to fill you with it, ask for My forgiving flame clothed in the color violet to purify your body and illumine your mind. And it will set you eternally free from the shadows of human creations.

How do I know when I will be perfected and become a being of love alone?

I answer you again in St. Bernard's words: "When the Lord comes as a consuming fire and His Presence is understood in the power by which the soul is changed and in the love by which it is inflamed; when all stain of sin and rust of vices have been consumed in that fire."

And these are a few of the expressions which fill his pages as he describes the experience of the mystical marriage of the soul with God: "an inpouring of the sweetness of holy love;" "a virtue which changes the heart, and a love which fires it;" "an inpoured savor of heavenly sweetness;" "a taste of the Presence of God;" "the soul is inwardly embraced;" "sweetly refreshed with delicious love;" "experiences joy ineffable."[35] These are some of the effects of the union which is a prelude to the ascension by the fire of My Love.

I know that when you and the mystics speak of the fire of divine love it is not a figurative expression but the highest and ultimate reality. I learned that physical fire has always been a symbol of central importance for its rich association with earthly life and what lies beyond. As ancient peoples settled into agricultural village life, fire, as representative of the sun, became a fundamental element in their religions. There are many rites in which torches, bonfires, and burning embers are believed to be endowed with the power to stimulate the growth of cornfields and to promote health in man and animals. The Celts' early summer festivals involved kindling a fire and dancing sun-wise around it; since contact with the flame was thought to further health and fertility, people drove their cattle through the fire or between two fires, and they themselves darted through it.

Aspects of fire-festivals persist today in bonfires, fireworks, and the illuminated Christmas tree. Two expla-

nations are given for it: one purports that they function as imitative magic in order to assure the supply of light and heat from the sun. The other is the view that their aim is the prevention and the protection from the forces of evil in the understanding that light is the annihilation of darkness.

However, these two hypotheses can be considered complementary; the great power and the fiery energy of the sun are tantamount to victory over the shadows of negative forces. The fire as a means of purification is considered the necessary sacrificial means of achieving the sun's triumph and, consequently, well-being The Chinese, in their solar rites, utilize a tablet of red jade which symbolizes the element of fire. In Egyptian hieroglyphics, fire is also related to the solar-symbolism of the flame as spiritual energy bestowing power and authority. The upward rush of fire suggested to the Zoroastrians that it was the lightest, most spiritual of the other elements, air, water, and earth, and represented their Deity. The perpetual altar flame signified to the worshipers the trinity of life, light, love, imparted by the supreme Source, and in many faiths a candle or lamp stands for the very presence of the Godhead whose nature is, in reality, fire or light which is its radiation. For the Greeks the torch is a symbol of the continuity of noble human effort, a secular, collective immortality achieved when, as in a relay race, outstanding individuals passed on their gifts to others. The torch also occurs in many allegories as the emblem of truth.

Unfortunately, it is difficult for the average person to understand the meaning of myths and symbols, and they are, thus, deprived of the riches that they contain.

My favorite mythical character, besides Hercules, is the culture god Prometheus, who went up to heaven to light a torch and bring the fire to mankind. He is considered the great benefactor and supreme hero, being responsible for the presence of fire on earth, and is the patron of all the arts and sciences.

I like also the story of the goddess Demeter who went in disguise to the house of Metaneira, who asked her to nurse the child "whom the gods gave me late in life, fulfilling my desperate hopes and endless prayers." Demeter accepted the request and with her immortal hands would take the child to her breast and nursed him. On being nourished, not on mortal food but by the divine ambrosia, he grew like a god. At night she enfolded him in the power of her sacred fire, without the knowledge of his parents. And she would have made him immortal if the mother had not discovered what was happening. Metaneira in her lack of understanding was terrified, and cried out in her agony, "My child, this stranger buries you within the blazing fire to my anguish and grievous pain." As a consequence the goddess impatiently snatched the child from the fire and with a feeling of strong displeasure said, "Mortals are ignorant and stupid for they cannot foresee the fate both good and bad that is in store for them. Thus, you in your foolishness have done something that cannot be remedied. I would have made your dear child immortal and never to grow old all his days, and I granted him imperishable honor; but now, as it is, he will not be able to escape death and the Fates. Yet everlasting privilege will always be his because he has lain on my knees and slept in my arms." Then the goddess revealed herself in all her shining beauty and glory, filling the house with her light. After she disappeared from the room, the

mother was crushed and kept crying for a long time for the loss of the divine blessings.[36]

How often people, in their ignorance, doubt and fear, interfere with the fulfillment of the divine plan because they misconstrue events and circumstances in their lives and prevent, by their erroneous judgment of external appearances, the greater good intended for them. Human beings have almost entirely forgotten the true nature of the inner fire, which is the very life, light, and love of the Creator.

In Christianity there is a recognition of the Fire that descended on Pentecost which is called the Holy Spirit, but how many pray to it to come again to purify and free their lives from all limitations?

I am always pouring it, like the sun, otherwise mankind and all of creation could not survive. But who recognizes and accepts it as the source of every good thing? Those who open themselves to it will receive its infinite blessings because it contains all that one could ever desire, and infinitely more.

Fire is the metaphysical foundation of the secret practice of the alchemists, for it is the element which operates in the center of all things as a unifying and cohesive factor.

Because it is love. In fact, they referred to it with the emblematic name of the Philosopher's Stone, finding which was their central aim, the Magnum Opus (Great Work), because it possessed the power to transmute the baser metals into pure gold. They attributed the value of gold to the fact that it is a receptacle for the fire from the sun: according to alchemy, the quintessence of gold is fire, that is, the flame of that color.

The Philosopher's Stone symbolizes the principle of transmutation by means of the inner fire of the lower or animal nature of man into his spiritual or divine.

"In Christian alchemy the Philosopher's Stone was held to correspond to Christ, the Messiah of Nature, who has the apocalyptic function of restoring both fallen and divided man and the disintegrated world to the perfection of their original unity."[37]

I can see again the operation of the principle of polarity. As the occult work *Mysterium Magnum* states, "No thing can rest in itself, unless it returns into the One out of which it has come."[38]

Also in Hinduism the fire element has a prominent role. The god Vama tells Naciketas the secret of the fire that leads to heaven, a fire that can be referred to either as a ritual fire or a mystical fire produced by *tapas (ascesis)*. This fire, he explains, is the bridge to the supreme Brahman, the image of the bridge signifying passage from one mode of being to another.[39]

According to a method of yogic meditation, one concentrates on the fire before him, then he visualizes and feels his body as if made of fire at one with the sun and with all manifestation that fire takes, from stars and lightning to the infinitesimal spark. He unifies them into one, all-pervading, all-vivifying element and realizes universal life and every form of existence in it as the action of fire.

Thus, the meditation becomes an instrument for penetrating into the essence of life behind the phenomenal veil, leading to wholeness and mastery by absorbing and blending with the cosmic fire.

One becomes what he meditates on. Fire being the highest vibratory action is master over all the energy and substance in the universe; and since the nature of love is fire, you see the process of purification and transformation leading to union with the divine Reality.

However, fire is also associated with natural disasters like forest fire, volcanic eruptions, and predictions of world cataclysms are not unfamiliar to many, in fact it is an accepted subject of our belief system. For instance, St. Peter wrote in his letter, "But the day of the Lord will come like a thief, and the elements will be dissolved with fire, the earth and everything that is done on it will be disclosed, the heavens will be set ablaze and dissolved, and the elements will melt with fire."[40]

Considering the destructive trend and immoral conditions of our society there are those who honestly admit that people deserve as their just reward, either through personal or planetary disaster, the cause – effect sequences which they have set in motion.

The nature of divine love is such as to always provide the way and means for mankind to turn away from their wrong doing before it is too late, and give them the opportunity to face the Light.

"When sin increased, grace abounded all the more."[41]

In order to prevent people from destroying themselves, the Earth is given at this time the greatest possible assistance as ever before. The planet is entering into its final cycle and a new dispensation has been released to awaken as many as possible to their responsibility to life.

What do you mean by final cycle?

As we continue our dialogue, and the subject becomes more complex, remember the words of Francis Bacon: "The universe is not to be narrowed down to the limits of our own understanding, which has been the practice up to now, but our understanding must be stretched and enlarged to take in the image of the universe as it is discovered."[42]

I will think about them as I keep listening to you.

About your question, it would take too long to explain that subject in detail, and it is not necessary for you now.

But you should know that planets, solar systems, and universes move through cosmic cycles of time of different length as the Infinite Ground, which underlies all that is or can ever be, manifests itself by the interplay of spirit and matter.

"There are cycles in orderly repetition in ever-ascending spiral, under definite laws. The same quality in tone will be called forth by the spirit as it indwells the form of matter, but the key will ascend by gradual degrees. It is similar to the effect produced in striking the same note in different octaves, beginning at the base."[43]

What is the new dispensation?

This is the best of time although it appears to be the worse, because those who are sincerely seeking the truth may learn the instructions on the "I AM" Presence as God individualized, how to activate the sacred fire of love, and attain the ascension which is the purpose of human embodiment.

Anyone can complete the journey on the earth if he or she so desires and is determined enough to make the necessary effort. If the individual will accept the teaching of the Ascended Beings who are humanity's elder brothers and sisters, and turn his attention to Me, with the call to be free from his limitations, by the practice of the Sacred Fire, and the creative word "I AM," I will raise him into the ascension at the close of this embodiment by the magnetic power of My love.

Where our attention is, our life energy flows and we become one with its object.
Yes, the attention directs your energy, and if you turn it to your Source of life, I will fill you with the fire of My love which will purify you as it dissolves your Karmic debts and sets you free from the wheel of birth and rebirth. When you understand the meaning of the word "Presence," and realize that it is your true Self within and above you, ever waiting to give you the Flame of its love and its very Being to you, the door is wide open to your ascension.

Is the ascension accomplished after we die?
No one can die.

I mean after we leave our physical garment?
No, when you ascend, you overcome so-called death, which was never intended to manifest and never part of the divine plan.

It is the consequence of our separation from our Source: how absurd to think that life and death are interdependent and one cannot be without the other.
The concoctions of the human intellect are legion and they make a travesty of life. If death were a natural law, why does everyone dread it, even animals? The very repulsion in mankind, and their desire to prevent it as much as they can, should prove that it is a fallacy, and it is not part of God's creation.

I read this passage:

> "The instinct of self-preservation has its roots in our in-nate fear of death ... which is a part of the Great Illusion, and only exists because of the veils we have gathered around ourselves."[44] And I am reminded of the Scriptural statements, "death came through sin."[45] "For the wages of sin is death."[46] Then we have the glorious promise: "Death will be no more; mourning and crying and pain will be no more."[47]

There is an ancient saying that sleep is the sister of death.
It is true, most people do not realize that every night, while the body sleeps, they die to the physical plane and are alive and functioning elsewhere.

Alice Bailey agrees with you: "The process of daily sleep and of occasional dying are identical, with the one difference that in sleep the magnetic thread, or current of energy, along which the life force streams, is preserved intact, and constitutes the path of return to the body. In death, this life thread is broken or snapped."[48]
It is done by Me when one's life is over but the individual is more alive than before, and free, at least for awhile, from the cage of his physical body.

I think of the analogy of a diving suit which one wears to explore the depth of the ocean.
Death is the entrance into fuller life and it should be a cause of rejoicing instead of grief, because you live in the realms of light.

I assume you are referring to those who have lived a decent life; what about the others?
Those who pass away with evil tendencies or enslaved to vicious habits are in a state of great distress because they are facing their own demons and their cravings are now experienced with more intensity without the possibility of gratification by the physical senses.

This is like hell.
You are right, suffering also in the afterlife is not the result of divine judgment, it is self-created under the action of the impersonal Law of cause and effect. Those people are earthbound and, since they do not have a physical body, they try to gratify their desires through those who have similar habits.

Like attracts like.
I will tell you more about it later on. However, everyone is continually helped to rise out of his predicament and distress, in order to learn the lessons which life teaches, so that eventually progress will be made toward the goal of human existence on this Earth.

The individual must come back into earthly existence but I think I am ready to cross over to the other bank of the turbulent river of death and rebirth.
I have been waiting a very long time for the hour of your decision.

Will you provide for me the chariot of fire in order to ascend?
Because of My Mercy, under the new dispensation it will not be necessary to purify completely the fleshly body which can be

done by cremation. The understanding of My Presence as your I AM Self and the use of the fire of My love will enable you to consume and transform all the negative energy accumulated from the past and present; and you are gradually raised in vibratory action as the light within you expands. Then, at the end of your earthly life I will pick you up and you will never forget in all eternity the ecstasy of the moment when we become one.

It could have been accomplished long before and without the limitations and distress of the centuries past. However, I should be grateful for your limitless patience and ceaseless giving of yourself until the walls of selfishness were broken down and I was willing to respond to the call of your love.

Remember that I long for the purification and restoration of My creation. Try to follow My instructions so that you will know the truth about yourself and your relation to the rest of the universe and how to cooperate with the Law of Love. Of fundamental importance is the understanding that this inner fire, being love, is the Source of all creativity and genius. On the physical level it forms a new body for the incoming soul by the reproductive process; it illumines the mind, and enables the humanist, the scientist, and the philosopher to give their contributions to humanity.

When it flows through the heart and the solar plexus, the creative fire finds expression in works of art, spiritual aspirations, and service to others, carrying the individual to higher realms of consciousness. However, when the fire of life is perverted, especially through the misuse of sexual energy, the consequences are not only the loss of the life-force and the enslavement to the senses, but the degradation and distortion pervading every field of human activity and creativity.

As you begin to understand, things do not exist independently; in fact, they are nothing in themselves as their being and nature, and are sustained in their mutual interactions by My love. I explained to you that relationship is based on polarity, which is the fundamental principle of all manifestation originating from the Father-Mother God. This is the process in which all beings and things participate and to which he who is wise attunes himself in order to realize wholeness, happiness, and immortality.

You speak of your nature as being the fire of love. I understand that it gives us the power not only to be free from our limitations but we can overcome the last enemy. I seem to hear the words,

> "So shalt thou feed on death, that feeds on men,
> And death once dead, there's no more dying then.[49]

The fire of which I speak corresponds to the Holy Spirit of the Christians, the *prana* of the Hindus, and the life-breath of ch'i in Taoism. Without this vital force that animates and energizes it, the body would merely be a corpse.

I would like to also quote another of my favorite poets on the same theme whose message fills me with boundless gratitude to our infinite Source of love, wisdom, and power.

> That light whose smile kindles the universe,
> That Beauty in which all things work and move,
> That Benediction which the eclipsing Curse
> Of birth can quench not, that sustaining Love
> Which, through the web of being blindly wove

> By man and beast and earth and air and sea,
> Burns bright or dim, as each are mirrors of
> The fire for which all thirst, now beams on me,
> Consuming the last cloud of cold mortality.[50]

Your poet also says:

> ... the pure spirit shall flow
> Back to the burning fountain whence it came,
> A portion of the Eternal.[51]

Ah! I suddenly see the significance of his wonderful image of a "burning fountain"! It unites fire and water in an eternal wholeness as symbols and instruments of purification. More often in the Christian literature one hears about the "water of life." But the references to fire in the Bible are so numerous they fill a book, from the "burning bush" encountered by Moses to the descent of the Holy Spirit like "cloven tongues of fire," from "The Lord your God is a consuming fire" and "The Lord will come in fire ... For by fire will the Lord execute judgment" to "The Lord Jesus shall be revealed from heaven with his mighty angels in flaming fire."[52]

I find also interesting that for the early Christians the phoenix was the symbol of resurrection and immortality. It is a legendary bird about the size of an eagle, graced with certain features of the pheasant. After living five hundred years (or one thousand according to different versions), as death draws near, the phoenix builds itself a nest of fragrant wood and resins and exposes itself to the full force of the sun's rays until the nest burns as a funeral pyre. Consumed in the flames, the bird rises anew from its own

ashes and, on the third day, flies off to live for another five hundred years. This can be interpreted as referring to reincarnation.

It is very meaningful, but people are ignorant of the sacred fire and, therefore, lack the knowledge not only of what love is, but how to love. It is the fire of creation and it has the power to purify, illumine, heal, and transform every type of energy and raise it from the lower to the higher level of perfection. It is the power by which so-called miracles are done.

Why "so-called?"

Because, what people refer to as miracles are, in reality, the operation of the Law of Love. Therefore, there is nothing supernatural, but mankind has fallen even below what is natural. They must learn what the sacred fire of love is or they will perish, destroyed by the reaction of their own evil.

In this context I'd like to quote the descriptions from four different periods in the literature of mysticism, fourth, fourteenth, seventeenth, and twentieth centuries, by those who had the actual experience of the divine fire. They make one feel how real and sublime true love is.

> 1. "Of Him alone [the fire of the Holy Spirit] it is said that it is Your 'gift' (Acts 2:38). It is in Your gift that we find our rest. It is in Him that we enjoy You. Where we rest, there is our place. Love lifts us up toward that place; and 'Your good Spirit' (Psalms 142:10) raises 'our lowliness from the gates of death.' (Psalms 9:15) In a good will is our peace. A body tends toward its proper place by its own weight. A weight does not tend only downward, but moves toward its own place. A stone falls, fire rises. Each

thing acts according to its weight, seeking the place where it belongs. Oil poured under the water comes up to the surface above the water; water poured on oil sinks under the oil. Things which are not in their own place are restless. Once they are where they are intended, they are at rest. Love is my weight. Wherever I go, love is carrying me. By the gift of Your Holy Spirit we are set aflame and borne aloft, and the fire within us carries us upwards. We climb the 'ladder which is in our heart,' (Psalms 83:6) as we sing the canticle of the ascension. It is your fire, your sweet fire, that sets us aflame and carries us upwards. For we are raised "to the peace of the heavenly Jerusalem"(Psalms 121: 6), and we will desire nothing more than to dwell there forever."[53]

2. Oh eternal Trinity, fire and abyss of love, dissolve this very day the cloud of my body! I am driven to desire, in the knowledge of yourself that you have given me in your truth, to leave behind the weight of this body of mine and give my life for the glory and praise of your name. For by the light of understanding within your light I have tasted and see your depth, eternal Trinity, and the beauty of your creation. Then, when I considered myself in you, I saw that I am your image.

O abyss! O eternal Godhead! O deep sea! What more could you have given me than the gift of your very self? You are a fire always burning but never consuming; you are a fire consuming in your ardor all the soul's selfish love; you are a fire lifting all coldness and giving light. In your light you have made me know your truth: You are that light beyond all light who gives the mind's eye supernatural light in such fullness and perfection that you bring clarity even to the light of faith. In that faith I see that my soul has life, and in that light receives you who are Light ...

O eternal God, light surpassing all other light because all light comes forth from you! O fire surpassing every fire because you alone are the fire that burns without consuming! You consume whatever sin and selfishness you find in the soul. Yet your consuming does not distress the soul but enriches her with insatiable love, for though you satisfy her she is never sated but longs for you constantly. The more she possesses you the more she seeks you, and the more she seeks you the more she finds and enjoys you, high eternal fire, abyss of love![54]

3. From about half past ten in the evening to
about half an hour after midnight.
    Fire.
God of Abraham, God of Isaac, God of Jacob,
Absolute certainty: beyond reason. Joy. Peace.
Forgetfulness of the world and everything but God.
The world has not known thee, but I have known thee.
Joy! Joy! Joy! Tears of joy![55]

4. All at once, without warning of any kind, I found myself wrapped in a flame-colored cloud. For an instant I thought of fire, an immense conflagration somewhere close by in that great city; the next, I knew that the fire was within myself. Directly afterward there came upon me a sense of exultation, of immense joyousness accompanied or immediately followed by an intellectual illumi-

nation impossible to describe. Among other things, I did not merely come to believe, but I saw that the universe is not composed of dead matter, but is, on the contrary, a living Presence; I became conscious in myself of eternal life. It was not a conviction that I would have eternal life, but a consciousness that I possessed eternal life then; I saw that all men are immortal; that the cosmic order is such that without any peradventure all things work together for the good of each and all; that the foundation principle of the world, of all the worlds, is what we call love, and that the happiness of each and all is in the long run absolutely certain. The vision lasted a few seconds and was gone; but the memory of it and the sense of the reality of what it taught has remained during the quarter of a century which has since elapsed. I knew that what the vision showed was true. I had attained to a point of view from which I saw that it must be true. That view, that conviction, I may say that consciousness, has never, even during periods of the deepest depression, been lost."[56]

I have a deeper understanding that there is no substitute for the fire of your love, which is what everyone really desires and is seeking, and I realize that lack of anything good and beautiful in life is the lack of the sacred fire.
Your authors agree with me on the nature of love as fire.

All the mystics do because they know you by personal experience.
You see, beautifully described, the nature of love as the magnetic force that draws everything to its proper place.

This is how Scotus Erigena explains the unifying and cohesive power of love: "Amor is the bond and chain which joins together all things in the Universe in an ineffable friendship and an insoluble unity."[57]

For the individual, the perfect state is its original home, and the natural tendency is to return there, raised by the magnetic power of My love.

Unfortunately, we interfere with it and deviate from the true way; and although you continue to pour the fire of your love into us, instead of using it creatively, we willfully or unintentionally misuse and dissipate it, creating havoc in our world.

Since I have revealed Myself to you, you can expand and raise the flame in your heart, just by giving your attention and love to Me. This is not a strenuous practice.

It sounds so simple — and safe!

It is. Allowing the flow of your life-force to reach up to Me, returning it to complete the circuit of love, is the greatest joy you will ever know. And this is not the ephemeral and passing sensations the outer world offers, which are here today and gone tomorrow. The love I pour forth is always expanding with every heart-beat and is everlasting. No one can take it away from you, and where that love is, there is freedom and happiness.

But I don't have any worthy feeling to give to you, only a smoldering fire with no warmth or light.

You can ask for the flame of My love and you will receive it without any limit, for I AM infinite. But "ask it of grace, not of doctrine; of desire, not of intellect; of the fervor of prayer, not of the teachings of the schools; of the Bridegroom, not of the

Master; of God, not of man; not of illumination, but of that Fire which enflames all and wraps you in God with great sweetness and most ardent love. The which Fire most truly is God."[58]

Call to Me to fill you with My forgiving flame of love, peace, and whatever you need. Ask for it in My name, "I AM," and you will receive more than you may ever desire. Repeat often: "I AM the divine fire of love and peace. I AM the protection and freedom of God. I AM the flame of love and peace at all times. I AM the healing flame of all-forgiving love."

Try it, knowing that "I AM" is the infinite power that created the universe, and you will know what My love can do for you and through you. A long time ago I challenged everyone to *prove* Me, and I promised to open the windows of heaven and pour out such a blessing that there shall not be room to receive it.

Yes, it is in the Scripture but how many are aware of it and of its meaning? "... put me to the test, says the Lord of host; see if I will not open the windows of heaven for you and pour down for you an overflowing blessing."[59] I know with the feeling of absolute certainty which you give me that the victory of the light is inevitable.

> And all shall be well and
> All manner of thing shall be well
> When the tongues of flame are in-folded
> Into the crowned knot of fire
> And the fire and the rose are one.[60]

The fire of My love can never fail.

[1] The *Talmud.*

[2] *Confessions* VII, 17, 23.

[3] J.E. Cirlot, *A Dictionary of Symbols* (NY: Philosophical Library, 1962), p. xvi.

[4] Ibid., p. xvi.

[5] Ibid., p. xxx.

[6] *Speaking of Beauty*, p. 130.

[7] Cirlot, p. xxxi.

[8] B.J. *A. Contemplation Upon Flowers* (Portland, Oreg.: Timber Press, 1999), pp. 312, 316.

[9] *The Two Noble Kinsman*, act 2, scene 2.

[10] *Speaking of Beauty*, p. 38.

[11] "Modern Beauty," quoted in *Speaking of Beauty*, pp. 59-60.

[12] *Cirlot*, p. 136.

[13] Ehrman, *Lost Scriptures*, p. 105.

[14] Underhill, p. 134.

[15] Underhill, p. 135.

[16] Julian of Norwich, *Showings*, (NY: Paulist Press, 1978), ch.6, p. 186.

[17] Francis Thompson, *The Hound of Heaven.*

[18] *Inferno*, Canto 1; 1-3, 10-12.

[19] *Paradise*, 31; 79-90.

[20] *Measure for Measure*, Act 2, Scene 2, Lines 117-122.

[21] *A Treasury of Great Poems*, ed. L. Antermeyer, L. (NY: Galahad Books, 1993), p. 1.

[22] Marvin Pope, *Song of Songs* (Garden City, NJ: Doubleday & Co., 1977), p. 19.

[23] *Paradise*, 31; 79-90.

[24] John 19:30.

[25] *Abrams*, p. 45.

[26] *Meditaciones sobre los Cantares*, in *Obras Completas*, (Madrid, 1844).

[27] Underhill, p. 137.

[28] White, p. 114.

Fire and the Reality of Symbolism

[29] Ibid., p. 115.

[30] Don Cuthbert Butler, quoted in *Western Mysticism* (Mineola, New York: Dover Publications, 2003, 2nd edition), p. 112.

[31] Ibid., p. 112.

[32] Jeremiah 2:12-13.

[33] Butler, p. 112.

[34] Ibid., pp. 103, 104.

[35] Ibid., p. 104.

[36] Cf. M. Morford and R.J. Lenardon, *Classical Mythology* (NY: Longman, 1971), p. 257.

[37] Abrams, *Supernaturalism*, p. 160.

[38] Quoted in Abrams, *Supernaturalism*, p. 502, n.38.

[39] M. Eliade, *Yoga*, p. 118.

[40] 2 Peter 3:10-12.

[41] Romans 5:20.

[42] Quoted in E. Norman Pearson, *Space, Time and Self: Three Mysteries of the Universe* (Wheaton, Illinois: The Theosophical Publishing House, 1990), p. 33.

[43] Alice Bailey, *A Treatise on Cosmic Fire*, (NY: Lucis Publishing Co., New York, 1973), p. 274.

[44] *Esoteric Healing*, p. 444.

[45] Romans 5:12.

[46] Romans 6:23.

[47] Revelation 21:4.

[48] *Esoteric Healing*, p. 444.

[49] William Shakespeare, Sonnet 146:13-14.

[50] Shelley, "Adonais."

[51] Ibid., Stanza 38

[52] Exodus 3:2; Acts 2:3; Deuteronomy 4:24; Isaiah 66:15-6; 2 Thessalonians 1:7-8.

[53] St. Augustine, *Confessions*, XIII, 9.

[54] St. Catherine of Siena, *The Dialogue*, p. 365.

[55] Blaise Pascal, quoted in F.C. Happold, *Mysticism: A Study and an Anthology*, (NY: Penguin Books, 1971), p. 39.

[56] William James, *The Varieties of Religious Experience, A Study in Human Nature* (NY: The Modern Library, 1936), pp 390-1; Dr. R.M. Bucke, *Cosmic Consciousness: A Study in the Evolution of the Human Mind*, Philadelphia, 1901.

[57] Abrams, *Natural Supernaturalism*, p. 294.

[58] "De Itinerario Mentis in Deo," cap. vii.

[59] Malachi 3:10.

[60] T.S. Eliot, *Four Quartets*.

NOTE: *For ease of reference, all quotations from* Hosea, Jeremiah, Ezekiel, Isaiah, *and* Psalms *in this chapter were offered in-line with the citations rather than as an endnote.*

CHAPTER 15

The Nature of Consciousness

*The unfoldment of individual life in the universe has no other
aim apparently but to become conscious of its own divine essence, and since this process goes on continuously, it represents a
perpetual birth of God or the continuous arising
of Enlightened Beings, in each of whom the
totality of the universe becomes conscious.*
Lama Anagarika Govinda

**I must confess that you gave me an explanation which I
didn't understand; you said that who we are, our existence,
and how we view the world and reality depend on our state
of consciousness but the truth is, I still don't know what
consciousness really is.**
Consciousness! Wonder of all wonders! What a miracle it is,
and yet only a few individuals are aware of it; can there be anything more wonder-full than just "be"?

Certainly not, if you are what you want to be.
You are a sculptor of destiny! You have the power to be what
you choose to be, it is your birthright and your divine privilege,
the gift of God to you.

Think deeply on this: the Infinite becomes conscious of
Itself through you offering in love all that It is and has for the
creation of beauty and perfection. You are not only conscious
of yourself and be able to say "I," an individualized focus of life
as a Self, but you can be aware of the Source of your own existence and of the universe around you, whether infinitely great
or infinitely small.

You are the door of the unfathomable treasure house of
unseen visions and unheard melodies, to ineffable feelings of

ecstasy and endless flow of ideas, to limitless hidden riches and unimaginable secrets. They are all waiting to come forth and become manifest at the sound of My name, "I AM," spoken by you as My individualization on Earth. Can the Infinite give you more than all of Itself to do what you will?

Yes, the knowledge to do what is good for me.
Is it not innate in the very substance of your being? Your heart knows the truth; the difference between love and hate, harmony and discord, beauty and ugliness, is not self-evident?

Not always, one can be so confused that he doesn't know anymore what is positive and negative, true or false; and even if he should have some idea of if, he doesn't care or cannot act accordingly because of the weakness of his personality.
That happens when the individual forgets Me and My teaching because, then, he closes the door and does not let Me illumine his consciousness.

But you have not answered my question: this amazing consciousness of yours, what is it? I still do not understand it.
I may talk to you for all eternity and still you will not be able to comprehend My words because you do not realize who you are.

That has been the main purpose in all that you have told me, and I can see that it is the key to my understanding of everything else, including you. I beg you to be patient, I am like an infant or a man soundly asleep, at least I know this. I am still not at home, living outside myself, while you are teaching me how to shatter the walls of my prison and re-

veal to me who I am. Call me and cry out louder, it takes more than many thunders to penetrate my deafness; set me on fire and purify my mind that I may attain the truth which you are and be free. I have done extensive research in the field of consciousness but what I have learned seems worthless.

I know that the word consciousness derives from the Latin *cum* (with) and *scio* (know); in its original sense to be conscious meant to have knowledge of or be able to respond and react to external factors and the environment. In its common usage it may refer to a state of awareness – the two terms are often used interchangeably – of one's experiences or inner states and processes. However, despite a long history of speculation, research and talk about it, it is still a mystery.

How can we explain the existence of the world within us and that around us, one made of our thoughts, feelings, images, reflections, desires, memories, and the other of the visible reality of the earth, water, the sky, clouds, trees. How does our hidden and private realm, where one is the only actor, fit into the nature of the "ten thousand things" that surround us and creates our boundaries and limitations.

And if this condition were not already a challenge to our understanding, our very being is constituted of two different entities, variously called mind and matter, body and soul, self and not-self, or inner and outer self. The apparent dual nature of the individual has been, in fact, the perennial "great question," debated by thinkers in every age with a wide variety of answers, or none. No one can dispute or deny the reality of consciousness, and even evolutionists have to admit that "it is the most god-awfully potent evolutionary invention ever developed."[1]

However, they cannot explain how it happened and why it came into existence. The question is, in what way has it evolved and how can this inner world of ours derive out of mere matter? And if it is not a property of matter, it must originate with animal life, not at the beginning, as it was originally asserted, but at some stages in evolution by natural selection. But can it be possible that our conscious faculties with their preponderant influence and determining factor and power over our lives be derivable from animal behavior? One can say that, "A conscious animal might be a knower, and we might extend the epithet "Knower" to machines if they receive information from the world and modify their responses accordingly. But only a self-conscious being knows that he is a Knower."[2]

A cat does not know that it is a cat and I am sure a machine does not know what it is. "Alone of species, all alone! We try to understand ourselves and the world. We become rebels or patriots or martyrs on the basis of ideas. We build cathedrals and computers, write poems and tensor equations, play chess and quartets, sail ships to other planets and listen in to other galaxies. What has this to do with rats in mazes or the threat displays of baboons?"[3] Moreover, we can expand and raise our consciousness to a higher level wherein one has the immediate and experiential knowledge of the sameness of his or her self-identity with the infinite Creator.

In order to explain the complex interiority of consciousness so different from a mere aggregate of molecules and a collection of cells developed from matter with the help of chance and survival, it was proposed that a metaphysical force of some kind was responsible for the direction of its evolution.

However, according to the rules of natural science, this is considered anathema. As a reaction to it, consciousness was denigrated to the level of a helpless spectator without any causal efficacy on the life of the individual. It is like the shadow which accompanies the person but unable to influence his way, or the sound coming from the harp but cannot pluck its strings.[4]

For the materialist consciousness is "a quirky accident"[5]... it just happened as a fortuitous and unexpected by-product,"[6] therefore we can live without this strange new faculty.

What does it have, some scientists say, that neural signals and physical brain activity do not have? But then they are confronted with a paradox: if it is useless and without survival value, it should not have developed in natural selection. If consciousness is causally impotent and it doesn't help the neural circuits in the brain, then its development cannot be accounted for by their theory. This evolutionary novelty is, indeed, so exceptional that they must recognize their inability to explain its origin. Therefore, as a commentator once wrote, we will never understand how a pattern of electrochemical impulses in our nervous system is translated into the rich experience of, say, watching an opera or flying an airplane.[7]

Without mentioning the undeniable fact that one's consciousness allows him "to experience and express what has been referred to as 'non-computable elements,' things like compassion, morality, and many others, that mere neural activity is extremely hard pressed to explain."[8]

Within the evolutionary community some of the descriptive terms used with reference to consciousness are: problem, mystery, riddle, challenge. Although it is admitted that it is the highest manifestation of life, its origin, destiny, and the nature of its connection with the physical body and brain are questions that remain unsolved.

The brain is accompanied by consciousness but scientists don't know why it should be so. The emergence of full consciousness is considered by some thinkers as one of the greatest of miracles; but the difficulty arises in explaining why. With consciousness has come the unprecedented power to be in control of one's life, but it also carries tremendous responsibility because actions always have consequences.

And this is true whether the human being is considered a child of God, a species of primate, or matter in motion. Some materialists have suggested that a machine can do everything we can do.[9] For example, an eminent physiologist asserted that there is nothing that could not be copied by machinery, nothing therefore that could not be brought within the framework of physical science.[10]

His remarks were made at a scientific symposium held at the Vatican; following his speech, the seminar participants engaged in a discussion centered on the lecture. A renowned neurosurgeon in attendance dryly addressed the speaker: "I had in mind to ask whether the robot could, in any conceivable way, see a joke. I think not. Sense of humor would, I suspect, be the last thing that a machine would have."[11]

However, it has been proved that consciousness is not necessary because we can do things, even as essential and indispensable, like thinking and learning, without being conscious of them.

But that is the problem! People are not really awake and their usual condition has been called, as you know, *sleepwalking.* It seems that you forgot what I said about identification; go back and read it again. To be truly conscious is that only rarely achieved state in which you are in a position of freedom and mastery, and from which you can direct your life without taking on conditions from anybody or anything and be subject to them. There is no question that the main cause of human mistakes and distress can be attributed to the fact that people are mostly not conscious of what they do, reacting instead of acting. They are not living from the center of their being, putting inner wholeness in their decisions, needs and wants. It has been said that humans are gods in exile, and it is true, they are exiles from their own homeland, the core of inner experience, "I AM."

However, to be conscious, for instance, of the way we walk, one foot after another, or of our fingers when we play the piano, or of every letter and the punctuation when we read a text, it would be an obstacle and painfully slow down the pace and process of our existence.

Before being able to do anything you must certainly be aware of it at some level; the body itself has its own consciousness and responses, and you can train it to perform what you want. Only afterward, the action becomes independent of volition and spontaneous, called automatizations or habit. You may also be hypnotized by outside suggestions, which is often the case. But many times, and I would say most of the time, you do things unknowingly but never unconsciously because you are either conscious or not. If you were totally unconscious you could not be alive, which is impossible. You may act and do things unknowingly, that is, without the intellect being aware of it, however there is also the capacity of knowledge in the feelings.

I think I understand what you mean; this is the case when, on a deeper level, we are sure that something is true and real without an intellectual explanation or rationale for it. Then I was amazed to learn what is perhaps the most astonishing theory of all: consciousness does not exist, it is nothing. And even more astounding and unbelievable was the fact of the acceptance and success of that preposterous idea. "It allowed a new generation to sweep aside with one impatient gesture all the worn-out complexities of the problem of consciousness and its origin."[12]

How can anybody believe that he is not conscious? To say that consciousness does not exist without being conscious of it is quite a feat. As I said, it is like the fish that lives in and by the water saying that water does not exist. However, they are right.

I am shocked! Do you agree that consciousness does not exist?

For them it does not, they have killed it; did not the German philosopher Nietzsche say that God is dead?

They don't know who God is.

Because they do not know themselves; if they did, they would know Me, for I AM the more advanced consciousness of themselves.

There has been in recent years a serious and remarkable increase of interest in the subject of consciousness, accompanied by a flood of publications and scientific meetings. One would think that an explanation and a definition of what the nature of consciousness is would be a simple matter. However, a dictionary of psychology had this to say: "Consciousness is a fascinating but elusive phenomenon; it is

372

impossible to specify what it is, what it does or why it evolved." And the conclusive sentence was disheartening: "Nothing worth reading has been written about it."[13]

The so-called mind/body problem has proved so elusive that it has been considered "a mystery of ultimate significance." In fact, it was admitted that "We are glorious accidents of an unpredictable process with no drive to complexity, not the expected results of evolutionary principles that yearn to produce a creature capable of understanding the mode of its own necessary construction."[14]

I made reference to my research because people are scientifically minded, or they think so, and look to science as the source of truth.

But we should not talk anymore of these opinions because that is what they are, merely opinions. Both scientists and philosophers cannot even agree on the meaning of the term, let alone on the origin and the nature of what they try to explain. The fact is that the brain, or matter, cannot generate consciousness (but let me interject here that to degrade matter for the sake of the spirit is worse than mistaking matter to be the only reality). Neither can consciousness create matter as the idealists claim, nor according to the dualists are mind and matter separated and working in parallel, like a pair of identical clocks without causal connection.

Then, if we exclude all those explanations, what is the alternative? "Human history is a process of ascent to godhead," writes John White, and "We cannot create higher consciousness from electrochemical reactions. Consciousness is immaterial; it cannot be squeezed from test tubes or neurons. It operates *through* them but cannot be reduced *to* them. As a plant grows toward the light, so does humanity

yearn for God and greater awareness because, like a plant's inherent capacity to perceive and respond to light, there is a teleological design at work in us from the start."[15]

There is a general consensus that consciousness is a relational concept, called intentional, that is, it implies someone who is conscious and something of which to be conscious.

Therefore, only the principle of polarity, as the dynamic relation between spirit and matter, can provide us with the final answer to the nature of consciousness. Nobody knows how anything material could be conscious, and evolutionists cannot close the gap between the physical and the subjective realms of this issue. It will surely remain baffling and insolvable as long as it is regarded as an exclusively natural process in an exclusively materialistic world.

The existence of consciousness implies an interrelation between the two essentials aspects of the underlying ground of being. However, it is not an undifferentiated unity, in which both sides are lost, nor is it the duality of two separate things. This twain-in-one, spirit and matter, are ever inseparable, complementary, and interdependent; consciousness is a force like electricity that exists everywhere and is active only by the connections of two poles. Both are necessary to generate electric energy; a link must exist between them. This is true also in the case of a magnet: it has two poles, never one, with the magnetic lines forming a *continuous* path through them. It is the same with the polarity of spirit-matter generating and giving rise to the phenomenon of consciousness.

As I have explained before, there is no spirit which is not enveloped by matter or form, and no matter which is not animated or vivified by spirit. Consciousness has been opposed to matter without understanding what it is and how it originated, and a gulf has been created between them. This has been the result of an erroneous approach to such fundamental issue. According to the principle of polarity there is no gap between spirit and matter because they are not two separate entities and are not fused and confused either. Therefore, the origin and nature of consciousness is no more a mystery or an insoluble problem. As you need so-called physical light in order to see, the light of consciousness is the necessary condition in order to be and to know. Consciousness is identical with life, existing everywhere; it is the primary, all-pervading constituent of reality and there is no place where it is not. The universe is an aggregate of states of consciousness as the matrix of universal manifestation and of all experience.

From the mineral to the plant, from the animal to the human and the divine, nothing exists which is not in some measure both alive and conscious; differences are only in the degree of dominance of one side, or pole, over the other with spirit and matter interacting at all levels. Le me emphasize that consciousness is light, not in a metaphorical sense but in the reality of the highest form of energy-vibration. This light of which I speak is also the pattern of your physical form, and it emanates about you as your aura.

I know there have been pictures made of it by a sophisticated kind of photography.
In the beginning you were created a luminous being, referred to as My own image.

I don't look any more like that.
You should know why; every thought, feeling and spoken word that is not the vibration of the light of My love creates a shadow or a cloud. When it is constantly repeated, it condenses and covers over the radiance of the light, until it reached the

density of your physical body. For the sake of clarity, I will use this form:

Spirit • Consciousness • Matter
Father • Son • Mother
Thought • Word • Feeling

The point of union, whether it is called consciousness, son, or the Word, is "I AM", the creative principle of love (I use the traditional term "son" but it refers naturally also to daughter).

Consciousness is the expression of that which might be regarded as the focal point of manifestation; it is produced by the relation between the two poles and their interaction. You are the link or point of union between spirit and matter, the focus of consciousness of the Infinite, the individual of absolute free will, the spiritual pole being your connection with the infinite and the material pole with the finite.

By the power of your self-determination you can turn to one or the other dimension of your being, the divine and the human, but if you have attained wisdom, you will live in the heart-center of your Being, holding your connection with Me, and thus be master of your world. My plan is to bring you to the realization of your "I-Am-ness," and to the fullness of your complete Self-Consciousness.

I am not sure I understand what it is.
The term self-consciousness needs clarification because of its ambiguity; it may refer to a disposition to be embarrassed in association with others, or an awareness of being aware. For instance, when you eat you are aware of the food, its taste, its texture, etc. and, at the same time, you can also be aware of yourself eating; unless you are identifying with the food.

That's one reason why I eat too much. I feel myself through the food.

A self-conscious person not only experiences thoughts, emotions, sensations, and mental pictures, but he is aware of them. This is the uniqueness of the human being as an individualized focus of consciousness: he is not only aware of his environment and the world, he has a sense of self, he is conscious of himself. On a higher level, self-consciousness refers to the capacity of the individual not only to be aware of himself but also of the Source of his life, his God Self.

This is the highest expression of the principle of polarity; you said that all life is conscious.

Yes, but in different degrees or levels; according to each particular nature there is a relation and interaction with the surroundings. Because of its relational nature there must be an objective world responding to consciousness in order for it to act. A tree, a dog, a flower, a rock they all have the capacity to feel and to be aware of their environment but lack a sense of identity, or self-awareness; they cannot have a sense of I, as I said, they do not know who they are.

But we don't know either, I think that's the point of your discussion.

Yes, with the difference that you have forgotten it and, therefore, you have the capacity to remember it, and they do not. Moreover, minerals, plants, and animals do not have any knowledge of the Source from whence they come for they are not made in my image and do not have an individual identity.

I think one can recognize individuality in the human being and its absence in the animals by observing their behavior under certain conditions. A group of animals surrounded by similar circumstances will act, or rather, react in the same way. Their behavior is determined by the external situation; none will try to adjust its action to change or alter it, but they act all alike. If you know the nature of the animal and its surroundings, you can predict the behavior of the whole class by the action of only one or two. This shows definitely the absence of individuality. In the case of human beings, you cannot know in advance that they will act in the same way.

There are situations in which one loses himself and identifies with the crowd, especially in case of mass hypnosis. Otherwise, according to one's development and character of the individuals there will be different decisions and actions taken under the same circumstances.

With regard to animals, I should mention that they have a group soul which is the cumulative consciousness of the species. That is what determines the herd instinct – the gregariousness of cattle, the formation of birds in flight, the movement of a class of fish, and the migratory patterns of many species.

I was thinking of what you said before; it is hard to believe that everything feels, even a mineral.

You may think it is not something animate, but where does it come from? All the energy in the universe is My energy, therefore there is intelligence and will acting everywhere.

I can think of the determination and the struggle of a tiny plant to grow in the fissure of a rock.

Reference is made to it as the fire of the Holy Spirit, *prana,* *t'chi,* or cosmic light, but in reality it is My life by which I create and sustain everything in manifestation.

Imagine what a transformation in the consciousness of mankind if they understood that the light of the sun, the air they breathe, the food they eat, the vegetation, electricity, the water, and the earth are the energy of My life and the gift of My love. It is entrusted to each one for the fulfillment of My plan designed for his or her happiness.

Since it is the nature of love to give of itself, it must have something to love. I am reminded of these words by Zarathushtra to the sun: "Thou great star! What would be thy happiness if thou hadst not those for whom thou shinest! For ten years has thou climbed hither unto my cave: thou wouldst have wearied of thy light and of the journey, had it not been for me ... But we awaited thee every morning, took from thee thine overflow, and blessed thee for it."[16]

This understanding would enable the individual to overcome the sense of separation and its selfish attitude toward life, which is the cause of all limitations, and attain the state of at-one-ment with its Source. Then life would become, once again, sacred.

Even in your imperfect world people do not realize the extent to which they depend on each other. From the builders of their homes and cars to the manufacturers of their clothing to those in the postal service, to teachers, the garbage collectors, and so on and on.

But they are paid for what they do.

That is not the point. Your mind is still clouded with wrong concepts. If you are hungry and need food, can you eat money? It is only a means of exchange, after all.

Unless it becomes an end in itself.
It would be a form of misdirected love.

You are trying to teach me that love is the root cause of everything and the motive force behind every action. Certainly it makes easier to forgive those who, as the prayer says, "trespass against us."
The ignorance of that truth has dragged the people into the distress and limitations they experience in their lives.

I understand that we should be aware and appreciate what everyone does to build and sustain a civilization, but are we supposed to depend on others?
That is not what I am saying. You can only be free when you depend completely on Me. But since each one is part of the all, like the cells in the body doing their specific work, people should be neither dependent nor independent.

Is this another conundrum?
Not at all. My truth is always simple, I am simplicity itself for there is nothing more simple than One. Meditate on it. Think of your question in the context of My explanation of the principle of polarity.

Oh, yes, like the rest of the universe we are all interdependent.
And since I AM all there is, consciousness is everywhere; if I were to withdraw it the universe would disappear. Another im-

possible act of Mine because all that exist is My creation and the expression of My love, but I am present as the "I AM-Self" only in the individual human being. As the "I AM," I AM conscious of Myself in and through you on the physical plane and enable you to be conscious of yourself and, hopefully, of Me.

I think Meister Eckart referred to what you are saying when he wrote: "the Father gives birth to His Son without ceasing; and I say more: He gives birth not only to me, His Son, but He gives birth to me as Himself and Himself as me and to me as His being and nature. In the innermost Source, there I spring out in the Holy Spirit, where there is one life and one being and one work."[17]

He expressed well My thoughts. In the infinite ground of being, your consciousness of "I AM" as the Son is identical with the consciousness of the Father, the two united by the love of the Holy Spirit. I AM present in and through you as your individualized "I AM-Self."

Your explanation of the fundamentality of polarity has helped me to understand life, but how did it originate?

I will repeat, in a slightly different way, what I said about the Trinity; I do not blame you if you still do not understand it, you have to meditate on it and call to Me to illumine you; worded explanation is not enough. Think of the formless, undifferentiated Infinite in a latent, quiescent state, like static electricity. By an inner impulse it becomes active and two poles emerge, spirit and matter, the inner and outer side of Being. That is how the infinite Ground becomes conscious of It-self, that is, a Self, the "I" or "I AM.

It becomes Self-conscious, that is, acknowledges and con-templates its own Being, and therefore becomes an individual Self, in other words, It feels and loves Itself.
Yes, polarity, as you have learned, means a relation between two complementary and interdependent poles.

The Infinite becomes conscious of Itself as the Father-Mother God giving birth to the Son, the individual human being.
It is a truism that in order to be a Creator God must be Self-conscious or it could not be the Source of creation both transcendent and immanent in it.

I needed to hear again this explanation; I am not a superficial person but these are profound issues and it takes time to grasp them. I begin to understand the principle of polarity. I remember that according to Hindu Tantrism the Deity is explained as being polarized into feminine and masculine, respectively called Shakti and Shiva. Their ecstatic union originates the event (referred to as *lila* or play) causative of the creation of the universe.
The Infinite as the formless primordial Ground cannot create because it is not in a reciprocal state, since consciousness and love are both relational: they imply a subject and an object, again not as a duality but an inter-subjective process of relationship. Therefore, the One rising out of its undifferentiated state becomes two, not the sum of one plus one as in mathematics, but polarized as spirit-matter or Father-Mother. Their interaction and intercourse generates the flow of energy, which is love, the cause of all manifestation.

Dante's sublime tercet comes to mind:

O Light Eternal who alone abidest in Thyself,
Alone knowest Thyself, and, known to Thyself
And knowing, lovest and smilest on Thyself.[18]

Yes, the Source knows and loves itself, and it must have something on which to bestow its love; therefore creation, or the desire for form which is beauty, is manifested.

Because, love, by its very nature, is self-giving.
It certainly is! It radiates like light from the sun. Each individual, male and female, can say: I am a projection or emanation of the Father-Mother God, an individualized focus of consciousness, infinite life aware of itself through me.

The infinite is the infinite of my-Self and what is called "enlightenment" is the "condition of being aware of the universe *as* the universe – being cosmically conscious...the transcendence of all separateness and all boundaries in the extraordinary, yet perfectly ordinary, experience of the cosmos being conscious of itself through an individual."[19]
      And this is your Divine Presence focused in my heart which makes me conscious of my existence and of yourself as One life in the word, "I AM."
I am delighted to see that you are beginning to wake up to your divine Reality.
      In order to quicken your intuitive faculty, I turn your attention to the laws of nature. They are, in reality, all one, operating at different levels from the lowest to the highest. The emergence of the manifested universe out of so-called "nothingness" cannot be grasped by the intellect, but something similar can be seen acting in your everyday experience.

383

I use again the example of electricity. It is everywhere present in its static state, and no one knows what it is; yet, although its nature is unknown, you can observe the effects it produces. Like the formless primordial Ground in its latent state, electricity must be considered to exist behind its myriad phases even though unmanifest. For instance, it flows through the wires in your house, but you do not see it until the switch is turned on and the light appears. By analogy, on a cosmic scale spirit and matter are hidden, and no one knows what they are or even *that* they are, in their infinite, primordial state.

Also, electricity requires two poles in order to become active.
Right, then it "individualizes" as a light bulb, with the filament as My 'I AM" Presence in you, and the glass as your personality. Unfortunately, the human being has collected a lot of dust which has covered over the transparency of the glass and does not allow anymore My light to shine through, as it was originally intended.

That's why we need to clean up and purify ourselves.
I have used electricity as a crude illustration but it is closer to the truth than you think. All life-energy is, in electric parlance, an electric circuit.

Do you know that, fundamentally, there is nothing but electricity in manifestation, the "mystery of electricity?"[20]

I read that everything in the natural world is electrical in nature; "life itself is electricity, but all that we have contacted and used today is that which is only physical and related to and inherent in the physical and etheric matter of

all forms."[21] And it has been stated that, "the human being is electrical in origin and nature."[22]

And in another text, "All that can be seen in manifestation is fundamentally *physical electricity* ... We know of no natural phenomenon in nature – entirely unconnected with either magnetism or electricity since, where there are motion, heat, friction, light, there magnetism and its Alter Ego – electricity, will always appear, as either cause or effect – or rather both if we but fathom the manifestation to its origin."[23]

Electricity is another name for the fire of My love. Yes, esoterically it may be referred to as "electric fire" which correspond to Spirit, the Father, the first aspect of the Godhead and of manifestation. Then there is the "fire by friction" which is Matter, the Mother, form and latent heat.

I assume that from the interplay and blending of the two fires is brought forth the Son.

Which is called "solar fire," its radiation as light and consciousness. I am explaining in a different way, although this can only be evocative, who you are: the meeting place of the poles of spirit and matter, the union of the two, the child born of their marriage. Thus, we have individuality in order to express that which is in each of the two plus the result of their merging in himself. This may seem at first somewhat abstruse and vague by lack of adequate terms; however, when meditated upon it will prove very illuminating. Let me try to elucidate it adding a few thoughts:

1. Electric fire is the divine flame, the manifestation of the will-to-be, the vital principle of existence and the intelligent purpose underlying all.

2. Fire by friction is the electrical cause of vibration animating the atoms in the manifestation of matter; it generates the inner activity of heat and radiation by intercourse with the pole of spirit.
3. Solar fire is the electrical manifestation of form from a God to human being, and an atom by magnetic power, and is the animating principle of the human race.[24]

Therefore, the fire of My love is always flowing through every individual and pervading all creation. It is the cohesive power holding every manifested form together by the Law of Attraction, which is another name for love, and, at the same time, moving and sustaining all that is in ever expanding glory, beauty, and ecstasy.

I'd like to quote Julian of Norwich:

> "See! I am God. See! I am in everything.
> See! I never lift my hand off my works,
> Nor will I ever. See! I lead everything
> toward the purpose for which I ordained it,
> without beginning, by the same Power,
> Wisdom, and Love by which I created
> it. How could anything be amiss?[25]

With her sublime simplicity she conveyed the truth of My words. Love, wisdom, and power acting as one in perfect balance are the threefold flame of divine love. If you have only love without wisdom you may desecrate it. Wisdom without love becomes degraded into intellectualism. Power acting by itself leads, as you know, to unimaginable tragedy and destruction.

One must be balanced by the other two or you cannot manifest perfection.

Divine love is referred to as the Breath of the Eternal.
But very few understand that the fire of My love is as close as their breath, in fact, it is in the very air they breathe in all the time, or they could not live.

No one would think of the polluted atmosphere of our cities as the fire-breath of your love.
Mankind has contaminated and imposed their impure emanations upon it, but the reality behind the chemical names of oxygen, hydrogen, etc. that has been given to it is eternally pure.

After your explanation I keep repeating, " I AM" the fire of love, and begin to feel it.
Good! Remember, what you think upon, and what you affirm with the creative word "I AM" you become: it is the way to expand your consciousness until it embraces all you desire. If every human being were to acknowledge that statement, the Earth would be transformed in a very short time. The planetary consciousness would change from the shadows of selfishness, hate and violence to the light of love and peace.

You said earlier that life is one, consciousness is one and energy is one.
Yes, but not a total merging and fusion into oneness, with each entity lost in it like a raindrop in the ocean. Life is energy and vibration, it consists of a to-and-fro movement between the two poles of spirit and matter; without their interaction it is not possible to have motion because there would be nowhere to

move, and if motion were to cease, the result would be inertia or a return to the primeval formless state. The Mother-God is the pole of matter, which coalesces and encloses the diffusion of the energy giving visible form to the ideas, or spiritual thoughts, of the Father-God.

I don't understand. How can matter enclose energy? Aren't they the same thing? Or do you mean something different by energy?

I use the terms energy or light or light-energy with reference to the radiation of the fire of love generated by the interrelation or intercourse of spirit-matter or cosmic male-female polarity.

Remember that the traditional expression spirit-matter is intended to be suggestive or evocative; it is fitting to convey My ideas to you since I have to use words from your limited language. By matter I mean the outer side or the form, and by energy the light filling all space out of which everything is created, including your body. The word substance can also be used with reference to condensed energy in its countless variety of vibratory action.

From the light of the sun to electricity and to God, many are the meanings of the light which in the Bible was the first command.

Yes, it is the primordial fiery energy generated by the relation of Father-Mother God. Try to realize that it implies the cosmic Law of Attraction, as the power of the unifying life, acting everywhere from one unit to another, be it atom, individual, solar system or galaxy.

Then, is love related to magnetism?

Magnetism and the capacity to express love are, from the inner standpoint, synonymous; love is the greatest magnet in all creation. Therefore, if you want something you must love it in order to draw it to you and keep it permanently because it becomes part of you. Remember that love owns all.

I can understand that polarity is the activity of love, but how can we relate to it?
My child, polarity is only a word from the science of magnetism which I use from your limited vocabulary to explain the nature of love and the Law of life. However, you do not relate to it, it relates to you.

Because we are the children of love; then we should learn to love love.
Yes, knowing that love is not merely an attribute, and not even just a relation, but a Being.

It is you!
Yes, I AM love, and so are you, although you are not conscious of it, yet.

You said that consciousness originated from the polarity of spirit-matter.
Yes, the same as love.

Do they have the same origin?
There is only one Source of life and creativity; consciousness is light, therefore you have another trinity, life-light-love, three in one and one in three.

But you said that love is fire.

Fire and light have nearly the same meaning, as fire radiates light, and they are used interchangeably by the mystics.

Also by those who temporarily died and after returned to their bodies; they employ the imagery of the light to describe their apprehension of the intensity and the splendor which characterizes their experience. I would like to quote this description:

> And then, before you is this most magnificent, just gorgeous beautiful, bright white or blue-white light, it is so bright, it is brighter than a light that would immediately blind you, but this absolutely does not hurt your eyes at all ... The next sensation is this wonderful, wonderful feeling of this light ... It's almost like a person. It is not a person, but it is a being of some kind ... then the light immediately communicates to you ... this communication is what you might call telepathic. It's absolutely instant, absolutely clear ... and for the first time in your life is a feeling of true, pure love. It can't be compared to the love of your wife, the love of your children, or to what some people consider love from an intense sexual experience ... it couldn't even begin to compare. All these wonderful, wonderful feelings combined could not possibly compare to the feeling, to the true love. If you can imagine what pure love would be, this would be the feeling that you'd get from this brilliant white light ... As a result of that experience, I have very little apprehension about dying my natural death because if death is anything, it's got to be the most wonderful thing to look forward to, absolutely the most wonderful thing.[26]

Notice the identity of light and love; as I said, in reality, light is the radiation of the fire. The flame in your heart, which is an extension of My heart-flame, radiates the light-energy that enables you to live as a self-conscious being.

But isn't all life conscious?
I think I answered that question but I know that your awakening must be gradual for you can only absorb a little light at a time without hurting you. Try to be aware that My light-energy interpenetrates everything in the universe; there is One Presence which "I AM", acting everywhere with myriads variety of different grades and levels of consciousness and forms of manifestation.

I remember the immortal verses of the beginning of Dante's *Paradiso*:

> The glory of the One who moves all things
> Penetrates through the universe, shining
> In one part more and in another less.
> I have been in the heaven that most receives
> Of His light, and have seen things that
> No man, once returned from there, can tell.[27]

As I said in My explanation, I have to deal with the limitations of your vocabulary.

And of my intellect.
But as I radiate My light into you I will make you will feel the truth of My words, because it is the feeling that unites you with its object. The human mind may be filled with all kinds of con-

cepts and ideas but in order to really know, one must become one with the truth by feeling it, and for that, love is required.

After your instruction with regard to that issue, I am convinced of it. Very few comprehend that the universe is a magnificent manifestation filled with wonders, beauty, and music indescribable, where perfect Beings of light and love live in a state of eternal and ever-expanding joy and ecstasy. The so called scientific theories about black holes, colliding planets, and vanishing stars must be childish in your eyes.
They are the concoctions of the fallen human intellect, disconnected from its Source, drawing conclusions from fragments of data based on the world of appearances mistaken as reality.

As the Scripture says, "They grope in the dark without light, He makes them stagger like a drunkard" (Job 12:55) "... they became futile in their thinking, and their senseless minds were darkened. Claiming to be wise, they became fools." (Romans 1:21-22).
Try to recognize the universe as a divine creation, and yourself as a God-Being. I revealed Myself to you and My purpose in our dialogues is to return you to the remembrance of who you really are, of your divine origin, divine destiny, divine heritage, and of the divine use of your creative faculties for your victory over this world in the attainment of the ascension. Therefore, realize that you are a conscious Self, and the consciousness that is in you as you is greater than that which you recognize as the intellect or mind. Let me tell you more about it.

Where you are in consciousness at any moment is what you are at that moment; life is a state of consciousness, you are and you have and you act according to it. Your physical body is a vehicle of your consciousness, your family and home are its extension, and your occupation (whether you love what you do or it is a drudgery that you hate) is an activity of your consciousness. Therefore, unless you change your inner state, nothing else can change; the objective is to expand and raise the level of consciousness of who you really are because it determines and attracts the kind of existence that you live every moment.

I heard this story: the movies came to the large cities first, and finally arrived in a remote mining camp in the Rockies. The picture was announced and the tent was put up. The residents had never been to a movie before. The place was packed with cowboys and miners, and at a given moment during the showing of a blood-curdling melodrama the villain began to choke the heroine. An old cowboy in the front row pulled out his gun and fired six shots into the villain. Everybody laughed, because in those days a gunshot didn't mean much. There were only a few bullet holes in the wall, and of course the picture went on as scheduled.

If the man wanted to prevent any harm, instead of firing at the screen, he should have turned around and fired into the projector to stop the film. Your story is a good illustration of the subject I was discussing.

How can I apply this to my life?

The world is the screen, and you must place on it whatever you desire to experience. Your thoughts and feelings create the film pictured on the screen by the light of your consciousness. If you want to change your existence or any circumstance, change the film of your thoughts and feelings about it. The key to life is not somewhere outside of you; it is not the world that you must change, but yourself. Do you not know the statement, As within, so without? People think that changes in the government, society, economy, and so forth, will solve their problems; for them, that is the real world, and they depend on it and are, therefore, conditioned by it.

When someone considers what constitutes a happy life, he usually thinks of external factors, like friends, family, degrees and awards, career, property, etc. He does not realize that happiness is a state of consciousness by the quality of his thought and feelings. If I ask you where you live, you will tell me your address and hometown, but in reality, you live in your consciousness because it is precisely there, in your inner world, that you feel and experience your hopes, fears, happiness, dejection, love, anger, etc. People want to improve their life-style or try to escape the boredom and worries of their day to day existence by various diversions, such as entertainment, travel, new acquaintances, clothes and so on, but the only permanent change must come from within.

As you know, there are people who are considered very successful in life, the so-called rich and famous; everybody admires and envies them, yet even though they are celebrities they may be quite unhappy and miserable. On the other hand, someone, in very different and even adverse circumstances, may be contented and satisfied because he is rich within himself.

This is true. In the words of Jalalu'd Din, "With Thee, a prison would be a rose garden, oh Thou ravisher of hearts; with Thee Hell would be paradise, oh Thou cheerer of souls."[28] I now realize that one's real life consists not of external events, but of inner states which reveal who we really are; events enter us from outside, and then, there is our inner attitude and reaction to it. To mention a trivial exam-

ple, I have been at parties and other festivities, and I certainly didn't always enjoy myself at all. In fact, most of the time, the greater the expectation, the deeper the disappointment and frustration. I am sure everybody has experienced that.

According to research evaluating the subjective well-being of people around the globe, happiness has little to do with material possessions and a lot to do with attitude. However, one may object that there is no sunny side of life.

He should not say that. As long as he breathes and his heart beats, I AM present within and above each individual. I will never leave or forsake him because he is part of Myself and I am part of him. I AM the sun of each one's life; if the individual will remember Me the shadows will never be able to approach him.

Unless the person turns his back to you and creates a shadow himself, and then has to walk in it.

That is the only way evil is created.

This is confirmed also by scientists; in the study I mentioned, religion's contribution to well-being appears to be nearly universal across various faiths and ethnic groups. Although, not surprisingly, those who are single, elderly, or in poor health gain the most. Still, faith seems to succor the young as well; teens who attend services, read the Bible, and pray, feel less sad or depressed, less alone, less misunderstood and guilty, and more cared for than their nonreligious peers.[29]

Everyone wants to be happy, they expect it especially when they are young, feeling that happiness should belong to them and be the natural condition of their existence. That desire and expectation is true because it comes from Me, it is innate since I have placed it in their hearts. Happiness is the essence of life, also called beatitude or bliss, and it was the original condition of mankind on this planet.

But we forgot you, and therefore forgot how to be happy. However, as you implied, it depends on our choice and inner attitude. We may look at life as the old aphorism teaches us using the example of the glass half-empty or half-full.

What really creates lack and closes the door to the abundant supply that is always pouring from the Source, as the sun gives light, is the feeling of ingratitude. If one were grateful for what he has, he would not fail to receive more.

It would be in accord with the Law of Love.

Exactly, but if one becomes negative and resentful, he will lose also the little he has. In your experiences remember that unless an event helps you to learn, grow, and become more conscious of your "I AM" Self, and therefore, more free and wise, it creates more obstacles on your path and will obstruct the natural tendency of life to love and happiness. There is no such thing as standing still or a middle ground, you go either up or down. You should not allow your thoughts and feelings to rule you or deceive you, because they are the determining factor in your life. Everything depends on how you use them. Unfortunately, people are used by them, and the result is a house in disorder.

What is the relation of thought and feeling to consciousness?

They are the instruments by which consciousness finds expression together with the spoken word. You, as the Self, are meant to be the master in the house and to make them obey your order according to your will.

What about our physical senses?

They are not physical, you do not see, for instance, with your eyes; you see through them. The eyes may look and stare at something for a long time but if you are not conscious of it you will not be able to see. It is the I, your Self, who is conscious of what the eyes see, and of that which the ears hear; they are your tools, the same as the other sensory organs:

> The Self wishing the wish to hear, became
> the ear; to see, the eye, to smell, the nose ...[30]

In the same Hindu Scripture you read,

> Hearer of the ear and Speaker of all speech,
> Seer of the eye and Mentor of the mind,
> The Self is verily the Life of life.[31]

And in the Koran, "Eyes do not see Him, but He sees the eyes."[32]

Then, the Self is the primal cause and the source of manifestation.

Yes, "The Self is self-luminous because, clearly, nothing else can illumine it. It illumines all else. Eyes see sights, and ears hear sound; but who sees the eyes and who hears the ears? They obviously do not see and hear themselves. I am conscious of the eyes and of their objects, of the ears and their objects. Indeed I see and hear, rather than the eyes see and the ears hear. They are only the instruments I use."[33]

Moreover, when your body sleeps, where did your so-called physical senses go? Are they sleeping also? I think not.

I learned that the senses of sight, hearing, smelling, tasting, and touching involve specialized cells that send impulses directly to the brain to be interpreted, and interpretation is necessary for anything to be perceived and to actually exist for us.
But ask yourself: who is the interpreter? It is the "I" not the brain; you do not think with the brain, but through it, you use it only on the physical side of life. In fact, people do not think clearly and the faculties of their mind do not function as perfectly as I originally intended because their negative attitudes, wrong food with preservatives and additives, artificial vitamins, substances like drugs, tobacco, alcohol, meat, they all contaminate their brains. Every negative thought and emotion sends a corresponding vibration to the brain, and it is like a shadow which obstructs the inflow of the finer vibrations of the stream of light coming from Me. The individual does not realize that what enables him to think is My light penetrating his brain, and if he interferes with it, he is bound to experience difficulty and limitations in the use and control of the mind.

However, the "I", or the self, can misinterpret or have a mistaken notion.
Again, it depends which self you are referring to; do not forget that at present, there are at least two selves in you. When I speak of the "I", I mean the real one, that is, the I AM-Self acting through the heart which is My direct interpreter. The trouble is that the intellect, as we discussed may, and it often does interfere and hinders the action of the heart. What I am explaining with regard to your physical form applies also to your

inner side, because what is called the soul is affected. However, you must realize that the body is merely a shell, or an overcoat, although people are so identified with it that they believe it is who or what they are.

I know, we think of ourselves as physical beings, and perhaps, those less superficial have the vague idea of a soul somewhere within them. But is not the body the temple of the Holy Spirit? That's what I learned in my Bible study.
It is intended to be, but people have made it their God and have sacrificed everything on its altar. You know how deeply concerned they are with their physical appearance, preoccupied with their weight and blood pressure, and careful with their caloric intake. Everyone sees his doctor regularly, and they give more time to physical exercises than to prayer and meditation. Only when something happens to their temple, without hope of recovery, they turn to the true God within whom they have ostracized.

You are right, we go to the gym as religiously and faithfully, perhaps even more so, than to our houses of worship.
No wonder the world is in such a mess!

[1] Bert Thompson, Ph.D. and Brad Harrub, Ph.D., *The Origin of Consciousness* (Part I), p. 1, Apologetics Press, January 2004.

[2] Ibid., p. 8.

[3] Julian Jaynes, *The Origin of Consciousness in the Breakdown of the Bicameral Mind.* (Boston: Houghton Mifflin, 1976), p. 8.

[4] Ibid., p. 11.

[5] Thompson and Harrub, p. 16.

[6] Ibid., p. 18.

[7] Ibid., p. 17.

[8] Ibid., p. 25.

[9] Ibid., p. 14.

[10] Ibid., p. 14.

[11] Ibid., p. 14.

[12] *The Origin of Consciousness in the Breakdown of the Bicameral Mind*, p. 15.

[13] Thompson and Harrub, p. 6.

[14] Ibid., p. 24.

[15] *The Meeting of Science and Spirit*, p. 149.

[16] Friedrich Nietzsche, *Thus Spake Zarathushtra*, transl. T. Common (Mineola, NY: Dover Publications, 1999), p. 1.

[17] Quoted in J.A. Bracken, *The Divine Matrix. Creativity as Link Between East and West*, (Maryknoll, N.Y., 1995.), p. 42.

[18] *Paradiso*, 33:124-6.

[19] White, p. 15.

[20] *Esoteric Healing*, p. 377.

[21] Ibid., p. 377.

[22] Ibid., p. 379.

[23] *A Treatise on Cosmic Fire*, pp. 312, 310.

[24] Ibid., pp. 241, 316.

[25] Quoted in J.C. Pugh, *Entertaining the Triune Mystery* (Harrisburg, PA: Trinity Press International, 2003), p. 83.

[26] Ken Ring, Heading Toward Omega. In Search of the Meaning of the Near-Death Experience.(NY: William Morrow, 1984) pp. 57-59.

[27] *Paradiso* 1:1-6.

[28] Underhill, p. 389.

[29] *Time*, January 17, 2005, p. A48.

[30] *Upanishads*, quoted in Das, p. 115.

[31] *Afranishads*, in Das, 114.

[32] Ibid., p. 114.

[33] Das, p. 114.

CHAPTER 16

Spirit and Matter

The spiritual creature which we are has need of a body, without which it could nowise attain that knowledge which it obtains as the only approach to those things by knowledge of which it is made blessed.
St. Bernard

The intuitive mind is a sacred gift and the rational mind is a faithful servant. We have created a society that honors the servant and has forgotten the gift.
Albert Einstein

In order to reach a higher state of consciousness it is necessary for me to reunite my spiritual and physical poles. We understand, more or less, what matter is, but the notion of spirit is unclear. It would be helpful if you would explain.
There is a great deal of confusion with regard to terms like, spirit, soul, mind, self, and consciousness. Often they are used interchangeably, but they are not the same. As I mentioned, the word "soul" in English is referred to by various words in the Hebrew and Greek languages in which the Old and New Testaments were originally written. It is also used in at lease four different ways with several meanings.

By spirit I mean the finest essence and highest form of energy; you may call it divine because all energy in its pristine purity is God's. We saw already that the word "spirit" derives from the same root as "breath;"[1] in fact, what the breath is to your body, the spirit is to all life.

That is the meaning of the statement in Genesis, "God breathed into man's nostrils the breath of life and he became a living being."[2]

The word "spirit" presupposes the primordial polarity with matter and can only be understood in its relation to it. I am not referring to the Holy Spirit, which is love, but to one of two poles of the Source as the divine magnet that cannot be active unless is united to the other pole.

Spirit represents the inner or invisible side of life and matter is the outer, external aspect. Therefore, for the universe to manifest it is required to have both in order to generate, by their relationship, the light energy out of which all forms are created.

How do spirit and matter come into being?

I thought I had explained it to you, but I will elaborate on it until you are able to apprehend it, at least intellectually. The infinite Ground is that of which nothing can be said because it is unmanifested and transcendent. It emerges from its quiescent and latent state and becomes conscious of itself. Remember that consciousness is relational, one is always conscious of something, but since the Infinite is One, without a second, it can only be conscious of itself, now notice, it-Self.

It gives birth to a Self by knowing and feeling itself.

Yes, and it loves itself.

That's why God is love, by the self-feeling of the Infinite.

Therefore, being related to itself becomes a bipolar being, the inner side as spirit and the outer as matter. Their union and interaction generates the fire which radiates or emanates the universal light-energy filling all space.

The two poles are interdependent and complement one another; are they the primordial polarity of male and female?
Yes, that is another name for it, like the Father-Mother God. Thus, you have the divine matrix or the symbolic cosmic womb out of which everything is created.

Let me repeat to see if I have understood it correctly:
Two poles arise out of the self-contemplation of the Infinite, and the flow of energy generated by their union becomes the fire of creation or the cosmic light, which is its radiation , filling all space out of which everything is made in the manifested universe.

It is interesting to note that the Latin word "*materia*" (matter) is related to "*mater*" (mother) for she brings into form the ideation of the spirit as the father. I see the necessity of matter, in her various degrees of vibratory action and condensation, complementing spirit and be the envelopment to delimit the diffusion of the energy in order to bring forth and create form.
Yes, matter in its sevenfold state, from the densest to the finest, should be thought of as mater or the feminine aspect of creation. The polarity of male-female exists throughout the universe as the one inseparable and complementary principle, since without their dynamic interrelation all is quiescent, in a latent state, like static electricity. It is impossible for the Infinite to manifest with only one of them, and it becomes active in both of them because the creative power of life, which is love, is kindled by their being joined and related to each other.

When the principle of polarity is recognized, one finds in it the explanation that the physical or material world and the inner spiritual reality are two sides of the same fabric, in which the threads of all forces and of all events, of all forms of consciousness and of their objects, are woven into an inseparable network of endless, mutually dependent relations, giving rise to the totality of the universe.

"It is erroneous to create a gap or a duality and to think of spirit wholly immaterial and body or form wholly material, i.e., two things neither of which exists."[3] They cannot be separated and exist independently, just as you cannot isolate the positive from the negative pole of an electric or magnetic field. The spirit can express itself only by its unity with matter which becomes its outer manifestation.

There is no spirit that is not clothed in matter or "matter-enveloped," there is no matter that is not animated by spirit or "spirit ensouled." Life cannot manifest and find expression without a form of some kind, that is, without a body of matter, however fine and subtle it may be, which gives it a distinct and unique existence. Therefore the body is often referred to as an instrument or a vehicle, that which carries the life making it individual. Even the Highest Being in the cosmic hierarchy of the infinite universe has its vestment or film of matter. "And though such a Self is called spirit because its aspect is so predominant, none the less it is true that it has its vibrating sheath of matter."[4] Otherwise, it could not be an individualized focus of consciousness which "I AM" and therefore be a creator. Life is perpetual motion and a constant flow or stream of energy based on the Law of polarity and the poles represent, as they emerge from the infinite ground of being, the Fatherhood and the Motherhood of God.

They are the source of light which empowers the world process by the moving force of love.

Does your explanation have relation to the Trinity?

Yes. Did you ever ask yourself why there are three persons in God?

It is a mystery and a dogma.
Do you find that an adequate and satisfactory explanation?

No, but it seems beyond human comprehension.
You are made in the image and likeness of God, whereby you must have the capacity to know your source, your divine blueprint.

How is it possible?
By simply knowing who you are.

I see that you always go back to the same point.
It is the only way. "I AM" is the way, the life, and the truth!

Are you referring to Jesus?
Not the personal Jesus, but to the "I AM" in Him, with whom He was one. You must realize that you, too – your true self-identity – are that "I AM." Have you ever thought why the omnipotent Father needs a Son? Obviously, there can be no father without a son or daughter, and there should be a mother as well. However, He is supposed to have the power to create the universe by Himself.

I don't know why, then, He would need a Son.
God, in order to create, must be conscious, especially when creating out of nothing. But consciousness, as I said, is a bipolar relation; it implies something of which to be conscious, and someone to be conscious of it. Since He is One, and there is no other, the Father can only be conscious of Him-self and by that

406

act of self-acknowledgment, or individualization, He brings forth the son. Thus the Son is begotten as the self-consciousness of the Father, expressed in the words "I AM." Furthermore, since no creation of any kind is possible without Love, the relationship between Father and Son will provide it abundantly, and that will be the third person, the Holy Spirit.

This explanation of the Trinity is so simple that it is hard to believe.
Then be content with the mystery or the dogma; after all, I am not a theologian. But you must agree that My exposition makes more sense than the "big bang" or the "chemical soup" from which you supposedly sprang.

I didn't mean that what you said is not true; knowing, at least a little, who you are, I try to have an open mind.
You need also an open heart.

That's right. It has been suggested that the world needs two modes of thoughts, one that cares about truth and what it is, and one that concerns itself with the logic of truth.
You should not fall into the trap of believing that man's one-sided intellect which as I said, tries to assume the role of a judge over the very forces from which it originated, can explain the nature of the ultimate reality that gives meaning and depth to your existence. There are two fundamental attitudes that characterize the intentional flow of consciousness, inwardly or outwardly.

They are the subjective and objective poles and we are drawn to favor one or the other. In fact, the history of Western civilization can be described in terms of the con-

flict between them, also referred to as religion and science or idealism and materialism.
And which one chooses depends on what kind of a person he is, for it is not a dead thing which you can reject or accept as you wish, it is rather animated by the consciousness and the attitude of the individual who holds it. It is a decision made deliberately.

Or ignorantly.
But that is not an excuse. Both views and their positions are essentially one sided as it is evident from My explanation to you.

They should be interrelated according to the principle of polarity. Progress has been made in the field of science as attested by this quote: "Changing one's paradigm is not easy. Millennia passed before humankind discovered that energy is the basis of matter. It may take a few more years before we prove that wisdom and knowledge are the basis of – and can actually create – energy, which in turn creates matter."[5]
And, after that, it may take a few more years to find out that love is the source of energy, matter, and all that is.

Philosophers want to know how God thinks, but they should rather learn how He *loves*.
The truth is not in your head or the world outside, but in your innermost Being, the cause of your heart-beat. Instead of getting entangled in beliefs and opinions, theories, and abstract ideas, you must go beyond what the intellect has accumulated from external appearances, based on outer perception and rely on inner awareness, the intuition or the teaching from within

which arises when you feel yourselves connected with your Source.

Take, for instance, your body. If you perceive it in its outward material form or appearance, you are dealing with an object among other objects of the external world. You can dissect it, analyze it, dissolve it into its chemical or molecular constituents, or observe its mechanism and measure the electrical impulses that operate it.

From this point of view, you can dissociate yourself from the body, using or abusing it as you like, and deny all responsibility for your physical existence. But from the inner standpoint, if you are inwardly aware of your body, even though it is only a covering or a vehicle, you are no more dealing with a merely material object, a thing among other things; instead you are confronted with a living entity that is a reflection of the basic tendencies of your consciousness, acquired through your growth, maintained and modified by your thoughts, feelings, words, and actions.

Religion and science seem always to be in conflict.
They need not be, although their methods are different. One is inwardly directed, based on devotion and the inner experience of the ultimate reality; the other consists in observation and deduction from sense data.

I'd like to quote these pertinent words by John White: "Our endless accumulation of scientific facts does not add up to wisdom and understanding of the human situation in its cosmic aspect. Every new bit of information, every new answer we get raises a dozen new questions. Gathering scientific data is an endless process, and unless we are properly grounded in the *moral* foundation of the universe we will

continue to find new ways of misusing science so that knowledge only leads to greater unhappiness."

Then he relates a passage by Krishnamurti: "Knowledge is only a part of life not the totality, and when that part assumes all-consuming importance, as it is threatening to do now, then life becomes superficial ... More knowledge, however wide and cunningly put together, will not resolve human problems; to assume that it will is to invite frustration and misery. Something much more profound is needed."[6]

Science is the endeavor to gain power over nature; religion is the effort to conquer and transcend oneself.

As you have explained it to me, the heart must illumine the head. A physicist writes: "To paraphrase an old Chinese saying, mystics understand the roots of Tao, but not its branches; scientists understand its branches, but not its roots ... Mystical experience is necessary to understand the deepest nature of things, and science is essential for modern life. What we need, therefore, is not synthesis but a dynamic interplay between mystical intuition and scientific analysis."[7] It sounds like the principle of polarity.

Yes, the gap is closing in the growing understanding that the scientific approach based on the dualistic mode of separating the subject from the object is essentially a set of models and metaphors giving only a picture or a map of the territory, not of the nature of Reality itself. The view of the universe which has emerged from modern atomic physics is that of an interconnected web of relations and the interdependence of all things and events, which can only have a possible explanation by their at-one-ment with the whole.

The crucial feature of quantum theory is that the observer is not only necessary to study or investigate the properties of an object, but he is necessary even to define them. It was remarked that in atomic physics one can never speak about nature without, at the same time, speaking about oneself. In fact, it has been suggested that we replace the word, "observer" with the word, "participator."

According to Heisenberg, "Natural science does not simply describe and explain nature; it is a part of the interplay between nature and ourselves."[8] The individual "is found to be both physical and spiritual, both aspects being 'real' and neither fully describable in terms of the other. 'Scientific' and religious' metaphors are complementary; neither contradicts the other."[9]

But I would like to emphasize that what is really important is not intellectual analysis and theories, but intuitive feeling and deep insight. When something is categorized or defined, it becomes circumscribed and limited; it loses its grounding in infinity and is uprooted, as it were, from its deeper reality and its incommensurable nature.

I have read that "When the critical intellect looks at anything carefully, it vanishes. This is true of the solid substance of bodies as of historical generalizations, of entities such as nations ... The reason is, of course, that things exist only relatively — for a point of view or for convenience of description. Thus, when we inspect any unit more closely we find that its structure is more complex and more differentiated than we had supposed. Its variety comes to impress us more than its unity. As a historian of science once put it, 'Isn't it amazing how many things there are that aren't so'?"[10]

A mystery may remain incomprehensible and ineffable to your human faculties but, as witnessed by mystics, saints, and artists throughout the ages, it can be envisioned and experienced.

It is a mystery, not because it is hidden or out of reach, but because it appears so to your limited intellect, which is an inadequate and inappropriate instrument to penetrate the ultimate reality.

For Einstein, the source of all true science is the sensation of the mystical, which he considered "the most beautiful and most profound emotion we can experience." For him, the person "to whom this emotion is a stranger, who can no longer wonder and stand rapt in awe, is as good as dead."[11]

I am very grateful for your elaboration of these fundamental principles of life because I receive a greater understanding as you repeat and explain them in a little different way. I feel that I am really growing up when I contemplate the Infinite as the transcendent ground, and how it becomes immanent in every being and an all-pervading activity from atoms to galaxies all interconnected in hierarchical orders.

Yes, knowledge exists in relationship rather than in an objective reality or in a subjective experience because your energy and the energy of the universe as God is an energy of love.

Just as each cell and organ of the body contributes and shares in its own distinct way in the life of the total organism, so we have and are the same life, nature and energy of the Infinite One. It makes me think of the hologram: if I take a holographic photo, for instance, of a bird and cut out one section of it, let us say the head or a wing, and then enlarge that part to the original size, I will not have a large

head or wing but a picture of the "whole" bird. That is, each individual section of the picture contains the whole picture as the part is in the whole and the whole is in each part.

Does it not remind you of the principle of polarity?

Yes, and the lines:

> A robin redbreast in a cage
> Puts all Heaven in a rage.
> .....
> A skylark wounded in the wing,
> A cherubim does cease to sing.[12]

That explains our innate sense of the Infinite and our effort to know it whether we refer to it in mathematical terms like boundless, unlimited, immeasurable, or to metaphysical concepts of oneness, universality, completeness. There is, more or less unknowingly, a deep longing for it as we face and struggle with the experience of our fundamental and pervasive finitude. That's why our desires are insatiable and never fully satisfied, or only temporarily, and we change them constantly, or at least their objects. We are afflicted by the tragic irony that the happiest moments are also the most fleeting and short-lived making our existence a "useless passion."

Try to realize that life is a continuous ongoing process of both being and becoming, a never-ending conversion of one into the other.

Another type of polarity.

However, human experiences are polarized in the activity of becoming because the attention of the individual is totally involved and almost engulfed in the external world that is changing all the time.

Therefore, we are like a wheel off center, and without the connection with the Ground of being we are bound to end in futility. But how can we make the experience of being and becoming one in our life?
Think of My name because it is the spring of the divine activity of life flowing freely and uncontaminated by human discord and negative energy.

Your name is the creative Word that was with God and was God and spoke the first command, "Let there be light; and there was light." In the simple and profound comment of Meister Eckhart, "All created things are God's speech. The being of a stone speaks and manifests the same as does my mouth about God."[13]
Yes, "I AM" is the creative Word of love and it is both being and becoming in dynamic interrelation and perfect harmony. "I" is being, the divine storehouse of all patterns and ideas; "AM" is the substance and the moving force of becoming which bring them into manifestation. The consciousness of My name will give you the experience of infinity and eternity because for it there is no separation of before and after but only a continuous ever-present now without beginning and with no end. You are no longer troubled by your past mistakes or worried about the future once you realize that I AM, as your true Being, enables you to become who and what you want to be.

I would begin by affirming that I AM your forgiving Presence, that is, giving-for my shortcomings the consuming fire of your love.

I AM also the magnetic power acting everywhere always drawing the lesser into the greater in ever-expanding beauty and perfection.

Does the cosmic principle of expansion refer also to you?
Rather than an immutable and fixed entity, as some thinkers assume God to be, I AM in the fullness of the act of being and becoming always capable of further actuation.

But are you not infinite?
Yes, I AM always infinitely beyond the limited capacity of the human intellect to understand, but not to love. Life involves passage from potentiality to actuality, that is, transit from one stage of existence to another in ever-expanding creativity. I AM is the eternal principle of that activity in My interrelation with each individual sharing with them My love, wisdom, and power when they recognize that I AM their greater Self, and that I AM that I AM.

Then you enable the divine seed within each of us to grow and unfold by the light-rays of your sun-presence.
Most certainly, for I express Myself through you when your thoughts, feelings and words are in accord with the Law of love. You may think of yourself as a finite being within the confine of your physical body but why not as a co-creator with Me?

Unfortunately we humans have become groundless like a tree uprooted by the storms of our passions.
Yet I AM still shining on it. Unlike the tree, although fallen, humanity is not forgotten and left to rotten. With their acceptance of My presence they can be the salt of the earth, without whom "This world would smell like what is – a tomb."[14] Every-

one has the power in their heart to rise because "I AM" is their immortal life.

In a Christian context each individual possesses the same being, substance and nature as the eternal "Son of God." I quote again Eckhart: "The Father gives birth to His Son without ceasing; and I say more: He gives birth not only to me, his Son, but he gives birth to me as himself and himself as me and to me as his being and nature. In the innermost source, there I spring out in the Holy Spirit where there is one life and one being and one work."[15] This boggles my mind.

Do not allow that or we cannot continue our dialogue. It is not so difficult as you think: the Father represents the Infinite I referred to, from whom emerges the Son "In the innermost source," that is, by its self-knowing and self-loving, and you are its individualized focus of consciousness.

I am one of his sons, but the Father "gives birth to me as himself and himself as me ..."

Yes, because you are, as I said, an extension or projection of itself on Earth, that is, its self-consciousness, sharing the same identity, "I AM." Therefore, you were himself before coming-to-be who you are now.

Before I was, I was you. That's why Eckhart can speak of the soul as its own creator: "For in the same being of God were God is above being and above distinction, there I myself was, there I willed myself and committed myself to create the man [i.e., me]."[16]

You are a duplicate of Myself, that is, My image.

One life-stream flowing from the infinite Ground of being.
Through the sevenfold universe, as I will elaborate on this later on.

But how can he say that the soul created himself?
I see that you still have difficulty understanding it and I think very few people do. Let me try again, but do not be discouraged because it takes time, study, and meditation to grasp it. In what is referred to as the Infinite or Ground before anything existed we were all One "above distinction." And you were that before it became by self-acknowledgement, the God Self that individualized in you on the physical plane.

But you said that we are still one life, one consciousness, and one energy.
Now no more in a static and formless state. Let me use the analogy of the electric lights in a room. There might be a chandelier suspended from the ceiling, a standing lamp, one on the desk and other devices as means of illumination.

However, they have and use the same source of power.
Right, there is one energy-principle and activity immanent within each of the light fixtures that does not exist apart or separable from them. Yet, at the same time it is transcendent of all of them as their ultimate ground.

This reminds me of the beginning of Dante's Paradiso which I'd like to quote again:

> The glory of Him who moves all that is
> penetrates through the universe and shines
> in one part more and in another less.[17]

I am sure that you inspired that beautiful poem. That's why the creative process is difficult, if not impossible, to explain in human terms. Even with regard to a simple thought we don't know where it comes from. Thoughts are constantly streaming through our mind, each following swiftly the other, by conditioning and association, and even those we create we are not aware how they arise. It is, indeed a mystery the way they appear apparently out of nothing.

Nothing comes out of nothing, you should know who is the Source of all that is true, good, and beautiful.

It is you! I know that those individuals considered most creative, like composers, artists, writers, even scientists, recognize that they are not the doer and that the process is mysterious. "Whence and how they come," writes Mozart of his compositions, "I know not; nor can I force them ... All this fires my soul, and, provided I am not disturbed, my subject enlarges itself, becomes methodized and defined, and the whole, though it be long, stands almost complete and finished in my mind, so that I can survey it, like a fine picture or a beautiful statue, at a glance."

He tells us that the parts are not heard successively but all at once and how delightful it cannot be described. The creation is compared to a "pleasing lively dream ... What has been thus produced I do not easily forget, and this is perhaps the best gift I have my Divine Maker to thank for."[18]

The description by Tchaikovsky is similar to that of Mozart: "... the germ of a future composition comes suddenly and unexpectedly ... It takes root with extraordinary force and rapidity, shoots up through the earth, puts forth branches and leaves, and finally blossoms ... I forget every-thing and behave like a madman: everything within me stands pulsing and quivering; hardly have I begun the sketch before one thought follows another."[19]

This "supernatural and inexplicable force" does not exclude the human effort of giving expression to the exter-nal form, although, we should not believe that the composi-tion is "only a cold exercise of the intellect. The only music capable of moving and touching us is that which flows from the depths of a composer's soul when he is stirred by inspi-ration."[20]

According to Giacomo Puccini the opera *Madame Butterfly* was "dictated" to him by God: "I was merely in-strumental in putting it on paper and communicating it to the public." But he recognizes that one must acquire "by laborious study and application the technical mastery of his craft ... God does not do for man what he can do for him-self."[21]

He is right, I have endowed everyone with My divine faculties and the individual must use them because he is a co-creator.

Wagner believed that "there are universal currents of Di-vine Thought vibrating the ether everywhere ... I feel that I am one with this vibrating force."

He is referring to the music of the spheres to which one can attune and receive a fragment of its tremendous power and beauty.

"I believe," Wagner explains, "that it is this universal vi-brating energy that binds the soul of man to the Almighty Central Power from which emanates the life principle to which we all owe our existence. This energy links us to the

Supreme Force of the universe, of which we are all a part. If it were not so, we could not bring ourselves into communication with it. The one who can do this is inspired."[22]

To the question of why only great composers are able to connect with that transcendent Power, Wagner referred to Beethoven and said that he was much more aware of his oneness with Divinity than another because "we all have at birth the same relationship to that Power." However, we may be subject to some conditions that obstruct or even prevent that relationship. And he made clear that "an atheistic upbringing is fatal. No atheist has ever created anything of great and lasting value."[23]

I would like to mention the words of one more composer that is in agreement, as they all are, with the earlier quotations. In fact, I am tempted, with your permission, to write part of a conversation between the famous violinist Joseph Joachim and Johannes Brahms because it touches on some ideas of our dialogues. The great composer refers often to the words of Jesus with regard to our oneness with the Creator. "Not I, the Father that dwells within me does the works" is one of his favorite statements because "when He said that, and when I am at my best while composing, I too feel that a higher power is working through me."[24] "To realize that we are one with the Creator, as Beethoven did, is a wonderful and awe-inspiring experience ..."

Brahms explains about his creative process, "when I feel the urge I begin by appealing directly to my Maker ... I immediately feel vibrations that thrill my whole being ... Above all, I realize at such moment the tremendous significance of Jesus' supreme revelation, 'I and my Father are one' ... Immediately the ideas flow in upon me, directly from God ... All true inspiration emanates from God and He can reveal Himself to us only through that spark of divinity within."[25]

Then we have an interesting interpretation of sacred scriptures that seems to be in accord with your teaching. He was asked if he believed that the divine power which Jesus called the Father is in all of us, and whether any composer could create immortal works. Brahms quoted Jesus' words, "The Father that dwelleth in Me, he doeth the works ... He that believeth in Me, the works that I do shall he do also, and greater works than these shall he do." (John 14:10-12)

"That is one of the most momentous of Jesus' many significant utterances," adds the composer, "and is one that the Orthodox Church ignores. Did you ever hear a sermon preached in the pulpit on that text? Joachim answers, 'I must confess that I never heard a sermon based on the text of John 14:12.' And you never will," continued the composer, "because it is a flat contradiction of John 3:16," [For God so loved the world that he gave his only Son, so that everyone who believes in him may not perish but may have eternal life] and that is the cornerstone on which the whole Orthodox Church is built."[26]

Joachim agrees with Brahms that he could never reconcile himself to the belief that Jesus was "the only begotten Son of God," and remarks that John 14:12 are Jesus' words while John 3:16 are those of the Evangelist.

"Then you do not believe that Jesus was the Son of God?" the author questioned the composer, and he replied: "Certainly I believe He was the Son of God; we are all sons of God, for we could not have come from any other source. The vast difference, however, between Him and us ordinary mortals is that He had appropriated more of divinity than the rest of us have." And he continues to explain that "The power from which all truly great composers like Mozart, Schubert, Bach and Beethoven drew their inspirations is the same power that enabled Jesus to work His miracles ... It is the power that created our earth and the whole universe, including you and me."

According to him Jesus taught us that we can appropriate that power when He said, "Ask and it shall be given you, seek and ye shall find, knock and it shall be opened unto you ... When I compose I always feel that I am appropriating that same spirit to which Jesus so often referred."[27]

I think the word "appropriate" is not very appropriate, though in your limited vocabulary is used also in the sense of "to take possession of."

In reality, it is you who appropriate the individual when he allows you to do it. Thomas Wolfe referring to his novel, *Look Homeward, Angel* said: "I cannot say the book was written. It was something that took hold and possessed me ... Upon that flood everything was swept and born along as by a great river. And I was born along with it."[28]

Let us say that you and I appropriate each other because attunement and cooperation are necessary.

It is the principle of polarity, the outer self responding to the God Self. De Musset wrote, "It is not work, it is listening; it is as if someone unknown person were speaking in your ear."[29]

Another poet, Goethe, said: "The songs made me, and I not them; the songs had me in their power." Dickens' statement is similar: when he sat down to write, "some beneficent power" showed it all to him. George Eliot told a friend that, "in all she considered her best writing, there was a 'not herself' which took possession of her, and that she felt her own personality to be merely the instrument through which the spirit, as it were, was acting."[30] This is true especially concerning mystical poets and writers. Blake described the composition of "Jerusalem" in these verses:

> I see the Saviour over me
> Spreading his beams of love
> dictating the words of this mile song (I, 4-5)

And Rimbaud in the disordering of all his senses to reach the unknown, wrote, "It is false to say: I think. One ought to say: I am thought ... For I is an other. I attend at the blossoming of my thought: I look at it, I listen."[31]

"All was ordered according to the direction of the Spirit, which often went in haste," wrote Jakob Boehme, "... the burning fire often forced with great speed, and the hand and pen must hasten directly after it; for it goes and comes like a sudden shower." One would assume that the procedure is different with the methods of scientific investigation and discovery since it deals with "objective" reality, but it is not so. The mathematician Karl Gauss described in a letter how he proved a theorem he had been working on for four years: "At last two days ago I succeeded, not by dint of painful effort but so to speak by the grace of God. As a sudden flash of light, the enigma was solved ... For my part I am unable to name the nature of the thread which connected what I previously knew with that which made my success possible."[32]

Helmholtz, the great German physicist, said that after previous investigation of the problem "in all directions

... happy ideas come unexpectedly without effort, like an inspiration."[33]

In looking back over these passages they seem to be a variation on the same theme. The worded expression of the creative process may be different but they all point to the same source which either dictates, possesses or inspires them. My increasing desire is to receive more light into myself because I realize that all depends on it. How can I be a vessel of Grace?

By your attention to Me and your call; it is as simple as that.

That is the magnetic power of love.

Yes, the God Self is constantly trying to draw the individual on and up but he is not responsive because of the pressure and pull of the outer world which absorbs all his time and energy.

I have noticed that in our dialogue you are more interested in my personal experience with the divine reality than the conceptual understanding of God derived from intellectual reflections.

Yes, because the inner activity, through the feeling, can teach you more than any conceptualization or theories of either philosophy or science. I am not so much concerned with what you think but how you feel that which is embedded within you so that once awakened it never occurs to you to question it. The essence is not what you hold in your head but the depth at which you hold it, hopefully in your heart's core, in your heart of heart.

It is where you speak to me, because the key to the understanding of life is love, your love. The words of St. Catherine of Genoa strike a sympathetic chord. "O love, can it be that

thou has called me with so great a love, and made me to know in one instant that which worlds [sic] cannot express?"[34]

That is what I try to bring more clearly into focus because everything in life, both at the human and divine level, depends on the fire of creation. Only by it you can be purified, set free, enlightened, and raised into the ascension.

It is my eternal freedom from the wheel of birth and rebirth and the glorious return to the Father's house as the divine being I AM predestined to become.

[1] See Chapter 11, p. 135.

[2] Genesis 2:7.

[3] Annie Besant, *A Study in Consciousness* (Wheaton, Ill.: The Theosophical Publishing House, 1972), p. 28.

[4] Ibid., p. 28.

[5] G.L. Schroder, quoted in, G.E. Schwartz, *The G.O.D. Experiments* (NY: Atria Books, 2006), p. 169.

[6] *The Meeting of Science and Spirit,* p. 65.

[7] F. Capra, *Beyond Ego: Modern Physics and Eastern Mysticism,* p. 69.

[8] Werner Heisenberg, *Physics and Philosophy.* (London: George Allen & Unwin, 1963), p.75.

[9] *Beyond Ego,* p. 244.

[10] A.W. Watts, *The Two Hands of God: The Myths of Polarity.* (NY: Collier Books, 1969), p. 1.

[11] Quoted in A.L. Govinda, *Creative Meditation,* p. 203.

[12] William Blake, "Auguries of Innocence."

[13] Meister Eckhart, *The Essential Sermons, Commentaries, Treaties and Defense.* Transl, by E. Colledge O.S.A. and G. McGinn, (NY: Paulist Press, 1981), p. 205.

[14] P.B. Shelley, Letter to Maria Gisborne, l:209.

[15] Meister Eckhart, op. cit., p. 187.

[16] Ibid., p. 52.

[17] *Paradiso,* 1, 3.

[18] *Creativity,* ed. P.E. Vernon, (Baltimore, MD: Penguin Books, 1970), p. 55.

[19] Ibid., p. 57.

[20] Ibid., p. 58.

[21] A.M. Abell, *Talks with Great Composers* (NY: Carol Publishing Group, 1994), p. 117.

[22] Ibid., p. 137.

[23] Ibid., p. 138.

[24] John 14:10; Abell, p. 4.

[25] Abell, p. 5.

[26] Abell, pp. 9, 10, 12.
[27] Ibid., pp. 11, 14
[28] Quoted in *Nonduality*, p. 155.
[29] Underhill, p. 23.
[30] *Nonduality*, p. 155.
[31] Quoted in Abrams, p. 418.
[32] *Nonduality*, pp. 155, 159.
[33] *Creativity*, p. 91.
[34] Quoted in Underhill, p. 182.

CHAPTER 17

The Sense of Wonder

Concepts create idols, only wonder can understand.
St. Gregory of Nyssa

*If I want to fix my mind on what I mean by
absolute or ethical value ... one particular experience
presents itself to me ... I believe the best way of
describing it is to say that when I have it
I wonder at the existence of the world ...
It is the experience of seeing the world as a miracle.*
Ludwig Wittgenstein

*We need a renaissance of wonder. We need to renew, in our
hearts and in our souls, the deathless dream, the eternal poetry,
the perennial sense that life is miracle and magic.*
E. Merrill Root

*There are only two ways to live your life.
One is as though nothing is a miracle. The other is
as though everything is a miracle.*
Albert Einstein

To the awakened individual, Nature can indeed be a source of
wonder, the visible realm shrouded in the mystery of the invisible. The physical side of life, what you call matter, should
not be considered of a lower and lesser value unless its inner
light is eclipsed by clinging to its temporal forms with the desire to possess them and use them for personal ends.

The finite is as necessary to the infinite as the infinite to
the finite, no part can be understood except with reference to

the whole because they are the two inseparable, or bipolar, aspects of the same reality.

As you said, the process of perception depends on the state of consciousness of the individual. How meaningful these words are: "Whether man shall live his old life or a new one in a universe of death or life, cut off an alien or affiliated and at home, in a state of servitude or of genuine freedom, all depends on his mind as it engages with the world in the act of perceiving.[1]

Yes, if you see with the feeling of love the eyes capture and emit light illumining everything. You will discover that the simplest thing in the sensible world, like a stone, a snowflake, or a flower, can speak to you of that deeper relationship that reveals the whole creation as the family of God.

This divine reality found its voice in the Canticle of St. Francis of Assisi, in which he raises his song of praise to the Most High for His gifts. And in his mystical vision of all creatures in God, and God in all creatures, he calls the sun, the moon, stars, water, fire, air, earth, and every created thing, even death, with the loving attributes of brother and sister.

Sometimes I wondered about the relationship of love and beauty, and I'd ask myself whether I love something because it is beautiful, or is it beautiful because I love it. I think that to the eyes of a mother, for instance, her child is always beautiful. "Beauty is simply Reality seen with the eyes of love," says Evelyn Underhill.[2]

Love and beauty are germane, they are intimately related and, I would say, interdependent. Can you think of anything more beautiful than the light? Spiritual light also can be visible and tangible to the feeling and it is Reality itself.

It was the first command, and you said everything is made out of it.
Yes, and on it is recorded everything, whether in the life of the individual or localities.

St. Theresa of Avila said that compared to it the light of the sun is dull.
It is beauty itself, and the source of it, because it is love. If you visualize the light, it penetrates the physical veil and reveals the inner side which is the original divine creation.

You mentioned the trinity of life-light-love. Even in our experience whatever we love is beautiful, even though we may be aware of the flaws and the defects which become irrelevant or non-existent. I am reminded of William Blake's lines:

> Love to faults is always blind;
> Always to joy inclin'd,
> Lawless, wing'd and unconfin'd,
> And breakes all chains from every mind.[3]

The insight of another of your poets is also close to the truth:

> A thing of beauty is a joy for ever:
> Its loveliness increases; it will never
> Pass into nothingness ...[4]

Love transfigures the object by its light, bringing forth its inner form and you see My creation as I see it. I said in the beginning that it was "very good," and it still is. Mankind has largely spoiled and disfigured its appearance, but can never destroy its Reality, which is made of the eternal substance of My light.

And the mystic agrees when he addressed the speaking face of heaven and earth:

> And I said to all the things that throng about the gateways of the senses: "tell me of my God, since you are not He, tell me something about Him." And they cried out in a great voice: "He made us." My question was my gazing upon them, and their response was their beauty.

Then he turns away from the attraction of the world to the Source of beauty itself and cried out:

> Late have I love you, beauty so old and so new: late have I loved you. And see, you were within and I was in the external world and sought you there, and in my unlovely state I plunged into those lovely created things. which you made. You were with me, and I was not with you. The lovely things kept me far from you, though if they did not have their existence in you, they had no existence at all.[5]

Nature is in truth so beautiful, notwithstanding all that has been imposed upon her, that were we to see her, as Adam originally did, her appearance would amaze us.
It may seem a paradox to you but the more one is conscious and understands life the deeper is the feeling of the marvelous and awesome. Emerson said, "the wise man wonders at the usual" and sees "the miraculous in the common."[6]

In his novel *The Fountain,* Charles Langbridge Morgan discusses this very idea:

> I supposed that ignorance was what chiefly separated the mortal from the immortal state, and I believed that death would be a door to secrets that after it everything would be made plain. Nor do I suggest now that the greater knowledge and understanding are not attained to in the immortal state; but that they are the distinguishing essence of God I no longer believe. What I have hitherto called omniscience is better thought of as infinite power of wonder. Knowledge is static, a stone in the stream itself, in common men a trickle clouded by doubt, in poets and saints a sparkling rivulet, in God a mighty river, bearing the whole commerce of the divine mind. Is it not true that, even on earth, as knowledge increases, wonder deepens?[7]

No one can say what life is, you can only know it by being it; that is why My true name is "I AM." Real knowledge does not consist in the intellectual accretion or accumulation of information and data gathered from without. People believe in their concepts, while only wonder can penetrate the mystery of life.

This reminds me of a lovely poem:

> Flower in the crannied wall,
> I pluck you out of the crannies,
> I hold you here, root and all, in my hand.
> Little flower -- but if I could understand
> What you are, root and all, and all in all,
> I should know what God and man is.[8]

"Therefore, it is the glorious paradox of our existence that all conceivability of the world is only the footstool of its inconceivability."[9]

When your senses are purified by the fire of My love can you recover the capacity to see without distortion, not the mere surface but into the inner life of things, and realize "God in all creatures, and also in the herbs and grass."[10]

The writer echoes the mystic, "The object achieves its epiphany," that is, a spiritual manifestation, by revealing its luminous soul "from the vestment of its appearance."[11]

You need the inner eye, the clairvoyant mode of sight which opens the mind and heart to the infinite within the finite, to the eternal within the temporary and transient, to the divine within the human.

We are told of St. Douceline that "out of doors one day with her sisters, she heard a bird's note; 'What a lovely song!' she said; and the song drew her straight to God. Did they bring her a flower, its beauty had a like effect." "To look on trees, water and flowers," says St. Teresa of her own beginnings of contemplation, "helped me to recollect the Presence of God."[12]

I think that the statement, "Unless you change and become like children, you shall not enter into the Kingdom of Heaven,"[13] beside becoming humble, refers also about recovering the capacity to see without veil and distortion. Only by the purity of our feeling can we truly see that everything that lives is holy because God created it.

You are right. The vision of the child is not corrupted like an adult carrying the burden of the past, involved in the world, which tends to keep him enslaved to his fallen state. This human condition causes a lack of awareness, a deadness of the sensibility, and a visual deficiency by which people "have eyes, yet see not, ears and hear not" and a heart so hardened that it can neither feel nor understand the Reality of life. The result for a person so desensitized is that

> A primrose by a river's brim,
> A yellow primrose was to him,
> And it was nothing more.[14]

In contrast, this is the way that Wordsworth addresses the child: "Thou best philosopher ... Mighty Prophet! Seer blest!"[15]

Yes, because of its innocence the child possesses the freshness of perception and the sense of wonder and novelty that Adam and Eve enjoyed in Paradise.

For Emerson "infancy is the perpetual Messiah, which comes into the arms of fallen men, and pleads with them to return to paradise." And Thoreau remarked that "Every child begins the world again." The height of his own experience had occurred in childhood, "before I lost my senses" and "my life was ecstasy."[16]

The genius of a poet is to carry those feelings and state of mind on into his adult life, combining them with the developed faculties and culture of maturity. Do you know these verses?

> "A child said, 'What is the grass?' fetching it to me with full hands;
> How could I answer the child? I do not know it any more than he."

No, but I remember a poem similar in feeling the wonder of Nature:

> Happy those early days, when I
> Shin'd in my angel-infancy ...
> When on some gilded cloud, or flower
> My gazing soul would dwell an hour,
> And in those weaker glories spy
> Some shadows of eternity.[17]

According to some thinkers, particularly in the period of Romanticism, the cause of the eclipse of the child's celestial light was less the fallen condition of man than the fetters of bad habits, the manners and customs of so-called civilized people. As Wordsworth wrote in his sonnet "My Heart Leaps Up When I Behold A Rainbow,"

The child is father of the Man.

And, of course, the child is also mother of the woman. It seems a paradox but it is not, because if the child, as it grows to adolescence, were protected from the negative influences imposed on him and the domination of discordant suggestions and impressions which affect his or her character, My light flowing into his mind and body would remain untainted and its energy uncontaminated by earthly vibrations. Thus, the individual would be able to complete his journey and return home, as it was originally intended, without passing through the dark forest of human limitations.

Remember: My Divine Plan contains only harmony and happiness for every one of My children.

As an American, I know that in the literature of my country there has been a strong emphasis on the purity of childhood as the norm for a true relation to life and the universe. In *The Reign of Wonder: Naivety and Reality in American Literature,* the author has demonstrated the persistence, from Emerson to Henry James and J.D. Salinger, of the ideal of the child's innocent eye which, by freeing perception from wrong habits and prejudice and sustaining the sense of wonder, transforms the old world into a new Eden.[18]

From its earliest period – in fact, even in the writings of Christopher Columbus — the New World has been identified with the new earth of the Book of Revelation. The belief that America is the land of the promised millennial Kingdom had been brought to these shores both by Franciscan missionaries and the Puritan fathers.

"This way of thinking was re-aroused by the American revolution, and to some extent again by the Civil War – singers of the Battle Hymn of the Republic echoed the millennial expectation of their Puritan ancestors in the English Civil War: 'Mine eyes have seen the glory of the coming of the Lord!' The doctrine of Manifest Destiny in the 1840's and later decades derived its impetus from the continuing myth of America as the elected theater for the fulfillment of eschatological prophecy." William Gilpin wrote in 1846 that the providential future of the American people is "to regenerate superannuated nations ... to confirm the destiny of the human race – to carry the career of mankind to its culminating point ... to cause a stagnant people to be reborn ... to absolve the curse that weighs down humanity, and to shed blessings round the world!"[19]

The American is represented as the "new Adam" inhabiting (if he would but open his eyes and be aware of it) a garden-land in its Eden-like purity. He is endowed with the power of renewal to give mankind a fresh beginning. Motivated by his desire for freedom to worship God, he has awakened from the sleep of centuries and emancipated himself from the encumbrance of history and the corruption and decadence of the Old World. With regard to America, Hegel, the influential German thinker, wrote in the introduction to his lectures on the Philosophy of World History:

> "It is the land of desire for all those who are weary of the historical arsenal of old Europe."

The conviction and expectation that America is the nation that will usher in the Golden Age is recorded on our Great Seal and one dollar bill: *Novus Ordo Seclorum,* from Virgil's Messianic eclogue.
My plan for your people is to be responsive enough to fulfill their divine mission; for "Were the Americans to fail in their experiment in self-government, they would fail not only themselves, but all men wanting or deserving to be free."[20]

And we Americans should also listen to the words of Walt Whitman:

> I say no man has yet been half devout enough,
> None has ever yet adored or worship'd half enough,
> None has begun to think how divine he himself is, and
> How certain the future is.

I say that the real and permanent grandeur of these
States
must be their religion,
otherwise there is no real and permanent grandeur.[21]

And there is no real and permanent peace or happiness either, because the essence of religion is love and without it, as I have emphasized throughout our dialogues, you have nothing but misery, failure and, ultimately, disintegration. That is why there is nothing more harmful and self-defeating than a self-centered attitude, and the answer is simple.

The person who is concerned with himself alone goes against the very tendency of life. Therefore, he creates a wall of separation and loses precisely what he tries to possess, for he obstructs the flow of his life-stream and turns its living waters into a foul smelling marsh.

I begin to realize that, if one would only sweep away by the power of love the illusory world of the little self, "his eyesight would be unsealed and his heart set flaming in the light-sea of celestial wonder!" Then he could recognize that "Through every grass-blade ... the glory of a present God still beams."[22]
Yes, without love he will fail to know and feel the greatest wonder in the universe, that which is the most wonder-full of all: love.

Now I wonder why I have the great privilege to be instructed by you on the fundamental questions of life, despite all the errors of my past.
It is because in all you ever did you were, in reality, searching for Me, ever conscious of your exile, in search of light, of the

soul, of the beloved, of that higher something which you sensed as existing and capable of being found. You did strive after recognition of and by the divine. You are one who loves the seemingly unattainable, the Other-Than-Yourself. You will learn that the magnet which attracted you, and the apparent dualism that colored your life and thoughts, and which gave motive to all you sought and did was your true Self, the one Reality.

I hope that you will recognize, if you are willing to listen to My words and put them into practice, that assimilation into and at-one-ment with that one Reality enables duality to be transmuted into the unity of polarity, and the sense of search to be transformed into the effort to become what you essentially are — a member of the family of God.

It is both a homecoming and a reunion.
You came from the One, and from it arises the desire to return to the oneness you once knew and which, as love, contains all. This is the purpose and goal of life in its quest for self-fulfillment and all-ness. When you have accomplished that, you will find that you are One with Me, and I am One with thee.[23]

You have shown me the vision of the final end. I'll guard it in my mind and heart and it will be the beacon-light of my life because, as the Scripture says, "without the vision, the people perish."[24]
Remember also the admonishment of the ancient wisdom, "What thou seest, that too become thou must; God if thou seest God, dust if thou seest dust."[25] What you see refers to both the world outside and to your inner world because you have images and pictures in your mind which you have collected from your past and present life.

I can understand it, the eyes are like the camera of the mind because whatever I see is photographed instantly on it.

As I said, even into your flesh, but you are not aware that you can create a picture from within your own mind. In fact, every picture you have that is beautiful and constructive comes from Me.

It is You seeing it in and through me.

Yes. It is My plan of perfection for you and for the rest of life.

How terrible it is to think that we desecrate it with negative and destructive pictures!

It is very unfortunate that human beings do not know what they are doing with My attribute of sight. Yet, it is the major cause of their limitations because wrong images steal your life and torment you.

I remember you saying that we are creating something every moment, waking or sleeping, by our thoughts, feelings, pictures, and words.

You are also visualizing something all the time, and since the mental image is part of the matrix of manifestation, you can see how great are the consequences of what is going on within you.

Pictures are magnetic and bring to you what correspond to them. And they will manifest very quickly if you love them. It is the creative Law of cause and effect.

I think I understand what you mean by creating a blueprint in the mind. It is what an architect or an engineer does when he or she wishes to build something.

Exactly. Unless one has a mental picture, nothing can be brought into visible and material form. The picture in your mind is an essential part of the creative process going on constantly in the life of the individual. It is important, therefore, not to hold negative or wrong mental images, but to see and visualize only what you require and desire.

Rather, what *you* desire.
That would be the perfect thing if you want to experience happiness and fulfillment.

But how do I know what you desire?
It is very simple because innately within life there is the tendency toward the good, the true, and the beautiful in accord with the Law of love, and it is the plan I always see for everyone. But in order for the individual to allow it to come through he must see it without shadows as I do.

The I, or eye, by which God sees is the I, or eye, by which I see.
Congratulations! To be the channel of the gifts I want to bestow on you, it is necessary that you hold the mental image of the perfection you want, which is the pattern of that which is to be manifest. Your love to the picture becomes the magnet that draws it to you. Therefore, affirm "I AM' instead of I am not or have not.

Remember, everything you see or think is photographed in every cell of your body, and then becomes a physical thing or condition. It is of great importance to realize that every form you contact carries with it, like a living presence, a quality that is good or evil, angelic or demonic, and when you look at it you absorb that quality into yourself.

I must think deeply on the statement you made:

What I see, become I must;
God if I see God,
Dust if I see dust.

It sounds simple like every truth.
And it is, because I gave you the power of free will and you, being a co-creator, can choose what kind of picture you want to create. And it does not take more effort to create or visualize what is good than its opposite.

I should visualize only what I want to experience; if one needs supply of money he must hold a picture of it?
Absolutely, instead of accepting a condition of lack and limitation. Do you think I want My individualities to be poor and not be able to fulfill My plan for them? If I can give the energy of My life to them, certainly I would not deny what they require for their comfort and harmonious existence. In fact, I want to give them more than what they desire for themselves.

There is abundance everywhere in the universe, and the source of it is infinite, but mankind by ignorance of the use of their faculties create their limitations.

As within, so without; but it is not easy to keep out of one's consciousness what is not good. We are not only filled with negative pictures from our past experiences but are surrounded by them, especially of violence and corruption. How can we be free from the pressure and the constant suggestion impinging on us from everywhere?
I can appreciate that because the energy of your feeling is one with that of mankind and you can be easily affected by it. I have already explained to you what you should do, but I will repeat it

since the human self seems very slow to understand what is good for its progress towards the final goal.

You told me that when I visualize the light, the shadows of imperfection and discord are forced to disappear.
Therefore, see and feel yourself as a luminous Being, which you really are, each cell of your body like a miniature sun, and your aura blazing forth in rays. Since every limitation is a lack of love, whether mental, emotional, or physical, it means also a lack of light.

If I have difficulty in visualizing, may I ask you, as my source of light, to fill me with it?
Absolutely! That is the essence of what I am trying to teach you, not merely as an intellectual knowledge but a practical application. Because you can never be permanently free until you depend completely on Me.

Like a small child on its mother. I think the admonition of the Beloved Master to become like little children means just that.
Above all, demand that you be permeated with the fire of My love, which is the power of purification, the forgiveness of healing, and the wisdom of illumination. Feel it pass through you and penetrate every atom of your Being raising its vibratory action and making you feel closer to Me.

This is the harmonious and perfect way, instead of the fire of suffering, because divine love is the greatest force in the universe. Therefore, it will dissolve and transmute, like physical fire burning up debris, all negative energy accumulated from the past, and like an armor of light, preventing the shadows also to approach and connect with your life.

Then I will again be the shining image I was made in the beginning and I will remember,

> How like an angel came I down!
> How bright are all things here!
> When first among His works I did appear.
> The world resembled His eternity,
> In which my soul did walk;
> And everything that I did see
>   Did with me talk.[26]

1 Abrams, *Natural*, p. 375.
2 *Mysticism*, p. 258.
3 "Gnomic Verses," VII.
4 John Keats, "A Thing of Beauty."
5 *Confessions*, 10:6, 10-27.
6 Abrams, p. 413.
7 Charles Langbridge Morgan, *The Fountain*, 1932.
8 Alfred Lord Tennyson, "Flower in the Crannied Wall."
9 Martin Buber, in *Creative Meditation*, p. 208.
10 Jacob Boehme, in Abrams, p. 383.
11 James Joyce, *Stephen Hero*, ed. Theodore Spencer, (NY: New Directions, 1944), p. 211.
12 Underhill, p. 216.
13 Matthew 18:3.
14 William Wordsworth, "Peter Bell," Stanza 12.
15 Abrams, p. 525 n. 18.
16 Quoted in Abrams, pp. 412, 413.
17 Walt Whitman, "Song of Myself"; Henry Vaughan, "The Retreat."
18 Tony Tanner, *The Reign of Wonder: Naivety and Reality in American Literature* (Cambridge, England, 1965).
19 Quoted by Henry Nash Smith, *Virgin Land: The American West as Symbol and Myth* (Boston: Harvard University Press, 1971 [reprint of 1957 edition]), p. 40.
20 C. Rossiter, "The American Mission," *The American Scholar*, 20, (1950-1).
21 Walt Whitman, "For You, O Democracy."
22 Thomas Carlyle, *Sartor Resartus*, ed. C.F. Harrold, (NY: Odyssey Press 1937), pp. 186, 264.
23 Cfr., Alice Bailey, *Esoteric Healing*, (NY: Lucis Publishing, 1972), pp. 116.
24 Proverbs 29:18.
25 Brother Angelus.
26 Thomas Traherne, "Wonder."

CHAPTER 18

The Meaning of Self-Love

Having realized his own self as the Self, a man becomes selfless; and in virtue of selflessness he is to be conceived as unconditioned.
Maitrayana Upanishad

It is the nature of extreme self-lovers, as they will set a house on fire, and it were but to roast their eggs.
Francis Bacon

I am still troubled. When I listen to your words, challenging me to accept your love and live fully within its flame, I feel my spirit rising – I feel inspired. I know in my heart that we came from love, and love is what, knowingly or unknowingly, we are craving – we are starving for it! I don't understand why, then, it seems so difficult to love as you love. We were created not only with that capacity but also as a channel for it; and then in our abasement, we have enslaved ourselves to the human law of selfishness and lost the liberty of love. We hug to ourselves the light-energy we receive from you, using it to serve our self-will. Then the life-force, thus misused, holds us bound until it is purified by the flame of your love. Our egotism cannot destroy the power of free choice, which is identical with our will but cloaks it in a veil of darkness which deprives the individual of the freedom with which love endowed him —

— causing the confusion and self-deception that make people believe that they are free to do what they want, while in reality they are serving the wrong master. The problem is not with love itself but with its motivation and aim, in the ignorance of its true object.

446

Our wrong habits and tendencies are the signs of a love in contradiction with its nature which does not recognize its self betrayal.

We are dominated by the enemy within, whose only intent is the gratification of its own desires by which we are thrown into conflict with ourselves. There is a myth about the fascination with our personality and our bondage to it that has always intrigued me, perhaps because I identified with it. It is the story of Narcissus.

According to it, all the nymphs were attracted to him and would fall in love with him; but he, being very conceited and proud of his beauty, rejected and shunned them all. One of those he spurned cried to the gods, "May he feel what love is and not be reciprocated." The avenging goddess, Nemesis, heard and granted the prayer.

There was a clear fountain with water like silver, untouched by shepherds or beasts, nor defaced with fallen leaves. Grass grew fresh around it, and the rocks and the woods sheltered it from the sun. The youth, tired from hunting, hot and thirsty, was attracted by the beauty of the place and lay down there. While he was trying to quench his thirst, Narcissus saw his body reflected in the water and was captivated by its beauty. He fell in love with it, believing that what was only an image to be a real thing. He would lie enraptured, hour after hour, gazing into the pool, inflamed by the desire for his own self.

How many times did he bestow vain kisses on the deceptive water, and plunge his arms into it to grasp the form he saw! Yet he could not hold in their embrace his own appearance. He did not understand that he cherished the very flame that consumed him, and his deceived eyes aroused his passion. Poor, deluded, Narcissus! Why do you try to love and possess your fleeting image? What you desire is not real — in itself it is nothing! It is but an appearance that with you comes and stays, and with you it will go, if you can bear to leave it.

No concern for food or rest could take him away, but stretched out on the shady grass he kept looking at this deceptive beauty with insatiable longing. And, in so doing, he was destroying himself through his own eyes. He raised himself up a little and lifting his arms exclaimed, "Has there ever been anyone tormented by a more cruel love? Tell me, oh trees, can you remember anyone who is wasting away as I do? I behold my beloved, but what I see and love I cannot have; such is the torment of my unrequited passion. I am you! I realize it; my reflection does not deceive me; I burn with love for myself, I am the one who fans the flame and bears the torture. What am I to do? Should I implore or be implored? What then shall I ask for? What I desire is with me, all that I have makes me poor. O how I wish that I could escape from my body! A strange prayer for one in love, to wish away what he loves! And now grief consumes my strength; the time remaining for me is brief, I am cut off in the flower of my youth, but death does not weigh heavily upon me, for it will bring an end to my misery. My only desire is that he whom I cherish could live a longer time. As it is, we two, who are one in life, will die together!"

He finished speaking and, sick with longing, turned back again gazing to his own reflection. His tears disturbed the water causing the pool to ripple, and the image became dim. He saw it disappearing and cried: "Where are you fleeing? Cruel one, stay here, do not abandon him who loves you! If I am prevented from touching you, let me look at you that I may have at least this nourishment of my misery and ill-starred love." As Narcissus beheld himself in the water, after the pool returned calm, he could endure it no longer; then, as yellow wax is wont to melt under the touch of fire and the gentle frost under the warmth of the sun, so he was enfeebled, worn, and wasted away by love, gradually being consumed by its hidden flame. He lay down his weary head on the green grass as he pinned away and his former comeliness disappeared and was lost; until the night closed once and for all those eyes that had so admired the beauty of its owner. Then too, after he had been received in the home of the dead below, he gazed at himself in the waters of the Styx. Echo and the other nymphs were avenged but the Gods looked compassionately down upon the dead body and changed it into a yellow flower, with a circle of white petals in its center, bearing the youth's name. It has ever since flourished beside quiet pools, wherein the pale image is reflected. The nymphs wept and grieved; the pyre and streaming torches and the bier were being prepared, but the body was nowhere to be seen.[1]

Poets and writers have related this tragic story of self-love and the self destruction that inevitably ensues more often than any other fable of antiquity.

> A lonely flower they spied,
> A meek and forlorn flower, with naught of pride,
> Drooping its beauty over the watery clearness,
> To woo its own sad image into nearness,
> Deaf to light Zephyrus it would not move;
> But still would seem to droop, to pine, to love.[2]

The notion of love as the cohesive and unifying power of the universe and the bond that connects not only human beings with one another but everything in existence has a long history. The antithesis and opposite of this unitive love is self-love, for which the center of reference is not the All but the part – or the separative self.

I understand that the latter causes many selves out of one true Self, whereas love as an integrative force makes One out of the many – as it is engraved on the Great Seal of the United States: "E pluribus unum."

This difference is reflected in the Augustinian division of the two cities: the earthly city built by self-love, reaching the point of the most extreme estrangement and denial of God, and the heavenly city which represents the love of God as one surrenders himself and becomes the instrument of divine love.[3]

You can return to the source of love only by the way you came forth from it in order to complete the cosmic *circuit* or circle, for separation presupposes an original union. From that love you turned away by the selfish desires of the personal self, and the circuit was broken.

It has been stated that:

> "Love was the cause of our being created ... From that love we have been separated, forsooth by the love of ourselves ... By love, i.e. by our love to God, we are to return to our source, which is also our end; for nothing else is able to bind together ... to make one out of many, except love."[4]

According to Hegel, "Evil generally is the self-centered being-for-itself, and good is selfless simplicity." For Coleridge the opposite condition to that of the man who feels "himself, his own low self the whole," is to make "the whole one Self! Self that no alien knows! ... Oblivious of its own;" and this latter condition will effect the universal redemption.

The poet Blake agrees that the liberation from selfhood is the essential act which effects a redeemed, or reintegrated humanity. Therefore he prays, "Annihilate the Selfhood in me, be thou all my life!" for "Man liveth not by Self alone but by Brotherhood and Universal Love" — and in his "offering of Self for Another" Jesus manifested that "This is Friendship and Brotherhood; without it Man is Not."

The oriental mystic Jalan d'Din concurs, "O let me not exist! For non-existence proclaims in organ tones, 'To him we shall return'."

In Shelley's vivid imagery, "the dark idolatry of the self" is the "Mammon of the world," and constitutes that mental state which is the only hell. According to him, man should transcend his individual ego, transfer the center of reference to others, and thus transform self-love into love.[5]

This is how a mystic of our time explains it: "Mankind is a single body comprising many individuals ..."
Let me interject that the universe is also a single body of a countless number of Beings.

He continues: "Individual self-love is unnatural, as is the self-love of one cell in our own body. When one cell puts itself first and before the organic functioning of the whole body, when it declared war on the other cells, this is cancer. Self-love is the cancer of the whole mystical body."[6]

However, the subject of self-love can be very confusing, its lack of conceptual clarity is evident in the fact that the term can be used in different and even contradictory senses. For some authors it is essential to love oneself in order to maintain one's mental health and lead a balanced life. More importantly, they also affirm that one cannot love others unless one loves oneself.

As we shall see it depends on their understanding of what the "self" and love are.

A contemporary author and lecturer, M. Scott Peck, claims that there is a significant connection between self-love and love for others. According to him love is "The will to extend one's self for the purpose of nurturing one's own or another's spiritual growth." He points out that his statement includes self-love with love for another, in fact "They are indistinguishable."[7]

His definition is not only very inadequate but incorrect; the will is one of the powers and functions that love possesses and should not be identified with it. Love is the moving force of life and he is referring to the effect, among myriad, it can produce and manifest.

People recognize it as the determining factor in their lives: a man says, "I love Mary, therefore I will marry her," or a woman who loves to take care of others makes her decision, "I will be a nurse." I love grand opera and I will buy tickets for the opera season. Love is the cause of our actions using the will as an instrument.

His definition is also ambiguous because he does not explain what he means by "self."

Later on we are informed that "we have a sick self and a healthy self," and toward the end of the book, adding to the confusion, he uses the term "ego." Our author makes the amazing claim that the purpose of spiritual growth is not to become egoless, "Rather it is to develop a mature, conscious ego which then can become the ego of God."[8] And he supports his unbelievable assertion with a specious argument that, in a spiritual context, is totally meaningless. "You must have something in order to give it up...You must forge for yourself an identity before you can give it up...You must develop an ego before you can lose it."[9]

This is like saying that one must necessarily be an egoist in order to become an altruist, or that one cannot be a good person unless he is first wicked or an evil-doer. And what does he mean by spiritual growth since it is his basic subject? What is it that is supposed to grow?

It is the evolution of an individual and he considers it a "miracle," and this is why: according to the second law of thermodynamics it should not occur because the energy flows from a state of greater organization and higher differentiation to a lesser and lower one. "In other words, the universe is in a process of winding down." Ultimately, in billions of years it will reach the lowest point as an amorphous, totally disorganized and undifferentiated blob in which nothing happens any more. This state is termed entropy.

This upside down way of thinking is compounded and reinforced by an analogous wrong theory.

The flow of evolution is against the force of entropy and that is why effort is necessary. In fact, for him, evil is leth-

453

argy. From a virus to a bacterium, from a paramecium to a sponge, to insects and a fish and so on, there are increasing and higher states of complexity and organization, with man at the top. Our author calls this process the "miracle" of evolution because without it, "We who write and read this book should not exist."[10]

I do not see how miraculous it is except for the benighted human intellect and its concoctions.

But what follows is even more astonishing. In order to explain evolution, "we hypothesize the existence of a God who wants us to grow – a God who loves us."[11]

I commend him for his reference to a deity, but what is the nature of that God?

It is intimately associated with us, in fact "We were part of God all the time." And now we have an astonishing revelation: "Our unconscious is God. God within us."

This is one of the most peculiar explanations I ever heard of who "I AM."

In case we are "horrified" by the notion that our unconscious is God ...

We should be!

... he reminds us that "it is hardly a heretical concept, being in essence the same as the Christian concept of the Holy Ghost or Holy Spirit which resides in us all."

Who is, incidentally, not a concept but one of the persons of the Trinity, and I am sure it is highly conscious for it is the feeling of love between the Father and the Son.

But the supreme irony is that for him love is not a feeling. In agreement with most Catholic theologians Dr. Peck asserts that "Love is an act of the will," because it can be made permanent only if it is "a committed, thoughtful decision."

He emphasizes that commitment is inherent in any genuinely loving relationship. "Anyone who is truly concerned for the spiritual growth of another knows ... that he or she can significantly foster that growth of another through a relationship of constancy. The source of this commitment that enables love to be constant is not a desire, a need or something emotional because it would be only temporary." For him, the person who truly loves does so because of "a decision to love," that is, he has made a commitment to be loving whether or not the loving feeling is present.[12]

But what does he mean by feeling?

"The feeling of love is the emotion that accompanies the experience of cathecting...the process by which an object becomes important to us."

What is wrong with that?

Once cathected, one of the reasons is that the object becomes a "love object"... "invested with our energy as if it were a part of ourselves ... The misconception that love is a feeling exists because we confuse cathecting with loving." And one of the reasons is that: "we may cathect any object, animate or inanimate, with or without a spirit."[13]

I think one should love life, in all its forms because it is My energy.

Cardenal recognizes it when he writes, "Things are God's love become things."[14] But Peck has a different opinion, and he continues, "Second, the fact that we have cathected another human being does not mean that we care a whit for that person's spiritual development."[15]
This is true but it does not prove that the feeling of love is absent, though requalified as possessive and selfish.

Yes, like the third example he makes of two strangers who meet casually in a bar; "In such a way that nothing – not promises made, or family stability – is more important for the moment than their sexual consummation." Immediately following the fleeting and momentary experience of cathecting, the couple may find each other unattractive and undesirable.
Unfortunately human beings may misuse their capacity for love and pervert its energy.

The rejection of love as feeling is based on the fact that it does not last, for it has beginning and end. Therefore, "falling in love" is the most powerful and pervasive misconception about love. The problem is that such experience is sexually motivated and, invariably temporary. "The honeymoon always ends. The bloom of romance always fades."[16] He uses another example: "It is not only possible but necessary for a loving person to avoid acting on feelings of love. I may meet a woman who strongly attracts me, whom I feel like loving, but because it would be destructive to my marriage to have an affair at that time, I will say vocally or in the silence of my heart, 'I feel like loving you, but I am not going to'."[17]

This is very praiseworthy but he confuses the issue. The problem here with the feeling is not its transitory and impermanent nature. But because his action is unethical or would disrupt his marriage. Although he claims to be describing the nature of love he is really making a moral judgment which is commendable since it is about a sexual attraction. He thinks his action is motivated by genuine love rejecting the false or improper one. However, love is one, there are not different types but qualities, that is, the energy of love is subject to the qualification of the individual according to his attitudes.

We impose on your pure light-essence the quality of our thoughts and feelings, thus creating a shadow; we contaminate it by the misuse of our free will.

Obviously our author does not recognize that fundamental notion.

This is how he explains it: "Many, many people possessing a feeling of love and even acting in response to that feeling act in all manner of unloving and destructive ways. On the other hand, a genuinely loving individual will often take loving and constructive action toward a person he or she consciously dislikes, actually feeling no love toward the person al the time and perhaps even finding the person repugnant in some way."[18]

This reminds me of the episode in the life of St. Francis of Assisi when he kisses the leper to prove his love for Jesus, and of Mother Theresa of Calcutta who continued to serve the derelicts while she was in the dark night of the soul.

But does it mean that there is no feeling of love in them even though they may not experience it? It is impossible! All life feels and is conscious in various degrees and levels. The sun is always there and continues to shine even if one may not feel its warmth.

"All life is love! ... Love is. All else *is not*, because in the same measure in which things partake of being, they partake of love. All that is not love, *is not*. All that which is, has its being and its action in love."[19]

Yes, love is the moving force of life; in the individual experience of love the nature of life become manifest. Dr. Peck asserts that love is an act of the will and that we do not have to love. "We choose to love." This is tantamount to saying that one chooses to breathe.

Of course, like Hamlet, one may ponder about "to be or not to be," but that is beside the point.

The problem is about our author's concept of the nature of feeling. For him "true" love is not feeling because he does not know what "true" feeling is.

It is a common problem.

He fails to distinguish between the inner feeling coming from the heart and the outer emotional feeling that belongs to the personality. People do not discriminate which of their feelings are of divine or human origin, and this is very unfortunate because they may differ as light and darkness and be the cause of good or evil.

This has reference to the principle of polarity, and how we have lost contact with the core of our being. And we are so confused that we make decision based on feelings that may be wrong and have dreadful consequences. Our author reiterates that love is not a feeling, "it is a committed, thought-

ful decision." However, he does not clarify the notion of what love is, rather he makes it more nebulous when he says that if the feeling of love is present, "so much the better but if it isn't, the commitment to love, the will to love, still stands and is still exercised."[20]

Then, after all, the feeling of love is not to be disparaged, but what is seriously lacking is the understanding that the individual has the capacity to love because I love him or her *first*. It is "I" who love them into existence, and it is My love that, wave after wave, constantly gives them the light of My life. The truth is that no one really knows what love is unless he *feels* it in the flame of his heart for, then, he experiences it at the very source.

St. Catherine of Siena makes it very clear when she conveys to us God's instructions to her. "The soul cannot live without love. She always wants to love something because love is the stuff she is made of, and through love I created her. This is why I said that it is affection that moves the understanding saying, as it were, 'I want to love, because the food I feed on is love.' And the understanding, feeling itself awakened by affection, gets up, as it were, and says, 'If you want to love, I will give you that good that you can love' ... In the dignity of her being she tastes the immeasurable goodness and uncreated love with which I created her ... On the other hand, if sensual affection wants to love sensual things, the eye of understanding is moved toward them. It takes for its object only passing things by self-love, contempt of virtue and love of vice ... This love so dazzles the eye that it neither discerns nor sees anything but the glitter of these things. Such is their glitter that the intellect sees and affection loves them all as if their brightness came from goodness and enjoyment... But vice is disguised as something good and the soul cannot tell the difference because she does not know the truth. So she wanders about searching for what is good and enjoyable where it is not to be found."[21]

The ambiguity of our author's explanation is evident also in this passage: "When love exists it does so with or without a loving feeling. It is easier – indeed, it is fun – to love with the feeling of love. But it is possible to love without loving feelings."[22]

For him love is something that we choose and the commitment involved in love, or its constancy, is the result of a deliberate act of the will and the determination to nourish endlessly one's own or another spiritual growth. However, his assertion that "genuine love is volitional rather than emotional," because it would be only temporary, is a fallacy. In reality the distinction between the will and the feeling might not make any difference with regard to the constancy of love.

There is a comment by a philosopher who agrees with you: "the decision to love does not seem to guarantee, any better than it is guaranteed if love is emotional, that the commitment will endure. What is it about a decision to love that implies that one will stick to that decision? Choices are reversible, under all sorts of conditions and for all sorts of reasons, in which case love-by-decision is just as vulnerable to termination as love-as-feeling."[23]

Considering how weak and unreliable human nature is when separated from its Source how can one be so sure that his will is immovable like a mountain and, to use a poetic image, "steadfast like a fixed star"?

We have free will but it seems more inclined to error, in fact there are theologians who deny our freedom because we are enslaved to sin.

Dr. Peck affirms the reality of "grace" as "a powerful force originating outside of human consciousness which nurtures the spiritual growth of human beings."[24] Is it not remarkable that it is unconscious? However, why not believe that this "force" may nurture and sustain the feeling the same as the will toward the attainment of godhood, as he calls it?

This is another bewildering statement: "I have said that the ultimate goal of evolution is for the individual to become as one with God ... to become God while preserving consciousness ... then God will have assumed through our conscious ego a new and potent life form." And he presents a peculiar interpretation of the mystical experience; because the goal is not to become egoless, "Rather it is to develop a mature, conscious ego which then can become the ego of god."[25]

If he is referring to the true self, it is a long way from being a virus. I must confess that it is beyond My comprehension, even to an all-knowing mind, why God would not make the process less "involved" and more direct. I know from personal experience that the infinite Ground does not need a "swamp" to emanate gods and goddesses out of Itself.

I don't understand how we can have "the joy of communion with God"[26] envisioned as the "collective unconscious."
Neither I.

And is it possible to have a sense of union without feeling? Then he tells us that, "Mental illness occurs when the con-

scious will of the individual deviates, substantially from the will of god, which is the individual's own unconscious will."[27]

I agree with the first part of his sentence which explains why there are so many cases of insanity in the world today. And I sympathize with psychiatrists because they deal with disturbed people's mind, and are expected to explain conditions and solve problems which they do not understand.

And of which they might be afflicted, too. For our author the root of evil is not selfishness but laziness, which I find an original idea.

There is some truth in it because, after the personality has created its limitations, it does not make the necessary effort to be free from them by turning to Me for assistance.

In another section of the book he says that "Everyone in our culture desires to some extent to be loving, yet many are not in fact loving. I therefore conclude that the desire to love is not itself love."[28]

It is not the right conclusion because desire and love are closely joined and, in many cases, they overlap and coincide. In fact, it is impossible to see where one ends and the other begins. In reality, like love, I am the beginning and the end of all desires.

You are alpha and omega.

I'd like to quote the following passage: "Desire is a word which has been prostituted to cover the tendency of humanity to crave material things or those pleasures which bring satisfaction to the sensuous nature ... but in the last analysis, desire is essentially love. This desire expresses itself by attractiveness, by its capacity to draw to itself and into the radius of its influence that which is loved."[29] It is significant that in religious texts desire and love, in their figurative expressions, are almost indistinguishable. The imagery of thirst and hunger cannot possibly refer to the will as they are not intentionally experienced.

As the deer longs for the flowing streams,
so my soul longs for you, O God.
My soul thirsts for God,
for the living God. (Psalm 42:1-2)

They feast on the abundance of your house,
and you give them drink from
the river of your delights. (Psalm 36:8)

I am the bread of life.
Whoever comes to me will
never be hungry, and whoever
believes in me will never be thirsty. (John 6:35)

The bread that I will give
for the life of the world
is my flesh. (John 6:51)

We were all made to drink
of one Spirit. (1 Corinthians 12:13)

They shall hunger no more,
and thirst no more. (Revelation 7:16)

As I mentioned earlier, a desire from the heart is prayer and I always answer it. I would say that desire and love are the two wings of the self, their magnetic power is without limit and they represent the Law of attraction.

Dante, in the final hours of his ascent to the last sphere of Heaven, tries to explain how he focused all the energy of his being to contemplate the beatific vision.

> As I was drawing near
> the end of all desires
> my burning desire reached its zenith.[30]

I hope before the end of our dialogues to make clear what I mean when I say that love is a feeling, not an easy task to explain it in words that you can understand. But always remember that there is no greater power in all the universe than the fire of My love, and it should be your lode-star.

As Mechthild of Magdeburg says, "Orison draws the great God down into the small heart: it drives the hungry soul out to the fullness of God. It brings together the two lovers, God and the soul, into a joyful room where they speak much of love."[31]

As I will elaborate later on in our chapter on "What Is Love," the true feeling is experienced by those referred to as God intoxicated, who love Me not in a sentimental manner but with "passionate emotion." Mysticism cannot exist without it," writes Evelyn Underhill, "We must feel and feel acutely, before we want to act on this hard and heroic scale. Together with art, they correspond to the two eternal passions of the self, the desire of love and the desire of knowledge: severally representing the hunger of heart and intellect for ultimate truth."[32] St. John of the Cross, perhaps the most austere and rigorous disciplinarian in any religious order, uses poetry in his *Song of the Living Flame of Love* as the least inadequate means to express his feeling:

> Oh, flame of living love
> kindled tenderly
> in the deepest center of my soul.
> ... Oh, suave cautery!
> Oh, delicate wound!
> Oh, softhand! Oh gentle touch
> that tastes of eternal life
> and pays all debts!
> By killing, you transform death into life![33]

Another passage by our author that perplexes me is this: "Because genuine love involves an extension of oneself, vast amounts of energy are required and, like it or not, the store of our energy is limited as the hours of the day. We simply cannot love everyone."

We cannot love everyone? Forgive me Dr. Peck, I thought that love in order to be "genuine" or "true" must be unconditional. I must have misunderstood you.

Then, again, we have this unclear statement: "True, we may have a feeling of love for mankind, and this feeling may also be useful in providing us with enough energy to manifest genuine love for a few specific individuals. But genuine love for a relatively few individuals is all that is within our power."

"Our power?" What power do you have unless it is given? That is why your capacity to love is limited. Do you not know that love comes from Me, and that you could not live unless you are first loved by your source of life?

Then he says that those chosen few must be responsive to your interest in them: "To attempt to love someone who cannot benefit from your love with spiritual growth is to waste your energy."³⁴

I see why you are perplexed, first with regard to loving only those who deserve it, (but how can one pretend to judge?) He should be reminded that God "makes his sun rise on the evil and on the good, and sends rain on the righteous and the un-righteous. For if you love those who love you, what reward do you have?"³⁵ Second, there is a contradiction with regard to the limited energy of love after declaring emphatically, "When I genuinely love I am extending myself and I am growing. The more I love, the longer I love, the larger I become. Genuine love is self-replenishing."³⁶

Yes, love is, indeed, an inexhaustible fountain, self-creating, constantly giving of itself to all, not only to a selected few because of their merit. Love will exist when the lover finds no merit, because he attributes merit on the basis of his or her love.

I have a question: Kahlil Gibran wrote, "Think not you can direct the course of love, for love, if it finds you worthy, directs your course."³⁷ Then why are the effects of love not always conducive to good and constructive? Evil is pervasive, both in the inner and external life of individuals and nations.

The reason is that the feeling of love which I constantly give with every breath and heartbeat can be perverted by selfishness, becomes possessive, misdirected and turned to the wrong object. But even in its negative and destructive manifestation, love provides the motivation without which the will of the personal self is inactive and the intellect merely a servant, often an arrogant one.

It has been said that we become what we love.
Yes, because love is transformative, and by its unifying power, you become one with whatever you love. My people on the Earth do not have even a fragment of an idea of what love is and what it can do for them, that love which gives all and owns all, without which nothing can exist.

Love is the power of cohering, that is, of holding everything in the universe together in harmonious and perfect motion and creative activity. Without its magnetic attraction, there would be no form, and no manifestation. My love is always flowing in and through the individual, and he can easily connect with its radiant current by his attention to Me. Then he will be able to attract everything he desires. Conversely, the moment he becomes negative, it is like turning out of the stream of love. As a consequence the discord continues to increase and becomes a repellent force.

Never forget that everything you can think of is made of love because it is the energy of My life, even though the light might temporarily be covered over by the shadows of human creation.

People may seem to turn away from Me, but they cannot evade their desire for love, no matter how disguised it may appear to be, because it is inherent in every atom of their being, and it is the connection of their life-stream to the Source which

I AM feeding life into their body, even though they are abysmally ignorant of it.

Lao-Tzu expresses a similar idea when he compares the human being to a low valley through which rivers flow, or to a channel of universal forces. "A river or a channel has two functions: that of receiving and that of giving, but not that of keeping. He who tries to keep life or any of its gifts to himself thereby loses both."[38]

Selfishness and greed do not allow the stream to flow and the result is stagnation changing it into an evil-smelling pool, a breeding ground of death and decay. St. Teresa of Avila says that without love, all is nothing — *"Sin amor todo es nada"* — and with it, all is bliss. In her vision she describes it like an arrow that transfixes her heart:

Beside me, on the left side, I saw an angel in bodily form. He was not large but small of stature, and most beautiful - he must have been one of the highest ranks of angels we call Cherubim who seem all on fire. In his hands I saw a long golden spear, and at the iron's point there appeared to be fire. This he plunged into my heart several times so that it penetrated to my entrails. When he drew it out I felt that he took them with it, and left me all on fire with the great love of God.[39]

But is it not the will of the archer that shoots the bow?
Yes, but it is the love that moves the will and everything else.

This reminds me of the end of Dante's *Paradiso*:

> Here power failed the lofty fantasy;
> but already my desire and my will were turned,
> like a wheel that is evenly moved, by the love which

Moves the sun and the other stars.[40]

If you remember, the word "stars" is also at the end of the Inferno, "and thence we issued forth to see again the stars," and in the final verse of Purgatory, "I came forth ... pure and ready to rise to the stars." The final injunction in each case is to look upwards, "up" being the right direction of your mind and heart. Thus, love returns to its Source where the individual experiences the fullness of all he desires, the circle or circuit is complete and never-ending.

As another poet said

Love is a circle that doth restless move
In the same sweet eternity of love.[41]

But I am still confused. Since love implies a relation, a love and a beloved, how can one love himself? Who is loving whom?
You are right, the relation between the self and the other is fundamental: self-love is contradictory, it acts in opposition to its own nature, and even though the person still loves, his love has turned against itself. Beset by anxiety and conflict, it carries a taste of death and is bound to disintegrate.

However, there must be someone who is loving; how can love be selfless?
By being "selfless" is meant not being self-seeking or egocentric —without an acquisitive tendency — as contrasted to a totally free and spontaneous self-giving.

I see that the fundamental difference between the two kinds of love is possessive and non-possessive.
Yes, it is basic for the understanding of whether an action is done for the self's sake or for another's or God's sake. An act may appear the same but it can either have an acquisitive or benevolent quality.

How do we know the difference?
The act is judged by the motive. Two people may give money for charitable purposes and have opposite intent.

Is the desire for salvation and to go to Heaven a selfish one?
No, because in order to reach those goals you must purify yourself of all selfishness; and the desire to perfect oneself is, in fact, very good, as it means to become more God-like.

It is obvious, then, that the expression "self-love" as opposed to "selfless" means "evil."
Not necessarily. Now it may seem to you that I contradict Myself which is, of course, impossible. These two ways of thinking, or rather, attitudes, are both right and wrong.

How can that be?
You still do not comprehend (and it must be partly because I have to deal with the limitations of your language to make understandable what I say) that there are two selves in you, let alone many others on account of numerous identifications.

I am aware that I am fragmented — not one but many selves.
Let me remind you again that you are like a magnet with two poles called spirit and matter, the inner and outer side of your

470

being, God Self and personality. There are also other terms with reference to your bipolar nature; but these are merely names and are unimportant, you must rely on your intuition which is the teaching from within.

From you.

As I explain this, I am trying to raise your level of understanding and receptivity. You are an individual, meaning the nexus or link between your human and divine nature in their complementarity and essential oneness — rather that is who you are supposed to be, and what your free will consists of. I should not be surprised, however, that you still do not realize it. It has been a long time since you left Me and wandered away from home. But I will make things clearer to you as we go on.

I hope you will forgive me.

I always do. Forgiveness is inherent in love and it is the action of the Law. Moreover, I have nothing to forgive because no one can affect Me adversely in any way, and I never condemn. You see, the very word "forgive" means "to give for."

This is true also in other languages.

Therefore, all I do is to dissolve the wrong or evil and free the individual by the fire of My love. The same should be with everyone who has suffered injury; he should replace his feeling of hurt or injustice with one of benevolence.

It is easier said than done.

Then he can ask Me to do it for him.

As the Divine Master did, and how he taught us to do; because we don't know what we do when we hurt life. And unless we forgive how can we be forgiven?
But for most people it is difficult to forgive, even though they sometimes struggle because they know it is the right thing to do. Those who are not willing to forgive, however, stay bound by their discordant feeling. Whether it is your Karmic accumulation or that caused by others, make the demand to be consumed and I will do it. " I AM" the truth that sets you free.

But don't we have to make adjustments person to person?
As I said, it is not always required by the Law, because, if one is not willing to cooperate, the condition can never be balanced.

I can see the Law of Love always acting since you are the Love Self of each human being.
Remember also that unless you forget the discord, especially by not feeling it, you have not really forgiven. In fact, it will disappear if you forget it.

Many people say, "I have forgiven but I have not forgotten."
Unfortunately, they are deceiving themselves. If you still remember the wrong you suffered, and hold a feeling of injustice, the wound has not healed and you will continue, perhaps unknowingly, to be resentful and feel hurt.

But should we not expect reparations for the wrong done to us?
Let the Karmic Law take care of it. After all, you do not know whether it could be your own misdeed coming back to you for redemption.

I understand, but I hope and trust in your forgiveness.
You must never doubt it; if I had not forgiven you, I would not be talking to you right now. Do you not recall the poem your mother taught you?

> When all thy mercies, O my God
> My rising soul surveys,
> Transported with the view, I'm lost
> In wonder, love and praise ..."
> When worn with sickness, oft has thou
> With health renew'd my face;
> And when in sins and sorrow sunk,
> Reviv'd my soul with grace.[42]

At least you have a good memory for poetry.

I love it, together with a few spiritual books it was my only consolation.
But you did not learn enough to know the truth about your true self, though, like beauty for the romantic poet, it is all you need to know.

Why did you say that those two opposed viewpoints about self-love are both right and wrong?
Because it depends on what their idea of the self is — which self they are referring to. You know now that there is more than one self in every person, and only one is real. Therefore, the expression "self-love" can have at least three different meanings. As an illustration, let us take Jesus' second great commandment, "Love your neighbor as yourself."

I know that it has been interpreted in several ways.

Then you must see that there is a problem, and with good reason. The first meaning is to love your neighbor as much as you love yourself, and you would be surprised how intensely you love yourself. That is what you have been doing in your life seeking to gratify your personal desires and ambitions.

This would be the love of the false self, the rebellious personality, the egotist who thinks only of himself. It is the story of Narcissus loving his own image.

If by "self-love" they are referring to the personal self, their attitude is wrong and it is the cause of all evil. Instead, if by "self-love" they mean love of Me, their God Self within and above them, they are expressing the truth. Now you can see why I said that they are both right and wrong.

> The ancient wisdom have I taught to thee,
> Highest, most sacred, holy; yet again,
> Hear thou the secret-most of mysteries,
> The final word of all that "I" can speak:
> Place thy whole mind in Me, the Supreme Self,
> And place Me in thy mind (and nothing else);
> Love Me, the Universal "I," all-one,
> The "I" will save thee
> By giving thee its own infinity.[43]

And the third meaning?

It is like the summation or synthesis of the previous two, on a higher level. In order to love your neighbor as yourself, you must see your neighbor as your own self; that is, you must recognize that your self and your neighbor's are one, rooted in the same infinite Ground individualized in each human being, as the I AM Self.

Then you can truly love all in your self, and your self in all for in both you are loving the One God. As Jesus instructed his disciples, "I and my Father are one ... As you, Father, are in me and I am in you, may they also be in us ... so that they may be one, as we are one, I in them and you in me, that they may become completely one."[44]

This is true self-love, when you realize, "I am in my Father, and you in me and I in you." Then you love yourself in God and God in yourself and in everyone as the I AM Self present everywhere.

"For then the soul is in God and God in the soul, just as the fish is in the sea and the sea in the fish."[45]
But there are those who are like fishes which do not know that they live, move, and have their being in the sea.

We deliberately refuse to recognize and accept that we depend on it, and even blame God for the tempest and our shipwrecks while we sail upon it.

1 Paraphrase of Ovid, *Metamorphoses* 3:342-510.
2 Keats's poem, quoted in H.A. Guerber, *The Myths of Greece and Rome* (NY: Dover Publications, 1993), p. 98.
3 St. Augustine, *The City of God.*
4 Juan Luis Vives, *On Education*, in Abrams, p. 295.
5 All quoted in Abrams, pp. 295-6.
6 Ernest Cardenal, *Love*, (NY: Crossroad, 1981), p. 75.
7 M. Scott Peck, *The Road Less Traveled: A New Psychology of Love: Traditional Values and Spiritual Truth.* (NY: Touchstone, 2003), pp. 81, 83.
8 Ibid., p. 277, 283.
9 Ibid., p. 76.
10 Ibid., p. 265.
11 Ibid., 269.
12 Ibid., p. 119.
13 Ibid., 117.
14 Cardenal, p. 43.
15 Peck, p. 117.
16 Ibid., p. 85.
17 Ibid., p. 119.
18 Ibid., 116-7.
19 Cardenal. p. 9.
20 Ibid., p., 119.
21 *Dialogue*, St. Catherine of Siena, p. 103-4.
22 Peck, p. 118.
23 Alan Sobel, ed., *Eros, Agape and Philia: Readings in the Philosophy of Love* (NY: Paragon House, 1980), p. xviii.
24 Peck, p. 260.
25 Peck, p. 283.
26 Ibid., p. 286.
27 Ibid., p. 282.
28 Ibid., p. 83.
29 *Esoteric Psychology*, vol. 1, p. 45.
30 Paradiso 33:46-48

[31] Underhill, p. 344.

[32] Ibid., p. 72.

[33] *Song of the Living Flame of Love.*

[34] Peck., p. 158.

[35] Matthew 5:45-6.

[36] Peck, p. 160.

[37] Kahlil Gibran. *The Prophet.* (NY: Alfred A. Knopf, 1995), p. 13.

[38] *Creative Meditation*, p. 211.

[39] Vida, Ch. 10.

[40] *Paradiso*, 33:142-5.

[41] Robert Herrick, "What Love Is."

[42] Joseph Addison, "An Hymn."

[43] *Bhagavad Gita*, quoted in Das, P. 100.

[44] John 17:21-23.

[45] *Dialogue*, ch. 2.

CHAPTER 19

Deliverance Comes from the Woman

Motherhood is the tenderness of God.

Woman remains the guardian of moral and religious values.
Paul Evdokimov

The fact that we perceive reality through our conditioned states of consciousness is it related to the way men perceive female friends when we fall in love?

What is commonly called falling in love is an instance of the repeated act of a thought form, that is, keep thinking about someone. I can explain it in two ways: there is love at first sight that could be the recognition of someone known in previous incarnations. Such a person is referred to as a soul mate. The other kind is the process of growing into love. It can be attributed to the power of thought-feeling.

I myself wonder why I would choose a particular woman, among so many, to be the embodiment of my unique female companion and the epitome of all beauty and virtue.

This is an innate tendency within each individual because every man is created with his female counterpart, every woman with her other male self. They are referred to as twin flames from one original fiery body, as I will explain later on. Their meeting in the world is extremely rare, unless it is My plan for them, considering the hundreds and sometimes thousands of incarnations in so many different places and ages. However, because of the polarity which is inherent in the essential nature of each individual, man and woman are attracted to each other.

I can see that the cause far transcends the physicality of sex.

They are drawn by the magnetic power of love that pervades all manifestation.

You said that love is the greatest magnetic force in all the universe and it is based on the principle of polarity.

Yes, spirit and matter, male and female, Father-Mother God are the two poles of the cosmic magnet of creation. In the absence of the other true self, in order to find completeness and overcome the sense of separation, one tends to project the ideal counterpart onto someone else. Except in the case of acquaintances from past lives, to fall in love is a matter of meeting a woman, for whom one has a liking, several times.

Then it depends on circumstances to bring them together.

If they meet only once, even if the woman makes a good impression on a man, after awhile she is forgotten. However, if the man continues to see her, the thought-form which he has created of her becomes more alive and vivid. He projects his own ideal and transcendence onto her.

I remember reading that "woman represents everything in the world when a man is in need of a vision that would make him complete."[1]

Eventually he will see in her the divine reality of his female other self. For him, she has taken that form, and he then confers on her all the splendid qualities that exist in his twin flame. Their presence in that particular woman may not be superior to many others, but she becomes uniquely perfect to him because it is through her that he realizes his ideal.[2]

As it has been beautifully expressed, "The concrete being rises to heaven like a most brilliant star," and "The destiny

of woman is to make the hearts of men beat at the right moment."[3]

But will it not be a bitter disappointment when he finds that she does not correspond to his ideal? Kierkegaard wrote, "It is woman's misfortune to represent everything one moment, and to represent nothing in the next moment, without ever truly knowing what she properly signifies as a woman."[4]

This may happen, and it does happen to everyone, not only female but also male, who does not know who they are. The positive aspect is that his perception and feeling for her will help the woman to live up to her lover's ideal. She may not possess all the attributes and virtues he sees in her, but she will try to be worthy of his love by developing and bringing them out of their potential state. Since every individual possesses the divine image, she can be what he believes she is as nearly as possible. This is true, of course, also in the case of the woman who projects her ideal onto a man.

I remember remarking to my friends how could someone fall in love with or marry a woman who seemed to us homely and unattractive. Now I understand what happens.

The lover is able to see through the veil of the flesh the luminous being which is hidden to others. The woman then becomes the mediatrix through whom one can reach God.

I read that many men became a genius, a hero, or a saint through the love for a woman.

Yes, the woman indeed possesses the power to raise the consciousness of the world if she is true to her calling. She is the Eternal Feminine, the essence of womanhood that leads man to Heaven, like Beatrice for Dante.

You said that feeling is the feminine side of life, which has three times greater power than the thought which is the masculine. It is true that when the woman was honored and revered, a civilization reached a high level of perfection. That's why it has been said that a nation is worth the value of its women.

I agree with this comment:

> While man extends himself in the world by means of tools, woman does so by her gift of self. In her very being she is linked to the rhythms of Nature, attuned to the order that rules the universe. It is through this gift that every woman is potentially a mother and carries the world's treasure in the depths of her soul.[5]

The spiritual principle is expressed by the woman. For instance, a man does not have the paternal qualities to the same degree that a woman possesses the maternal attributes and virtues. Prevalently, man's aim is to act and woman's is to feel and to be, which is the preeminent religious category since "I AM." "She will always uphold the primacy of being over theory, of the operative over the speculative, of the intuitive over the discursive ..."[6]

Woman could accumulate intellectual values, but such values provide no joy. The excessively intellectualized woman, man's equal and constructress of the world, will find herself despoiled of her essence, for what woman is meant to contribute to culture is femininity as an irreplaceable mode of being and way of living. Man creates science, art, philosophy, and even theology as systems, but all these lead to a frightening objectification of the truth of being and existence, Woman, fortunately, is present; she is predestined to become the bearer of the values obscured by this objectification, the place where they become flesh and live.[7]

The woman has the power to protect and save your present civilization if she chooses to introduce into its dehumanization the tender qualities of caring and grace with which she is endowed and which she represents. It is possible for her to do it because the ultimate source of morality lies in the feminine principle: self-sacrifice, purity, nurture, the protection of the weak. Woman remains the guardian of human and divine values for she is the feeling side of life, which has the power of unification. However, if she betrays her nature, and degrades her humanizing force, there is no hope for mankind, nor the planet. "Woman now makes her own living; but then, even in the domain of love, she rapidly gravitates toward the masculine way from which all spiritual meaning is altogether absent."[8]

Each woman also possesses in latency masculine qualities, but at present the need is for the essence of her feminine affectivity. She may become the equal of man or take his place, but this does not add anything special to her or her vocation. On the contrary, "an enormous deviation is created, aggravated by her incorporation into the masculine world at the very moment of its decadence." ... In his adventures, man dominates everything by his reason. He can consciously risk his life, which means he has the power to dispose of it. Woman does not risk her life; she gives it."[9]

She can infuse her nurturing ethos into every level of society, and raise it to counter-balance the excesses of the male tendencies to intellectualize existence. Through her spiritual nature she represents the act of life-giving, the only one who can prevent the subversion of the feeling by the modern masculine "genius."

Lapsing into abstractions, man has uprooted and disconnected himself, not only from God and Nature, but also from the feminine which is both the counterpart and the mystery of his own being.

According to Dr. Pearce, whom I quoted with regard to the dialogue between brain and body, "patriarchy has failed us ... Surely fathers are indispensable for this sea change, but we must start with mothers and women at large. Males, it seems have lost their moorings, leaving Plato's words more time today than ever: 'Give me a new mother,' he said, and 'I'll give you a new world'."

And there is the fairy tale of the noble King who falls into error, causing his consciousness to sink so low that he became imprisoned in an animal body. Another tale relates also how a fair prince was led astray by undesirable and perverse inclinations and as a consequence was transformed into the body of the lowly frog. I know that fairy tales are not just stories for children but convey deep and meaningful truths about our life. The lesson they teach in this case is that freedom and regeneration comes "not from Knights in shining armor and mighty exploits of strength and courage, or even the wisdom of sages and seers, but through the gentle gesture of the eternal She, whose nurturing kiss alone saved him from himself."[10]

Given the disintegration of the emotions in the experiences of the masses, obsessed by sex but abysmally ignorant of its meaning, the body is nothing more than a physiological mechanism. The sacredness of love disappears and the animal nature leads to the destruction of femininity. The divine Eros, instead of raising the consciousness and leading the individual to the contemplation of celestial beauty, has degenerated into the futility of sexual technique and the meaninglessness and emptiness of the ability to "perform."

"So called 'free love' where the body is offered in the absence of the soul, causes a disquieting number of neuroses. With the destruction of interiority, the human being, delivered to the wretchedness of the flesh, becomes the possession and the sport of demonic forces."[11]

It is imperative that woman who represents the capacity to love and to feel, comes to the rescue of the human race. "This is her vocation: to protect the world of humans as mother, and to save it as a virgin, by giving to this world a soul, her soul."[12]

It has been said that love is all she has to give, but it is the only earthly thing which God permits us to carry beyond the grave. I can understand why it was a woman who received the message of salvation, and it is significant that the risen Christ appeared first to a woman; and it is "the woman robed with the sun" who represents the Heavenly City. She is the "Amen" of all of humanity who responds, accepts and receives in her womb the divine "I AM."
The destiny of the future civilization lies in the heart of the mothers; if their love were withdrawn, the earth would collapse.

"The modern, profoundly masculine world, where the feminine charism plays no role whatsoever is more and more a world without God, for it has no mother and God cannot be born in it."[13]

As the Koran states so beautifully, "Paradise lies at the feet of the mother."

There is a deep truth, more than many can understand in the expression, "Motherhood is the tenderness of God." What is most characteristic in the divine nature is present in the woman.[14]

Julian of Norwich refers to Jesus and God as mother: "The mother can give her child to suck of her milk, but our precious Mother Jesus can feed us with himself ... The mother can lay her child tenderly to her breast, but our tender Mother Jesus can lead us easily into his blessed breast through his sweet open side, and show us there a part of the godhead and the joys of heaven with inner certainty of endless bliss ... This fair lovely word 'mother' is so sweet and so kind in itself that it cannot truly be said of anyone or to anyone except of him and to him who is the true Mother of life and all things."[15] " O that you would tear open the heavens and come down," the prophet cries.[16] It is the vocation of the woman to bring forth the divinization of man.

1 For this chapter I am indebted to: Paul Evdokimov, *Woman and the Salvation of the World: A Christian Anthropology on the Charism of Women*, tr. Gythiel, A.P. (Crestwood, NY: St Vladimir Seminary Press, 1994), p. 174.

2 C. W. Leadbeater, *The Hidden Side of Things*, third ed., (Adyar, India; Wheaton, IL: The Theosophical Publishing House), pp. 373 ff.

3 Evdokimov, pp. 174-5.

4 *The Seducer*, p. 79.

5 Evdokimov, p. 184.

6 Ibid., pp. 152, 260.

7 Ibid., p. 185.

8 Ibid., p. 182.

9 Ibid., p. 183.

10 Pearce, p. 247.

11 Evdokimov, p. 184.

12 Ibid., p. 185.

13 Ibid., p. 251.

14 Ibid., p. 167.

15 *Showings*, 60th Chapter (NY: Paulist Press, 2001), p. 209.

16 Isaiah 64:1.

CHAPTER 20

Mother Nature, Fairies, and Angels

In all things of nature there is something of the marvelous.
Aristotle

Angels and ministers of grace defend us!
William Shakespeare

There are fairies at the bottom of our garden!
Rose Fyleman

My question is now this: since the four elements, both in Nature and in the individual's bodies, are of divinely created origin, how can they become destructive? As you know, we experience all kinds of disasters, from earthquakes, hurricanes, droughts, to devastating fires, floods and other catastrophes.

The answer is simple, and I pose it to you as a question: have you ever considered the effects on Nature of the tragedy of war after war throughout thousands of years, and the destructive use of energy by mankind's selfishness and hatred that has disfigured the face of the planet? Let me refer you to one of your books, The Hidden Messages of Water that you either forgot or of which you did not understand its message.

You are right (of course you are!) The research work and experiments of Dr. Emoto has drawn global attention because he has scientifically proved by thousands of photographs how water responds to our attitudes towards it. In the context of your explanation I'd like to elaborate how he discovered that crystals formed in frozen water reveal changes according to the quality of our thoughts. When ex-

posed to loving words the molecules of water show brilliant, complex, and colorful snowflake patterns. In contrast, negative thoughts result in distorted, asymmetrical forms, with dull colors. Since humans and the earth are composed mostly of water, his message is one of personal health, global environmental renewal, and a practical plan for peace that starts with each one of us. "Our emotions and feelings have an effect on the world moment by moment," writes our scientist; "If you send out words and images of creativity, then you will be contributing to the creation of a beautiful world. However, emitting messages of destruction, you contribute to the destruction of the universe."[1]

What is true of water must also be true of the other three elements, air, fire, and earth. It is no wonder we experience natural disasters.

We refer to Nature as Mother, but very few understand its deep meaning. Yet mankind's bodies are formed from the substance of the earth; and Nature, through the beings of the elements, feeds, clothes, and houses billions of people and enables them to take embodiment here. When Mother, human and divine, is not respected and honored, the Spirit, which finds expression through Her as the pole of matter, is neglected too. By Her image as Mother, man is not bound and limited by matter as an end in itself, but as a divine counterpart for the full realization of his I AM-Self.

People have not been taught, or rather, have forgotten the innate truth that they must appreciate and have reverence for the Earth as the motherly expression of life. They should recognize Her gifts and comprehend Her sacred language, but only the poetic soul

Finds tongues in trees, books in the running brooks,

Sermons in stones, and good in everything.[2]

Unfortunately, modern man sees Nature only as something to be conquered and exploited for his personal selfish ends. But why should relations between the mind and the natural world be qualified as something which is against or in opposition instead of the union and bond of polarity?

Why should there be a necessary struggle and domination for mastery of the subject over the object viewed as a hostile force?

The aim of so-called civilized man is to subjugate Nature; yet in her self-giving, She is present in every aspect of the universe, above all in the beings of the elements and the bodies of mankind. No form, from an atom to a planet or a whole system of worlds comes into manifestation without the receptive, responsive, creative attributes of matter-Mother.

No wonder that all ancient cultures recognized the preeminence of woman and worshipped goddesses!
The Mother embodies the divine ideation from the Source, and She is as the giver of form which becomes through Her the expression of beauty.

How could we survive without that which Nature provides for us?
The inhabitants of the four elements are Her faithful servants and instruments to take care of mankind and bless them with Her boundless gifts, giving them lovingly and freely the fire for heat, the air to breath, the water to drink and be clean, and the food to eat.

Are they what are spoken of as "elementals" or "nature spirits"?

Yes, they are like the soul, the inner life, or the essence of the four elements and the builders of forms; the unseen inhabitants and little workers of earth, water, air, and fire are called respectively gnomes, undines, sylphs, and salamanders.

According to tradition, this is the common classification of the fairy kingdom, but there is an endless variety of them. I know that the first reaction of those who slumber, enveloped in the fog of their intellectual concepts that buffer them from reality, will obviously be that the whole thing is nonsense.

I would tell them, as Hamlet already did, that "There are more things in heaven and earth than are dreamed of in their philosophy."[3]

Before somebody can say that anything is impossible or absurd, he should reflect for a moment on how sorely limited the human being is in comparison with a universe of billions of stars, which the intellect can not fathom, does not know why they exist, and in a poetic mood, imagines that they are solely for decoration.

Man doesn't even understand what Reality is. I heard this fitting anecdote: "They asked Rabbi Levi Isaac of Berditchev: 'Why is the first page number missing in all the tractates of the Babylonian Talmud? Why does each begin with the second?' He replied: 'However much a man may learn, he should always remember that he has not even gotten to the first page'."[4]

I do not mean that people should be gullible or naive, but only have an open mind in order to be receptive to the truth that is always trying to reveal itself to the earnest and sincere seeker

490

who is determined to pierce the veil of the world of appearances.

It has been said that "Truth is stranger than fiction."
Does not My love, wisdom, and power transcend anything that humans can conceive? I will say again that the truth of the teaching I am giving for your illumination and that of others cannot be understood except it finds a response from within. Faith need not be blind. Everyone is endowed with the capacity and faculties necessary to discover the truth concerning both himself and the universe. It abides in the heart of every human being, and I am always speaking through it. But who is ready and willing to hear My voice?

The incessant noise and clamor of the world makes us deaf. Of one thing I can be sure: the vortex of desires and appetites of the personality, the waves of emotion tossing us to and fro, will always prevent your voice from reaching us.
I will repeat these words as an indictment to every age of human history:

> "You will indeed listen, but never understand, and you will indeed look, but never perceive. For this people's heart has grown dull, and their ears are hard of hearing, and they have shut their eyes; so that they might not look with their eyes, and listen with their ears, and understand with their heart and turn — and I would heal them."[5]

Let us continue: it is foundational to recognize the oneness of life and the seamless fabric of reality underlying all phenomena. I told you that you live in a universe where everything is interrelated and interdependent by a system of correspondences, not as a mere causal time–space relationship, but one of common ground, and all is one consciousness, from the so-called Matter and Nature to Humanity and the Godhead.

A universe, moreover, is actuated throughout by the dynamic interplay of bipolar forces that not only sustain its present existence but also keep it moving in an ever-ascending spiral toward greater harmony, joy, and perfection. Behind the painted veil of Mother Nature there is a vast network of nature spirits devoted to mankind, created to serve their needs and obey them for good or ill. They are part of the hierarchy of higher and lesser Beings comprising gods and goddesses, archangels, angels, and, on the lower rungs, the elementals. They are the little inhabitants of the four elements, who formed your bodies in the beginning under My direction in their divine purity, beauty, and immortal perfection.

Even as the Father in Heaven is perfect.[6]
Their function is to be the receivers and transmitters of waves of creative energies from Myself through the sun, and are commissioned to bring into manifestation both the divine and human ideation of thoughts, feelings, and spoken words. They are the expression and objectification of God's love, endowed with the mandate to multiply and expand the beauty and harmony of His plan in the blissful feeling of sharing and belonging to one another.

The nature spirits, after receiving the life-force from the sun, absorb, contain, and then release it in their creative work, whether in the formation of a rock, a jewel, a flower, a plant, a metal, a cloud, or a snowflake. They are instrumental for the creation and maintenance of all that is in the sanctuary of Nature, in perfect attunement with the divine Word.

Unfortunately, they are also subject to the maleficent influence and abuse of man.

Can you tell me something about their appearance?
Brownies, elves and gnomes appear in Western countries much as are described in folklore. In some Eastern, Central and South American countries their forms are more archaic, and even grotesque. Undines or nereids, associated with the element of water, resemble beautiful, and generally unclothed, female figures, femininity being suggested by roundness of form, there being diversity of polarity but no difference of sex neither in the angelic nor in the fairy kingdom.

Varying in height from a few inches to two or three feet, undines are to be seen playing in the spray of waterfalls, reclining in the depths of deep pools or floating swiftly over the surface of river and lake. Fairies and sylphs, associated with the element of air, generally appear to clairvoyant vision much as represented in fairy-tale. They look like beautiful maidens with brightly-coloured wings, not used for flight since these beings float swiftly or slowly at will, their rosy, glowing forms partly concealed by gossamer, force-built "garments." Salamanders, associated with the element of fire, appear as if built of flame, the form constantly changing but suggestive of human shape, the eyes alight with fiery power. The chin and ears are sharply pointed and the "hair" frequently streams back from the head, appearing like tongues of flame, as the salamanders dive steeply into the flames of physical fires and fly through them.[7]

Variation of these forms are to be seen in different countries of the world and in different parts of the same country.

I will introduce you to the undine living in the locality of a waterfall.

She looks like a tall and graceful young girl, unclothed and of a singular beauty. Auric forces flow out behind her in wing-like form and on every side. She seems to ensoul the rocks, trees, ferns, and mosses, in addition to the waterfall and pool. Her whole form is of a soft rose pink; her hair is fair and shiny, her brow broad, her features beautifully modeled, her eyes large and luminous.

Even more striking than her form is the rainbow-like aureole that surrounds her, as a halo sometimes seems to surround the moon. This aura is almost spherical in shape and consists of evenly arranged, concentric spheres of colors of the spectrum in their palest shades, with rose, green, and blue predominating. Some of the spheres of color are outlined with a golden fire, and beyond the outer edge a shimmering radiance of pearly white adds beauty to the aureole and lovely form within.

Over the head a powerful upward flow of forces interpenetrates the aura in a fan-shaped radiation. This appears to come from a point in the middle of the head, where there is a brilliant golden center, slightly below the level of the eyes and midway between them. The whole region of the waterfall is vibrant with her life. Later she reemerges; this time she is wearing a jeweled belt, the ends of which cross and hang down on the left side. The jewels are not like any known to us, being large and of fiery luminosity and the belt is made of something that shimmers like golden chain-mail of extremely fine texture.[8]

What a lovely, wonderful being, like the Fairy Queen described by a clairvoyant: "We are surrounded by a group of joyous, dancing fairies. The leader is some two feet tall, clothed in transparent, flowing draperies, and has a star on

her forehead. She has large, glistening "wings" of delicate shades of pink and lavender. Her "hair" is light golden brown and streams behind her, merging with the other flowing forces of her aura. The form is perfectly modeled and rounded, like that of a young girl, and the right hand holds a wand. Her face stamped with a decided impress of power, especially noticeable in the clear blue eyes which, on occasion, glow as with living fire. Her brow is broad, her features small and rounded, the tiny ears a poem of physical perfection. The bearing of head, neck and shoulders is queenly, the whole pose being full of grace. A pale blue radiance surrounds this beautiful creature, while golden flashers of light play around and above her head. The lower portion of the aura is shell pink, irradiated with white light."[9]

In their original form elementals are indeed beautiful because they are divinely created. When you see them portrayed in unnatural and grotesque appearances and characterizations, it is really the human thought-forms imposed upon them which produce the distortion of their figure.

Nature spirits have a permanent astral body that consists of an oval or spherical aura of prismatic colors surrounding their delicate light-built fairy form within. They also clothe themselves in etheric matter which offers them closer contact with the physical world. Their size varies considerably, from very tiny to full human stature; they have no organs and are, as I mentioned, asexual, but they do have a heart made of golden light that is the center of their vitality, circulating the currents of their energy.

It is interesting, and very significant in the context of your teaching that there are not differences of sex, but of polarity.

The beings of Nature do not need to sleep or slumber, and they do not eat, although they have mouths — in fact, they smile and sing — and other facial features. They feel through their heart, as people should, with the capacity to commune and blend with their surroundings. Their feelings control the rhythm of their hearts and vitality; accordingly, they can change their shape and color, together with their clothes and covering.

Elemental's thought is strongly formative upon astral and etheric matter, and they possess an extraordinary ability to imitate and mimic, often playfully, human activities, habits, and dress. Nature spirits are totally dedicated to their labor of love, and whether it involves opening a bud, the growth of a leaf, or the coloring of a flower, they feel responsible for it and take a maternal pride in their accomplishments. Although their work is a serious activity and life-giving, it is also an act of play because of the pleasure and enjoyment they derive from it.

An important difference between humans and elementals rests in their modes of perception. When you look at a tree, what you see is its shape, size, and color; in their case, they actually experience the nature of the tree as a living and breathing entity. Their world is not that of surfaces and appearances — of skins, husks, and barks — with definite, separate edges. To them, everything is made of flowing energy, pulsating and filled with motion and feeling.

It is more like the reality you have explained to me where there is no separation but interrelation and continuity in the oneness of the universal sea of light.

There is no such thing as either dead or blind matter, just as there are not inactive principles or Law. How could mankind act and create a civilization, or anything for that matter, if there was not intelligence in the material world to respond to them and to work with?

I must remember that all energy is God's energy.
Everything is a living combination of light, sound, and color. For the elementals, a stone thrills with life and they feel affection for all of Nature as if it were part of themselves.

There is no struggle, suffering, or discord in their experience except what mankind imposes upon them; this explains how the forces of the elements can become destructive. When God created man and commanded him to be fruitful in service, to multiply His gifts and to become master of the elements, He gave him helpers to assist him in the creation and expansion of His Kingdom.

Nature spirits depend on human beings who are God's coworkers and stewards on Earth. In the beginning the elementals carried out the divine plan which flourished everywhere in glorious fulfillment, as the manifestation of divine care in action. It is recorded in the Bible as the Garden of Eden, and in tradition as the mythical Golden Ages.

After man rebelled against the Cosmic Law he cut himself off from the flow of everlasting life with consequent disruption of the intimacy and harmonious relationship with God and Nature. And he brought upon himself the so-called divine judgment: "Cursed is the ground because of you; ... thorns and thistles it shall bring forth for you."[10]

The beautiful rose began to appear with thorns, not as a divine creation, not even for protection, but as the result of man's stinging thoughts and his sharp feelings. During the long period of his exile from Paradise, man's discriminating faculties dimmed, and he misused his divine powers.

This resulted in the energy-veil that shut off the original luminosity and glorious beauty of the divine manifestation of this world, which caused the densification of both his body and the planet that, mark you, is a living organism. The destructive vibratory action of the human miscreation increased its momentum and the consequences are the conditions of unbalance and continued disturbances on the surface of the Earth. Throughout the ages, the negative Karma escalated in intensity and the accumulation of destructive energy of mankind's thoughts and feelings imposed its discord on the beings of the elements. It is not well to recall the human rebellion against the Law of life, but for your illumination I only mention that many inventions and sophisticated technologies were known long before your present time. In fact, another dire consequence that caused the suffering of the fairy kingdom was the perverted practices of scientists in past civilizations more advanced than yours, like Atlantis.

They misused their knowledge, and their manipulation of the forces of nature caused the elementals to be imprisoned in the form of animals.

Which are the materialization of mankind's negative thought forms. In the life readings of Edgar Cayce about fifty percent of different people had incarnations in Atlantis that influenced their present lives. And there are references to "atomic forces, machines of destruction that sailed through either the air or under water, the creating of high influences of radial activity from rays of the sun, and applications of spiritual things for self-indulgence and material gains." The language is not accurate as he tries to describe

devices, like lasers and atomic bombs, that were unknown at the time of the readings.[11]

All nature is groaning under the negative energy created by the human defiance of the Law of Love and harmony. If man persists in sowing the winds of violence, discord, and darkness, he is bound to reap the whirlwind of chaos and self-annihilation.

Nature cannot tolerate indefinitely man's injustice and destructive activity. She is made of the substance of light which, by its very essence of purity, only for a time can be subjected to the discordant energy imposed upon it. Since all the universe obeys the Law of Love and ever expanding perfection, when a certain point of pressure is reached, Nature overthrows all opposition to the tendency of God's life toward purity and harmony.

Mankind, in its selfishness and ignorance, creates by thoughts and feelings, the discordant vibratory action that is impressed on the four elements of their bodies and the body of the Earth.

But Nature is My direct creation and has the power to purify Herself, returning to mankind what has been forced upon Her.

Ask yourself who creates storms of anger and tornadoes of violence and war. Do you think that I cause earthquakes to destroy My handiwork? That would not be a very intelligent act on My part.

The legend of the sinking of Atlantis under the Atlantic Ocean, or of Lemuria under the Pacific, is all that remains of the records of those great civilizations destroyed by the recoil of their own evil, and present humanity should read the handwriting on the wall. The mercy of God is holding in abeyance the retributive effects of the Law, giving mankind a little more time to awake from the sleep of the senses and turn away from his downward path.

But the elementals can, at any moment, become the instruments of Karmic judgment and explode in earthquakes, atmospheric disturbances, the raging of the seas, the roaring of uncontrollable fire, and shifting of landmasses.

We are already experiencing them.
There is only one way to deter the unleashing of the destructive momentum and prevent its recoil: purification.

How can this be done?
By the fire element, the only purifier, for both the individual and the Earth. People can turn to God, as they understand it according to their belief, and call for the fire of My love, or the Sacred Fire or the Holy Spirit, to consume all evil and bring again peace and harmony.

But people are usually afraid of fire because it can burn and destroy everything. I remember the words, "Lord do you want us to command fire to come down from heaven and consume them?"[12]
The physical fire, which is the outer aspect or manifestation of the spiritual fire, can only cause damage and destruction when it is charged with the discord and negative energy imposed on it by mankind.

We don't realize that the Law of cause and effect is acting in the elements of Nature, earth, air, fire, and water, and that what we send out is bound to come back to us.

People think of them as inanimate or dead substance, but I assure you that all life feels, in different degrees, and there is will and intelligence everywhere.

Because, as you said, life, consciousness, and energy are one.
Yes, and it is God-life, God-energy, and God-consciousness they are receiving and using, or misusing, all the time in every way they think, feel, and do.

We are not aware of it, and go through our daily existence blindfolded to the true purpose of why we are on this planet as the guest of God. And we think we can ignore the Law of Love and not be responsible for it. Certainly we need the illumination that only your sacred fire can give.
When the individual draws it into himself by his desire to be free from his Karmic debts and be perfected, the fire, which remember is love, loves to do it because that is its nature. It can only purify, heal, transform, and perfect whatever it touches.

It is described by the saints as the giver of heavenly joy, peace and ecstasy. It reminds me of the descent in tongues of flames at Pentecost, when it filled the house and everyone of those present with its divine powers.
Yes, what is referred to as the Holy Spirit, which is one person of the Trinity, is another aspect of God. That is why the sin against it is unforgivable.

Instead of the forced purification by suffering, called purgative, caused by the return of the individual's miscreation into itself, the harmonious and perfect way for its release is as I said, to call to Me, and draw it into you by your love and devotion, because it is My desire to give it and it can only bless you with its infinite gifts.

The counterpart or the physical side of the fire can only become devastating and destructive when its elementals become subject to the human discord and negative energy created by human beings.

This is what happened with Sodom and Gomorrah. My burning desire is to cry out: fill me with your heavenly fire and love me free!

I will, this is your opportunity because the end of the cycle is here and now, and people must clean up or they will be cleaned out. I have watched a long, long time men's waywardness, inhumanity, and deliberate viciousness, patiently awaiting the moment of their return home. Now it is the requirement of the Cosmic Law that the Earth be purified by fire and come into accord with the other planets of the Solar System and the rest of the universe. Then the Earth and its inhabitants will be free from all discord and limitations, the divine plan is fulfilled as it was originally intended and every child of God will know again the joy of living in paradise. Your planet will become again luminous as it was in the beginning and no longer called the dark star.

How are the angels related to the nature's spirits?

The whole cosmos is under the charge and guidance of hierarchies of Divine Beings, each having a service to give and a mission to perform.

I remember the dream of Jacob in which he saw "a ladder set up on the Earth, the top of it reaching to heaven; and the angels of God were ascending and descending on it."[13]

Using the same image, I would say that the beings of the elements are on the lower rungs and above them in the hierarchy are the angels. Unfortunately, mankind has lost its contact not only with Nature's hidden life, but also with the angelic host, although they always minister to them.

Most people think that they do not exist, that they are figments of the imagination or merely symbolic.
The angels are more real than humankind because they are beings of light, clothed in a glorious radiance, directing dazzling rays of various quality according to their field of service. Their love, beauty, and power are so transcendent that there are no words to describe them. Streams of fiery energy of intense brightness flash constantly through and around them. Their flaming aura extends outwards to a considerable distance, shining with delicate colors of many hues which veil the beautiful form within. They are My messengers, immortally pure and perfect. The angels are continually active as channels and expression of the creative fire of love, giving service and assistance to the people of Earth in countless ways.

Were the angels involved in the origin of hell?
There is no such thing as "fallen angels" for the simple reason that they never descended into physical embodiments and have not been through human experience. Therefore, the angels cannot fall, only human beings are subject to that condition because of the misuse of their free will. The angels always do My will, as they are the carriers and the outpouring of the fire of My love, and their service is to bless all life.

The angelic host are your eternal friends and, being one with life, they enable you to feel the desire to reach up for greater good and make you victorious over evil.

503

Are there angels of different order and groups?
There are angels of protection, peace, purity, freedom, music, healing and of every divine attribute and activity. If you could see them how by the radiance of their love and light they can prevent, control, and change a destructive condition bringing safety and harmony in place of danger and injury, you would be in awe and could not help to worship them. They give assistance by the outpouring of the flame of love from their heart, hands, and the auric forces of their body.

Certainly we need to associate with them and feel their presence rather than the discord of the outer world.
They will be with everyone who is aware of them and opens the door to their company by love and prayer. Their service includes the assistance given to those who leave their body at so-called death to escort them into the realms of light.

Can you elaborate with regard to the healing angels?
Yes, since mankind needs healing of the mind and body so desperately. One or more of the angelic host stands above every hospital in the cities of the world pouring their healing light to cure all kind of illness. The medical world may deny or ignore them but without their service and assistance the number of healing would be very small. Yet others take the credit.

Benjamin Franklin was right when he said that God heals and the doctor gets the fee. There are those who believe in the guardian angel, is it real?
Absolutely; in the beginning of your individualization on Earth, I provided an angel in order to give the protection needed according to your Karma, and it has always been with you. Every

human being has an unseen body guard and personal physician called "guardian angel" which accompanies him or her through every embodiment until the individual accomplishes the ascension by fulfilling the divine plan or, if he fails to obey the Law of love, will meet the second death.

Is the guardian angel involved in the process of birth?
Very definitely; every time you take a new body it is the function of the angel, at the time of conception, to attach or join the divine spark, which is the heart center, to the twin cell that has been newly formed. The presence of that flame and My descending creative force upon the twin-celled organism causes it to grow, in harmony with the body of the mother, into a definite form. In the pre-natal stage, soon after conception, the baby-body shows itself as an ethereal living being almost self-luminous, the ether being the mould and matrix of every form as the womb of Mother Nature. The whole process of birth, like the origin of a planet, can be described in terms of frequency, sound, and color. Each type of tissue and organ has its own vibratory rates varying according to the Karmic law. Health means that every part of the body is in tune and harmonized; a dissonance or a note out of tune produces illness.

I realize the importance of harmony, especially in the feeling which is the determining factor in our lives. I am very interested to know the appearance of the angels; for example, do they have wings?
Whatever I create it is made of light, which is the primal energy and substance, therefore, the angels are self-luminous beings. Their forms are built upon the same model or divine archetype as the physical body of mankind in its original perfection. The outline of the angelic form is less clearly defined, resembling

fiery flowing forces. They differ in appearance according to their Order but, again, like the elementals, there is no sex differentiation among them, their diversity being of polarity.

Therefore, the angels appear as very beautiful ethereal human-like beings. "Their faces, however, wear an expression which is distinctly non-human, for they are stamped with an impression of dynamic energy, of vividness of consciousness and life, with a certain supernal beauty and an other-worldliness which is rarely seen among mankind."[14]

Then, the master painters were right in portraying their form closely to ours, but why give them wings?
The flame-like energy flowing within their bodies and radiating through their shining aura takes the shape behind them of outspread wings of prismatic colors. However, the angels do not need wings as they can move very swiftly, floating gracefully through the air.

What is their mode of communication?
It is a communion of thoughts and feelings which is the perfect way not limited by words which are the cause of misunderstanding and deception. The angels' feelings of the oneness of life is so deep that they always express that fundamental truth. Since their bodies are composed of light every activity of their consciousness causes a corresponding change of the shape and color of their aura. When pouring love the angel is all aglow with rose-pink flames streaming out and enfolding the object of its affection. Mental activity suffuses its head with brilliant golden light forming a crown set with a jewel for each thought.

Also our thoughts and feelings produce color and forms or pictures, but unfortunately the vibration of our body is too dense for us to see them.

Much evil could be prevented and avoided if human beings were aware of what they create, most of which is a desecration of life. It is also the mercy of God that they do not see their negative thoughts and feeling forms because they are so hideous as to make the person faint.

I suppose that the angels are present during religious services.

Every religion has an archangel and angelic beings who bestow, protect and expand the spiritual power called forth by the faithful. Each church, temple, shrine, monastery and convent is under the care of a directing angel of a specific Order. Their function is to receive the uprising streams of prayers and songs. After gathering the devotional feelings of the congregation they offer them to God. Then they distribute the outpouring of divine force carrying the response and fulfillment of every sincere desire.

I read this description by a clairvoyant: "The Eucharist Ceremony is under the care of an exalted angel, sometimes called the Angel of the Eucharist. At the moment of the Consecration of the Elements, a glorious Angelic Being in the likeness of the Lord Christ, known as the Angel of the Presence, descends upon the altar as His messenger. At the chanting of the Preface, when reference is made to the Nine Orders of the Angels recognized in the Christian angelology, a representative of each Order responds to the Invocation and bestows the power, light and benediction of his

Order upon Officiants, congregation, Church and surrounding regions."[15]

I wish you to know that also every nation is presided over by an angel of elevated rank in the hierarchy. Accordingly it has full knowledge of the Karma and the destiny of its people, and its service is to minimize and possibly prevent errors and bestow blessings in response to each heart's desire and call. Then, inspire and assist them to fulfill the divine plan. If mankind would cooperate with the angelic host, and recognize their service, and invite them into their lives, it will hasten tremendously the coming of the Golden Age of the Earth.

[1] Masaru Emoto, *The Hidden Messages in Water* (Hillsboro, Or.: Beyond Words Publishing, 2004), p. 84.

[2] Duke Senior in William Shakespeare, *As You Like It,* Act II, Scene 1, Lines 15-18.

[3] William Shakespeare, *Hamlet,* Act I, Scene 5, Lines 173-175.

[4] Marc–Alain Ouaknin, *Mysteries of the Kabbalah* tr. Bacon, J., (NY: Abbeville Press, 2000), p. 244.

[5] Isaiah, quoted by St. Paul in Acts 28:26.

[6] Matthew 5:48.

[7] Geoffrey Hodson, *The Kingdom of the Gods* (Wheaton, IL: Theosophical Publishing House, 1999), p. 57.

[8] Hodson, pp. 117-8.

[9] Ibid., pp. 125-6.

[10] Genesis 3:17-18.

[11] See Edgar E. Cayce, *On Atlantis* (NY: Warner Books, 1968), ch. 4.

[12] Luke 9:54.

[13] Genesis 28:12.

[14] Hodson, p. 87.

[15] Ibid., p. 79.

CHAPTER 21

The Seven Bodies

Wisdom has built her house,
She has hewn her seven pillars.
Proverbs

The universe is the individual on a large scale.
Lao-tzu

He made this world to match the world above, and
Whatever exist above has its counterpart below...and all is one.
Zohar

    I am not disparaging your physical form, but it is the least important of your bodies.

    I would like to emphasize that it is not a principle, and by it I mean the germ or the seed on each plane carrying all the potentiality of divine consciousness. The physical body constantly remains that which is worked *upon* and not what has an innate influence of its own. It is not important in the active process being only a recipient and not that which originates activity. What is fundamental is the unfolding consciousness, that is, My "I AM" Presence in the individual. The physical body merely responds, or it should when healthy. When it becomes, erroneously, the focus of attention it is similar to the worship of an idol. "It has not true life of its own, it is always conditioned by inner causes. It is never, intrinsically, itself a cause. Its achievement and its triumph is that it is an automaton."[1]

What do you mean by bodies? Do we have more than one?

You certainly do, and they are far more real than your flesh form because they are not transitory and perishable. You are familiar with the states of matter called solid, liquid, and gaseous; however, there is a higher condition than gaseous referred to as etheric, in which all substances and forms exist. Beyond that there is another realm of nature called the astral, and a still higher and more refined state of matter with the name of mental. From each one of them there is made, a corresponding body and there are, including the physical forms, four of them.

These realms of different levels of consciousness and rates of vibration and degrees of density are spoken of as planes. However, the name can be misleading because they are not lying one above the other but interpenetrate and interact with each other, all filling the same space.

I am not sure I am following you.
Repetita juvant, says a Latin proverb; let me repeat some of the basic ideas to help you understand the magnificent universe in which you live. The infinite Ground emerges from its static state to acknowledge its own being giving rise to a dyad. The two complementary poles, by their interplay, generate the flaming light that is the matrix of the unfolding universe.

The cosmos, meaning "order," is a bipolar continuum, or a series of interrelations based on the primordial polarity of:

> spirit / matter
> Father / Mother God
> universal / individual
> one / many
> infinite / finite
> life / form

511

Can you clarify the meaning of "form"?

Does not anything in manifestation, including you, have a form of some kind? Let me answer with the definition from your dictionary: "External appearance of a clearly defined area; the shape of a thing or person."[2] Between the pole of the finest and most rarefied light-energy down to the pole of the densest degree of matter, seven planes come into being, each with its own seven sub-planes, connecting the God Self with the individual as one life-stream.

I can see why the number seven has been considered sacred as it underlies manifestation in various ways. There are seven days of the week, seven colors of the spectrum, seven notes of the diatonic scale, seven planets, the seven capital sins and their opposing virtues, the seven gifts of the Holy Spirit, the Seven Spirits before the Throne, the seven rays, the seven centers in the body, and so forth.

Numbers are not merely expressions of quantities, they are the outer garments or symbols of principles, essences, and of the harmony of beings and the universe. The number seven is present in religion, myths, legends, folk-tales, and works of art,.

With regard to colors, I would like to say a few words about them because of their importance in the life of everyone. Every color you see or that surrounds you has a definite effect on all facets of your being, whether it is your health, prosperity, or happiness.

The frequency and vibratory action of a color is its quality, and it is either constructive and beneficial or harmful and destructive. You should know that every feeling has its own color, which is its essential nature and produces a corresponding result on the person and his world. For instance, if you are angry, the radiating vibration shows flashes of red; if you are in a state of depression, it is grey. Selfishness and hate create darkness.

But the fire is red.
Not always. It depends on what is burned. The red in the fire is the impurity in the substance which is being consumed; when burning dried leaves, for instance, its color is golden.

How do we know which color we should wear and use in our surroundings?
Look at the rainbow. Mother Nature shows you which colors are life-giving because you absorb their rates of vibration (or wave-lengths) into your emotional body.

However, the red in the rainbow is really rose-pink, which is a very beneficial color because it is the radiation of love. The color white, like light, includes all the colors of the spectrum.

In Revelation, we read, "They will walk with me, dressed in white, for they are worthy. If you conquer, you will be clothed like them in white robes, and I will not blot your name out of the book of life.[3]
The seven planes are also called "spheres" or "heavens," transcending the experience of ordinary sense-consciousness. Some of your saints and mystics have had a glimpse of them in their moments of ecstasy.

I should also mention that color and sound go together. They are two aspects of the same phenomenon. Much could be said on this subject but I do not want to digress further from our topic.

St. Paul mentions "someone" (who is really himself) being raised "either in the body or out of it" he couldn't tell, to the third heaven.
You know that your physical body has the same composition as the earth; each of your inner bodies is also part and made of the same matter of the plane to which it belongs.

The four lower bodies corresponding to the four basic elements, earth, water, air, and fire (although fire is not a body but the inner essence), constitute the personality or outer self. They are your instruments for the mastery and expansion of your consciousness acting on the lower planes.

As a crude analogy, you use different vehicles like an automobile to travel on solid ground, a ship on the water, and a plane to fly through the air. Similarly, you, as the individualized "I AM," and an extension of Myself on the planet Earth, use your bodies as vehicles or instruments to experience life and relate to the outer world.

But I am not aware of them.
You may not realize that they are bodies, but you use them all the time because they are your outer side of consciousness, your pole of matter, and make up your personality or outer self. When you are hungry or thirsty, it is your physical body that demands attention, and it is the etheric body that vitalizes and energizes it.

If you are excited, irritated, depressed, or happy and at peace, you are focused on your emotional or astral body. When dealing with intellectual matters or solving an abstract problem you act in your mental body. Each of them are related respectively to the inner side of the element of earth, water, air, with the fire of love pervading and permeating. They are, however, interconnected and interpenetrate each other; you are one life-stream, flowing from the Source of all, one I AM-Self, acting on different planes.

One consciousness becomes sevenfold clothed in seven bodies.
Yes, and what is lesser and lower always tends to rise and move upward toward the greater and higher vibratory action responding to the magnetic attraction of the love from the Source of all.

According to the principle of polarity, instead of the gravitational pull downward of our worldly desires. I think there are not many people who are aware of their inner bodies — we are too occupied, or rather preoccupied, with our physical form and are attached to it like a clam to its shell.
To identify with it would be as unreasonable as to think that you are the clothing you wear.

Remember that even your inner bodies are not who you are, although they are of much greater value and significance to your life experience than your physical body, that could not exist without its etheric counterpart. It is also called the "double" because it is the pattern or the mould upon which the flesh structure is built and held, and enables it to be healed in case of injury. This substance, which underlies all forms, is a transferring and transmitting agency of vital energy to the outer dense physical body. In fact, it is the ether that makes electrical and chemical activities possible.

The etheric body can be described as a web or network of a thread of forces and interlacing channels which underlie the nervous system and the entire body. It is the cause of sensation and power of growth and reproduction to what would otherwise be an empty shell or an aggregate of minerals. In a healthy person the lines of force radiating from it are straight and shining, while in one who is ill they are grayish and drooping.

I assume that they appear in what is referred to as the aura or the energy field of the individual.

Yes, it is present around everyone, in fact, everything, and shows the development of the consciousness, the nature of the character and the qualities of the one who occupies the physical body. Moreover, it contains the etheric records or counterpart of all the life experiences and activities, past and present, of the individual. It is the same with every locality. The etheric body not only vitalizes and energizes the physical body but integrates it into the energy body of the Earth and of the solar system as a web of energy streams, of lines of force and of light. Along these lines of energy the cosmic forces flow, as the blood flows through the veins and arteries.

This constant, individual — human, planetary and solar-circulation of life — forces through the etheric bodies of all forms is the basis of all manifestation, and the expression of the essential non-separateness of all life.[4] With regards to the etheric records of everyone, you are familiar with folk tales relating how an individual's experiences flashed in front of them as they were drowning, perhaps falling or facing sudden accidental death. In an astonishing short time one sees all the detailed events of his earthly existence.

They might also have retrospective views of their past lives in series of pictures.

I read of a case about the fall of a man that lasted only a few seconds but his time sense expanded tremendously. This is how he described it:

516

I saw my whole past take place in many images, as though on a stage at some distance from me. I saw myself as the chief character in the performance. Everything was transfigured as though by a heavenly light and everything was beautiful without grief or anxiety, and without pain. The memory of very tragic experiences I had had was clear but not saddening. I felt no conflict or strife: conflict had been transmuted into love. Elevated and harmonious thoughts dominated and united the individual images, and like magnificent music a divine calm swept through my soul.[5]

May I ask why that happens?

Let these words be engraved on your mind: One day, when you return to the invisible world, you will be examined on how you have applied the Law of Love ... you will find yourself confronted by the film of your earthly life, you will see the smallest details and notice the tiniest errors and you will have to reform yourself. You must therefore reflect and concentrate on what you are saying and how you are saying it. Here, you are an actor on stage, being photographed and recorded all the time.[6]

Now to answer your question more fully I have to digress, but I do not mind if it will benefit you.

First let me make a distinction; the case you mentioned may be called "panoramic memory" where there is no emotional involvement, the individual is more a spectator than a participator, being the recipient of redemptive grace and the purgatorial refining fire. Instead, what is referred to as a "life-review" is a deeper event, characterized by a degree of self-judgment of the consequences of one's thoughts, feelings, and actions.

Oh, I remember that those who temporarily died, many of them, had that experience, and I'd like to quote a few passages from their description:

☯ Instantly my entire life was laid bare and open to his wonderful presence, "GOD." I felt inside my being his forgiveness for the things in my life I was ashamed of, as though they were not of great importance. I was asked – but there were no words; it was a straight mental instantaneous communication – "What had I done to benefit or advance the human race?" At the same time all my life was presented instantly in front of me and I was shown or made to understand what counted. I am not going into this any further but, believe me, what I had counted in life as unimportant was my salvation and what I thought was important was nil.

☯ ... as the light came toward me, it came to be a person – yet it wasn't a person. It was a being that radiated. And inside this radiant luminous light which had a silver tint to it – white, with a silver tint to it – (was) what looked to be a man ... Now, I didn't know exactly who this was, you know, but it was the first person that showed up and I had this feeling that the closer this light got to me the more awesome and the more pure this love – this feeling that I would call love ... And this person said, "Do you know where you are?" I never got a chance to answer that question, for all of a sudden – quote, unquote – *"my life passed before me."*

But it was not my life that passed before me nor was it a three-dimensional caricature of the events in my life. *What occurred was every emotion I have ever felt in my life, I felt.* And my eyes were showing me the basis of how that emotion affected my life. What my life had *done so far to affect other people's lives using* the feeling of pure *love that was surrounding me as the point of comparison.* And I'd done a terrible job. God! I mean it. You know, I'd done a horrible job, using love as the point of comparison ... Looking at yourself from the point of how much love you have spread to other people is devastating. You will never get over it. I am six years away from that day (of his NDE) and I am not over it yet.

❧ He, (the Being of Light) then asked me, "Do you know where you are?"... I said, "Yes." ... And he said, "What is your decision?" When he said that ... it was like I knew everything that was stored in my brain. Everything I'd ever known from the beginning of my life. I knew everybody else in the room knew I knew and that there was no hiding anything — the good times, the bad times, everything ... I had total complete clear knowledge of everything that had ever happened in my life — even little minute things that I had forgotten ... just everything, which gave me a better understanding of everything at that moment ... Everything was so clear. ... *I realized that there are things that every person is sent to earth to realize and to learn.* For instance, to share more love, to be more loving toward one another. To discover that the most important thing *is human relationships and love and not materialistic things.* And to realize that every single thing that you do in your life is recorded and that even though you pass it by not thinking at the time, it always comes up later. For instance, you may be ... at a

519

stoplight and you're in a hurry and the lady in front of you, when the light turns green doesn't take right off, (she) doesn't notice the light, and you get upset and start honking your horn and telling them to hurry up. Those are the little kinds of things that are recorded that *you don't realize at the time are really important*. One of the things that I discovered that is very important is patience toward other human beings and realizing that you your-self may be in that situation sometime.[7]

A seemingly trivial event it is here given to demonstrate how easily human beings, in their ignorance of the power of emotions and lack of consideration, may hurt other parts of life and, therefore, hurt themselves.

It is the Law of polarity: what we do to others, we do to our-selves.
The same energy vibration sent out from one pole must inevi-tably return to the other pole because they are two in one.

If life is based on polarity, and that is our relation to the rest of creation, it has universal application from the smallest to the greatest, from the way I relate even to so-called inani-mate things to God.
Yes it is always, operative in every field of human activity, whether religion, family, politics, science, medicine, education — it includes all that is. And let me sound a warning, especially to those in public office and representatives of the people: if you have certain inner convictions and beliefs, you cannot deny or go against them for expediency's sake or self-interest with-out experiencing the consequences.

How can we separate our inner side from the outer? We split ourselves in two and become false to our self, an aberration. But I have a question on this quotation:

> You are shown your life – and you do the judging. Had you done what you should do? You think, "Oh, I gave six dollars to someone that didn't have much and that was great of me." That didn't mean a thing. It's the little things – maybe a hurt child that you helped or just to stop to say hello to a shut-in. Those are the things that are most important ... You are judging yourself. You have been forgiven all you sins, but are you able to forgive yourself for not doing the things you should have done and some little cheaty things that maybe you've done in life? Can you forgive yourself? This is the judgment.[8]

That last sentence seems to be a contradiction, forgiveness and judgment are they not opposites?
You do not understand; if you do not forgive yourself it means that you are condemning yourself.

I see why to forgive oneself is often harder than forgiving others.
The purpose of the life-review is to make people learn from their mistakes and failures and see what they have done with their lives.

It is the self-revelation of the underlying motives by stripping away the masks, wrong motives, and deceptions of the personality. Scene and event are re-experienced especially with regard to their emotional content, including the effects of one's actions on others.

Is this not evidence of the principle of polarity governing all life? It is as if the feeling comes back from the individual that was helped or harmed.

It certainly is, the sense of responsibility toward life is thus enhanced with the realization that everything is infallibly recorded and not even a thought will escape.

This is true, it is made very clear by another passage I want to quote:

> For me it was a total reliving of every thought I had ever thought, every word I had ever spoken, and every deed I had ever done; plus their effect on everyone and anyone who had ever come within my environment or sphere of influence whether I knew them or not (including unknown passers-by on the street); plus the effect of each thought, feeling, word and deed on weather, plants, animals, soil, trees, water, and air.[9]

When there is the Presence acting, and I think I know who it is, there is absolute love and forgiveness, never a condemnatory sign.

I recall this accurate comment: "Yours is the judgment. You stand at your own bar of judgment. You make your own decisions, you take your own blame ... You are the accused, the judge, the jury."[10]

The result is the desire to know more about the meaning of life and death, a thirst for true love, wisdom, and the understanding that human existence is a gift of infinite value not to be squandered.

Returning to the explanation of the etheric body, I should mention, as an illustration, that the lack of sensitivity that one experiences under anesthesia is due to the displacement, partial or otherwise, of the etheric body, although it is still connected by a fine thread or cord of light to the physical form. There is some evidence of its reality in the fact that if an arm, for instance, is severed from the body, pain may still be felt in the non-existent limb.

You are referring to what is called the phantom limb. I was intrigued by something I read about it:

> Most amputees report feeling a phantom limb almost immediately after amputation of an arm or a leg. The phantom limb is usually described as having a tingling feeling and a definite shape that resembles the real limb before amputation. It is reported to move through space in much the same way as the normal limb would move when the person walks, sits down, or stretches out on a bed. At first, the phantom limb feels perfectly normal in size and shape — so much that the amputee may reach out for phantom leg. As time passes, however, the phantom limb begins to change shape. The arm or leg becomes less distinct and may fade away altogether, so that the phantom hand or foot seems to be hanging in mid-air.[11]

When the body is sleeping you actually take off in your etheric body, usually without knowing where you are going.

This explains why sometimes I have the sensation of flying that I attribute to dreams. There was a lady who was able to function consciously out of her physical body. This is how she describes one of her episodes:

... I had gone to bed but not fallen asleep, and felt myself slipping out. I found myself with a mother and her babe. They were in bed. A state of distress showed in her aura and I became aware that she was calling for her husband. I soothed her until she ceased to weep, and then soothed her to sleep. But she did not see me as the dying ones (whom I helped) had done. Almost at once I saw the sea; this sea was the Astral World. I saw one coming across the sea and realized it was the husband. I assisted the mother to leave her physical body and she stood beside me in her Astral [soul] Body and became aware of me. With a great cry, she saw her husband. They embraced and the happiness which they felt glowed through them. When in her physical body, her loved one could not make her aware of himself because of her great grief; but once out of her body, he was able to meet her in the Astral World. She would wake out of that dream, as she would call it, and remember having seen her husband. This might be enough to stop her grieving - her dream would have been very vivid and so would be stamped in her memory for ever. Grief prevents our loved ones manifesting to us; it also keeps them near the earth and this retards their progress.[12]

What she says about grief is very true; people think that it is an expression of affection for the departed but it is, in reality, the effect of attachment and a form of selfishness. They are concerned about themselves feeling the loss of the loved one and are filled with self-pity. Thus, the magnetic pull of their emotions does not allow the departed one to leave the discordant stratum around the planet and experience the happiness of the etheric realm. It shows the ignorance of the human mind, which mistakes the physical body for the individual who, at least temporarily, is free from the limitations of the flesh structure and will rest in the light and love of the higher planes of life between embodiments.

Since mankind turned away and even forgot the source of their life, they have imagined in their state of separation that their existence has beginning and end. In other words, the individual became identified with his physical form. In reality, by leaving his body he is more alive than before because he is not imprisoned by its density. It can be compared to the difference between wearing heavy winter clothes and those in summer time.

When one rises above the atmosphere of this planet, which is charged with discord and impurity, he is free from the gravity pull and can move with the speed of thought wherever he may desire. Moreover, he lives in the joy and peace of the heavenly realms of light because no negative energy exists outside of the Earth.

It is laughable, if it were not tragic, to think that in a universe of love with the glory of billions of stars shining above us, we, on this speck of dust, are so absorbed by and concerned with our little self to think that we can be left alone or be isolate.

True love overcomes the sense of separation from the loved one because it holds everyone and everything within its embrace; everyone is part of and lives in the "I AM," or God-consciousness. The case of the lady you mentioned is exceptional because she was able to retain her consciousness and memory out of the body and render assistance to another. Ordinarily, when sleeping, you are in a dream state and may have unpleasant encounters.

That is a mild way to express it. I have often had all kinds of either absurd and even repulsive experiences.
The atmosphere or aura of the planet, up to approximately seven thousand feet, is peopled and filled with all kinds of discordant forces and destructive thought-forms, some of them very vicious. It is the accumulation of all the negative and misused energy of mankind from time immemorial. These miscreations try to attach themselves to anyone they possibly can in order to absorb and steal his energy and feed on them like vampires.

This explains the nature of horrible dreams and nightmares when one finds himself surrounded by loathsome and distressing conditions and attacked by beastlike creatures.
Incidentally, you should not watch horror movies before going to sleep because like attracts like. However, if you are able to penetrate and pass through that dangerous layer or stratum around the Earth, you may reach the higher planes and enter into the light with the result of pleasant, peaceful sleep and illumination of your consciousness. I should mention that sleep, which people take for granted, is one of My greatest blessings because it allows the body to rest and be filled again with My light-energy.

"When a person sleeps" says the Chandoya Upanishads, "he has gone to his own."[13] And the Muslim poet concurs, "Every night Thou freest our spirits from the body."[14] I realize now the importance of the etheric body. I am anxious to know about the others.

Next to it is the emotional body that, as its name implies, is the seat of desires, passions, and feelings. It is also known as the astral body because of its luminosity, at least in the more advanced individuals.

Then again, in the case of a sensual and immoral type, it is like a dark cloud and murky colors, and the vibrations very slow. This body is the main cause of your troubles because it is very difficult to control; in fact, it controls you. It is the most important of the lower bodies and is the determining factor of your life because it contains three times more energy than the others and fluctuates constantly like the waves of the ocean.

This is a truthful analogy because it is composed of the inner or finer side of the water element; when it is disturbed by negative feelings it becomes agitated and violent, leading the person astray in his thinking and actions. It is very restless in its craving for stimulation and strong vibrations, and likes to change them frequently for greater excitement. Mankind lives almost entirely in the sense-consciousness instead of the God-consciousness and, as a result, people are dominated and driven by their emotions.

That's why it is so difficult to be still. I read this passage in a book written by a scientist:

> Since the advent of written language there have been more words recorded about emotions, in every language, than almost any other single object. Why not, when emotions are the experiences we know most intimately. They are etched in our minds, indelibly recorded in our awareness as pleasant or distasteful. Emotions carry the essence of our unique and collective consciousness. Our thoughts and behaviors are basically directed by emo-

tions which either permit or prohibit what we think and how we act.[15]

All the gamut of the feeling world, from the most negative and destructive to the noblest and sublime, is played in the emotional body. Since it is the seat of desires it is oriented in the masses of the people toward the plane of physical experience with the focus on the gratification of their sensuality.

With the deplorable consequences prevalent in our society.
The physical self was originally a wonderfully sensitive instrument of the inner bodies, and gifted with great magnetic power. The tendency and habits of expressing negative thought-feelings like criticism, condemnation, dislike which is a form of hate, and similar qualities are embedded in the personality and affect not only its conduct but the energy is transferred and attached to its relationships, career, possessions, and home.

We humans are indeed strange creatures, as many of us are prone to an inferiority complex with regard to ourselves, but to a sense of superiority where our relations to others is concerned.
Ordinarily, the astral vehicle is the coarser and most gross because of its earthly appetites and passions, keeping the individual enslaved, and stifling any higher aspiration. It is the root cause, with the etheric body, of ninety percent of physical diseases and limitations. I suggest that you quote a passage from one of your books for the benefit of those who do not have an understanding of the inner causes of disease and do not know how to deal with them. It may be of encouragement.

"Disease is a purificatory process, carried out in order to produce a purer expression, like aroma, influence and soul usefulness. It is the working out into manifestation of undesirable subjective condition ... sometimes this working out and elimination may well bring about the death of that particular body. But the soul goes on. One short life counts for very little in the long cycle of the soul, and it is counted well worthwhile if a period of ill health (even if eventuates in death) brings about the clearing away of wrong emotional and mental conditions. They make a horror out of death, whereas death is a beneficent friend. Disease can be the sudden and final call to the body to relinquish the soul and set it free for other service."[16]

St. Francis of Assisi addressed death as sister. The medical establishment is slowly beginning to realize the importance of the power of the mind over the body and that a physical disorder may be influenced by emotional factors. They call it "psychosomatic."
Very slowly, but unless the cause is removed at the inner level, there can never be a permanent cure. The emotional body is, indeed, a testing ground; but if the awakened individual is determined to rise out of his limitations and wants to be master of himself, he will unquestionably succeed.

You said that nothing is impossible if in our God-awareness, we continue to make effort to express the dominion over the outer self.
Try to remember that you are a projection, like an extension cord, of Myself on the physical plane, clothed in bodies made of the matter of the lower planes in order to gain experience through the instrument of your personality. Then, as you unfold the consciousness of your creative powers you attain the

ascension and become a Divine Being. That was your decision when you chose to come into incarnation and you took the responsibility of the use of life-energy for that purpose. Now only you can prevent it, by the use, rather misuse, of your free will.

By turning to Me and calling My luminous essence into your bodies you can purify and transform them, making them your obedient servants. Then, they will become for you, instead of a prison, the cup that holds My love, the chariot of fire that carries you into Heaven where you belong.

That's why the divine Eros is portrayed with wings; but we must allow him to fly.
The mental body, like the others, follows closely the outline of the physical form extending outside it from three to eight inches. Its vibrations are more refined as it is composed of a finer material than the astral, as the astral is finer than the etheric-physical.

Keep in mind that the inner bodies vary, whether coarser or finer and more or less luminous, according to the state of consciousness of the individual. The mental body can have a definite form, radiating its beautiful pastel shades of color, or be underdeveloped, rudimentary and cloudy. Its matter belongs to the mental plane and is continually active because the individual thinks all the time, waking and sleeping.

Rather, his mind does the thinking, most of the time by itself.
Contrary to the assertion of some healers, it has less impact on the personal life unless by thought they mean also feeling as they are closely related; only ten percent of all the diseases originate in the mental body because of negative thoughts. Like the other vehicles, these discordant vibrations defile and injure

the delicate fabric of the mental matter and, if continued, affect the physical body with illness and disabilities.

I should be careful what kind of thoughts I create.
Yes, try to be aware, that is the key; your thoughts are the material by which the mental body is built day by day. You should use your faculties to develop and expand your consciousness and raise the vibratory action of your bodies by your attention to Me as often as possible.

Your original nature is to be a creator according to the Law of Love and Harmony, and your mind should be the cup into which I may pour the light of My wisdom. Unfortunately, the average person, instead of thinking from within himself, becomes the playground of other people's thoughts, especially the media, which he unknowingly, through suggestions, accepts and assumes to be his own. Try to focus on what is good, true, and beautiful so that you become a magnet for them in your life.

At the same time you will become stronger and able to repel, by your inner light, all evil forces that try to influence you and try to steal your energy. You ought to obey the Law of Life and use your faculties constructively, keeping your feelings calm and harmonious by the power of My love. Then, after your passing from the physical plane, since you take with you the content of your consciousness, which is light, you will live in the heavenly world with the treasure you have gathered.

I begin to understand the meaning of that esoteric statement: "God needs a body."
It is the way and means by which It can reveal Itself as the individualized "I AM" and express Its love as a creator in the manifested universe.

You emphasized the fact that we too are creators.
Absolutely. In fact, the Infinite creates through the individual, that is, through its own individualities.

Does this mean that you create through me?
Yes, that is why I endowed you with the creative powers of thoughts, feelings, and spoken words, the same as I have. You are My channel on the physical plane. But I should qualify this by saying that you are My co-worker when you create according to My plan designed by love. What is called the manifestation of genius, let me say that potentially everyone is a genius, for the individual is My own image. The faculties of Michelangelo, Shakespeare or Mozart are the same as those of a savage or an idiot who still have the divine spark buried under their human mis-creations. The difference consists in the way, by the use of his life energy, one is able to make himself the proper instrument for the expression in word, form, and sound of the divine artist.

This is understandable. Even a great performer like Paganini could hardly play on a broken or stringless violin. Our limitations are the consequences of the operation of the Law of cause and effect, as you already made clear. People think that it is a matter of heredity because it is a known fact, for example, that many famous musicians and singers have been born in families of the same profession.
Those who accept the theory of hereditary factors think, as the intellect usually does, in the reverse of the right way. The characteristics of a child do not derive from the parents, rather the parents are the choice of the child.

I thought that one's parents depend on the Karmic Law, or magnetic attraction.
Yes, an individual can choose or be attracted to the family into which he will be reborn according to his or her Karma.

I'm not sure I understand clearly the relation of our faculties with the events of our life.
You should know by now, but I do not mind repeating it, that thought, feeling, and the spoken word are creative. The light-energy which I constantly give you with every heartbeat is pure and contains only the perfection of love and wisdom. But as it flows into your body you qualify it by the use, or misuse, of your faculties. That divine energy by which you live, move, and do what you please, takes on the qualities which you create by your thought, feeling, and spoken word. In other words, if you become negative you change the quality of the light, you impose on it your discord which then, determines the experiences of your existence in the future. Therefore, you should let My luminous essence flow through you in its natural purity and perfection, without discoloration and wrong qualification.

I must not contaminate it with my negative attitudes.
Exactly, then it will manifest in your being and world its divine qualities without interference.

The action of the Law of cause and effect.
Right, that is how you shape your destiny.

According to some religious teaching, there are individuals predestined to heaven and others to hell.

That is nonsense! They do not know who I AM. As I told you, My plan is happiness and perfection for everyone because "I AM" love and I can only do the will of love.

That's why the Law of life is always acting everywhere. But in our free will we misuse our faculties and create our limitations. I comprehend now the Biblical statement, "What a man thinks in his heart, he is." And the same principle is found in the Eastern scriptures: "What a man thinks on, that he becomes, therefore think on the Eternal."[17] The Buddha said, "All that we are is the result of what we have thought: it is founded on our thoughts, it is made up of our thoughts."[18] Similar statements we find in Hinduism and Islamism.

> All this, the Object — world that we call "This."
> It is made up of Thought; he who knows not
>   This truth, his actions bear not wholesome fruit.[19]

> Men who are living here are in a dream,
> And when they die then shall they be awake;
> For all this world is a mere thought — the thought
> Of Him who is the True, whose thought is Truth.[20]

Let me repeat that you are endowed with the same faculties of the Creator. The difference is not in their nature or quality but in their magnitude and power. It is not easy for the average person to understand that thoughts and feelings, although they are invisible, are as real as your car, your furniture, trees, or anything else in the physical world, and even more so.

They are powerful forces and have a definite and decisive effect on your bodies and lives.

According to Plato, behind every created thing there is an idea that is its prototype or pattern; the physical world is like the shadow or an imperfect copy and imitation of the ideal world.
You do not have to be a great thinker like him to understand the truth of it; for instance, your house was first conceived in the mind of the architect, was it not? He had an idea which was the blueprint upon which the house was built. The books you read — where did they come from? How were your radio and airplane invented? An entire civilization is created by thought.

And also destroyed by it.
Yes, discordant emotions, rooted in selfishness, can derange the mind and debase the consciousness because, as I said, they represent seventy-five percent of the individual's energy. You may think of doing something but if your feelings do not like it, they force you to change your mind. However, when I speak of thought I refer to both since thought and feeling interact and affect each other. Creation takes place by their combining activity: thought is the form and the feeling provides the substance that makes it a living entity.

I remember your saying that feeling is the feminine side of our nature and that thought is the masculine aspect.
The thought must be infused with the universal energy drawn and coalesced by the magnetic power of the feeling that, after all, is the radiation of love.

And love is the animating force of all that is.
Absolutely; now follow Me closely.

I will try because I didn't realize before you talked to me that we possess these divine faculties and how, in our ignorance, we tend to misapply them.

The use of energy and power always implies responsibility. I explained to you that every human being uses a body made of substance, or matter, corresponding to the planes of the universe (or more exactly, of your solar system), which is the body of a Cosmic Being: as above, so below, there is the polarity of infinite and finite.

Thought creates a vibration that affects the matter of the mental body, causing it to respond and making it oscillate at the same rate as the nature and quality of the thought. By repetition of the same thought, whether good or bad, a habit is created.

Keep in mind the fact that the four lower bodies interpenetrate each other and what affects one is transmitted to the other vehicles of consciousness. A similar phenomenon takes place also in the natural world when, for instance, a storm causes the air to produce waves in the sea. The vibrations of your thoughts influence not only your mental body and the surrounding sea of mental matter, but they act also upon other people's minds: The action of this undulation is eminently adaptable. It may exactly reproduce itself if it finds a mental body which readily responds to it in every particular; but when this is not the case, it may nevertheless produce a decided effect along lines broadly similar to its own.

Suppose, for example, that a Catholic kneels in devotion before an image of the Blessed Virgin. He sends rippling out from him in all directions strong devotional vibrations; if they strike upon the mental or astral body of another Catholic, they will arouse in him a thought and feeling identical with the original. But if they should strike upon a Christian of some other sect, to whom the image of the Blessed Virgin is unfamiliar, they will still awaken in him the sentiment of devotion, but that will follow along its accustomed channel, and be directed towards the Christ.

In the same way, if they should touch a Muhammadan they would arouse in him devotion to Allah, while in the case of a Hindu the object might be Krishna, and in case of a Parsi, Ahuramazda. But they would excite devotion of some sort wherever there was a possibility of response to that idea. If, however, they should touch the mental body of a materialist, to whom the very idea of devotion in any form is unknown, they would still produce an elevating effect. They could not at once create a type of vibration to which the man was wholly unaccustomed, but their tendency would be to stir a higher part of his mental body into some sort of activity; and the effect, though less permanent than in the case of the sympathetic recipient, could not fail to be good. The action of an evil or impure thought is governed by the same laws.

A man who is so foolish as to allow himself to think of another with hatred or envy radiates a wave tending to provoke similar passions in others, unless they are free from them, which is rare; and though his feeling of hatred be for someone quite unknown to these others, and so it is impossible that they should share it, yet the radiation will stir in them an emotion of the same nature towards a totally different person.[21]

This explains how thoughts are contagious, even hypnotic, and how masses of people can be brainwashed by the media, propaganda, and publicity. For instance, we are influenced at present by a mental climate that hypnotizes us into thinking that only the material world really exists and that truth is relative, that is, a personal opinion.

I told you that there is one life, one consciousness, and one energy; therefore, your bodies are made of the same elements as those of all mankind and are one with them, the same as the element of water is one, whether in a river, a lake, or the sea.

I understand how we can affect each other for better or for worse.
People are bombarded and assailed by thought-waves all the time, both from within themselves and from without; they feel their impact but do not know their meaning. Mental telepathy can give you some idea of it.

Yes, it happens; for instance, I think of someone and a moment later he calls me on the phone.
A good thought is a continual benediction which everyone can radiate "like a fountain spraying forth sweet waters."[22] The reverse is, unfortunately, also true: a malevolent or vicious thought can injure more seriously than a bullet. What is called "black magic" is based on this. Very few people know how to protect themselves, especially with regard to the emotional body, which is the most vulnerable and is open to any destructive vibration that can easily enter through the door of the solar plexus and affecting the stomach.

How can we prevent that?
Observe yourself — I mean your inner world. Self-observation is different from observation. People are more or less aware of the external world but very ignorant of what is going on within themselves. Be a detached observer – that is, do not identify with your negative thoughts. Remember, you are not your thoughts even though you created them or accepted them from outside.

But you said we are what we think.

Yes, you use them to shape your life, like a sculptor with clay or marble, but if you do not like what you experience, then, you must change it. You are the master in the house; if a stray dog enter into it, you can chase it away.

I remember that Hindu aphorism, "A bird may land on your head but you don't have to let it build a nest there."

Use strong language if necessary because thoughts and feelings can be very stubborn; say, "Get out!" And they will if you are firm enough. Use the light of your consciousness and affirm, "I AM free from this discordant creation!"

Or, even better, call to Me to dispel the shadows which harbor within you or try to lodge there and harm you. I will as surely take care of them with the fire of My love as you ask, and will clothe you in an armor of light which is invulnerable.

You mentioned also that thoughts create a form.

Yes, they have a double effect; every thought produces not only a radiating vibration but a definite objective shape whose vitality depends on the intensity and the charge of the accompanying feelings. The thought-form is more limited in scope than its vibratory action but more precise. As the thought is sent out it immediately clothes itself in the matter of the corresponding bodies, that is, mental and astral, and becomes a living creature. According to its quality, it can be angelic and bestow blessings, or devilish and cause only destruction.

If it is connected with another person by sending love, envy, or sorrow, it will radiate vibrations that reproduce themselves and influence other people's minds. But the thought-form will go directly to the intended person and, if it finds an attunement, it will discharge itself upon him, provoking a similar undulation and, if it already exists, it will intensify it. In case the mind of the recipient is occupied with a different subject, the thought-form will wait about him or in his aura for the opportunity to be connected and become part of him.

For instance, the desire to protect a loved one creates a thought-form that will stay in his aura and acts as a shield and preventive force.

This is similar to an answered prayer.
To a lesser degree. If the desire is turned to Me, you will agree that My power is greater than that of any human being. I should remind you of the Law of magnetic attraction: if you create a negative thought-feeling it will attract others of the same kind. If you send it to someone else, it will affect him if there is a similar thought-vibration to which it is attuned. But in the case of a spiritual person, it cannot influence or hurt him because it will be repelled by the higher frequency of his aura and inner bodies.

That's why those saintly people who minister to the sick with infectious diseases, even during a plague, are not affected.
The luminous halo or nimbus around or above the head that you see in paintings is very real. Love, which is light, is the greatest protection because it is the highest vibration and form of energy and therefore is master of all the elements.

This reminds me of the episode when Jesus stilled the storm.

If you are master of the elements within you, then you are also master of them around you and everywhere because they are one.

What about the person who is concerned only with himself? Unfortunately, this is often the case. Most people are wrapped up in selfish thoughts about their personal aims, concerned with financial matters, or brooding over their unhealthy conditions. A corresponding vibratory action radiates in every direction and will spread around, but the thought-forms fluctuate about its creator, and their tendency is constantly to react upon him, as they repeat and intensify themselves. Everyone lives in a shell or cocoon of thoughts that he or she has created and cannot help feeling their influence and pressure. In fact, they can become so disruptive that, in some cases, he may believe he is tempted or possessed by the devil, while in reality it is only the reaction to his own mental creation. However, whether you call it the devil or a thought-form, it is the same destructive force created by mankind. Another kind of thought-form is neither directed at someone nor hovering about the thinker, but remains floating where it was created.

The atmosphere is filled with them and they fasten upon those minds that are responsive and of the same vibrational quality. Occasionally, even when we are not disturbed by negative thoughts, we may encounter them when, for instance, passing by a bar. Such places are filled with the radiation of the people who frequent them and I assure you that the monkey-like figure that fastens to the back of an alcoholic is no figment of the imagination. It is an actual creation of the mind to which the person gave birth and now it seems to be external and harass him.

Not only people and their aura, but inanimate objects and localities are impregnated and magnetized by thought-feelings possessing a great influence for good or its opposite.

I heard of a bridge where several people committed suicide and everyone crossing it would feel that same impulse and inclination acting upon him.
A very negative influence is produced by such places as a prison, a cemetery, or a funeral home because of their radiation of gloom, depression, and sorrow, which react strongly on those present.

On the other hand, places of worship, such as churches, temples, shrines, and religious items like statues, pictures of divine beings, votive offerings, and other decorations, even in-artistic, can inspire profound devotional feelings since they are charged with the radiant vibrations and the beautiful thought-forms of the faithful and pour them out again.

I wonder which thoughts originate from myself and how many come from outside.
As an average, not even one-fourth of all your thoughts are originally created by you.

Does this mean that we think with other people's thoughts?
Yes, most of the time, as no one realizes the power of sugges-tion. It is unfortunate because the quality of the thought-feelings charged into the atmosphere of the planet is decidedly negative and discordant. Consider also the fact that everyone perceives life and the world through the typically chaotic mass of his habitual thoughts and, therefore, naturally he tends to see everything not as it really is but modified, or qualified, by

their rates of vibrations. It is as if everyone wears a pair of colored glasses.

[1] Alice A. Bailey, Esoteric Healing (NY: Lucis Publishing, 1972), pp. 613-4.

[2] *Random House Unabridged Dictionary*, 2nd edition, p. 751.

[3] Revelation 3:4-5.

[4] *Esoteric Healing*, pp. 2-3.

[5] *Whole in One*, p. 9.

[6] Ibid., p. 44.

[7] *Heading Toward Omega*, p. 67, 68-9, 71.

[8] Ibid., p. 70.

[9] P.M.H. Atwater, *Coming Back to Life* (NY: Dodd, Mead, 1988), p. 36.

[10] *Whole in One*, p. 58.

[11] R. Melzack, "The Puzzle of Pain." (Harmondsworth: Penguin, 1973).

[12] Robert Crookall, *During Sleep* (London: Theosophical Publishing House, 1964), pp.1-2.

[13] Chandoya Upanishads, 6:8, 1.

[14] Masnavi Rumi, in *Wisdom Is One*, p. 52.

[15] Valerie V. Hunt, *Infinite Mind. Science of the Human Vibrations of Consciousness* (Malibu, CA: Malibu Publishing Co., 1996), p. 104.

[16] *Esoteric Healing*, pp. 41-2.

[17] Annie Besant, *The Riddle of Life.* (Wheaton, IL.: The Theosophical Publishing House), p. 59.

[18] *Dhammapada*, tr. Max Miller. (Mineola, NY: Dover Publications, 2000), p. 1.

[19] Manu-Smirti, Hindu law book, quoted in Das, p. 254.

[20] Hadis, *The Sayings of the Prophet Muhammad*, quoted in Das, p. 253.

[21] *The Hidden Side of Things*, pp. 418-19.

[22] Annie Besant, "Elementary Theosophy: Thought-Power and Its Use," in *Theosophist Magazine April 1911-June 1911* (Whitefish, Montana: Kessinger Publishing, 2003), p. 456.

CHAPTER 22

Androgyny and Twin Flames

Then God said, "Let us make man in our image, according to our likeness" … God created man in his image, in the image of God he created them; male and female he created them.
Genesis

The One, alone, knew no delight and so he desired and originated for himself a second, the female partner, whose function was to present to him a reflection of his own splendor manifested in time and space.
Brihadaranyaka Upanishad

"Why did God punish not only the guilty pair, but also the innocent unborn generations?" I totally agree with this question about Adam and Eve asked by a disciple to his guru, who answered:

> Genesis is deeply symbolic, and cannot be grasped by a literal interpretation.
> The tree of life is the human body; the spinal cord is like an upturned tree, with man's hair as its roots, and afferent and efferent nerves as branches. The tree of the nervous system bears many enjoyable fruits, or sensations of sight, sound, smell, taste, and touch. In these, man may rightfully indulge, but he was forbidden the experience of sex, the "apple" at the center of the body ("in the midst of the garden"). As Eve told the serpent, "We may eat of the fruit of the trees of the garden: but of the fruit of the tree which is in the midst of the garden, God hath said, 'Ye shall not eat of it, neither shall ye touch it, lest ye die'."[1]

The serpent represents the coiled-up energy that stimulates the sex nerves. "Adam" is reason, and "Eve" is feeling. When the emotion or Eve-consciousness in any human being is overpowered by the sex impulse, his reason or Adam also succumbs. "The woman whom thou gavest to be with me, she gave me fruit from the tree, and I ate it. The woman said, 'the serpent beguiled me, and I did it'."[2]

God created the human species by materializing the bodies of man and woman through the force of His will; he endowed the new species with the power to create children in a similar "immaculate" or divine manner.[3]

At this point in the book I was confused, because the teacher stated that in order to assist the first human pair in their upward evolution, God transferred to them the individualized souls or divine essence of two animals. He continues:

In Adam or man, reason predominated; in Eve or woman, feeling was ascendant. Thus was expressed the duality or polarity that underlies the phenomenal world. Reason and feeling remain in a heaven of cooperative joy so long as the human mind is not tricked by the serpentine energy of animal propensities.[4]

Then he said, adding to my confusion, "The human body was therefore not solely a result of evolution from the beasts, but was produced through an act of special creation by God." Divine Consciousness present within the first created pair counseled them to enjoy all human sensibilities, with one exception: sex sensations. These were forbidden

**lest humanity enmeshed itself in the process of animal re-
production. "Now the serpent (sex force) was more subtle
than any beast of the field (any other sense of the body)."⁵
Adam and Eve yielded to the temptation and following the
way of brute procreation fell from the state of heavenly joy
natural to the original perfect man. When "they knew that
they were naked," their consciousness of immortality was
lost, even as God had warned them; they had placed themselves under the physical law by which bodily birth must be
followed by bodily death.⁶**

He is right about the first part of his explanation — that certainly makes more sense than the literal interpretation of the
text — but I can appreciate your confusion about the second
segment. There are some misconceptions: first, he said that
God created man and woman by materializing their bodies by
an act of His will. Then he refers to the evolution from the
animals which is entirely erroneous and a clear sign of the intellect thinking backward.

As I mentioned, animals do not have an individual soul
or divine essence, they are not self-aware, but are part of what
is called group soul, which is the collective or cumulative consciousness of the species.

It is the group soul that accounts for the herd instinct, like the
migratory patterns of birds and fish, the gregariousness of cattle, and so forth. Your author makes no distinction between
polarity and duality, which is a crucial one. And I would clarify
that what is predominant in man is the intellect, and in the
woman is the feeling with the reason holding the balance between the two faculties.

**Some people may not like what you said about the animals
lacking a sense of individual identity.**

I can sympathize with them because their love for animals exceeds often even their love for other people and God. But, let me emphasize, it is disconcerting to see the different and contradictory attitudes in the masses with regard to the animal kingdom, from total indifference to shameful abuses like hunting and fishing, from wholesale slaughter for food to one of care and adoration. The truth is that animals, as they are known by mankind, are not a divine creation: it is imprisoned life in a distorted and limited form and this is the truth whether people understand it or not.

Regardless of their large size, like elephants or small like germs, they are the objectification of the vicious and destructive thoughts and feelings of mankind.

I know that every thought creates a form, beautiful or ugly according to its quality, there are pictures made of them because they can be clairvoyantly seen.
Then you should not be surprised when I say that humanity, from prehistoric times, have imposed their negative vibratory action upon Nature and the elementals. As I have previously explained, the vibrations of a thought make a picture on the etheric plane. It then becomes a sentient creation when infused with feeling and, in the last stage of densification, it manifests as a physical entity.

What about domestic animals, and others like the horse or a cow? They can be very friendly and helpful.
Man has the power to influence and train them to do his will. The love for pets is certainly praiseworthy because their consciousness is raised by it. Thus, eventually, they will be free from their imperfect nature and form. In fact, it is mankind's

responsibility to cease all their mistreatment of animal life, and purify and release them by the power of love.

I realize that thoughts and feelings are creative and are the cause of individual and universal manifestation on every plane of reality. You told me that God creates in the same way, by the same faculties: "In the beginning was the Word," the Bible says;[7] and in the first chapter of the Book of Genesis, before every creative act there is the statement, "And God said." There are ten sayings — ten is the symbol of perfection — and after every creation He affirms that, "It was very good." Certainly, creatures like flies, scorpions, and those preying on others for food, make it hard to believe that they were created by God as being very good.
I should add that the birds are closer to their original divine creation except, of course, those expressing rapacious qualities.

The teacher also said that the belief according to which only one man is the son of God is based on false humility and spiritual cowardice. People may think, Christ was a special being, uniquely begotten; how can I, a mere mortal, emulate Him?
In reality, everyone is divinely created, as is stated also in the Scripture and reiterated by Jesus: "You are gods and all children of the Most High," says God in Psalm 32:6, and Jesus reminded the Priests of what they seemed to have forgotten: "Is it not written *in your law*," I said, 'you are gods'? If those to whom the word of God came were called 'gods' and the Scripture cannot be annulled ..."[8]; also in Matthew 5:45, and reference is made to the divine nature of human beings. "So that you may be children of your Father in heaven."[9]

The author stated that the early Christian Church accepted the doctrine of reincarnation, which was first declared a heresy in 553 AD by the second council of Constantinople. It seems that the decision was made on the assumption that reincarnation offers too many opportunities to the individual and would not induce or encourage him to strive and make the effort for immediate purification and salvation.

However, the truth suppressed or ignored leads to inconsistency and error.

The teacher ignored the basic difference between the two creations of man in Genesis, one in the divine image and the other from the dust. It is true that the sacred life force derives directly from God, but there the resemblance between the two accounts ends. In the first creation, male and female were created together as one, both were parts of Adam/humanity. Originally, he contained in himself the two constituent parts.

An old proverb states, Every man carries his Eve within.

It is also true that every Eve carries her Adam within.

The human being was created in the beginning androgynous, which is the male and female elements in their original unity. Genesis literally says, Let us make man (in the singular) in our image and let them (plural) have dominion.

So God created them, male and female created He them.[10] It is evident that originally the human being was both male and female, as God is because "He made them in his own image and likeness."

Your statement reminds me of a passage by a Bible scholar that I didn't understand but now it is clear. He wrote referring to Genesis 1:27, "The text stresses the gendered character of humans made in God's image: 'male and female he

created them.' This assertion that God made males and fe-
males in God's image strains against the logic of monothe-
ism." He asks, "How could it be that only one God could
create both men and women in God's image?"
Unless it is both?

The text does not go so far as to describe multiple gods –
male and female – creating both sexes of humans. It does
not say, "male and female they created them."
It does not have too. "Elohim," one of the names of God, is plural.

The only explanation the author has in mind is that of God
as the head of a group of divine beings, with whom he would
consult. This is found elsewhere in the Bible, for instance
Job 1:6; 1 Kings 22:19-23; Isaiah 40:1-8, Psalm 89:7-8. He
wonders whether this divine council in Israel like those in
neighboring cultures, could include both male and female
divine beings.
It certainly does, but who created them? I offer a more simple
explanation, and since it is simple it must be true.

"Only at this point," he concludes, "Genesis 1 diverges from
God in the singular to talk of God in the plural."[11]
I never change. Before I explain the true nature of the male-
female relationship I will relate how it has been erroneously
interpreted and misunderstood.

According to the traditional version of the Biblical
story, the Fall of man caused every division in Nature and his
separation both from God and within the depths of his consciousness. As a consequence, there is no longer a communion
of two beings in one soul. The polarity of man-woman was

broken and the original oneness of their interiority was lost, its two constituent and complementary parts were severed.

Falling away from their spiritual pole, they were drawn toward the pole of matter, where everything appears dense and heavy, with space that isolates, time that measures death, constrained by natural necessities, surrounded by absurdities and nothingness.

Out of their Creator's caring sight they are enfolded by the shadows and He cannot see them anymore: "Where are you?" God calls, and He addresses them for the first time separately: 'He said to the woman; and to the man He said'."[12]

From then on a sense of estrangement is insinuated in all relationships (Where are you?) Each one is hidden from the other.

The original nature of the human being as androgynous is also found in the discourse of Aristophanes in Plato's *Symposium*.

His fable on the origin of love coincides with the division of the original human sexes. The story begins with a depiction of the dual nature, or rather two bodies, joined in one spherical-shaped being, in a union of man and woman, called 'androgynous' (*andros* meaning male, and *gynos* meaning female).

Self-sufficient in their roundness — implying a state of wholeness — with their backs and sides forming a circle and consisting of two faces, two privy organs, four feet and hands, each of these primal beings could walk upright or roll and tumble with great speed. They had enormous strength and grand ambitions, and were so mobile and powerful that they dared to scale heaven and challenge the gods.

Zeus and the other Olympians deliberated about what they should do. They didn't want to destroy the human race because the honor and sacrifices they received from them would cease; but neither could they tolerate their outrageous behavior. Finally, Zeus declared that he had a good plan about how human beings can continue to exist and yet, by their becoming weaker, discontinue their indecent actions. I will have them cut in two; they will have less power and, at the same time, provide more offerings to us by becoming more numerous.

He then asked Apollo to sculpt a new form for each of them, one with two legs, two arms, one face, and one set of genitals. . From this division and the sense of incompleteness that it generated, desire and love were born, urging each of the new beings to search for his or her other half. And the reason is that human nature was originally one and we were male and female, and the pursuit of our wholeness is called love. We must praise the god Love, who is our greatest benefactor for both leading us in this life back to our own nature and giving us hopes for the future.

He promises that if we are pious he will restore us to our original condition and heal and make us happy and blessed. Aristophanes' myth identifies the androgyny as a state of completeness with two united halves. And it can be related to the original creation and the separation of Eve from Adam after the fall into disunity.

Is there a difference between the two terms "androgyny" and "hermaphrodite"?
They are usually used synonymously; but specifically, "androgyny" means having the characteristics of being both male and female in an asexual union to form a completed whole. A her-

maphrodite is an individual with male and female organs of reproduction physically represented.

This brings to mind the myth of Hermaphroditus, the son of Hermes and Aphrodite, told by Ovid in the *Metamorphoses*. It is interesting to see how the gods and goddesses, even in their degraded and anthropomorphic representations, always answer those who pray to them.
This is the passage I like:

The nymph Salmacis fell passionately in love with Hermaphroditus but was rejected and denied his company. After vain attempts, one day she was able to hold him in her embrace. She encircled him, as he strove against her in his desire to escape, like ivy is wont to weave around tall trunks of trees but he endured and denied the nymph the joys for which she had hoped. Salmacis continued her efforts, and her whole body clung to him and she cried: You may fight, cruel villain, but you will not escape. May the gods so ordain that we will never be separated in future time, you from me or me from you. The gods accepted her prayer. Their two bodies were joined together as they entwined, and in appearance they were made one, just as when one grafts branches on a tree and sees them unite in their growth and become mature together. They were no longer two but a single form possessed of a dual nature that could not be called male or female and appeared, at the same time, neither one but both.[13]

This is another poetic fable illustrating the profound truth that each human being possesses both male and female qualities. As I mentioned, the primal Adam, made in the image of God, was originally created with a nonphysical, or etheric body made of luminous substance; "he" was androgynous, that is both male and female.

Since God is light, everything which he creates must be out of the substance of light and therefore luminous. My question is, why is the evil and suffering of the human condition often attributed to woman?

Pandora, for instance, could not resist her eager curiosity to know what the box contained and, as she opened it, all that plagues mankind, like old age, sickness, insanity, vice, envy, revenge, etc., flew out in a cloud and attacked the race of mortals. Thanks to Prometheus, who had also enclosed the virtue of hope in the box, mankind could survive. Similarly, Eve is also considered the cause of all the evil that beset us.

Curiosity is a tendency rooted in the feeling nature of the human being which is, as I mentioned, the feminine activity, and thought is the masculine side of consciousness. The woman personifies the pole of matter: mater - mother — which provides the physical forms of the manifested universe. The individual became attracted to the material world, and having been drawn to the objects of the senses, he turned away from God, and even forgot its source of life.

Keep in mind that you, because of your polar nature, can be magnetically attracted to one or the other pole according to your choice.

In other words, we can be pulled either way, heaven or earth, the infinite or the finite, but it is very apparent the direction we preferred and to which side we became polarized.

The traditional explanations of the differentiation of the sexes according to myth, scripture, and esoteric philosophy is that "primordial man as a cosmic androgyne has disintegrated into the material and bisexual world of alien and conflicting parts."[14]

This is in agreement with what John Scotus Erigena, a theologian in the ninth century, wrote: "God, the source and cause and goal of all things, is one and undivided; and man, as originally created in God's own image, was also one and undivided, and hence exhibited no sexual differentiation. All division in nature was the result of the fall of man, which occurred with very little or no lapse of time after the creation and resulted in the separation of man from God, as well as the split of primal man into male and female sexes ..." Redemption is made possible by Christ, who in His risen form, like man before the fall, "united the masculine and feminine in his single person."[15]
Now listen carefully, because I must refute the traditional interpretations.

The explanations given concerning the separation of the sexes as a punishment by the gods or the result of the Fall of man are a fallacy. It is true that each individual is androgynous; however, he or she will forever remain so because that is the essential nature of their being.

Everyone is originally created in a state of wholeness; but after the descent into the physical plane the primal inner unity was impaired and disrupted. Through many embodiments and identifications with his or her bodily form, either the masculine or the feminine qualities became predominant in each individual.

And this is the consequence: in our culture epoch at least, the male attributes are strength, aggressiveness, assertiveness, dominance. The typically female qualities are submissiveness, self-sacrifice, gentleness. The will power of the superman, without love and wisdom, will always end in tragedy.

Without the inner balance and harmony of the faculties, there is self-division and conflict, the personality becoming one-sided and fragmented. However, *this condition has nothing to do with sexual differentiation*, which is not what defines the individual that is still essentially one and its identity is the same.

In fact, we may embody either as man or woman according to our Karma, and in the physical body there are even rudimentary organs of the opposite sex besides its own. According to the Cayce readings, "All human spirits were created sexless and divine. But the principles of polarity, or sex, was one of the architectonic principles of the universe. And when the spirits became entangled in matter they did so in many ways in relation to the laws of polarity. At first they were androgynous, containing both sexes within themselves. Then, they became bisexed. The early centuries of Atlantean history contain many strange examples of grotesque forms created out of the blundering use of the sexual power. The present bisexual division is only a phase in our development, which is probably tending toward the androgynous on a spiritual level."[16]

There is some truth in what the author says, but we should not confuse the element of sex on the physical level with the essential nature of the individual which is innately a perfect unity of thought and feeling characteristic of its male and female polarity.

The split into male and female sexes would mean that the human being is no longer androgynous.
Right, and that is absurd. Do you think it is possible for you to exist without your feminine side — that is, your feeling? Or for a woman to lack the use and power of thought which is the masculine activity of life? Such a condition would throw humankind into confusion and insanity.

Are we not already close to it? But I can see the importance, rather the necessity of the reincarnation process to restore the divine pattern of all-ness.
The purpose of successive incarnations, alternating between male and female bodies, is to provide mutually balancing experiences in order to attain completeness and again reach the state of original all-ness. The reintegrating process can take place to a certain degree through a loving and harmonious marriage, but this complementation, though a blessing is, unfortunately, not very common.

I read that "Masculine women and feminine men who permit themselves to become homosexual are perhaps taking the line of least resistance by reverting to a previous state of existence. It could be that they are refusing to learn the lesson of equilibration which their body is trying to teach them."[17]
I have a question, and it is a fundamental one: you said that the human being is androgynous, with no possibility of change in its nature, and the separation of the interpretations, the consequence of his rebellion to the Deity.

Then, can you explain the origin and the cause of the difference between male and female sexes?

In order to unravel this confounding mystery let me, first, make it clear that I treat this entire subject of sexual polarity as a mere incident of universal polarity, that is, from the perspective of divine reality.

It must be understood in terms of electrical polarity, analogous to magnetism, not in relation to the physical body which cannot be the foundation of sex and never the fulfillment of its purpose. The apparent difference between male and female is not based on the dense physical plane, which is not a principle but an energy veil, a shadow of true reality, the illusion of *maya*.

The dictionary's definition of principle is: "a fundamental primary or general law or truth from which others are derived."[18]

I have already explained to you that the physical body has no true life of its own but it is simply responsive to impulses and inner causes.

People do not understand that sex is not a matter of psycho-biology or merely reproductive organs, but the symbol of the universal Law of polarity. A symbol, as you know, is an external, visible sign of an inner and spiritual reality, and it has a complex of associated meanings. Unfortunately, the word *sex*, like the word *love*, has been trivialized, debased, and perverted with no thought of its true meaning. Cosmically speaking, sex is emblematic of the principle of polarity, which means the interrelation and complementarity of spirit-matter or life-form. The entire universe is created, sustained, and governed by male-female forces which are present and active in God as Father-Mother. Therefore, there are different orders of polarity but there is no sex separation in the reality of life because the physical body is only a vesture or a shell.

"And the Lord God made garments of skins for the man and for his wife and clothed them."[19] I see how much this differs from the common understanding and view of humanity with regard to the male-female relationship.
In other words, sex is an expression of the Law of Attraction, which underlies all manifestation. On the human level, it denotes the connection between man and woman and the desire for union. The natural function of sexual activity on the physical plane and its true purpose, according to the Karmic Law of this cosmic cycle, is to express and expand love in the procreation of a body for the incoming individual to be incarnated. Thus, sons and daughters of God can be provided with the necessary physical forms in which their divine qualities may unfold and be manifest on Earth. I must emphasize that the present attitudes and notions about sexual relations, which are the reverse of the truth, must be transmuted and elevated from their degradation as the craving for selfish pleasure and the debased gratification of the animal urge, to their true Reality.

The world situation concerning sex is extremely difficult and most serious, and there is no one who knows how to solve it. The physical results alone of sexual intercourse, whether within or outside marriage, have produced most of the disease, insanity, and evil tendencies afflicting people and have perverted impulses in every phase of human existence.

Your young people, especially the most intelligent, do not find a satisfactory answer to their questions and do not know what to think or believe. They may be offered sound, common sense advice about health and moral issues and be warned of the consequences that will inevitably follow when the laws of nature are broken and the body is prostituted to lower desires. However, the hope for and promises of a just reward through the exertion of self-control and sexual abstinence is not enough to help them resist the urges within themselves and the constant suggestions coming at them from every side. Those who are able to master their animal nature, whose wisdom and conscience guide their lives, and who can maintain their body and mind pure and uncontaminated are the glory of humanity.

Unfortunately, very few, even among the wise and godly, understand the real cause underlying the problems and distress that have proliferated around the male-female relationship. There must be a true comprehension of the meaning of the so-called sexual energy, its role in the universal scheme of creation, and the purpose of its existence. Or the human race will never be free from its self-created limitations.

From your explanation they are related to the ignorance of the Law of polarity which governs all creation.
Yes, there is neither balance between the inner and outer self nor harmony between thinking and feeling. Therefore the individual suffers from the unfulfilled desire to be himself or herself, as a whole, which is the only condition for happiness. Life is energy and vibration acting under Law, and there must be an harmonious connection between the two poles, God and the human self, with the flowing current of light and love returning to its source like an electric circuit.

Since the feeling from the heart, which is love, is obscured by intellectual fabrications, "assuming theories as facts"[20] and contaminated by sensuality and lust, we deceive ourselves and, in our fantasies, mistake sexual gratification

561

with joy and fulfillment. In the influential book by Boethius *The Consolation of Philosophy*, one of the luminaries at the dawn of Western civilization, we read:

> "It is the nature of all bodily pleasure to punish those who enjoy it. Like the bee after its honey is given, it flies away, leaving its lingering sting in the hearts it has struck."[21]

I begin to understand that without self-knowledge we don't know what we want or what our motives and desires, whatever their names, really are. If we are not aware of our need for food we would never know that we are hungry for it, and therefore we would never eat, of course with dire consequences. The same, even more so, applies with regard to spiritual nourishment.

Everyone is starving for love, which is God, but they are searching for everything else except for the only Source from which they can receive it. If the individual in his fogged mind and disorderly emotions fails to recognize the true nature, the real object of his yearning, the confusion is vast and inevitable. Bent on satisfying his desire and a passion intended for true love with its counterfeit on a too limited scale, he or she will strive to compensate a fundamental emptiness with an increasing variety of fruitless experiments.

Is this why there is such chaos and discord in the world?
It is certainly the main reason, the ultimate cause, as I told you, is the separation from me.

I realize that the desire for love springing from personal deficiency, craving and need, can never find fulfillment by

looking to the mirage and appearances of the external world. Therefore, the relentless hunger, the insatiable longing, the empty heart remained until you rescued me from my state of misery.

If you remember, I said that what you call "the world" is the reflection of the thoughts and feelings of humanity.

And they are the way everything in the universe is created. I should never forget such a simple truth and yet so enlightening and encompassing because it explains life and manifestation at the individual, social and cosmic level. How tragic their misuse!

You must understand the fundamental truth that love is life itself in its state of perfection; therefore, evil in all its forms can only exist because mankind breaks the Law of love. In other words, it is the absence of love which is the cause of mankind's limitations and distress.

The same as darkness is lack of light. I know this is not merely an idealized virtue or religious principle for it is recognized even by a psychiatrist like Erich Fromm according to whom, "Love is the answer to the problem of human existence ... Without love, humanity could not exist for a day." And his words resonate with your explanation: "Love is the only way of knowledge, which in the act of union answers my quest."[22]

It is especially the feeling, where most of the energy is focused, that is vulnerable and subject to destructive impulses like criticism, irritation, hatred, and resentment. But unless the emotions are protected, controlled, and kept harmonious, the individual is a playground for the discordant forces within himself, and from the world in which he lives. Discord means disintegration of mind and body.

I should add that this kind of social malaise is prevalent when a civilization is in a state of internal decadence and corruption and is making a transition from an old to a new order. It explains the present unbridled gratification of the appetites of the sense-consciousness and the obsessive interest in sex. You must know that from the Source of creation there comes periodically, according to cosmic cycles, an outpouring of spiritual energy to help the progress of mankind and raise the consciousness of the race. These streams of light affect the seven centers in the body and tend to temporarily stimulate, depending on the individual's susceptibility, their sexual organs and drive. As the Earth is entering into what is referred as a Golden Age, the planetary consciousness is aroused to a sense of universality and an urge toward union. There is, under these new energies, a definite movement forward into spiritual fields, but at the same time, you see a desire in the less advanced for experimenting in the field of sensuality.

It is a piteous condition we are in when we requalify and pollute the light-energy flowing into us with our lower desires.
Energy is impersonal and does not discriminate, it acts according to where it is directed and the way it is used and qualified by the consciousness.

Both the good and bad qualities in the individual are awakened like sunlight in a fertilized garden, which will produce more weeds together with flowers: the difference is in the seeds found in the ground.

Yes, the inflow of cosmic light and love arouses in some individuals divine aspirations, in others physical cravings and lust. It quickens the selfish desires for material possessions but also the feeling of brotherhood and the tendency toward at-onement. Eventually, it will bring the two poles of spirit and matter into closer unity, and this includes science and religions.

Can we, then, expect the "raising of Lazarus from the dead" and the emergence of humanity from the tomb of materialism?[23]

That is the work of My messengers who are trying to awaken as many as possible from the sleep of the senses, and enlighten them, at least those whose Karma permits it to their responsibility. The forces of darkness generated by mankind have only one intent, that is to destroy, and their main target is now the family.

In their decadent and benighted state people do not realize that a true marital relation should involve all aspects of human nature. There should be, on all levels of consciousness, a merging of the physical, the emotional, and the mental bodies, the realization of interpersonal union with another, in love.

I know that this desire is the most fundamental passion, "it is the force that keeps the human race together, the clan, the family, society. The failure to achieve it means insanity or destruction – self destruction or destruction of others."[24]

When the relation is merely physical, there will always be emptiness, incompleteness and frustration. Only when the two partners are united on all three planes will there be the solution of the male-female partnership and the elevation of the family as the nucleus of love to its intended place as the foundation of society.

Today, it is mostly the marriage of two physical bodies, and this explains its short duration: it is self-evident that love is absent because love's true nature immortalizes and conforms only to eternity.

The pseudo-etymology of the word *amore*, although unfounded, is meaningful: the letter *a* means "without"; *mor* means "death." Joining them, we have "without death," or life everlasting.

There may be the union of the physical body of one party with only the emotional body of the other attracted and participating. Rarely, indeed, it is a merging of minds.

How appropriate Shakespeare's sonnet on the celebration of love:

> Let me not to the marriage of true minds
> Admit impediments. Love is not love
> Which alters when alteration finds,
> O no, it is an ever-fixed mark
> That looks on tempests and is never shaken;
> It is the star to every wandering bark,
> Love's not time's fool, though rosy lips and cheeks
> Within his bending sickle's compass come.
> Love alters not with his brief hours and weeks,
> But bears it out even to the edge of doom.[25]

But even a marriage of true minds will not be complete and fulfilling because perfect union can be realized only by the blending of the flames in each lover's heart. Only the fire of love enables you to overcome the sense of separation without at the same time losing one's self-identity, the I AM, which gives you the experience of the feeling of oneness with the beloved.

This reminds me of the words of Walter Hilton: "God and the soul are no longer two, but one ... In this union a true marriage is made between God and the soul, which shall never be broken." Similarly Suso, "Earthly lovers, however greatly they may love, must needs bear to be distinct and separate from one another; but Thou, O unfathomable fullness of all love ... in virtue of Thy being absolutely all in all, pourest Thyself so utterly into the soul's essence that no part of Thee remains outside."[26] Why is this so?

I AM present everywhere, and the heart-flame of the individual is part or a focal point of the all-pervading cosmic fire, which is the real, eternal love, not time-bound or limited by space. It is indeed true that, as the proverb says, "a perfect love does last eternally."

This is as true as another saying, "love without end has no end" — that is, love with no ulterior motive. How tragic that the word love has been fused and confused with the word sex in its debased and erroneous meaning, and it is significant that what is written of one can be related to the other. "Love? It resonates as the most prostituted word there is — strictly speaking, it is the word for prostitution. Let's rehearse spontaneously the lexicon: one 'makes' love, like one makes war or makes deals, and all that remains to be determined is which 'partners,' at what price, for what profit, at what interval, and for how long."[27]

Few understand that under the symbol of sex, you have also the reality of love expressing itself. Both connote and imply a relation and are emblematic of the Universal Law of Attraction for, cosmically speaking, those two words represent the complementarity and interplay of the primordial poles. They include the polarity of spirit-matter, Father-Mother God, male-female, life-form, God Self – human self.

If one aspires to spiritual liberation from the prison of his body and the wheel of Karma, he must fix his attention beyond the bond of earthly marriage to the higher manifestation of love and sex in order to achieve the final goal of the victory of the ascension. The process of union and merging must take place, as I said, within yourself and with your God Self.

Is it not possible to accomplish the ascension in the marital state?
Yes, in fact, for some individuals it may be helpful, but as a rule, it requires more determination and effort to overcome personal differences. It depends also on the partner; if both have the same intent and desire to reach the same goal, it would be a great blessing, but it is rare.

In the Gospel of Thomas, when Jesus is asked by his disciples how they can enter the Kingdom, He replies: "When you make the two one, and when you make the inside like the outside and the outside like the inside, and the above like the below, and when you make the male and the female one and the same, so that the male not be male nor the female then you enter (the Kingdom)."[28] How can it be done? You have showered me with an abundance of knowledge, but my desire is growing for more.
Let me give you a synopsis or compendium of what I have been trying to teach you, and I will begin with a basic question.

Has it ever occurred to you that there might be two natures in you, or rather two sides, like the positive and negative poles of a magnet? You, as an individual, stand between them as the nexus, the combined nature of the two, which are in reality one and intended to remain one. I am present in you as the inner Self, and your outer aspect is the personality. The interrelation and complementary nature of the divine and human poles enable you to be self-aware and say I or I am, which is the expression of your identity — your sense of being one and the same individual underlying the constant flux of your outer consciousness and the ever changing conditions of the world around you. (By the way, this is reflected in your language: identity is a word from the Latin *idem*, which means sameness.)

You are thereby an inseparable part of Me, as your I AM Self, though you have totally ignored and even forgotten me.

Try to understand the difference between appearance and reality. One is temporary, always changing; the other is Being itself, permanent and immutable. As I have explained it, at present you are not a real person, you only *seem* to be one, shadowed by a false self. Yet I AM always with you, radiating every instant My very life in and around you as it flows through your nervous system like liquid light, bringing vitality to your bloodstream, and charging your physical structure with health and strength. For instance it is My light that heals the wounds or any condition within the body when the individual allows Me to do it.

And why do you think I do that? To perfect you and consume the discord which has accumulated preventing My love to come through, giving you the happiness I want you to experience. You do not realize that your every heart-beat is a wave of love from Me, and that what enables you to think, feel, and act is My energy, not yours: it comes from Me and is only loaned to you. You think it belongs to you, and that you can use or misuse it as you please without being responsible.

What a pitiful condition mankind is in! You heard the phrase, All is love, all is Law, but in their ignorance, people break the Law, and in so doing they break themselves by their disobedience to it.

I am beginning to see some light through the fog of my mental concepts and I am grateful for your teaching. Would you tell me where you abide?
I AM in the fullness of My being directly above you, and I AM present within you, referred to variously in the tradition of the mystics as the "spark of the soul," the "Trinity," "divine fire," the "Dweller in the innermost," the "diamond Self," and the "Ground of nature."

You cannot be separated from Me and live. Can you separate a ray of light from the sun? I am the sun of your individual world, connected with you by a stream of light called in the Scripture the silver cord: "Remember your Creator in the days of your youth, before the days of trouble come.... and desire fails, because all must go to their eternal home, and the mourners will go about the streets; before the silver cord is snapped... and the dust returns to the earth as it was, and the breath returns to God who gave it."[29]

It has also been described in these words: "It is as if a resplendent cord were hanging down from the height of Heaven to this world below, and we appeared to pull it down; but in very truth, instead of drawing down the rope we were ourselves being drawn upwards to the higher refulgence of the resplendent rays.[30] "And in 33:52-4 of Dante's *Paradiso*: "my sight, becoming pure, was entering more and more through the beam of the lofty Light, which in Itself is true." The silver cord or ray of light emanates or is projected from My heart to yours.

It causes, as you said, our heart to pulsate and our lungs to breathe.
It is the way you are connected with Me receiving the energy of My life, love, intelligence, purpose and the capacity for cosmic unity.

This explains why there is a soft spot on a baby's head, which is a visible sign indicating where the stream of light enters the physical body and initiates the activity of life after the umbilical cord is cut at birth.
Yes, after the infant is born as the body is growing, the bony structure of the head closes over; for once established within the heart, the action of My light can penetrate the protective covering of the cranium.

I urge you to give recognition to the fact that within your heart there is the point of contact with your God Self, a threefold flame extending from My heart that radiates as the trinity of love, wisdom, and power. Every time you acknowledge and give your attention with feeling to it, its light will expand within you and suffuse your entire being.

Are you what people refer to as the guardian angel?
Some of those who were granted, because of their intense love and devotion the vision of my Presence thought so, but in reality I am far superior to an angel. You knew Me in the beginning, but you do not recognize Me anymore; I am your Real-Self, your original Being, but your image of Me has been stained and covered with the mask and disguise of the personality, until you have become unlike Me, and therefore unlike yourself. However, I am still nearer to you than you are to yourself, although you are not aware of it. You could see Me if

there was no impure substance in your brain which veils your vision.

I recall the words of the poet Tennyson:

> Speak to Him, thou, for He hears, and Spirit with Spirit can meet—
> Closer is He than breathing, nearer than hands and feet.[31]

And I have a clearer understanding of passages like these: "I call Heaven and earth to witness that one day suddenly I saw the shape of my self standing before me and my self disengaged from me." And "The secret of prophecy consists for the prophet that he suddenly his self appears to him, talking to him, and he forgets his self, and it is released from his body, and he sees his self before him talking to him and predicting the future."[32]

I ask you to forgive my doubt and lack of understanding. You said that you are my real identity and have tried to explain it to me in many ways. But how do I know, I mean with real certainty or experientially, that you are present within me as my true Self. I am not a mystic.

You do not have to, but I am not surprised of your wavering feeling. It is the nature of the emotions to be like the waves of the ocean because their essence is the water element. I will give you a simple exercise that can be very helpful. Just keep in mind that what you observe, or that of which you are aware, it is not the real you.

I am the observer, not the object unless I become identified with it.

Something you do not want to do because as one of your books states, "We are dominated by everything with which our self becomes identified. We can dominate and control everything from which we disidentify ourselves. In this principle lies the secret of our enslavement or our liberty."[33] Let us begin with the body; you can be aware of it and its sensations, therefore you are not the physical form which is subject to constant change and can be young or old, healthy or sick, strong or weak, rested or tired.

I may even think of having a different body with other features, for instance, with blue eyes and light hair, or being taller.

Then you are not your emotions because, again, you can observe them as distinct and detached from you. Moreover, they are in a state of constant flux, often contradictory, alternating from one mood to another, from like to dislike, more changeable than the body.

They cannot be my identity which, by definition, means one and the same.

Right, they are not your permanent feeling of "I." Observe also the mind that is supposed to be your instrument but it is very difficult to control, a stream of thoughts flowing all the time and, as you know, very undisciplined.

It is, for sure, almost impossible to stop the mental chattering always going on, waking and sleeping.

This proves again that you are not your mind-stream. Then, who is the witness, the one observing the physical, emotional, and mental states and the myriad contents of your consciousness?

It must be my true Self, the permanent center of my being, that is part of you and enables me to say and to be the "I" or "I AM". But it cannot be defined because it is not an object of the mind, something that can be thought of.

Yes, it is not a function of the faculties of the personality. Only awareness can grasp the "I" knowing itself, " I AM".

This statement may seem surprising, even alarming to someone who has always identified himself with his mind and body. The Self or "I" to him would be non-existent, he may even think of vanishing or disappearing into empty space if he disidentifies from his personality. In fact, that's what a philosopher wrote: "For my part when I enter most intimately into what I call 'myself,' I always stumble on some particular perception or other, of heat or cold, light or shade, love or hate, pain or pleasure…We are nothing but a bundle or collection of different perceptions, which succeed each other with an inconceivable rapidity and are in perpetual flux and movement."[34]

It is understandable why he refers to himself as "nothing," because he is merely aware of his personal or outer consciousness, that is, the content rather than him-Self as the "I AM."

I can apply to him these lines of a Chinese sage:

> Why are you unhappy?
> Because 99.9 percent
> Of everything you think
> And of everything you do,
> Is for yourself –
> And there isn't one.[35]

The "I" is simple, the same always, without change, and self conscious; it is the source of unlimited potential and the foundation of freedom from the conditioning and the layers of negative energy accumulated from the past and present that imprison the individual.

But how do I know that the "I" is self-conscious? Is it possible to give an explanation of it?
The most perfect analogy I can use to make you understand it, is the light. Do you not need the light in order to see?

I certainly do, without light there would be nothing visible.
But how do you see the light? Does the light need something else to make itself visible?

No, the light reveals itself.
Because it is self-luminous.

Yes, I see what you mean, it is the same with the "I" by which I am aware of myself and of everything but it can be known only by itself because it is self-conscious, "I AM".
Congratulations! Think deeply on it, acknowledge and recognize it often as who you really are, it is the Word that abides in you, that created everything in the universe and it will reveal to you its infinity.

I begin to realize the permanent core of my being that is part of you and enables me to say and to be the "I" or "I AM", conscious of myself and of your Presence as One.
I AM very pleased with your progress; let us, continue.

The universe is a flow of energy from the Source of all that is, and the individual is a channel expressing it as he unfolds his divine attributes and manifests his creative powers. This cosmic current animates and motivates the human being into activity through the medium of force centers in the etheric body.

You should always remember that man is essentially (as regards the earthly plane) a being made of etheric matter, since his dense physical body is not considered a principle. I told you that the individual is a magnet and with regard to the body there are two poles or centers, one at the base of the spine which is the connection with the Earth and the finite, and the other at the top of the head which is his link to Heaven and the infinite. Between them there are five more centers, for a total of seven.

Again the number seven.
The centers correspond and are related to the seven major areas and glandular organs of the physical body. There are three of them below the diaphragm and four above:

BELOW
1. The base of the spine: Sacrum
2. Spleen center
3. The solar plexus: Pancreas

ABOVE
4. The heart center: Thymus gland
5. The throat center: Thyroid gland
6. The center between the eyebrows: Pituitary gland
7. The head center : Pineal gland

Would you describe their appearance?
Their shape can be compared to the bell of a flower of the morning glory family each with its own predominant dolor. The stalk of the flower springs from a point in the spine which may look from another view as a central stem. These force-centers or wheels are constantly rotating, and into the mouth of each is always flowing the energy of the life-stream from the infinite Source. The centers are active in every one and without them the physical body could not exist. In the undeveloped person they show themselves as small circles of a dull hue, about two inches in diameter in sluggish motion glowing with a faint light. When they are quickened and unfold in a more advanced individual, their size increases, and revolve spinning rapidly, resembling wheel-like vortices. Also their colors become brighter, flashing like miniature suns, therefore enhancing the faculties and raising the consciousness.

Where are they located?
They are visible on the surface of the etheric body, which serves as a bridge where thoughts and feelings are conveyed from the mental and emotional body to the denser vehicle. Think of these force centers as channels of divine energy from the higher planes, always flowing in everyone from one body to the other.

They are a replica, in miniature, of the sevenfold constitution of the universe and the medium of expression and connection with those referred to as the Seven Spirits around the throne of God. They are in the Bible signified by the Hebrew word *Elohim*, one of the names of the Almighty which is inexplicably plural. The Egyptians called them the Builders, depicted with great knives in their hand with which they carved the universe from its primordial substance. They represent the seven creative attributes of God that contain potentially all sound and color, issuing from the white light the musical notes and the spectrum.

Lao-Tse said that the universe is man on a large scale.
It is essential that the centers be interrelated and in harmony in an active interplay.

I assume according to the principle of polarity.
Yes, the inner and outer conditions of the life of the individual depend on his response to the inflow of My light and the use or misuse of the incoming energies.

The ultimate cause of disease and limitations is to be found in the lack of balance and arrested development of the centers because of the resistance and opposition to the magnetic pull of My love by the gravitational tendency of physical desires and negative attitudes.

Of this relation between the lower and higher centers, the polarity of sex is the symbol in one of its myriad forms. It should be noticed that the head center represents the spirit or masculine aspect, and the center between the eyebrows is the feminine aspect or matter. The pituitary and pineal glands (which can be considered negative and positive respectively) are the higher correspondences of the male and female organs of reproduction.[36]
You can see the enactment of the drama of sex on three levels of consciousness:

First, on the physical plane, it fulfills its divine purpose by creating a new form for the incarnating individual.

Second, in raising and transforming the lower energies into the higher, it reveals and manifests the threefold principle of good, truth, and beauty in the various fields of human activity and creativity.

Third, the at-one-ment of the heart and head with the magnetic attraction of My love culminates in the purification and deification of the individual who overcomes "the last enemy," death, in the victory of the ascension.

Unfortunately, the race-consciousness of mankind is acting predominantly in the lower centers, and people squander their most divine gift, the light-energy of My love, perverted to the gratification of the senses and the selfish ends of the outer personality.

I realize that the energies below the diaphragm must be raised and become one with those above the diaphragm.
Yes, what esoterically is called "initiation" or "rite of passage" really refers to the process of the life-force within the physical structure drawn up and raised from one center to another until it reaches the highest on top of the head, called the "crown".

Which is a symbol of authority, power, and victory, whose real meaning is rarely understood.
When I was in college, I took a course on Kundalini yoga. The Sanskrit word "Kundalini" means "coiled up," or at rest in circles, and is referred to as the serpent fire because the nature of her power is spiral-like.

Another definition of "Kundalini" is the curl of the hair of the beloved, and it can also mean to burn. It is the energy of the female principle existing in a latent state not only in every human being but in every atom and all substance present everywhere. In the physical body, this coiled energy is focused in one of the subtle energy centers at the base of the spine and is call Shakti, the feminine counter-

part of Shiva, whose seat is the center on the top of the head.

As I mentioned, these are the two poles of the human form, like the electromagnetic bodies of the sun and the earth, and they epitomize the polarized energies that exist everywhere, the fundamental forces that animate and move the universe.

Life is one, and all parts of its myriad manifestations are interrelated, forming an inseparable and perfectly integrated whole.

The individual is like a spark of the cosmic fire — he is the microcosm and contains in himself every element found in the macrocosm.

The complete play of the unfolding and expanding universe is duplicated in the human being, in the same way that in every cell is encoded the intelligence and information which make up the physical body, or like each piece of a hologram containing the whole image of the picture.

The goddess Kundalini is said to be as beautiful as a chain of lightning and delicate as the lotus' petals, shining in the minds of the sages. The purpose of life is to awaken her and cause her to rise, because her upward movement through the other centers aligned along the axis of the body inspires and radiates pure love and bliss. The embrace between Shakti and Shiva in the crown center generates light and draws by contact more of the divine essence from above, causing the expansion of the light in the body structure. By raising its vibratory action, it effects a gradual transformation in the ascensional process.

I used to think that it makes celibacy look really wonderful. However, I was not determined enough to go through the preparatory disciplines based on concentra-

tion, breathing exercises, postures, and the recitation of mantras. It requires perseverance, purity, and steady practice. We were told by our teacher that one must rise by that which may cause him to fall, but, unfortunately, instead of enlightenment and bliss, I took the downward path and experienced confusion and frustration.

Because of the close connection between the fire of Kundalini and the organs of reproduction, the raising process involves the transmutation of the life-force in the center at the base of the spine. With regard to the constitution of the human being, everyone is endowed with a limited supply of sexual energy during his lifetime. The semen is a life-carrying force, and, if it is allowed to flow out and be wasted, the individual depletes his vitality. There is a definite link between misuse of sex and degeneration and decrepitude. The loss of semen means loss of the life-force.

When Rollo May, a noted psychiatrist, writes that "the experience of love and death are interwoven," he refers also to the relation of death with the depletion of eros in the sex act. And he quotes Freud's words, "This accounts for the likeness of the condition of that following complete sexual satisfaction to dying, and for the fact that death coincides with the act of copulation in lower animals." Our author points out another side to the relationships between love and death. According to him the tremendous preoccupation with sex and the strive to prove one's potency serve to cover up contemporary man's fear of death. Because of the lack of defenses like the belief in immortality "the awareness of death is widely repressed in our day," therefore, "Repression of death equals obsession with sex." Since an obsession drains off anxiety from some other area...the clamor of sex

all about us drowns out the ever-waiting presence of death."[37]

Certainly it is not worth it to squander our energy, which is the fire of life, in temporary and fleeting sensations.

If the generative force is conserved and kept under control — I do not mean by repression, but transformation — it not only maintains the body youthful and beautiful, but intensifies all physiological, mental, and spiritual activities.

Kundalini yoga is the most advanced and difficult branch of yoga, which can be full of danger because you are truly playing with fire, that is, cosmic fire. If you have not attained inner purity and a state of harmonious attunement in all your centers, the Kundalini energy creates a mode of being stained with complexes, anxiety, depression, and fear, alternating with elevated, blissful periods, visionary experiences, and creative moods.

The same life energy, when raised, can lead you to a mystical state, but if it is contaminated by your carnal desires, it creates a frenzied excitement of the sex center, wild delusions, mental disorders, and even madness.

That's why it has wisely been said, "She gives liberation to the yogi and bondage to the fool", and in a more impressive way, "The Yogi gains his eternal salvation by the same act that causes some men to burn in hell for thousands of years."[38]

There are some teachers of Yoga who believe that when the Kundalini fire is raised every center will come into perfect alignment and activity, and your spinal cord will be cleared of all obstruction. This is the reverse of the truth and a serious mistake. The fire will rise and carry the consciousness to a blissful heavenly state when the centers are awakened and unfold removing all impediments from the channels. The centers themselves have the power to cleanse and "consume" all that hinder their radiation and expansion. This should be accomplished not by the sheer will of the personal self but by purity of life and mastery of the feeling nature. Above all, by the attention, with love, reaching up to Me; this is the perfect way.

Life is perpetual motion, it is not possible to stand still; you either ascend or descend on the ladder of being by the use or misuse of the life-force whose essence is fire. The ultimate reality is Oneness; there is in the individual, immersed in the gross material world of divisions and conflicts, both within himself and without, an unrecognized yet deep yearning to return to his original state. You live in a fortunate age, in spite of appearances to the contrary. Do you remember the beginning of one of your favorite novels? The opening of Charles Dickens' 1859 novel *A Tale of Two Cities* can refer to the present. "It is the best of times, it is the worst of times, it is the age of wisdom, it is the age of foolishness, it is the epoch of belief, it is the epoch of incredulity, it is the season of Light, it is the season of Darkness, it is the spring of hope, it is the winter of despair, we have everything before us, we have nothing before us, we are all going directly to Heaven, we are all going directly the other way."[39]

But it is hardly the best of times!
It seems the worst because all the destructive accumulation of mankind's discord and misused energy of the past is reaching its culmination. Like an avalanche that levels everything in its pathway, the masses cannot withstand the gravitational force of their past mistakes. Because of their disobedience to the cosmic Law, humanity is no longer attuned to love and they have be-

come the laggards of the solar system. However, they cannot delay longer the cyclic progression and the onward and upward movement of the universe. The Earth must be purified by the fire of love and come into at one-ment with the other planets of the system in order to rise to a spiral higher.

How is this to be accomplished?
The most simple and effective way is for people to turn the attention to God and call for the release of the light to annihilate the shadows.

Why God cannot do it without our request?
Instead of questioning, in their ignorance and confusion, why evil is allowed to exist, everyone should understand that mankind is responsible for the frightful condition they live in.

By the misuse of our free will and creative powers.
Therefore, if they want to be free they must turn the attention to the light and go back to their Source, the only hope for them, mark you, by making the demand by their free will!

I can see that it is the action of the Law of love.
You emphasize the power of the attention and the importance of keeping it on the good in order to attract it. But how can I focus and give my attention to you, the Source of all perfection, if I don't know where you are? What do you mean when you say that you are directly above me?
I told you that I am present within you, and My anchorage in your body is the heart. This is accepted by believers with some differences in their doctrines.

You told me that you are within every physical form as the immortal flame which is like a projection or like an extension cord from your heart. But your whole Being ... where is it?

I am pleased with your question because it is a sign of your progress and of your desire to know the full truth. Now I will disclose an essential aspect of it that was never explained except in a private revelation when the initiate was ready for it. Let me ask you: if I were within you in the fullness of My luminous Being do you not think that you would be perfect?

I am absolutely sure of it.

But you are not fully perfected, not yet.

You don't have to convince me of it.

Therefore, something has been missing in the various spiritual teachings of the world. You and I are one life-stream from the Infinite Ground of all, and I stand above you on a higher plane.

That's why you are also referred to as the Higher Self. I know that for you space doesn't exist, but can you give me an idea of the distance between us?

It varies according to the state of consciousness of the individual. In order to give an intelligible answer to your question, I must put on, again, the garb of the mathematician. According to your position on Earth, I abide, as an average, twenty feet above every human being. The distance is greater if the personality is destructive and depraved. I am always giving My light and energy without reservation but he would not be receptive.

You stand at the door and knock.

It is very true; when anyone turns to Me with a loving acceptance of My Presence and acknowledges My help, I can come very near to him or her because that is My greatest desire. They would give Me the opportunity to expand the light in every atom of their body-temple.

As you did in the transfiguration of Jesus.
Yes, I enfolded Him in My radiance and He became shining like the sun. Remember always that your attention is the flow of your life. Wherever it is directed, your energy must of necessity go, and you take on and absorb the quality of what is upon. Very few realize the tremendous power they possess in the use of their attention which is magnetic and draws you into its object and you attract it into your being and world.

But who has complete control and mastery over it, directing and sustaining it where he desires? Usually it is like a weathervane, turning one way and the other as the wind blows.
And it is easily possessed and attracted, through the pull of the feelings, by the constant suggestions of the negative forces, from within and without, which feed on your life-energy to sustain themselves. However, I remind you again of the wisdom of the ages: You become what your attention and vision are upon, God, if they are on God, dust, if they are on the dust.

I realize more and more the value of prayer and meditation to learn how to concentrate and direct our faculties upwards, with love, because when the life-current is raised, the actual physical body will follow. I read about individuals who may levitate in their ecstasy and devotional practices.

You can see the enactment of the symbolic sex process on a higher level of consciousness, when you raise your loving energy to Me and I return it amplified without limit by the fire of My love. Thus, displaying your spiritual objective and final goal, which is the union with the God Self. Every moment that you hold your attention on My Presence draws you closer to your ascension.

Remember always, there are only two ways to go, toward Me or toward troubles. Human problems will never be solved until people are purified and illumined and they begin to live in their higher centers, where they can express the potencies of their being using the creative word, "I AM," and the love of their heart-flame.

This is how the individual is transformed from the human into his divine Self.
Again, the polarity of sex is the symbol of this interrelation between the finite and the infinite, between Earth and Heaven, which are attracted and connected by the magnetic power of love.

And it refers also to the interplay and communion between our centers and you.
Yes, as below, so above; as above, so below.

I know that there is in us the deep desire for transcendence and the yearning for oneness because we come from the One, and we are restless until we find peace and fulfillment by becoming again one with it. That's what everyone is unknowingly seeking, but we are blindfolded by our false self and its selfish desires which have created such frightful

conditions, and it is very difficult be free from our human limitations

I can appreciate that, but I have never forsaken the children of the Earth, and have never left them without the light of understanding, even when the darkness seemed to engulf them. In fact, My love has saved them and the planet from total destruction.

Have I not, in every age, sent My messengers to remind them of the Law of Life and how to rise out of their problems and distress by simply turning to Me and ask for deliverance? And you know very well how they have been received and treated. This is because people do not want to know the truth and prefer to live in the darkness of their own concepts and emotions.

Unfortunately, self-gratification seems to be the determining factor of all actions originated by the personality, whether the fulfillment of a desire is accompanied by pleasure or satisfaction, or sought solely for the sake of such satisfaction.

Are all desires hedonistically motivated? According to some teachings we must kill all our desires, but that implies the desire to do it.

There is considerable confusion and misunderstanding with regard to this subject and I would like to clarify it. The truth is that there are physical or lower desires and higher or spiritual desires. By now you should know the difference between those that are constructive and oriented toward God, and bodily appetites which are habits acquired by the gratification of the sense-consciousness.

They are as far apart as selfishness and love. In the *Book of Common Prayer* we read, "O God, from whom all holy de-

sires, all good counsels, and all just works do proceed; give unto thy servants that peace which the world cannot give."[40] Desire is inherent within life as the moving force in manifestation toward greater expression of all that is in the womb of the Infinite. Like love, to which it is intimately joined, it is the principle of activity from the transcendent Ground of being which becomes conscious of itself in the entities that it empowers, mark you by the desire for the creation of that which is good and beautiful.

I can understand that desiring means a desire for what is good, or at least for what the individual thinks will do him good.
Yes, even if one acts out of compulsion, the compulsion itself is the consequence of a wayward search for goodness.

We may be aware that we have desires but we don't know what will satisfy us and keep using one object after another, until we die. We can say that the individual may be defined by what he desires.
That would be very helpful for the attainment of self-knowledge. There is no life without some form of desire and nothing can cause it to cease to be.

Like the desire to be free.
Very good! Everything depends on the nature of your desire because it will always fulfill itself, the time of manifestation depending on its intensity.

It is how we qualify, rather re-qualify, your pure energy.
It is the way you accomplish anything, good or evil.

An Indian sage, Shantideva, wrote: "All those who suffer in the world do so because of their desire for their own happiness. All those happy in the world are so because of their desire for the happiness of others."[41] I should remember it and apply it in my life because desire which is not followed by action may be useless. As William Blake says, "He who desires but acts not, breeds pestilence."[42]

I am talking about real desire, not wishful thinking. What do you suppose caused the fall of man?

The desire of the personality to have its own way contrary to God's love.

I am glad you have learned something.

I think the main problem is the male-female relationship:

> What is it men in women do require?
> The lineaments of gratified desire.
> What is it women do in men require?
> The lineaments of gratified desire.[43]

If that is the case they should not complain about the consequences.

Without an intense desire to perfect myself I can never do it.

That desire is one with Mine therefore you cannot fail. Or do you still want to experiment with the desires of your false self thinking that you have missed something or that you have to give up some of your pleasures?

I finally realize that the personality can never find true fulfillment trying to fill its emptiness from outside.
However, one can learn and awaken from the sleep of the senses seeking to gratify them as it happened to you. It seems a paradox but if one is satisfied and contented pursuing and indulging one's personal desires, he is completely lost, the darkness engulfs him. "Verily a polluted stream is man. One must be a sea to revive a polluted stream without becoming impure ... It is not your sin — it is your self-satisfaction that crieth unto heaven."⁴⁴

Is it because we don't know the meaning of the word "love"? Very few are awakened to the truth of these words: "The end of all our desires is God; hence the act whereby we are primarily joined to Him is basically and substantially our happiness."⁴⁵
The love of love, which is the source of life must dominate, not love of being loved or love of one's self.

Even those who recognize that love is a motivating force, a power which could be relied upon to impel us onward in life, are wondering what happened in our society. People are confused and don't know what love is any more. The motivating force itself is now called into question. Love has become a problem to itself."
The title of the chapter whose passage you quoted — "Our Schizoid World" — is meaningful. The author means, "the inability to feel," and he adds, "The schizoid man is the natural product of the technological man."⁴⁶

However, technology should not be blamed because it can be a blessing. It is rather man's dependence on it and his faith in science considered the depository and dispensary of truth; in fact, it has become the belief system of your society.

That is the cause of the inability to really feel and of all the artificial and mechanical means in the vain attempt to find a remedy. It is no wonder that sex has been defined "the new machine, the Machina Ultima,"[47] and reduced to mail-order technique.

Let us elevate the tone of our discussion above this sordid topic which is a reflection of "the contemporary emotional and spiritual wasteland."[48] The popularity of psychology indicates an interest in self-knowledge but betrays the fundamental lack of love in human relations. Psychological knowledge, even of the higher order, can never be a substitute for the wisdom and illumination which are experienced only through the unitive feeling of love. The sacredness of sex is contained in a proverb of ancient China: "Sexual intercourse is the human counterpart of the cosmic process."

This is what you have tried to explain to me concerning "the existence of maleness and femaleness as the expression of the fundamental polarity of all reality." The author I am quoting supports your view: "the smallest molecular particle gets its dynamic movement from the fact that it consists of a negative and positive charge, with tension – and therefore movement – between them ... Indeed, it could be argued that all of reality has a male-female character."[49]

Yes, this has been one of My basic subjects, in the attempt to raise the consciousness of mankind to a higher level.

But with reference to the Chinese proverb, there seems to be an infinite gulf between sex and the cosmic process.

Obviously, if you are thinking of sex as viewed on the physical plane it is like saying that a dipper is the earthly correspondence of the Big or even Little Dipper. But if you comprehend the principle of polarity acting everywhere in the universe, from the atom to a system of world, it would make perfect sense. Do you know that there are male and female galaxies? I should not expect that you do.

How profound is the truth of the ancient statement, "as above so below, as below so above."
In order to help you, I will take another approach based on the controversial subject of Eros and Agape, two Greek words which are translated "love."

I know that Eros is one of the prominent gods and personifies the creative force in nature, it is also a cosmic principle operative in the dealings of both human and divine life. Agape has its source in the Christian revelation that "God is love,"[50] and the sublime qualities that love contains.[51]
There is a long history of argumentation with regard to their relation, whether they are opposed or it is possible for them to be associated and reconciled. Eros has two basic forms, lower and higher, depending on its object.

Whether its arrow is directed downward or is aimed aloft.
I do not refer to its sensual aspect or sexual character, from which the term "erotic" is derived.

Otherwise there would not be the problem of its relationship with Agape.
Eros represents the desire, the longing or passion, and the upward movement toward the realm of the Good and Beautiful. It

originates as a response to visual beauty and affects the very way we see.

According to the Greek poetess Sappho, "whatever one loves is most beautiful."
However, the power of Eros is to lead us, in its ascent, from physical beauty which is merely a reflection, to beauty itself in the divine realm.

It takes us on its wings from the transient world of appearance to the permanent Reality. "We know the Creator's beauty through the beauty of His creatures ... St. John Climaco tells the story of a man who burned with love of God whenever he saw a beautiful woman, and burst into tears, praising God."[52]
I would advise you to do likewise, it is a good way to transmute the energy of the lower center and raise it into the higher.

I recall also Michelangelo's verses to the Source of eternal beauty:

> O make me see you everywhere!
> If I feel myself burn for mortal beauty,
> mine will be a dead fire near yours,
> and in yours I will be, as I was, on fire.

This tendency of Eros is viewed as self-centered and acquisitive, in contrast to Agape which "seeks not its own" and descends in compassionate love to the human level. It does not ascend to secure what is good for itself, but consists of a downward movement of self-giving because its foundation and prototype is God's own love.

It is asserted that Eros, originating from want and need, is determined by the quality, the beauty and worth of its object. It is non spontaneous like Agape but "evoked" and "motivated." "Eros recognizes value in its object – and loves it." On the contrary, "Agape loves – and creates value in its object."[53]

It is in Luther's words, "an overflowing love ... which says: I love thee, not because thou art good ... for I draw my love not from thy goodness as an alien spring; but from mine own well-spring."[54]

What about neighborly love?
According to that view, the desire of Eros is to love its neighbor "in so far as it can utilize him as a means for its own ascent." Even its love for God is acquisitively motivated because in its striving tendency it seeks fulfillment in the divine nature. "In loving God, the highest personal advantages are sought."[55] Agape, instead, is directed to the neighbor himself without ulterior motive, in fact it extends itself not only to friends but also to enemies.

It seems that no conciliation between these extremes is possible. The only thing Eros and Agape seem to have in common is that they focus all the significance in loving, rather than in being loved. But I think that the purpose of your explanation is to present to me the principle of polarity from another angle.
I told you that there is one life, one consciousness, one energy which "I AM"; and I said, also, that two poles are needed for energy to become active.

Like electricity and magnetism.

Therefore, Eros and Agape are one and the same love acting on two planes, divine and human, Agape is My life-energy or light descending from above into the individual, Eros rises from below on the return current, like an electrical circuit. Love, which is the essence of both, implies a tendency or motion toward the other or to an object. Even in the case of God loving itself. To view Eros and Agape as separated or opposed is a fallacy because one cannot be or exist without the other; they are complementary and interdependent.

Both are needed or love could not manifest by being divided because it takes two poles to generate light.
Yes, they are calling to each other to be re-united although, in reality, are not separated, except on the physical plane when the personality turns away from its Source and forgets that it is connected with it.

By the misuse of the free will.
Right, I cannot force Eros to aim its arrow only in My direction.

There is no true love without freedom.
And do you know what is the most perfect human relationship?

I assume that it must be the union of the human Eros with the divine Agape.
You have answered well. It is called friendship. I do not mean "friendship of pleasure" and "friendship of utility," for those are antithetical to the nature of true friendship. "Those who love for the sake of utility love for the sake of what is good for *themselves*, and those who love for the sake of pleasure do so for the sake of what is pleasant to *themselves*, and not in so far as the

other is the person loved but in so far as he is useful or pleasant.

Those friendships are only incidental for it is not as being the man he is that the loved person is loved, but as providing some good or pleasure. Such friendships, then, are easily dissolved, if the parties do not remain like themselves. For if the one party is no longer pleasant or useful, the other ceases to love him."[56] A true friend accepts the other *in toto*, as a whole, the individual himself. A "You" which is in reality, another "I," as part of the universal "I AMness."

A friend must be able to say, "I am loved for what I am," or more truly "I am loved because "I AM" one with your "I AM."

I think the greatest obstacle to that ideal lies in the relation between man and woman, much too often fraught with difficulties. You explained the nature and the problems of our sexuality, and you said that the cause of the separation into male and female sexes is not the sin or fall of man. Would you elaborate on it?

Yes, I will, however you must always remember in discussing these fundamentals that words but dim the meaning and are at most suggestive or evocative rather than elucidative or cognitive. Your language as a means of expression of the human consciousness cannot convey the reality of what is beyond its reach. Words are merely containers to communicate and interchange thoughts and feelings that often cannot be put into words. In fact, unless they are charged — I would say *transfigured* — by feeling, they can convey very little, no matter how eloquent and flowery the speaker or the writer may be.

I know that all the mystics struggle for expression; even Dante's poetic genius refers to the familiar theme of the ineffability of the divine illumination.

> O how scant is speech, and how feeble to my conception! And this,
> To what I saw, is such that it is not enough to call it little.[57]

It is not possible for Me to reveal to you the full truth because there exists neither the terminology nor the adequate state of consciousness to receive it. But I will make My words like cups of light and will assist you to drink from the transcendent source and thus quench your thirst

The subject of the sexual relationship has been sorely misunderstood and misconstrued because the reality concerning man and woman as twin flames or twin rays had been lost. Nothing will be so valuable and prevent so many problems and great distress as the knowledge I am unveiling to you.

Are they the same as soul-mates?
No, they are essentially different, a couple may become what are called soul-mates for having been related throughout many lives, generating a loving and lasting connection between them.

According to the Edgar Cayce material, soul mates are those who in the framework of reincarnation have been companions often before through fortunate or adverse conditions, creating, in various times and places, opportunity for growth and fulfillment in what should be service to one another. Here are some examples.

A young couple contemplating marriage were told that they had been together many times previously. During one embodiment in Persia their relationship was disrupted by dissension and conflicts. In another in ancient Egypt, although raised with opposing belief systems, they learned to be supportive and willing to cooperate. "As a result, in the present," Cayce told them, "they each, then, have that weakness of being able to be overpowered by the personality of the other ... Then if there is the agreement, if there is the coordination of ideals and purposes, and making the same work – it can be made a beautiful companionship!" But he warned them, "It also can be made to be the belittling of one or the other."[58]

To another couple he reminded them that, because of their troubled lifetimes together, their marriage "would become a burden upon each," and that they were simply meeting patterns they created in the past. "They each are faced with themselves! It is nothing but themselves they are faced with!" When asked what kind of relationship they should have in the present to heal the dissension and the problems of the past, the advice was, "friendship."[59]

However, if one has the desire and the commitment to make the marriage thrive, in spite of any difficulty, he or she can succeed. When a woman asked the possibility of meeting her soul mate she was told, "It is not necessarily true that any special individual may be called a mate, as there have been many..."[60]

Another lady who wanted to know whether there was another person other than her fiancé which would make her happy or happier, the reply was "...we might find twenty-five or thirty such, if you chose to make it so! It is what you make it!"[61] For Cayce, "...no greater office is there for an entity to fill than to be a channel through which a soul may find the way of experience into the material plane ... for the manifestation of God's love in the earth. Not as a duty or obligation, but as the opportunity for being a handmaid of the Lord."[62]

Soul mates are not limited to couples, they exist also among parents and children, friends, family, and even work associates. The real purpose of relationships is to enable the partners to know themselves, as each meets himself or herself in their experiences, become aware of their connection with God and be a "fit companion" for Him in their life. It is interesting that he refers to the individual as the " I AM": "Not in selfishness, not in grudge, not in wrath; not in any of those things that make for the separation of the I AM from the Creative Forces, or Energy of God. But the simpleness, the gentleness, the humbleness, the faithfulness, the long-suffering patience!"[63]

The Law of Love and cause and effect are acting all the time. "...each soul, each entity, *constantly* meets self. And if each soul would but understand, those hardships which are accredited much to others are caused most by self. Know that in those you are meeting thyself!"[64]

Cayce believed that learning how to love other people is what we're here to learn – "eventually all souls become soul mates with one another."[65] That is the realization of wholeness, as we expand our consciousness to embrace all life united to our Source.

He uses also the expression "twin souls" but it is not clear how they differ from soul mates. According to him there are no identical souls because God does not repeat Himself, "Not two leaves of a tree, no two blades of grass are the same."[66] "The primary distinction between soul mates and twin souls," comments our author, "is that soul mates are brought together as a means of assisting both individuals in soul growth, and twin souls often come together in an effort to achieve a joint task or a united work." At the heart of twin souls relationship is the "unity of purpose", the capacity to assist one another to accomplish their mission in life.

As a perfect example, "Cayce stated that Jesus of Nazareth and his mother, Mary, were twin souls." They may come together as a couple but should not be considered as halves of the same whole. Every soul is an individualized part in the oneness of God, and Cayce emphatically states, "One-One-One-One; Oneness of God, oneness of man's relation, oneness of force, oneness of time, oneness of purpose, oneness in every effort – Oneness-Oneness!"[67]

He is right with regard to the reality of the One life. But the twin flames to whom I refer are not "identical" because one is man and the other woman with their respective qualities corresponding to the original polarity of spirit and matter or life and form. Follow me closely:

The Infinite in its static, latent, and formless state, by an inner impulse to know itself, becomes self-conscious, giving rise to a primordial polarity as I have indicated.

I understand that consciousness implies a relation between a subject and an object but since the Infinite is One it becomes conscious of it-self.

I think you have finally grasped it. Yes, a Being with an inner and outer side, spirit and matter referred to, in some text, as self – and not-self. From their dynamic mutual interaction shines forth one flame as an individualized focus of consciousness which becomes a twinned flame, one masculine and the other feminine.

Why did the one flame divide into two?
They are not really two which would mean separated, yet they are not fused into an undifferentiated oneness. I use again the example of the two poles of a magnet, and that is the way by which love is generated and expressed. Each is both, one is the counterpart of the other and each is endowed with all the attributes and powers of perfection of the original flame.

I can see how two of the fundamental principles of life, androgyny and twin flames, have been fused and confused.
I hope that My explanation will be understood in spite of your human limitations. The twin flames descend on two rays of light from their highest realm into earthly embodiment, drawing from each of the seven planes the substance in order to form a corresponding body with the flame as its heart center, extending down into the
physical form as a lesser flame or spark.

The original plan was to unfold their divine seed and expand their heart flame of love through earthly experience, and enable them to master the elements and attain the ascension, by which they would become, respectively, a god and a goddess, in perfect union as the same "I AM Self."

Because there is the Fatherhood and Motherhood of the Supreme Source of life.
Yes, the primal polarity analogous to spirit and matter. Then, cycle after cycle, through the endless expansion of their I AM Self they become creators of a world, peopled by them with those who take embodiment there.

However, through their experiences on Earth their harmony was disrupted, they were disconnected and lost contact with each other. Then, like the rest of mankind, by the misuse of the free will, the shadow of their discordant thought-feelings, created by the desires of the outer self, gradually darkened their consciousness, lowering the vibratory action of their bodies who were originally luminous, making them as dense as the flesh body.

Thus, an energy veil was created that shut off the light of My Presence, and the negative Karma began to take its toll. Unfortunately, it seems that mankind does not learn the lessons of the past but keeps repeating the same mistakes. Yet I continue to provide them every day, month, year, and life after life with everything love can give and the Law of their being, by the use of their free-will, allows Me to bestow.

Again and again, even in one life-time, we go through the same experiences, groping in the darkness of our wrong desires. This is especially evident in the relation between man and woman.
I see that the male-female relationship is one of your main concerns and I am not surprised. It is indeed a mystery and I am trying to unravel it in our dialogues as clearly as possible considering the low-level of the human consciousness.

But why is it so difficult to find our twin flame?
The search is futile. I have explained to you the real cause of the mutual attraction between man and woman but no one knows who his or her other self is except Me.

Do we have to use the method of trial and error?
That is foolish! I never intended it as a way of knowing.

"In thy light we shall see light."[68] But why don't you illumine our way?
I am always doing it because it is My nature. Please, remember My words of long ago, "They need no light of lamp or sun, for the Lord will be their light."[69]

But ask yourself: is the individual willing to follow My plan? It is impossible to find your other half without My light, which must come from within in order to enable you to become who you are. You will never find completeness looking into the outer world because it is truly an inner experience. The union — or rather, reunion — with your female counterpart will take place after you have become, first, one being, centered in your heart-flame connected with Me.

It is the flame in your heart that is one with the flame in your twin's heart. I do not expect you to understand it with your intellect. Seek and feel your oneness with Me first, and eventually, it is not only possible but unavoidable for the divine encounter to become a reality because I decreed in the beginning your oneness.

But probably it will not be in this lifetime. As the Buddhist sage exhorts, "Instead of seeking union with a woman outside ourselves, we have to seek it within ourselves by the union of our male and female nature in the process of meditation."[70]
Yes, you must realize that the process of inner integration consists in the unification of the two sides of your nature in order to make yourself whole. How can you be reunited with your twin flame if you are not reunited with yourself first? Let me remind you that you are the nexus between two termini and you are nothing apart and separate from your God Self within

and above you. You must again find the connection of the outer with the inner for you are the combination of the nature of the two, the being of free will.

If I were you, I would not waste your time and opportunity to grow and ascend by searching for her by relating to other women. It would be more difficult than finding the proverbial needle in the haystack. Besides, she could be in a masculine embodiment or someone's wife (in which case you cannot break up her marriage), or she may even be already ascended — which would be the greatest happiness for both of you because she will be able to assist you.

I know, anyway, that the two of us are inseparable, and we will eventually be reunited "forever," which in this case it is true. Then I can say, "If ever any beauty I did see, which I desired, and got, 'twas but a dream of thee."[71]
Above all, do not forget that your purpose on earth is to return to Me, and if that is your decision, "all else will be given unto you."[72]

How can I do this? Perhaps I have already asked this question.
I do not mind refreshing your memory and showing you the way; in fact, I have done it many times in every embodiment, always hoping that you would answer My call. Now it is your turn to call to Me and for Me to answer you.

I want to know the way.
As I have explained it, there is only one way: love.

But I still don't know what true love is, although I always realized that it is the key to life, and tried in every way, to find it in my relation with people, in Nature, and in books.
You may read all the books in the world about that subject, and I do not have to tell you that there is an overabundance of them, without knowing what love really is.

It is true, but why?
Because love is not an intellectual concept. It is like explaining what music is by means of the science of acoustics or harmonics to someone who is deaf. And even if I refer to love as electrical fire or magnetism no one would understand because they do not know what they really are. I have given you an inkling of your ultimate destiny.

It staggers the mind.
You do not know the power of love and what it can do. Do not limit and do not withhold it, because I want you to be all that " I AM."

None of your desire and aspiration can be commensurate with the vocation you have received which is innate in the very energy of your Being. Worthless would be your ambition to be ruler of the world, and of little value even your longing to be one with the universe. Let your heart flame expand, and desire more of what you desire as I want you to have infinitely more. I have made you for Myself because without you I would not be who I AM, and without Me you cannot be who you are. Therefore, we are indissolubly bound in the fullness of all that love means and is.

Hold my attention and possess me for you are the only Source and the giver of eternal happiness.

[1] Genesis 3:2-3.

[2] Genesis 3:12-13.

[3] Paramahansa Yogananda, *Autobiography of a Yogi* (Los Angeles: Self-Realization Fellowship, 1971), p. 175-6.

[4] Yogananda, p. 178.

[5] Genesis 3:1.

[6] Yogananda, p. 177.

[7] John 1:1.

[8] John 10:34-35.

[9] Psalms 32:6; Matthew 5:45.

[10] Genesis 1:26-27.

[11] D.M. Carr, *The Erotic Word* (NY: Oxford University Press, 2003), p. 23.

[12] Genesis 3:9, 16, 17.

[13] *Classical Mythology*, pp. 216-7.

[14] Abrams, p. 155.

[15] Ibid., p. 153.

[16] Gina Cerminara, *Many Mansions: The Edgar Cayce Story of Reincarnation*, (NY: Penguin Books, 1991), p. 138.

[17] Ibid., p. 139-40.

[18] Op. cit., 1539.

[19] Genesis 3:21.

[20] Jean-Luc Marion, p. 9.

[21] Transl. R.H. Green, (Mineola, NY: Dover Publications, Inc., 2002), p. 48.

[22] *The Art of Loving*, (NY: Harper-Row Publishers, 1989), pp. 7, 17.

[23] See Alice A. Bailey, *Esoteric Psychology. A Treatise On the Seven Rays* (NY: Lucis Publishing, NY, 1979), Vol. 1, p. 283.

[24] *The Art of Loving*, p. 17.

[25] William Shakespeare, Sonnet 116.

[26] Quoted in *Mysticism in World Religion*, p. 249.

[27] *The Erotic Phenomenon*, p. 3.

28 Burt D. Ehrman, *Lost Scriptures: Books That Did Not Make It Into the New Testament* (NY: Oxford University Press, 2003), p. 22.

29 Ecclesiastes 12:1-8.

30 Quoted in *Mysticism in World Religion*, p. 279.

31 *Higher Pantheism.*

32 *Mysticism in World Religion*, p. 188.

33 *Psychosynthesis*, p. 22.

34 David Hume, quoted in Anne Bancroft, *Twentieth Century Mystics and Sages* (NY: Penguin Books, 1989), p. 159.

35 Wei Wu Wei, *Ask the Awakened* (London: Routledge-Kegan Paul, 1963), p. 1.

36 Cfr. Alice Bailey, *Esoteric Psychology*, p. 290.

37 Rollo May, Love and Will, (NY: W.W. Norton Co., 1969), pp 103, 106, 107.

38 *Yoga: Immortality and Freedom*, p. 263.

39 Charles Dickens, *A Tale of Two Cities*, bk. 1, ch.1.

40 Evening Prayer, Second Collect.

41 Bodhicaryavatara, ch. 8, v. 123.

42 William Blake, *Proverbs of Hell.*

43 William Blake, *MS NoteBook*, "Several Questions Answered."

44 Nietzsche, *Thus Spoke Zarathushtra*, p. 4.

45 St. Thomas Aquinas, Quodlibetal Questions, vol. 8, bk. 9, pt. 19.

46 *Love and Will*, pp. 15, 16-17.

47 Ibid., p. 47.

48 Ibid., p. 212.

49 Ibid., p. 112.

50 1 John 4:8, 16.

51 St. Paul, 1 Corinthians, 13.

52 Cardenal, pp. 76, 27.

53 Robert G. Hazo, *The Idea of Love,* (NY: Frederick A. Praeger Publishers, 1967), p. 120.p. 120.

54 *Eros, Agape and Philia. Readings in the Philosophy of Love*, p. 172.

55 Ibid., p. 121.
56 *Philosophies of Love*, ed. by D. K. Norton, and M. F. Kille,
    (Totowa, NJ: Rowman, Littlefield Publishers, Inc., 1971),
    p. 15.
57 *Paradiso*, 33:121-3.
58 Kevin Todeschi, *Edgar Cayce on Soul Mates* (Virginia Beach,
    Virginia: A.R.E. Press, 2007), p. 17.
59 Ibid., p. 109.
60 Ibid., p. 8.
61 Ibid., p. 9.
62 Ibid., p. 152.
63 Ibid., 183.
64 Ibid., 153.
65 Ibid., 189.
66 Ibid., p. 122.
67 Ibid., p. 181.
68 Revelation 22:5.
69 Revelation 22:5.
70 *Foundations of Tibetan Mysticism*, p. 103.
71 John Donne, "The Good-Morrow."
72 Luke 12:31.

CHAPTER 23

What is Love?

Love is a spirit all compact of fire,
Not gross to sink, but light, and will aspire.
William Shakespeare

And if I have prophetic powers, and understand all mysteries
and all knowledge, and if I have all faith so as to remove moun-
tains, but do not have love, I am nothing ...
Love never ends ... And now faith, hope, and love abide, these
three; and the greatest of these is love.
St. Paul

Only the soul that loves is happy.
Johann Wolfgang von Goethe

You explained to me that love is the only way to freedom, happiness, and the ascension. I have, in fact, searched the literature on love extensively, and what you said is, obviously, true. I'd like to recall, if you don't mind, some notes I wrote at the time that perhaps may be of some help to others.

I was faced with a bewildering diversity in conception and a variety of different and often contradicting theories that only increased the confusion in my mind. In addition, each writer has a vocabulary largely his own and words are often used in different senses. In their analysis regarding the origin and causes of love, some authors begin with God, others with biological needs or the desire to escape from feelings of loneliness and inadequacy.

For yet others, it can be an encounter with someone who is the occasion to remember eternal realities before birth; or they take feminine beauty for their focal point. There are writers who affirm that the aim of love is immortality, while others say it is the progress of the human race. There are also those for whom the purpose of love is physical pleasure, while others claim that it is the key to spiritual bliss and the way to Heaven.

Besides the diversity of views, there is the problem of using one and the same word to refer to immeasurably different emotional attitudes and affective states, such as love of parents, children, friends, sexual partners, food, money, power, clothing, pets, sport, flowers, sunshine, music, humanity, God. In fact, love can be directed toward any object, whether person or thing. The word love, so simple and composed of so few letters, recurs in so many widely diverse contexts that one is led to question if the writers have anything in common with each other. It has been asserted that love is the moving force of life and the motivation of everything in the universe, whether inanimate or animate, to do whatever it does. Stones love the center of the earth, the upward motion of fire is called a function of love, the attraction of iron filings to a magnet is described as the effect of love. Also the propagation of plants, the procreation of species, and the movement of planets and stars are all inspired by the cosmic power of love.

God Himself is said to be love. Such an idea of unlimited extent and meaning has induced some to doubt its reality, and love has been called a myth, a metaphor, an illusion, or just a word. However, in spite of the confusion, misconceptions, and perversions perpetrated in its name, love is still a magic word, and it seems to touch the deepest chord of the human heart.

In seeking what the diverse conceptions and different theories have in common, love is understood to be a tendency of some sort. Most authors think of it as a natural inclination or predisposition to move in a certain direction or react in a particular way, similar to the way the needle of a compass inclines toward the North Pole. Tendency in its general sense may take the forms of needs, desires, impulses, wants, or choices that can be physical or spiritual, innate or acquired, instinctive or deliberate, perverse or sublime, selfish or altruistic, emotional or intellectual. By saying that love is a tendency, which could be of different kinds, they mean to say that it is not a mental act or matter of thinking.

On the other hand, there are writers for whom love is instead a judgment about the nature and worth of the object, with elements like admiration, esteem, respect, or merit. Still, for others love must contain a valuational and emotional element, for it is a combination of both tendency and judgment, desire and thinking. According to them, feeling is part of seeing and seeing is part of feeling, the two somehow blending into each other; the lover then in his unique perception sees in the beloved what others do not see, or sees the same object differently.

The division between tendency and judgment is the most basic in the literature of love. From these two distinct spheres we can draw four characteristics common to all theories. First, love is an expression of interest; indifference is incompatible with love. Second, love always involves preference; to be loved is normally to be singled out. Third, love points toward action; it does not necessitate action, but there must be an inclination or readiness to act. Fourth, all authors speak of love as either good in itself or pointing toward some good. Many mention bad loves, illicit loves, low loves, and insane loves; but almost always the discussion of the love condemned takes place in the context of contrasting such love with love praised in its "higher forms." The capacity to love, or to love in a certain way, always is seen as a desirable or essential element in his notion of what life ought to be and how it ought to be lived. Although many will admit that love can be destructive, this kind of love has gone astray. When they mention "bad love," they conceive of it as a perverted form of good love. These four characteristics — that it implies interest, involves preference, inclines toward action, and is good or productive of good, form the nucleus of the idea of natural human love.[1]

But not every author agrees that all love is natural. According to some, mostly theologians, love is humanly impossible without the action and the grace of God, and it can only be explained and understood with reference to Him.

In every theory of supernatural love, although love is not entirely devoid of human participation, God is the focus, either as the lover, the beloved, or both. Creation is an act of love and an act of creating love; in creating us, God created our love by which we tend towards Him.

Our quest of God is God's very love in us, but the love of God in us is our finite participation in the infinite love wherewith God loves Himself. Borne on the current of divine love which flows through us and returns thence to its source, we can say with St. Augustine that to love God is to possess God.[2]

It is therefore the same thing to say that God moves human beings, that He causes their movement toward Himself, or that He creates in them the very love by which they love Him. The end or aim of human love is also its cause; a thing

that is made by God and for Him, by the mere fact that it acts, tends naturally to God by virtue of a law written in the substance of its very being.

Every mystic knows, or rather, experiences it:

God is love ... and out of love he gives existence and life to every Creature, supporting them all with his love. The color of the wall depends on the wall, and so the existence of creatures depends on the love of God. Separate the color from the wall and it would cease to be; so all creation would cease to exist if separated from the love that God is. God is love, so loving that whatever he can love he must love, whether he will or not.

There is no creature so vile that it can love what is evil; for what one loves must either be good or appear to be so.[3]

"Born of love, the whole universe is penetrated, moved, and vivified from within by love, which circulates through it like the life-giving blood through the body. There is therefore a circulation of love that starts from God and finds him again."[4] Divine beings, from nature spirits to angels, from archangels to gods, goddesses, and the Seven Elohim are the "arteries" and the "veins" which convey everywhere in manifestation the fire of love as the life-giving blood. This represents the cosmic crucifixion of the Logos, not however in suffering and death but in the supreme ecstasy of the act of offering completely itself to its creation.

Its self-giving love flowing in the four directions of infinite space form a cross.

Yes, the creative fire, or Holy Spirit, descends vertically to penetrate and impregnate the virgin matter, or Mother regarded as horizontal.[5] This is the act of the sacrificial love of Nature and motherhood that can truly say to the incarnating self, "you are bone of my bones and flesh of my flesh."[6]

What sublime images for contemplation! To think that we have the divine privilege to be the recipient of the limitless outpouring of such love and be filled with it just by asking and opening our hearts and minds as a cup or vessel.

Our misery lies in the fact that in our ignorance and confused desires we deceive ourselves as to the true object of our love and, therefore, are bound to suffer the consequences.

Whether natural or supernatural, the basic issue is that love implies a relation, someone who loves, or desires to love, and the other, the beloved; a subject and an object. We say, "I love you," or "I am in love," but who or what is the "I" that experiences this feeling called love?

They are certainly related, but I did not realize then, as I do now, that we cannot know what love is unless we understand who the individual "I" is. This is an important point and I'd like to elaborate on it. Love is a relational concept and the notions of self and other are pivotal and are based on the principle of polarity.

What love is follows from the nature of the human being. If one thinks that man is no more than an evolved animal then love is merely undifferentiated libidinal energy. Or if you hold the notion that every human being is destined to be born in a state of extreme loneliness and dire isolation, then love is the desire to escape from that miserable condition.

According to another conception I mentioned, not so narrow as those you referred to, love is the soul's contact with the divine realities contemplated before coming into physical embodiment. And it manifests through the encounter with someone who is the cause for recalling those realities.

615

Little attention has been given in the various commentaries to the scriptural passage where Jesus reminds his accusers of making himself God, "Is it not written in your Law, 'I said, you are gods'? "If those to whom the word of God came were called 'gods' — and the scripture cannot be annulled — can you say that the one whom the Father has sanctified and sent into the world is blaspheming because I said, 'I am God's Son'?"[7]

The truth is that you are life conscious of itself. I mean that the infinite Ground of being acknowledges, feels, and loves itself through you.

This is how each individual can say "I AM."
Therefore your nature is from God, and so it is love although its divine origin is forgotten.

The undying flame in my heart from the Father-Mother God. I recognize more and more that in my quest for truth and love, you were holding my hand and leading me on the right path. I was struggling with the love which I now recognize was selfish and possessive, and these lines come to mind:

> Love seeketh only Self to please,
> To bind another to its delight;
> Joys in another's loss of ease,
> And builds a Hell in Heavens despite.

as opposed to:

> Love seeketh not Itself to please,
> Nor for itself hath any care;
> But for another gives its ease,

And builds a Heaven in Hell's despair.[8]

People do not realize that whenever they try to possess, whether persons or things, they are being possessed. In reality, the possessor is the possessed because the desire to possess stifles the flame of love in the heart, whose natural tendency is to give of itself and expand.

The feeling of possessiveness goes against the flow of love and creates the very lack or absence of that which one tries to own. That form of perverted love, springing from personal deficiency, craving, and need can never find fulfillment by looking to the mirage and appearances of the external world. Therefore, the relentless hunger, the insatiable longing, the empty heart remained until you rescued me from my state of misery.
It may seem a paradox but love means to give and it is the real owner because you cannot give unless you have.

However, after you give it, you don't have it anymore.
That is what seems the absurd logic of the nature of love: the more you give, the more you have.

Because it is the source of all, it is you, the infinite giver.
The individual cannot exist without love, in fact love is more necessary than food; do you know why?

I can understand that a loveless existence is meaningless and barren, it is like a barnacle on life no matter how successful appears to be in the eyes of the world.
The physical self is made up, as I explained it to you, of the four basic elements which are the building blocks of all creation:

617

fire, water, air, earth. Therefore, it needs them in order to sustain itself.

We take in air through the breath, water and earth from our drink and food; and fire?
Fire is the fundamental and essential element because it interpenetrates the others and animates them with the infusion of life and motion.

Are you referring to the fire of love?
Yes, and now you understand why I said that people need love more than the food they eat. In fact, with enough love the individual can precipitate or materialize not only food, but whatever they desire.

As Jesus did when He multiplied the loaves and fishes.
The universal light-energy is everywhere present to be acted upon by the thought and feeling.

We live, move, and have our beings in it like a fish in the ocean.
Yes, it is a crude illustration but it is fitting because it is drawn, by magnetic attraction, into the thought form of the individual and by the feeling it coalesces and condenses into a physical manifestation. And it can be a thing of beauty like a flower if created by love, or something hideous and harmful like many animal creatures if generated by hate. Let me remind you that through the power of its faculties the individual produces definite effects on the planes of manifestation, including the animal kingdom.

How true it is! "The separative and maleficent thoughts of man are largely responsible for the savage nature of wild beasts, and the destructive quality of some of nature's processes, including certain phenomena, such as plague and famine."[9]

I must say that mankind is "totally" responsible for everything that is not the purity and perfection of the beginning of creation.

Creativity is a simple process, and that is how we bless life and ourselves or create distress and evil.

Let it be engraved in your mind that love is a flame, and it is self-creative. You know by the nature of the Holy Spirit and from the reading of the literature of the mystics that they all refer to love as fire or light. And since I have kindled it in your heart, and it is part of Myself, I can never extinguish it.

Another of your impossible acts.

But if you want to create the good which life contains you must be attuned to the feeling of love which is capable of responding only to the dimension of immortality. Your love to Me is of the same nature as My love to you; it is the very feeling that unites us, the feeling of the flame from My heart to yours. Try to realize that your feeling of love comes from the flame in your heart which is an extension from Mine.

Then love is a feeling? But feelings change, they are unstable and impermanent.

That which changes is not the feeling of love which is innate in your life as your heartbeat but its object, depending on the individual's choice and tendencies. Love is not a single feeling among other single feelings. One kind of emotional feeling is only a fragmentary part in the entire scale of the consciousness of life. In the feeling of love, the totality of life, which "I AM," is present and experienced as a duplicate of itself. In reality there is nothing else but love, and it is your purpose and aim for existing. In your experience of love the nature of life becomes manifest. It is the moving power of all that is. I remind you of the words in one of your books: "All else is not, because in the same measure in which things partake of being, they partake of love. All that is not love, *is not.* All that which is, has its being and its action in love."[10]

It is the feeling which is generated by the fire of the divine polarity.
Yes, all life emanating from Me is essentially the vibratory levels of the energy which is called "Love." "I AM" its source by My self-acknowledgment and self-love. Do you not think that I love Myself? And would I not love My creation so that other parts of Myself may enjoy its beauty? Therefore, the individual should feel itself through the flame which " I AM" and which is in everyone's heart. I did not make clear enough that the attracting and unifying power of love is the feeling. And you are what you feel yourself through.

You also said that true knowledge is to be one with the known and only the feeling of love can do it. And by it we co-exist and move in dynamic interrelation according to the Law of polarity.
Bravo! The fire of love is the self-perpetuating reality, giving unconditionally and creating out of itself what is transcendentally beautiful and perfect.

That is the love generated by the interplay between the primordial poles, spirit-matter or Father-Mother God, and from them, you, as my personal God Self, are a direct projection.

And you are My extension on Earth. The individual may refuse to accept it and not let it through, but love can never change its Law. Mankind does not want to solve their problems by the power of love and yet I could fill their being and world in no time with that which is eternal happiness if they would give me the opening. As I try to convey to you in various ways, the actual life flowing out from My Being is the energy of My love pervading all that is, manifesting at different vibratory levels, from the most resplendent to the densest.

It reminds me of the Biblical phrase, "God is love, and those who abide in love abide in God, and God abides in them."[11]

This explanation renders intelligible the application and use of the same word to so many discrete kinds of love, apparently not only diverse, but conflicting. It reveals the common ground of all forms of love making it one. A mystic of our time wrote:

> Things are related to one another, one is contained in another and that other in others still, so that the whole universe is one immense being. The whole of nature touches and intertwines. The whole of nature embraces. The wind brushing me, the sun kissing me, the air that I breathe, the fish swimming in the water, the far-off star and I who look up at it are all in contact. What we call the empty space between the stars is made of the same matter as the stars, except that it is thinner and more rarefied. The stars are merely a denser concentration of this

621

interstellar matter, and the whole universe is like one big star. We all share in this universe through one and the same rhythm, the rhythm of universal gravity, which is the force binding chaotic matter, joining molecules, bringing particles of matter together at any particular point in the universe, causing the stars to be stars. This is the rhythm of love.[12]

And that is the rhythm of your heartbeat in unison with Mine.

The answers to the question "what is love?" have ranged from the sacred to the profane, from the cosmic to the personal, from the scientific to the romantic, from the complex to the simple. Now I begin to understand in the feeling, not merely the intellect, that love is not an abstract idea or an intangible "something" as I believed but "someone" dwelling within and above us.

Love is a presence, your Presence. It is the feeling that we belong to someone and that someone belongs to us.

Love is a feeling that we are two but the two are one.

Love is knowing that we are loved first and feeling the presence of the other always loving us and smiling at us.

Love is wanting to be the divine other and knowing that we are the divine other, and that the divine other wants to be us and that it is us.

You are the only Source of love because love, absolutely speaking, is the nature of your Being. Therefore you always love us first. The most, and indeed the least, we can do is to allow that love to flow back to you and experience what love really is — like St. Catherine of Genoa, who wrote, "Sometimes I do not see or feel myself to have either

soul, body, heart, will or taste, or any other thing except Pure Love."[13]

Our love for whatever attracts and pleases us is, in reality, a love of God unaware of itself, and that is why nothing can ever fulfill us or content us. St. Teresa of Avila stated, "Only God suffices."

If you receive sincerely My love without self-interest you can drink it without any limit. It is like a cup that you fill at the fountain. If you take it out of the fountain to drink, it is soon empty. But if you hold your cup in the fountain while you drink, it will not become empty: indeed, it will always be full.

Everyone knows intuitively that he should love only that which exists eternally, or is bound to taste the bitterness of failure. Your existence is necessary for no other reason than because you are the only Being whose love can never die, and we are absolutely certain that you love us eternally and that we can love you forever.

That tiny flame in your heart can be fanned into a cosmic fire by your call, devotion, and loving attention to Me. This is the quickest way to your purification and ascension. All other practices are secondary, even useless, unless they help you to increase and expand your capacity to love.

Whenever you love something in this world, use it as a ladder, or a stepping stone, by sending that same feeling to Me. You can use the most common thing like, for instance, the food you eat, do you not love the food you eat when you are hungry? Or the warmth from a radiator when you are cold? Make it a ritual, send that feeling of love and gratitude to Me and I will return it amplified without limit with the fire of My love.

Fill me with it for nothing else can quench my thirst for happiness, that I may say:

> My bounty is as boundless as the sea,
> My love as deep; the more I give to Thee,
> The more I have, for both are infinite.[14]

Let me again make it clear that when I refer to love as fire I am not speaking figuratively. Fire is the highest vibration in the universe, the all-pervading inner essence of life itself, the causeless cause by which everything was created and sustained and in which all forms inhere. My very body is made of white fire, and I am not a figure of speech, either.

I am so bright that I would have to soften the radiance of My being if I were to appear visibly and tangibly to you.

You said that there are four lower bodies and three higher in the septenary scale of manifestation; can you explain the nature of the other two higher bodies beside yours?
What is called the higher mental body is also a white fire body, like Mine, that I use on the fifth plane as the channel through which My divine knowledge can reach you. It is the source of divine ideas, inspirations, and discernment.

How is it different from the mind?
The lower mentality gathers its knowledge from without through the senses and the intellect. The higher mental body is the teacher from within, referred to as intuition, insight, or the direct apprehension of truth.

I can understand the difference, also the medieval philoso-phers make a distinction between the active and passive in-tellect which sound similar to it.

The third body is called the causal body where are contained and preserved the recordings and the momentums of all the Good of your life-stream, carrying the result of all the benefi-cent thoughts, feelings, actions, and of every effort to expand your consciousness and perfect yourself throughout your many lives. All that energy, which is light, is gathered there at the end of each embodiment.

It is called the causal body because it is the receptacle and the storehouse of all constructive experiences. In it there are the causes , hence its name "causal," which manifest them-selves on the physical plane as the higher qualities of the indi-vidual which are different from one another according to the use or misuse, in their past lives, of their free will. It is referred to in Scripture by Jesus' words, "Do not store up for yourselves treasures on earth where thieves break in and steal; but store up for yourselves treasures in heaven ... For where your treas-ure is, there your heart will be also."[15] The causal body sur-rounds Me like a sphere of light, an aura of rainbow colors. It is truly your treasure by the wise investment of your energy in the use and multiplication of your talents. Because every thought, feeling, and word qualified with love ascend into it as a mo-mentum of your attainment and mastery. We partake of its glory for through it I can radiate, as a sun, My love to the rest of the universe in My creative activity at the cosmic level.

You are also the sun of my life.

Your body of causative Good is the determining factor of your life stream because, when it is filled with the light of love which you have given to Me and to others in your service to life, it will be like a powerful magnet in the process to become one with your God Self. It is your final victory over this world and the attainment of the ascension.

Sometimes, when I listen attentively to you and feel your love for me, I experience something like a pull upward.
Unfortunately human beings turn the flow of My energy downward through anger, resentment, and the perversion of sex creating havoc in their lives. What you feel is the magnetic power of My love because its natural tendency is always toward a higher level of the divine Reality.

This is evident just by looking at the physical fire, rushing up to return home.
It is much more evident in the experience of its raising force in your feeling when you return to Me the love which I am pouring into your being continuously; moreover, it connects you with its Source which is infinite and ever-expanding.

It is not like human love which has beginning and end, and it may be polluted and perverted.
The nature of divine love is a transforming, expanding, raising activity from the lesser to the greater, and it goes on infinitely into more glorious freedom, happiness, beauty, and perfection. It is the eternal way of life which "I AM."

That which draws the energy into the finite and into limitation is the gravitational force and the downward pull of the human consciousness. Therefore, it is really much easier to rise than to descend because the magnetic power of My love is irresistible to one who turns to it.

And if the members of the scientific community want to know what magnetism is, they should turn their attention to the flame of love within their hearts; this is the only way to know the truth about it because they will become it.

And do not forget the power of your attention, which is also part of the Law of Magnetic Attraction.

In reality we are like the two poles of a magnet! Why then it seems so hard to disconnect from negative conditions when we know they are wrong?
Because through habit of centuries you have accepted the belief that what you experience as limitations is the natural condition of this world, and therefore you are tied to it. But, My loved one, you can always, at any moment, turn your attention away from your problem and acknowledge, recognize, and accept My Presence that wants you to be free.

Is it not easier to think of someone who loves you, as I do, than of that which causes you unhappiness? If the personal self wants to have its own way when it is wrong, and most of the time it is, ask for My purifying Fire and we will educate it because nothing can oppose My love. Give Me your attention, you will feel connected with Me, we will never again be separated and you become the master of your world.

From now on this will be my all-consuming desire. You have revealed to me that I can be free from the wheel of Karma and re-embodiment, free from all limitations of the centuries, and live forever in my body of light in the supreme ecstasy of divine love as the immortal being which I AM.

I realize that this is the only real purpose of my long and strenuous journey on this earth. I see now that all the agony, the distress, and the struggle I went through are

nothing compared to the glory and the magnificence of my attainment of the ascension.

But how can I increase my divine inheritance in the causal body?

You must always be on the positive side of life, anchored in the I AM consciousness, if you are to achieve mastery over yourself and what surrounds you: never yield to the negative forces, do not give them power over you and do not be afraid of them because they rule by fear and are powerless before those who do not fear them.

I realize that only love can make us master: "Love conquers all: let us too give in to Love," stated the Latin poet Virgil.[16] I must keep calling and reaching up for the sacred fire of your love.

The feeling of love is always flowing from Myself into your heart, radiating with every pulsation a wave of light, and you can intensify and expand it by your attention to Me and your desire and call for it. Always remember that all is Law and all is Love which owns all and is the giver of all. Therefore you can make the demand in love, for whatever you require, whether protection, health, illumination, strength, and sustenance or the means of obtaining it, including money. Love, by its magnetic attraction, will bring them to you.

Even money!?

Why not? Do you not need it? Of course, if you waste it, you will be responsible. Keep in mind that love is light-energy and can be condensed into a substance as visible and tangible as dense matter. You do not yet realize that what you call "inanimate" things which you use all the time are, in reality, the condensation and manifestation of the Fire of My life and the gift of love to mankind.

I should never forget that fundamental idea which you told me: all energy is God's energy.
If people were aware of it, what a transformation it would bring to their lives! The floodgates of My infinite abundance would be thrown wide open because it would arouse in them the feeling of gratitude and reverence for life. Do you know that the main cause of poverty is ingratitude, which is a form of selfishness?

And you said that selfishness is the root of all evil.
Remember that love means to give, and I am the Source of all the good, in whatever form, visible or invisible, that comes to you. Without Me you can do nothing, not even think a thought or lift a finger; but the Law of Life, which is Love, requires that you first give some of your energy to initiate the circuit that in the return current will bring to you whatever you desire.

To give is to receive, but how may I know that I have fulfilled the requirement of the Law in order to receive your answer?
To explain very plainly how the Law operates, I will again don the garb of the mathematician. You must give one-third of your love-energy in your call to Me, and I will provide two-thirds. Make your request earnestly and sincerely, expecting and visualizing the fulfillment of your desire, and it will be done as surely as the universe exists.

Beware, however, of negative feelings like doubt, fear, depression, and resentment, which can delay or prevent the manifestation because they are a repellent instead of an attract-ing force and disrupt the flow of the current of life.

It is the action of the Law of the circuit or circle.
Yes, the energy vibration swings out and comes back to its starting point.

We know that emotions may cause congestion, which is disastrous to our health.
If you do not live in accord with the Law of Life, you go against it: there is no middle ground. Therefore, do not allow negative attitudes to interfere with the flow of My light-energy into and through your body.

How can I prevent it from happening?
By the recognition of My Presence; notice the word "Presence," knowing and especially feeling that "I AM" always with you. Be as aware of Me as you are of your hands; you use them all the time, do you not? Like them, I AM also always at your service; love loves to serve. But I can only give you what you can take –

> *Dio non alberga en core stretto,*
> *tant'è grande quant' hai affetto.*

> God does not lodge in a narrow heart,
> it is as great as thy love.[17]

You can offer Me your heart as a cup, small or large as you choose, and I will fill it accordingly. I told you that love cannot be forced, and I respect your free will.

That has been my problem: sometimes — rather often, actually – I'd prefer not to have free will because I run into troubles.

Remember that you are connected to the outer world through one pole, and the other pole lies open to the infinite and is the Source of the highest good in the universe. But when I give you My very life, and My limitless gifts, I must find the door of your consciousness open to Me. If people think or believe that I do not love them enough and complain that life will not give them what is good or what they need, it cannot be done.

"In the book of Hidden Things it is written," says Meister Eckhart,

> "I stand at the door and knock and wait." ...Thou needst not seek Him here or there: He is no farther off than the door of the heart. There He stands and waits and waits until He finds thee ready to open and let Him in. Thou needst not call Him from a distance; to wait until thou openst is harder for Him than for thee. He needs thee a thousand times more than thou canst need Him. *Thy opening and His entering are but one moment.*[18]

If I make myself receptive to love, I would become loving and lovable.

Do you not remember the proverb. "Love begets love"?[19]

The same goes for peace, health, protection, and prosperity: call for them in My name, "I AM," and you will find them coming into your being and world abundantly.

Please recognize My willingness to give because "I AM" infinite and My nature is the *summum bonum,* the greatest good one can possibly desire.

I understand that its attainment is not a one-sided aspiration but the fulfillment of a mutual desire; for no lover ever seeks union with his divine beloved but his beloved is also seeking union with him. When your love arises in My heart, it is you who feel love for me. I must acknowledge that I AM what I want to be and to have.

That is the way to keep the door open on your side; it is always open on My side.

I found an interesting explanation in the writings of Dame Julian:

> For as the body is clad in cloth, and the flesh in the skin, and the bones in the flesh, and the heart in the whole, so are we, soul and body, clad in the Goodness of God and enclosed. Yea, and more homely: for all these may waste and wear away, but the Goodness of God is ever whole.[20]

In your call to Me you are using a cosmic Law that has always existed, making it work for you instead of acting against you. The call is its own answer; cause and effect are two poles of the circuit of love. You are co-creator with Me.

I see the truth in the statement,

> "God can as little do without us, as we without Him," the wonder of wonders, that most real yet most mysterious of all individual experiences, the union of human and divine, in the flame in my heart which is "great enough to be God, small enough to be me."[21]

The Law must work in compliance with your demand. If all that "I AM" and have were not already yours at the inner level as the invisible treasure-house of life, it would be impossible for you even to have any desire for it.

Your thought and feeling of I AM molds the universal light-substance, present everywhere, and brings into manifestation whatever you hold embodied in your consciousness. When you say, "I am not," or "I have not," you deny the life, light, and love I am constantly pouring into you with every breath and heartbeat.

Since the Infinite is conscious of itself through you, the more your consciousness can embrace and embosom, the more it can pour into and express through you.

Someone said that at the heart of the universe is beatitude; and it is interesting that the Triune God in Hinduism is Being, Consciousness, Bliss. I recall the words of Dame Gertrude More:

> For what can be a comfort while I live separated from Thee, but only to remember that my God, that is more mine than I am my own, is absolutely and infinitely happy? For that soul that hath set her whole love and desire on thee, can never find any true satisfaction, but only in thee.[22]

The feeling of love contained in My Name is always giving of itself in its creative activity ever-expanding the beauty and harmony of the universe.

"By the word of the Lord the heavens were made, and all their host by the breath of his mouth. He gathered the wa-

ters of the seas as in a bottle; ... he spoke, and [the earth] came to be; he commanded, and it stood firm." "... He draws up the drops of water; he distills his mist in rain, which the skies pour down ... Can anyone understand the spreading of the clouds, the thundering of the pavilion?...to the snow he says 'Fall on the earth' ... From its chamber comes the whirlwind and cold from the north ... or who has begotten the drops of dew?"[23]

Open your eyes and Nature will reveal it to you. Is not the sun willing to shine and send out its rays? See the rapturous flight of the birds, the trusting opening of the buds, the color and fragrance of the flowers, the solemn rhythms of the sea, the silent majesty of the mountains. And only love is the cause of the music of the spheres that, I assure you, is very real and were you to hear it you could not stay in your body.

I can believe it, and it seems that the Chaldeans were the first to make reference to heavenly bodies joining in a cosmic chant as they majestically moved across the sky. In the Bible when God admonished Job he said, "Where were you when I laid the foundation of the earth...its cornerstone when the morning stars sang together and all the heavenly beings shouted for joy?" Also Shakespeare mentions it more than once:

"... look how the floor of heaven
Is thick inlaid with patens of bright gold,
There's not the smallest orb which thou behold'st
But in his motion like an angel sings,
Still quiring to the young-ey'd cherubins;
Such harmony is in immortal souls,
But whilst this muddy vesture of decay

Doth grossly close it in, we cannot hear it."[24]

Turn inwardly and listen to the song of love coming from the flame in your heart and contemplate the light of My Presence radiating through your outer form of clay. Do not let your negative thoughts and emotions interfere with it to create a shadow covering over its radiance and eclipse its light. A long time ago I revealed to mankind My name, "I AM," whose sound is an echo of the rhythm of the heartbeat in unison with the universal harmony.

In the Bible we read that when Moses was given the mission to bring his people out of Egypt he said to God: "If I come to the Israelites and say to them, 'The God of your ancestors has sent me to you', and they ask me, 'What is his name?' what shall I say to them?" God said to Moses, "I AM WHO I AM." He said further, "Thus you shall say to the Israelites, 'I AM has sent me to you' ... This is My name forever."[25]
The universe exists by My own self-pronouncement, the acknowledgement of My own Being through the individual. All life everywhere is "I AM," the all-embracing consciousness of life for "I AM" all there is, seen and unseen. "I AM" is the word of love and will give you the experience of the divine reality. If you suffer from bondage and confinement you will experience freedom and infinite expansion. If the individual is struggling in the darkness of fear and doubt, he will be enfolded by boundless light. Those who are restless and tormented by worry and anxiety, will enjoy peace and a sense of absolute security. If one is groaning under the weight of transitoriness and the thought of death, he will feel his immortality.

The All-pervading Self, Who bindeth all,

Knits them together, bides in every heart.[26]
"I am the Infinite;
What thou art that same am I"
Thou art all This, I am all This.[27]

I begin to realize what the mystics mean when they say that God is nearer to us than we are to ourselves. How meaningful are now the words I used to read without understanding them: "Thou wert I, but dark was my heart, I knew not the secret transcendent," says Te´wekkul Be´g, a Moslem mystic of the seventeenth century.

And St. Catherine of Genoa, "My *me* is God, nor do I know my selfhood save in Him." She also says, "my Being is God, not by simple participation, but by a true transformation of my Being." Another contemplative, Gerlac Peterson writes:

> Thou givest me Thy whole self to be mine whole and undivided, if at least I shall be Thine whole and undivided. And when I shall be thus all Thine, even as from everlasting Thou hast loved Thyself, so from everlasting Thou hast loved me: for this means nothing more than that Thou enjoyest Thyself in me, and that I by Thy grace enjoy Thee in myself, and myself in Thee. And when in Thee I shall love myself, nothing else but Thee do I love, because Thou art in me and I in Thee, glued together as one and the selfsame thing, which henceforth and forever cannot be divided.

And, finally, Jalalu'd Din tells us, like the writer of the *Song of Songs*, the secret of "his union" in which "heart speaks to heart."

With Thy Sweet Soul, this soul of mine
      Hath mixed as Water doth with Wine.
Who can the Wine and Water part,
      Or me and Thee when we combine?
Thou art become my greater self;
      Small bounds no more can me confine,
Thou hast my being taken on,
      And shall not I now take on Thine?
Me Thou for ever hast affirmed,
      That I may ever know Thee mine.
Thy Love has pierced me through and through,
      Its thrill with Bone and Nerve entwine.
I rest a Flute laid on Thy lips;
      A lute, I on Thy breast recline,
Breathe deep in me that I may sigh;
      Yet strike my strings, and tears shall shine.[28]

Try to remember that every breath you breathe is the release of a wave of love from My heart to yours, and My presence in you is your true Self, I AM.

1 Robert G. Hazo. *The Idea of Love.* (NY: Frederick A. Praeger Publishers, Institute for Philosophical Research, 1967), pp. 40-41.

2 Etienne Gilson. *The Spirit of Mediaeval Philosophy*, transl. A.H.C. Doucner. (Chicago:, University of Notre Dame Press, 1991), p. 276.

3 Meister Eckhart, translation by Raymond B. Blakney, op. cit., p. 244.

4 Gilson, p. 276.

5 Cfr. Hodson, p. 70.

6 Genesis 2:23.

7 John 10:35-36.

8 William Blake, "The Clod & the Pebble," *Songs of Experience.*

9 *Esoteric Healing*, p. 70.

10 Ernesto Cardenal. *Love.* (NY: Crossroad, 1981), p. 9.

11 I John 4:16.

12 Cardenal, p. 20.

13 Quoted in Underhill, p. 247.

14 Shakespeare, *Romeo and Juliet*, Act II, Scene 2, Lines 132-35.

15 Matthew 6:29-21; Luke 12:34.

16 *Eclogues* No. 10, Line 60.

17 Quoted in Evelyn Underhill, *Mysticism: A Study in the Nature and Development of Man's Spiritual Consciousness*, (NY: E.P. Dutton Co., 1961), p. 207.

18 Quoted in Underhill, p. 133.

19 Also cited by poet Theodore Roethke, who added "This torment is my joy" after it.

20 Julian of Norwich, "Revelations of Divine Love," in *Mysticism*, p. 35.

21 Quoted in Underhill, p. 100.

22 Quoted in Underhill, p. 88.

23 Psalms 33:5-7; Job 38:6, 9; Job 28:6-7.

[24] Shakespeare, *The Merchant of Venice*, Act V, Scene 1; *Pericles*, Act V, Scene 1, Lines 58-65; *Pericles*, Act V, Scene 1, Line 231.

[25] Exodus 3:13.

[26] Yoga Vasishtha, Das, p. 111.

[27] Upanishads, Das, p. 109.

[28] Underhill, pp. 99, 127, 129, 428, 426.

CHAPTER 24

A Glimpse of the Kabbalah

The point where philosophy ends is the point at which the wisdom of the Kabbalah begins.
Rabbi Nachman of Breslov

Never forget that you are a traveler in transit.
Edmond Jabes

There is a renewed interest in the Kabbalah, and the male-female polarity is one of its fundamental principles. Would you care to explain it to me?
I will be glad to because the Kabalistic teachings relate to some of the topics we have discussed.

Kabbalah literally means, "from mouth to ear," "tradition," and, "to receive," with reference to the five books of the Torah received by Moses from God.[1]

It is evident from the authority which the prophets claim for the words they utter that the oracles they communicated were not their thoughts; their words were revelations they received. According to the Kabbalists, symbolic mysticism is the true interpretation of the Scriptures:

> Woe to the man who sees nothing but simple stories and ordinary words in the Law! For were this so, we could even nowadays frame a law which would deserve higher praise. But it is not so; every word of the Law holds an exalted meaning and a sublime mystery.[2]

The literal reading of the Scriptures is compared to the clothing of the person, and the simple-minded do not know the soul that the vestment covers, and least of all, the spirit "which breathe in the Law."[3]

The secret is the foundation, says the Zohar, one of the basic texts of the Kabbalah, and the attitude of the initiate is "hearing the unheard/seeing the invisible/feeling the intangible."[4] The higher truth can only be transmitted esoterically, through a secret, encoded language, and not through intellectual concepts.

The Kabbalists teach that God built into the Hebrew language a sort of celestial code, whereby each letter communicates three kinds of meanings. The first is the numerical value, the second is its sound, and the third is its shape; and all three are necessary to decipher the code in which the Bible is written.

I heard this anecdote: "Rabbi Simeon began to weep, saying, 'Woe to me if I reveal these mysteries and woe to me if I do not reveal them'."[5]
By their veiled style they do not seek to make their teachings obscure or complicated, but to render them accessible only to those who are ready for it, so that they will not be misused.

It is written that, "Infinity must be both said and unsaid ... Understanding the Kabbalah is firstly an illumination or an intuition that transcends the signs by virtue of which thought is transmitted."[6]
There is the need to find a language "whose rhythm most closely expresses the fundamental vibrations of life ... The Kabbalist must also be a poet; you should insert in your writing a poem called, "May God Magnify My Soul," written by one of the last great Kabbalists, Rabbi Abraham Itshaq Kook:

To the open sea, to the open sea,
May God magnify my soul ...
That it may never be enclosed in a prison,
Neither material nor spiritual.
My soul is like a ship,
Under the expanse of the heavens.
The walls of my heart cannot contain it ...
It is above everything that one can name,
Above all pleasure,
Everything that is pleasant and beautiful,
It transcends that which is exalted.
O my God, may your help come to me in my pain.[7]

This is undoubtedly why the Torah is also called *shira*, "song" or "poetry."[8]

It is true that also other sacred writings, from the Bhagavad Gita to the Koran are closer to poetry than intellectual expositions. The treasury of the Kabbalah is known as "the wisdom which is hidden;" but it is also an art, the art of the heart and of knowing how to love.

What is necessary is the harmony and balance between the love of wisdom and the wisdom of love. This is the path of light. The key to the Kabbalah is always the light, offered with a wonderful promise:

If you desire, you can.
Son of man, look!
Contemplate the light of the Presence that resides in all existence!
Contemplate the joyful life force of the worlds above!

See how it descends and impregnates every particle of life
that you perceive with your eyes of the flesh and your eyes of the spirit.
Contemplate the marvels of Creation and the Source of every living thing
which is the rhythm by which every creature lives.
Learn to know yourself.
Learn to know the world, your world.
Discover the logic in your heart and the feelings in your reason!
Feel the vibrations of the Source of Life which is in your very depths
and above you and all around you.
The love which burns in you, let it raise its powerful root,
extend it to the whole soul and all the worlds.
Look at the lights
Look into the lights
Ascend and ascend for you possess a powerful force.
You have the wings of the wind, the noble wings of the eagle
Do not deny them lest they deny you.
Seek them and they will find you immediately.[9]

To understand the Kabbalah you must remember that it centers on the metaphysics of light.

Consider the titles of its basic texts: *Book of Clarity, Book of Splendor, Gates of Light, Light of the Eyes, Light of Sanctity,* to name only a few.[10]

Light is the first sign, the first word of creation. And God said, "Let there be light, and there was light."[11] It is the first and highest reality of the universe, the first path to the divine.

In the very beginning of creation, the word "light" is mentioned five times, and this light is self-luminous because the sun had not yet been formed. It is referred to by many names:

- infinite light
- divine desire
- cosmic vitality or current
- energy from above
- infinite influx
- desire to give
- positive desire

It is the supernal or primal light familiar to the mystics. In the Apocalypse of Abraham, written toward the end of the first century, Abraham ascends to Heaven and he sings a song of praise:

> Thou art He whom my soul hath loved [he cries to God], eternal Protector, shining like fire ... Thou, O Light, shinest before the light of the morning upon Thy creatures. And in Thy heavenly dwelling-places there is no need of any other light than that of the unspeakable splendor from the light of Thy countenance."[12]

A Kabbalist is a person who receives the light of infinity into himself and who feels light as his very life, like a stream of energy that flows through him and enables him to act. "Light, vibration, and energy are the key words and have a special place in the Hebrew alphabet: the letters become particles of tremendous luminous force by which it is possible to transform the world and even re-create it."[13]

In order to understand this concept you must remember that for the Kabbalists divine language is the substance of reality. The Book of Creation, referring to the Hebrew alphabet says, "The twenty-two letters, he has traced them, carved them, multiplied them, weighed, and permutated them, he has shaped from them all creatures and everything that has been created ... All of them move in a circle ... All the words emerge under a single name."[14]

The creative power of speech is the foundation of all there is; the universe is created and sustained by thought which becomes the manifestation of the Word. God, from the silent, non-verbalized state, becomes the Logos, I AM, invents the language in order to express Itself, and Its words become things.

I am reminded of two passages in the Scripture, "By the word of the Lord the heavens were made, and all their hosts by the breath of his mouth."[15] Also, "Is not my word like fire, says the Lord, and like a hammer that break a rock in pieces?"[16] I have a question: What is the difference between word and thought?

Their essence is the same; seen under one aspect this essence appears as thought and under another as the word, which means that, for the process of the human mind, they are inseparable. It is also said in the Zohar, the most authoritative text of the Kabbalah, that the Word assumed the form of the alphabetical signs, presumably because it is in this form that thought passes into written expression.[17]

Hebrew has no separate numbers, only letters, and every letter has a numerical value; moreover, each letter has two functions: to combine with others to form words and to assign numerical value.

The Hebrew word for "light" has the same numerical value, 207, as the expression of, "infinity"; and the Masters have remarked that 207 is also the numerical value of *raz*, "mystery." Therefore, there is a cosmic relationship between light, infinity, and mystery.

I am sure you are aware of the importance of numbers in the Scriptures, like seven, forty, twelve.

Yes, for instance, the twelve tribes of Israel, the twelve disciples who may correspond to the twelve signs of the Zodiac, and the twelve baskets.
And do you know why 13 is considered a lucky number? Because it has the numerical value of the word love.

I can understand that the world is created by the sacred letters, or archetypes, of which what we see on Earth is a reflection, but how did they come into manifestation?
They emanated from one another, and it is of the utmost significance that the first letter to be chosen was Beth (or Bet), not because it is the initial of the word Bara, which means "to create," nor of Bareshith, which signifies "in the beginning," but because it is the first letter of Barach (or Barakha) meaning "to bless."

This clearly explains, according to the Kabbalists, that fundamentally the universe is a work of supreme perfection, wisdom and goodness , and that no thing is absolutely wrong, evil, or condemned forever. Also, Beth is the second letter of the Hebrew alphabet which represents the figure 2 expressing both the chasm and the bridge, the wound and the benediction of the tension or dynamic relationship between God and man.[18]

Therefore, the cause and the instrument of creation is the divine power to bless all existence. "He who is mysterious and unknown ... unfolds Himself and passes continually from the unknown into the range of apprehension in the Voice of Blessing ... God said, "Let there be light," and it is affirmed that all celestial legions and powers emanate therefrom. When first manifested, its brilliance filled the world from end to end."[19]

Every form is created by the letters which are an image of the Word and the crown of the Tetragrammaton, the Sacred Name of four letters that are the molds of the work of formation, Yod, He, Vaw, He (YHVH), the synthesis of all worlds above and below which represents the Mystery of Faith.

What is that mystery? Perhaps I should not ask this question.
It is the hidden doctrine that there is male and female above, as there is male and female below.[20]

An important statement in the secret teaching is, "As above so below, as below so above," and in the Kabbalah it is said that the world below is a mirror, or it should be, of that which is above.
"By means of the Mystery of Faith He created the worlds. Now, in another place it is asked: What worlds? The answer according to the Zohar, is matrimonial unions. These are the worlds which God does not cease from creating. It follows that creation, as the story is told, is a veil of the sex mystery; it follows also that something is understood of which physical union is the shadow as it is known here: the intimations concern union

as the result of a law, which is literal on the plane of expression and mystical on a higher plane.

Another Key is given in these words: The union of the male and female principle engendered the world – as indeed it was impossible that it should do otherwise within the measures of Zoharic symbolism. So also in the emanation of the letters, Aleph and Beth are postulated, from which two come forth the rest of the alphabet, and hence it is said that these two are male and female. ... "Which letters are male and which are female we are not told."[21]

Because it was not possible for the world to subsist without the Law, He created it to rule and sustain all things above and below. "But because of the Law, in which the possibility of transgression is implied, He created also repentance as a path of refuge in Himself, of return at need to Him."[22]

Since the word Bereshith means blessing and goodness, it signifies also Divine Love, that Love of man for God, the correspondence of which is God's perfect Love for man. This Love of the Divine in man is not grounded on the self-questing hope of personal benefit, but in something constant in affliction and in joy, rooted in the perfection of God ... in the union between Divine Creator and the creature divinely fashioned by the hands of Him.[23]

The author I am quoting adds this interesting note based on the Zohar with reference to the Song of Solomon, "Let him kiss me with the kisses of his mouth;"[24] and these words are held to express the perfect and eternal joy which all worlds shall experience in their union with the Supreme Spirit. "The condition of this union is said to be the prayer of man."[25]

Of fundamental importance in the Kabbalah is the function of prayer which "rises to the upper spheres and is echoed by the angels."[26]

Prayer is the most perfect expression to enter into intimate relationship with the Source of light. According to the Kabbalah, the Creator Himself is also "praying from the other side of the universe."[27]

There is a mysterious formula, "God needs humans,"[28] intended to focus on the reciprocal desire for union: In order to generate and maintain His love, He must first acknowledge Himself and love Himself, but He can only do it in an intimate relation with His individualities, which every human being is.

The creation of the world is the process of His individualization from the state of undifferentiated oneness to a loving relationship with His people. Coming from God, they depend on Him, desire to imitate Him, and yearn to return to Him. To that end, prayer should not be a mere recitation of words; it must come from the heart. In praying, man does not merely ask; he shows that he is open to someone other than himself, that his person is always and already constituted "for the other." It is prayer that attaches man to Shekhina, and as the Holy One is united constantly to her, it follows that by prayer man is attached to the Holy One. All the angels open their wings to receive the Shekhina by prayer, and those on earth who wish their prayers to reach heaven should unite themselves with the Shekhina.[29]

Since she is the Divine Mother, the question arises naturally whether she occupies in Kabbalism the same position of intercession or mediatrix which is ascribed to the Blessed Virgin or Mother Mary by the devotion of the Catholic Church.

There are many resemblances in their rich and varied religious tradition. Also to the Shekhina can be referred the old Christian statement, *"De Maria numquam satis,"* ("about Mary there is never enough.")

This is testified by the extraordinary abundance of the names, forms of praise, rituals, prayers said and prayers answered.

All pointing to the undeniable truth and reality of the mother expression of God, rooted in the heart of every human being and in the ground of the universe.

Yes, the Shekhina in her innumerable designations is always feminine. She is called the Mirror of Jehovah; she is the Daughter of the King; she is now the Betrothed, the Bride and the Mother and again she is sister in relation to the world of man at large. There is a sense also in which she is or becomes the Mother of man. In respect of the manifest universe, she is the architect of worlds, acting in virtue of the Word uttered by God in creation ... Considered in her Divine Womanhood, in the world of transcendence, she is the Beloved who ascends towards the Heavenly Spouse, and she is Matrona who unites with the King, for the perfection of the Divine Male is in the Divine Female ... It is she who enables the Name (YHVH) to be expressed on earth, or God to be realized in the heart.[30]

On being asked why people pray without having their prayers answered, a Rabbi once said that it is because they do not know how to use the explicit Name.

But I thought that the name of God should not be pronounced because it is too sacred.

You are right: TETRAGRAMMATON, the so-called ineffable or unpronounceable Name, is the Name of Four Letters,

YHWH = YAHWEH or YAHAWEH, the Jehovah of our incorrect rendering, which Hebrew scholarship has characterized as philogically impossible, that is to say, inexpressible, because the vowels belonging to it are now unknown.

God is made to say in the Zohar: My Name is written YHVH but is read Adonai. Also, the word Elohim is substituted for the lost vowels.[31]

The proclamation of the Holy Name constitutes the apex and the perfection of prayer. That is why I explained to you the necessity of using My Name, which is more than a name, it is Who I AM.

I remember this anecdote: Seeing that the Rabbi went to the synagogue long before the service began, his disciples asked him: "Master, what do you do before prayer?" He replied: "I pray to be able to pray better."[32]

The purpose is to receive the light of infinity (en sof — "without end").

Since the focal point in the Kabbalah is the light and the act of receiving (qabbalah),[33] their relation is the same as that which exists between male and female.

This is proved by the numerical value of the word "male", which is "like the light," and the word "female", which corresponds to the expression, "like receiving the light." The words "male" and "female" mark you, do not refer only to men and women, but to the whole structure of the universe.

For the Kabbalah, *"the whole world is divided into male and female."*[34]

I can see some similarity to your explanation.

Yes also, for the Kabbalists, the principle of polarity is at the foundation of life, and each human being is androgynous; ac-

651

cordingly, "man is both male and female, and woman is similarly female and male. These are the two aspects of creatures in general. All life is based in this intimate duality."[35]

By that it means "polarity" since, as you said, sometimes they are used synonymously.
Which is not very helpful to one's understanding. Ultimately for the Kabbalah "the world rests upon this fundamental relationship between female and male, which is translated by love."[36]

I can see the reason for the secrecy of the teaching which can be easily misunderstood.
The outpouring or offering of the light is male and the "residence" of the light is female, known as the Shekhinah. "Thus, a man who receives and accepts is female, and a woman who offers is in the dimension of the source of light and in the 'male' mode."[37]

The numerical value of love is 13; therefore, the relation between male and female, which is 26 (13 + 13), is the numerical value of the word *havaya*, meaning existence.

And the word *havaya* is an anagram of the Tetragrammaton YHVH, a word that also has the numerical value of 26.

Thus, we have the identity of God, male-female, and existence.
Love "is the secret of secrets," and it is from love that the Name YHVH is revealed as the fundamental "middle" (*emtsa*).[38]

It refers to the love that descends from the Source of light to the world, and the love of the world that ascends to the Source of light. There is a mutual yearning between God and man for partnership and relationship. Man realizes his existential loneliness on this earth and the temporal delusions of his life. During his growth and development he discovers that, as a finite entity, he can cling to the Infinite and become one with Him.

And God, who appears in the Bible as the ultimate Source of life, who introduces Himself with the Name, "I AM that I AM," reveals the Infinite Being of Himself by His will to become the Creator of man and be one with him.[39]

"It is a shared principle, that constitutes that man is in search of God since by his nature he looks above to unite with the *concealed* God who grants him life; while God is in search of man since by His nature He looks below to unite with the *revealed* man who had received life from Him."[40] The existence of God as Creator of man begins, therefore, with the existence of man created by God. The co-existence of God and the human being, sharing the same destiny, is the most fundamental principle of the Kabbalah. They are partners in the same venture, travelers on the same journey, because they both seek reunion and to become One.

Men and women are also attracted to each other by the desire for companionship and intimacy, but their search is for someone who is not known to them.

How can we know someone else? We don't even know ourselves! I think this is the problem: unknowingly we search for our twin flame, but since this is an almost impossible endeavor, we should focus on our union with you, which must be accomplished first.

To enter into an unknown relationship can be a source of confusion and error, but not in a relation with God. In this case, the unitive process is not toward someone unknown but is rather a movement of return to the known. The person who is in search for God already knows Him because they are essenin search for God already knows Him because they are essentially part of each other; God and man have a shared identity and are mutually dependent.

"The Kabbalists describe the human being as a 'half' entity in search of his other missing 'half.' Whereas the first 'half' represents the psychological condition of the human being, the second completing 'half' is always found in the bosom of God Himself."[41]

There is no question that, knowingly or unknowingly we all have this feeling of incompleteness and the yearning to become whole.
"But the unique point of this mystical search for completion is that it ends with man's comprehension that a similar eagerness for completion and partnership lives in the hidden life of God Himself, his ultimate partner."[42]

This intimate bond will unfold in a perfect oneness that assures happiness and fulfillment in this world and in the next. Such mutually passionate desire is reflected in the form of marriage, family, society, and in the notion of human togetherness. For the Kabbalists marriage on earth is for the purpose of procreation, but that is only a symbol of its heavenly counterpart, the union with God. And only when that is accomplished will the sense of incompleteness be overcome and the yearning to become whole realized.

The creation of the universe occupies a central position in the speculation of the Kabbalists; they coined the name En-Sof, or Ayn-Soph, which means infinite, with no end, with reference to the ultimate source, the unmanifest One, beyond human comprehension, "in whom resides the essence or potentiality of all."[43]

It conveys the notion of a God that is not only the law-giver, the ruler, and the almighty, but the hidden and transcendent ground of being. It is the One which becomes the Father-Mother God, and by their relation and intercourse is the creative force that, like a fountain, flows endlessly, giving life to all that is.

Moreover, there is a corresponding process in the dimension of consciousness. The Kabbalists teach that the Hebrew word for "nothingness" (Ayin), written as AIN, has the same consonants as I, written as ANI. Ein-Sof, from its hidden "nothingness," became "I" (ANI), which is transformed into ANOKHI when God reveals Himself to the people of Israel in the first commandment: "I AM (ANOKHI) the Lord thy God." Thus, in His very first commandment He introduces Himself as a fully conscious God who requires recognition and demands acknowledgment of His unity."[44]

I can see how it is not possible for our mind, unless the infinite reveals itself, to conceive of a state prior to creation; I mean a period (which is not the correct word because there was no time or space) when nothing existed but the infinite alone.

In fact, the term *En* refers to its formless state of latency resembling nothingness; "The word "nothingness," of course connotes negativity and nonbeing, but what the mystic means by divine nothingness is that God is greater than any *thing* one can imagine, like *no thing*.

Since God's being is incomprehensible and ineffable, the least impious or irreverent and most accurate description one can offer is, paradoxically, *nothing*.

However, in the words of a fourteenth century Kabbalist, "Nothingness (ayin) is more existent than all the being in the world. But since it is simple, and all simple things are complex compared with its simplicity, it is called *ayin*."[45]

Having *postulated* the inconceivable reality of the Absolute called Nothing, the concern of the Kabbalists is the mode of its manifestation. They have to explain the relation of En Sof with the visible universe, and the human being as its representative. Moreover, they are faced with the problem of the connection between the transcendent and formless nature of the infinite and the anthropomorphic Lord of Israel, "whose stature and measurements were not beyond the ingenuity of rabbinical calculations."[46]

I am reminded of the similarity in the Indian philosophical tradition which distinguishes two aspects or modes of Brahman, nirguna and saguna.

Nirguna Brahman, or without attributes, is the transcendent state which defies all description and characterization. Nothing can be known or affirmed of it because of the limitation of human language based on phenomenal experience.

"Brahman comes to signify that which stands behind the gods as their ground and source ... the unitary principle of all being."

Saguna Brahman — meaning with qualities — can be interpreted by the mind and, more importantly, has its foundation not in mere speculation, but in the "content" of a loving experience of unity. The features of that experience of Oneness is described as being-consciousness-bliss.[47]

The problem of the incomprehensibility and hiddenness of the God who reveals himself as "I AM" to Moses and in Christ has been with Christianity from the beginning. Suffice to mention Meister Eckhart's distinction be-

tween the Triune God and the hidden Divine Ground, or Godhead. According to him God exists as "God" only in relation to the creature who invokes him. However, the ultimate source of all things is beyond God, called the Godhead. For Eckhart the two are as distinct as heaven and earth because one is personal and the other impersonal.

Since he seems to be one of your favorite authors, I should mention that he refers to My Presence in you as a "spark" ("Seelenfunklein" or *scintilla animae.*) It is the "foundation of the soul," uncreated and uncreatable, where the birth of the Word, "I AM" takes place. Therefore, the human being can realize his true essence and identity in Me.

How different your Reality from the idolatrous and false conceptions and images created by the intellect.

The Divine Plenitude pre-existing eternally was the substance, namely light, of every world which comes forth from En Sof; therefore, the Kabbalistic system is one of emanation. It must be also said, because of the identity of thought and existence, that there is much in the literature to support the view of divine immanence. At least this is the conclusion, "after due allowance has been made for the confusion and obscurity of the originals."[48] Therefore, it can be stated that "The Unknown Absolute manifested itself through an emanation, in which it was immanent, yet as to which it was transcendental."[49]

It is true that the terms emanation, creation, formation, and alike are used somewhat indiscriminately by the various schools and trends of the Kabbalists down the ages. But the doctrine of emanation rests on Zoharic authority, and it is appropriate to the Divine Ground unfolding from within itself, so that it may ultimately be revealed to and within an external universe, "of which God is the inward power and the abiding grace."[50]

You said that all energy is God's energy: there is a philosophical and theological tradition according to which God created the world out of nothing, *ex nihilo*.
The Kabbalists affirm the opposite, that is, " the world was created as nothing from something."[51]

It may be true, as it is contested, that in the Old Testament, God is always transcendent rather than immanent. However, to the prophets He reveals Himself as a Presence and, whether through vision or voice, they had an immediate contact with Him. Don't we read in Isaiah that, "the whole earth is full of His glory?"[52] And in the words of Jeremiah, "Am I a God near by, and not a God far off? ... Do I not fill heaven and earth?"[53] Also the psalmist recognizes the Divine Presence even in the underworld which is considered a region of darkness: "... if I make my bed in Sheol, you are there."[54]

There are some affinities in the prophetic Kabbalism represented by Abulafia (thirteenth century) who was influenced by the Book of Creation written in the early phases of Jewish mysticism, probably between the third and the sixth century.

Abulafia taught that the contemplation of the name of God leads to ecstasy: "The man who has felt the divine touch and perceived its nature," he says "is no longer separated from his Master [meaning God], and behold, he is his Master, and his Master is he, for he is so intimately united to Him that he cannot by any means be separated from Him."[55]

En-Soph, the infinite source of light, emanates from the indescribable radiance of its splendor ten Sefirot (or Sephirot, Se-
phiroth), which are its flowing essence, and through them it
gives form, sustains, and governs the universe. "They represent
both phases of the hidden life of the Godhead and means of His
self-revelation to man."[56] The Sefirot are its principles, powers,
qualities or attributes, vessels, and instruments, with the purpose, as they developed, of receiving, containing and transmitting the light which descends and expands upon the worlds below, animating and vivifying them with the breath or essence of
life.

"Taken as a whole, the Sefirot form 'the one great Name
of God,' Yahweh, which is equivalent to the divine Presence as
it is manifested in the order and harmony of creation. In themselves they constitute 'the world of union' — the highest of the
four unseen worlds intermediate between En-Sof and 'the
world of separation' in which man exists in his fallen state."[57]

The term singular is Sephira in which the idea of sphere
or circularity is involved as the circle is a Kabbalistic symbol of
En-Soph. There is a close relation between the sphere and the
circle, which is a symbol of the All, without beginning or without end, representing the ultimate state of Oneness.

**I am so thrilled by this explanation that I can't help to inter-
ject the description of the final vision in Dante's *Paradiso*:**

> Within the profound and shining substance of the super-
> nal light appeared to me three circles of three colors and
> of the same dimension; and one seemed reflected by the
> other, as rainbow by rainbow, and the third was like fire
> breathed forth by the other two.[58]

Among other etymologies, that of the precious stone sapphire has been proposed because of its purity and brightness. However, the circle, which is often an emblem for the sun, is also related to the number ten, the figure of the Sefirot, which represents the return to the one from the many. Therefore, the circle symbolizes oneness, heaven, perfection and eternity.

I am reminded also of the Chinese bipolar symbol Yin and Yang with the two modes of energy of male and female in a circle.

In the early phase of Jewish mysticism, the authoritative Book of Creation opens with the statement: By means of thirty-two mysterious paths did the Eternal, the Lord of Hosts, engrave and establish His name and create the world.

The thirty-two paths are the twenty-two letters of the Hebrew alphabet and the ten Sefirot. Later, the numerical significance decreases and the Sefirot becomes the central feature of the teaching of the Zohar. They are described as grades, or degrees of creative power and divine manifestation, and represent the hidden world of the divine language which underlies the phenomenal universe.

Since the beginning, God appears as Creator by the power of speech, clearly emphasized ten times in the first chapter of Genesis. Notice the recurrence of the number ten, corresponding to the ten Sefirot.

I can see the similarity with your explanation that thought, feeling, and the spoken word are the powers by which all is created, whether by God or human being. What is Nature according to the Zohar?

It may be called the garment of God. It is that in which He appears and wherein He is veiled, so that we can look upon Him and know Him in His vestured aspect.

However, it is not the body of God — which is more properly Shekhinah, at least in one of her aspects — and it is still less God manifested, except it is manifested in bright light, like the sun and the stars on the physical plane.

Is it not possible, then, to know God?

Yes, you can, but not as He is in Himself, your knowledge being made possible only through the manifestation of the Deity; it takes place after two manners — by the mediation of the Law of Nature, that is to say, in the physical universe; and by the Law of Grace which is the manifestation of God in his relation with the souls of his elect.[59]

What is the meaning of the "Tree of Life?"

The Kabbalists teach that everything in the physical world has a spiritual counterpart, and that they are both united. Their favorite symbol is the tree. Its roots lie in heaven and its branches are on earth. Thus, the spiritual and the physical are joined, *as above, so below; as below, so above.*

All that exists here below originates from its roots on the higher planes, except one thing: your free will is not dictated from above. The Tree of Life, also called the "Tree of God," or the "Cosmic Tree," is really a time-honored name for the way the Sefirot are arranged and presented. Each of them represents a branch which is rooted in the En-Sof which, as the Source of Life, is not only the hidden root but also the sap of the tree.

Remember that everything has been created by the divine power of the Sefirot, present and acting in and through them. They are equally balanced with one side of the tree representing the female qualities and the other side the masculine qualities.

Again the male-female polarity.
The tree is viewed as a spiritual ladder, which are the ten Sefirot, in the middle of the Garden; they form a ladder to Heaven because the individual can use them, that is, their qualities, for his spiritual progress and ascent.

They are divided in three triads, with a tenth which represents the harmony among them. The highest, the Crown, is indistinguishable from En-Sof, the primordial point, which is the Source and the beginning of everything in manifestation.

From it proceeds "Wisdom," the supreme masculine emanation of En-Sof, the fountain of divine thought, the root of faith, the active principle, the Father of the lower Sefirot and the husband of the supreme feminine, named "Intelligence" or understanding. She is the Mother, the passive or receptive principle, the divine womb, the origin of every existence, the "wife" of Wisdom.

This is referred to as the world of Emanation. From their union flows forth the seven lower Sefirot, beginning with "Love", or "Mercy" on the right and "Justice" on the left, balanced by "Beauty" in the center. The Beautiful is considered the expression and result of all moral qualities, or the sum of all purity and goodness. This is the world of Creation.

It may seem strange that "Love," or "Mercy" is male and "Justice" female, but I think they should not be taken too literally given the limitation of our language.
Noteworthy is the fundamental importance of the polarity of the Father-Mother God. Below them — the third triad — are

"Victory" or "Mastery," which manifests the divine patience, taken as masculine, the "Glory" or "Splendor of God," regarded as feminine, and then "Foundation", the ground of permanence and balance in the universe.

Finally, there is the "Kingdom" of God, also called the Shekhinah, which represents the feminine side or aspect of the Divine Presence. The Sefirot are said to be the offspring of the union between God and the Shekhinah, and She is often identified with the Holy Spirit. She is referred to figuratively as Princess, Matrona, Queen, and Bride, and other mystical names I mentioned previously. Originally, there had been a perfect and constant union between God and the Shekhinah, binding all worlds and everything in creation into one. This is the world of Manifestation or Action.

The Four Worlds are the stages, or degrees, through which the supernal Light descends from the higher to the lower planes.

Are they inhabited?
Yes, self-conscious beings, much more advanced than humans, live there, together with different categories of angels who constitute the links between worlds as messengers.

Are they described like the nine choirs of Dionysius?
There is no hierarchy of angels in the Zohar, but I will mention five of them because the Hebrew initials of the names arranged in order, form the word *argaman*, which means "purple":

> Uriel , the angel of light
> Raphael, the angel of healing
> Gabriel, the angel of power
> Mikhael, the angel close to God

Nuriel, the angel of fire[60]

Purple or violet is the color of spirituality and transmutation.
The Sefirot are both the concealed life of the Godhead and Its Self-revelation as the channels or emanations of the divine light whereby the transcendent En-Sof becomes immanent in the world, while remaining transcendent as the Infinite Source of all. Each Sefirot has multiple levels and its potential and possibilities are infinite. None of them appears separately, they are united with one another in an interpenetrating unity and, although each one has a predominant quality or key-note, all contain and participate in the qualities of the others. Their combined forces and interplay give rise to the limitless diversity and variety that you see in the universe.

And also to that which I don't see, which is infinitely much more. God never repeats Himself; it is reported that there are not two leaves or two snowflakes alike.
The Sefirot are also responsible for the laws and the order of the worlds below; in fact, there is a constant interaction between them, and they enable the human being — who is an emanation from them — to have a creative part in the divine plan and to have the capacity to unite himself with them and be able to attain the ascension.

With regard to the relation of the Sefirot to En-Sof, there is a description in the Gates of Heaven, a seventeenth-century work, which I'd like to quote:

> The Sefirot are the mirror of its truth, the ideas of its wisdom and concepts of its will; the reservoirs of its strength

strength and the instruments of its activity; the treasure-house of its happiness and the distributors of its grace; the judges of its kingdom who deliver their verdict; they are also the definitions, the attributes, and the name of He who is most high, and the cause of all things; these are the ten inextinguishable; ten attributes of His exalted majesty; the ten fingers of the hand; the ten lights by which He reflects Himself and the ten garments with which He covers Himself; ten visions in which He appears; ten forms thanks to which He has shaped everything; ten sanctuaries in which he is glorified; ten degrees of prophecy through which He manifests Himself; ten celestial cathedra from which He dispenses His teaching; ten thrones on which He judges the nations; ten halls in paradise for those who are worthy; ten levels which He gravitates downward and through which one can gravitate upward to Him; ten lights which illuminate all the intelligence; ten words through which the world was created; ten spirits which animate and maintain it in life; ten numbers, weights, and measures which number, weigh, and measure everything; ten sorts of fire which fulfill all desires.[61]

This is an eloquent depiction which can be a subject of meditation on the wonders of God's creation. The Sefirot are also called "the face" to convey the idea that the Infinite reveals itself in Its creation and becomes manifest through them.

It has been said that the face of man is evidence of the existence of God, which is very meaningful because the face is not only, as the word implies, that which is on the surface like features or aspects, which are seen. It is also that which

sees, by which a connection is possible, I see not only the
face of another, I also see him looking at me.[62]

I mentioned that there are ten sayings, before every creative
act: "And God said."

The tenth one concerns the food made available to humanity; for the Kabbalists there is something very special with
regard to food, the capacity to receive it, and how physical
nourishment can also have spiritual meaning. They instruct to
bless always what you eat in order to charge it with the divine
qualities of purity, health, and the illumination to be aware that
God created it for you, that it is a gift from Him. When you
taste the food and you like it, it is He who placed the taste there
for you to enjoy it.

**A meal should really be a ritual or ceremony when we think
of the wonder of each kind of food that we can eat to satisfy
our hunger, grown and provided for us by Mother Nature.
The variety of fruits and vegetables, their different shapes,
colors, textures, and tastes should fill us with amazement
and a feeling of gratitude. And what a miracle it is the way
the food becomes part of us and nourishes our body. Like
breathing, it is the most intimate form of communion with
universal life.**

You are right, but not as close a union as ours.

The Kabbalah teaches that true pleasure is not merely a
feeling or a temporary sensation, but that it has a spiritual
component, which means that the higher one rises in consciousness nearer to the divine realities, the greater the enjoyment because God is the Source of infinite bliss. Therefore, the
more you are united with Him, the more you know and experience what pleasure and happiness really are.

What the world calls ecstasy is merely intense excitation; you are referring to transcendent ecstasy, beyond human limitations, including time and space. I have heard the name "Adam Kadmon." Would you explain who he is?

The Sefirot form the figure of the primordial androgyne who, in his original form, like the planet Earth, was of a purely etheric substance, existing in union with God in Paradise. His body was of the nature of light, and he was endowed with all the divine powers:

> When our forefather Adam inhabited the Garden of Eden, he was clothed, as all are in heaven, with a garment made of the higher light. When he was driven from the Garden of Eden and was compelled to submit to the needs of this world, what happened? God, the Scriptures tell us, made to Adam and his wife tunics of skin and clothed them; for before this they had tunics of light, of that higher light used in Eden. The good actions accomplished by man on earth draw down on him a part of that higher light which shines in heaven. It is this light which serves him as garment when he must enter into another world and appear before the Holy One, Whose name be praised. Thanks to this garment he is able to taste the bliss of the elect and to look into the luminous mirror. That it may be perfect in all respects, the soul has a different garment for each of the two worlds it must inhabit — one for the earthly world and one for the higher world.[63]

In consequence of the Fall, the unity with God was broken, the Shekhinah went into exile, and throughout creation harmony was replaced by discord. Death, which is sin itself, is not a universal curse but only self-willed evil. It does not exist for the righteous who unite with God by a love-kiss; it strikes only the wicked who leave all hope behind in this world. Although man has fallen into separateness and mortality, he is still in his essence a divine being.

According to the Zohar, "Man is both the summary and the highest expression of Creation; hence he was not created until the sixth day. As soon as man appeared, everything was completed, the higher world as well as the lower, for all is summed up in man; he unites all form."[64]

This is the meaning of the term, "microcosm," which is based on the principle of polarity.

But the individual is not only the cosmos on a small scale, he is, above all, the image of God, in the totality of His infinite attributes. "Do not think that man is but flesh, skin, bones, and veins; far from it! What really makes man is his soul; and the things we call skin, flesh, bones and veins are but a garment, a cloak; they do not constitute man. When man departs this earth, he divests himself of all the veils that conceal him. Yet, the different parts of the body conform to the secrets of the supreme wisdom."[65]

Would you explain the nature of the soul?
While essentially a unity, the soul is threefold and the three elements are an emanation from the Sefirot. The lowest part is the life of the senses or sense-consciousness; above it the soul as self-conscious activity and the seat of the moral attributes and reason. Highest is the over-soul or spirit, the "divine spark."

Like the mystics, the Zohar recognizes it as an individualized expression of God.

Yes, "its name is Neshamah, which is literally 'breathing'; it is the breath of higher spirituality, the bridge which connects man with the heavenly world,"[66] where abides "the Supernal Soul, inscrutable and unknowable, veiled in a covering of exceeding brightness."[67] The soul is illumined by its light and is entirely dependent on it.

It reminds me of your divine Presence, the God Self.
As an emanation from the Sefirot, the *soul* pre-exists in the heavenly world, "hidden in the divine mind." Before its descent to earth, it vows to fulfill its task — to reunite itself with God. During its earthly life, it weaves the garment of light which it is to wear after death in the "realm of radiant splendor," as a result of acts of love. In its final blessedness, when it has completed its journey and grown to full stature, the human being ascends to his Source, and becomes one with God.

The union is described in terms of love; he is joined with the "Queen," the Shekhinah, or with the "King, the Holy One," in the Palace of Love. But it is only if a man is drawn towards the Holy One and is filled with longing for Him in this world that the soul is carried upwards towards the higher realms.[68]

Otherwise, men have to undergo reincarnation on earth, or to be purified in the fiery stream of Gehenna, or even destroyed. The aim and purpose of human existence is to attain union with God; and although its culmination is in the world to come, it is possible even during this lifetime to enter into a state of communion, joined in mystical ecstasy, and to be one with the Divine Presence in a continuous state.

According to the Zohar, two things are supremely necessary: the love of God and the practice of prayer which, if it is offered with concentrated attention and devotion, becomes a powerful instrument for good. It not only leads men towards union with God, but brings about in the realm above an added measure of peace and joy which descends to earth and is distributed to all receptive souls. One's responsibility is not only to become again united with God but to restore the universal harmony which sin had destroyed, and therefore to bring an end to the exile of the Shekhinah.

"The impulse from below," it is written repeatedly, "calls forth that from above." The power of the human being extends to the higher realms of life; "He who worships God out of love raises everything to the state where all must be one."[69]

By the principle of polarity and the magnetic power of love. I see that the supreme emphasis and focus is on the attainment of oneness.

Finally, I should mention also the importance of the celebration of the Sabbath. Each day of the week is subject to the influence of one of the Sefirot, and the Sabbath is related to the tenth, the Shekhinah, which unifies the power of them all.

The Sabbath has a mystical dimension. Throughout the centuries of Judaism, its observance has probably been the most central ritual. It is the only one mentioned in the Ten Commandments, and its laws are repeated in the Torah more often than any other law.

According to Genesis 2:2, on the seventh day God rested. However, the verse also says, "And on the seventh day God finished the work that he had done." There seems to be a contradiction; if it took six days to create the universe, then what did he finish on the seventh day? Creation should have been completed on the sixth day. But read verses 2 and 3 together:

2 And on the seventh day God finished his work that he had done, and he rested on the seventh day from all the work that he had done.
3 So God blessed the seventh day and hallowed it, because on it God rested from all his work which he had done in creation.

Kabbalists interpret this to mean that on the seventh day God "finished" by creating rest, like silence between tones, or contemplation after action.

God is changeless: "I AM God, I do not change."[70] Since He does not change, yet so many changes occur in the six days of creation (incidentally, you should not take the word "day" literally), the seventh day represents a day in which God and the universe are at one. It is a day when there will be no more changes; all is in perfect harmony with its Creator.

Therefore, the purpose of the Sabbath is to imitate God and to achieve a contemplative state of at-one-ment and peace. In view of the sanctity that the Zohar attributes to the sex-act, under the obedience of purity, which is marriage, it is affirmed that blessed are those who sanctify the Sabbath Day by intercourse with their wives, because their union becomes a house where the Divine Presence can dwell.

The union below, as an image of the union above, offers a point of contact with that on high between Matrona and the King. The principle of conception is that God and His Shekinah send down souls into this world while the father and mother provide the body between them — "heaven, earth and all the stars, being associated in the formation, together with the angels."[71]

In the words "male and female created He them,"[72] it is expressed that supreme mystery inaccessible to human intelligence, and is the object of faith.

By this mystery was the human being created, as also the heaven and the earth. It is inferred that every figure which does not represent male and female has no likeness to the heavenly figure.[73]

It is also said that woman is the image of the altar, from which it seems to follow that man is the priest, and therefore divorce makes a breach in the altar — in the altar below, because there is separation between male and female, and in the altar above, by the Kabbalistic conception of correspondence between things above and below.[74]

This is something that, I think, not everyone likes to hear and to believe.
The celebration of the Sabbath is a day of holy joy, not limited to man; it includes the supernal worlds in a divine reunion. And on that day, Judgment is suspended and gives way to the healing power of love and peace enfolding with its blessings the whole of creation.

Even those who dwell in darkness will find respite and relief from the expiating pangs of their sins. The Sabbath is thus an anticipation of the time when the Messiah Himself will come, when the exile of the Shekhinah will end, and all beings in heaven and earth will again be made one.

This is the consummation which is figuratively described as the resumption of the originally continuous marital union between the primordial male and female polarity, the Queen and the King, or God and His Shekhinah.

I think I may have given you at least a glimpse of the extremely complex symbolism and often mysterious teachings of the Kabbalah.

It is a fascinating secret tradition and, like all occult teachings, it is very difficult to penetrate the veils with which their symbols are clothed. I am grateful for giving me an explanation as clear as possible of the different interpretation of the various texts and their commentaries through the centuries. I would like to know more about some issues which the Kabbalists have left obscure.

However, I am reminded of the following anecdote: "One day, a non-Jew asked a Rabbi, 'Master, why do you Jews always answer questions with another question?' 'And why not?' replied the Rabbi."[75]

[1] Marc-Alain Ouaknin, *Mysteries of the Kabbalah*, transl. Josephine Bacon, (NY: Abbeville Press, 2000), p. 9.

[2] Adolphe Franck, *The Kabbalah. The Religious Philosophy of the Hebrews* (NY: Bell Publishing Co., 1940), p. 80.

[3] Franck, p. 80.

[4] Ouaknin, p. 100.

[5] Zohar, 111, 127b, quoted in Ouaknin, p. 9.

[6] Ouaknin, pp. 98, 100.

[7] Ouaknin, p. 101.

[8] Ibid., p. 101.

[9] *Mysteries of the Kabbalah*, pp. 43-4.

[10] Ouaknin, p. 45.

[11] Genesis 1:3.

[12] Quoted in *Mysticism in World Religion*, p. 176.

[13] Ouaknin, p. 45.

[14] Ouaknin, p. 301.

[15] Psalms 33:6.

[16] Jeremiah 23:29.

[17] A.E. Waite, *The Holy Kabbalah* (Mineola, NY: Dover Publications, Inc., 2003), p. 231.

[18] Ouaknin, p. 45.

[19] Waite, p. 226-7.

[20] Ibid., p. 223.

[21] Ibid., p. 231-2.

[22] Ibid., p. 224.

[23] Ibid., p. 227.

[24] Song of Solomon 1:2.

[25] Waite, p. 227.

[26] Ibid., p. 112.

[27] Ouaknin, p. 114-15.

[28] Ibid., p. 114-15.

[29] Ibid., p. 361.

[30] Ibid., p. 342-3, 346.

[31] Ibid., p. 617.

32 Ouaknin, p. 258.

33 Ibid., p. 105.

34 Ibid., p. 119.

35 Ibid., p. 119.

36 Ibid., p. 121.

37 Ibid., p. 119.

38 Ibid., p. 119.

39 Shimon Shokek, *Kabbalah and the Art of Being*, (NY: Routledge, 2001), p. 4.

40 Ibid., p. 7.

41 Ibid., p. 6.

42 Ibid., p. 7.

43 Waite, p. 139.

44 Shokek, p. 32.

45 *The Problem of Pure Consciousness. Mysticism and Philoso-
phy*, K.C. Robert Forman, ed, (NY: Oxford University
Press, 1990), p. 121; D.C. Matt, "Ayin: the Concept of
Nothingness in Jewish Mysticism."

46 Waite, p. 191.

47 Cfr. Eliot Deutsch, *Advaita Vedanta. A Philosophical Reconstruction* (Honolulu, Hawaii: The University of Hawaii
Press, 1973), p. 12.

48 Waite, p. 194.

49 Ibid., p. 192.

50 Ibid., p. 194.

51 Ouaknin, p. 195.

52 Isaiah 6:3.

53 Jeremiah 23:23.

54 Psalms 139:8.

55 Spencer, *Mysticism in World Religion*, p.188.

56 Ibid., p. 190.

57 Ibid., p. 191.

58 *Paradiso*, 22, 115, 120.

59 Waite, p. 135.

60 Ouaknin, p. 147.

[61] Ibid., p. 211.

[62] Ibid., p. 222.

[63] *The Kabbalah: the Religious Philosophy of the Hebrews*, p. 139.

[64] Ibid., p. 122.

[65] Ibid., p. 122.

[66] Spencer, p. 194.

[67] Ibid., p. 194.

[68] Ibid., p. 194, 196.

[69] Ibid., p. 194, 196.

[70] Malachi 3:6.

[71] Waite, p. 338.

[72] Genesis 1:27.

[73] Waite, p. 389, w.1.

[74] Ibid., p. 389, w.1.

[75] Ouaknin, p. 231

CHAPTER 25

The Creative Word "I Am"

"I AM that I AM...this is my name forever, and this is my memorial for all generations."
Exodus

"My first name is "I Am," my last is " I AM what I AM."
Zend-Avesta

The blossom disappears of itself as the fruit grows.
So will your lower self vanish as the Divine grows within you.
Vivekenanda

I AM" smaller than the atom.
"I AM" larger than the universe.
Da-Love-Ananda

From the dawn of history there is the record of a continual interrelation between humankind and a larger reality both outside and as an intimate part of its personal existence.

As century succeeded century people throughout the world have approached in a wide variety of ways, from the primitive to the speculative and contemplative, the mystery of the supernatural. We see the determined and purposeful effort of the individual to go beyond its given condition moved by the desire to establish and maintain a beneficial relation with the sacred realm. It is based not only on a belief or an idea but rather in the intuitive feeling and a sense of the wonder and awe-inspiring manifestation of the universe. Ultimately, it is beyond intellectual comprehension as proved by all the philosophizing in the world which remains of academic interest only. The spiritual quest, despite the bewildering diversity and discrepancies of its practices and creeds, have a common nucleus: the need for self-transcendence.

According to William James the cause is an "uneasiness" arising from "a sense that there is something wrong about us as we naturally stand."[1]
"Uneasiness" is too mild a word, like the Augustinian "restlessness," to describe the human condition. "Groundlessness," or "loneliness" and "anguish" have been referred too as more appropriate. The recognition of his finitude, the burden of his incompletion, and the open wound of his separation will give no respite to the personality impelling it, by the forward movement of life, to undertake the quest that leads beyond what he thought was himself. He cannot forswear the transcendent and limitless potentiality of his divine birthright without repudiating the original decision to fulfill My perfect plan for him and face, as a consequence, the agony of self-annihilation.

According to the same author the individual who suffers from his wrongness and reprove it, "is to that extent consciously beyond it, and in at least possible touch with something higher."
He begins to stir from his state of sleep; for some may take a long time while others wake up suddenly.

"He becomes conscious that this higher part is conterminous and continuous with a MORE of the same quality which is operative in the universe outside of him, and which he can keep in working touch with."[2]
You can keep not only "in touch" with Me but be the instrument through which I can express My perfection because, do not forget it, you are a co-creator.

As Swami Vivekananda said, ""This is the one prayer: remembering our nature ... Why does man go out to look for God?... It is your own heart beating, and you did not know, you were mistaking it for something external. He, nearest of the near, my own self, the reality of my own life, my body and my soul – I am Thee and Thou art Me. That is your own nature. Assert it, manifest it ... Every good thought which you think or act upon is simply tearing the veil, as it were, and the purity, the Infinity, the God behind, manifests itself – the eternal subject of everything, the eternal Witness in this universe, your own Self."[3]

The expression "I am Thee and Thou are me" is not the same as Jesus' "The Father and I are one?"

Yes, He referred to Me as the Father, according to the religious belief of the time, but I am also your Mother.

Julian of Norwich recognized it when she wrote:

> So Jesus Christ, who opposes good to evil, is our true Mother. We have our being from him, where the foundation of motherhood begins, with all the sweet protection of love which endlessly follows. As truly God is our Father, so truly is God our Mother, and he revealed it in everything, especially in these sweet words where he says: I am it; that is to say: I am it, the power and goodness of fatherhood; I am it, the wisdom and the lovingness of motherhood; I am it, the light and the grace which is all blessed love; I am it, the Trinity; I am it, the unity; I am it, the great supreme goodness of all kind of things; I am it who makes you to love; I am it who makes

you to long; I am it, the endless fulfilling of all true desires.[4]

From the interrelation and intercourse of the primal polarity
Father-Mother, the Son is born whose name is I AM.

That "was in the beginning with God and it was God."[5]
All knowledge of which the individual is potentially capable, no
matter what his path might be or the field of research, surely
leads him back to the Source of Being Itself that makes possible
the act of knowing and by whose intelligence everything is
known.

**Because to really know something is to be it. And how can
anyone know more about the creation than the Creator,
"without whom was not any thing made that was made"?[6]**
As I explain the fundamental subject of the name of God, I AM,
I want you to realize that it is the culmination of all knowledge
and of every endeavor to relate to and commune with the
Source of life. Whether it is the way of science, religion, poetry,
mysticism, occultism, their ultimate goal is for the individual to
become conscious of the meaning of the word "I AM" because I
AM is all there is. My purpose is to help you recognize that
THAT is who you are as the veils that hide the full truth are
removed.

**Then, there will be no one left to doubt or raise questions
beyond the limitations of my human condition. Once I become fully awake I will not cling anymore to my dream-self
which projects its dream-world in the make belief that it is
real. I call to you with the words of Al-Hallaj,**

"Between me and Thee
There is an I tormenting me.
Oh! remove by thyne own I this I of mine
from between us!"[7]

When the I AM within you illumines your understanding, the "I" that dared to usurp its place falls into nothingness. It cannot continue to live in the Presence of Being Itself when in your heart you hear the sound of My name.

And when I hear your name I will recognize who I AM. Indian folklore preserves a delightful narrative that illustrates it:

It is the tale of the lion cub whose parents had been killed by hunters and which was reared along with a flock of sheep. He learned to bleat and to eat grass, and grew up without suspecting that he himself was not a lamb. One day a lion fell upon the flock. Seeing the lion cub he asked him what he was doing among the sheep and why he was not ashamed of bleating and eating grass. "But am I not a lamb?" replied the astonished cub. Then the lion took him to a pool of water and told him to look at their two faces reflected in it and to compare them. "Are you not the same as I am? Is it not your nature to roar? Come, roar like I do ..." The cub roared, and he recognized himself ... [8]

Who you are, your real being is an extension of My Being, yet your origin is beyond your intellectual grasp for it is a question of love.

I must find and feel you at the source of my very existence, and to the extent that I know you I will know myself. Otherwise I have only a conception of your reality at the level of my thought instead of the experience of your living Presence as my I AM Self.

The impulse of love reaches directly to My heart because it is one with your heart. Only love can understand such communion, that is, how you can be one with Me and have, at the same time, a face-to-face dialogue.

It is according to the principle of polarity.

I see that you are making progress. However, My name seems incomprehensible and even mysterious to those who are still enveloped in the cocoon of the personality and identified with it. Thinkers may keep theorizing forever about the meaning of Being but they will never understand what it is, rather Who it is, until they feel it in their hearts as love.

The saying, "I AM that I AM" as the self-revelation of the nature of divine reality is misunderstood and interpreted by modern Scripture scholarship "more as a promise of God's covenantal fidelity" to the people than the identification of God with Being.[9]

Yet the individual is not made to remain forever on the rudimentary level of his sensory and intellectual consciousness, and he is not meant to turn to and depend on the outer world which draws and seeks to hold him captive.

I doubt whether the masses are ready to acknowledge and accept the reality of their divine identity.

The infant needs to be fed at his mother's breast but milk will not always be his food. Will the butterfly remain indefinitely at the stage of the chrysalis?

As the Hindu Scripture of the Purana states,

> Child-souls may find their gods in wood and stone;
> More grown-up souls in sacred lakes and streams;
> The older-minded in the orbs of space;
> The wise see Him in all-pervading Self.[10]

Jesus came to reveal again God's name, "I made your name known to them, and I will make it known, so that the love with which you have loved me may be in them, and I in them."[11] He left statements with the word "I AM" to overcome the self-created limitations of mankind but his teaching has been misinterpreted.

Christianity identified him with the Word as "the only begotten Son" and the "only" incarnation of I AM.
In reality it is everyone's divine birthright and predestination to realize the I AM Presence in him or her as the God-Self. When you say "I AM" you recognize that I am in you and you are in Me merging in our mutual love.

That was the meaning of Jesus' final prayer and the fulfillment of His ministry: "As you, Father, are in me and I am in you, may they also be in us ... so that they may be one."[12]
The oneness of life, consciousness, and energy to which I referred several times, finds its perfect realization in the infinite "I AM" individualized in every human being. There are differ-

ent individualizations but they all share and each is part of the One Source.

Like sparks or flames from the same fire or rays from the sun.
The individual must be aware not only that he exists but who he is by the recognition of the Presence that enables him to say I AM.

Not, however, the fictitious "I" of his identification with the bodily form bound to the shifting world of appearances, but discover within himself the being which is free from all conditioning and that never changes. In the words of Al-Allaj,

> "Thy place in my heart? 'Tis all of my heart!
> Naught beside Thee has any place ...
> I saw my Lord with my heart's eye and said:
> 'Who are Thou my Lord?' He replied, 'Thyself'!"[13]

"The Father who dwells in me does his works."[14]
There is no freedom without the understanding of the creative word I AM and its application. It is the Source from which the universe came into being and it can certainly create and bring to you whatever you desire to express and manifest.

But since we have this unlimited power it is still not clear to me why human beings are subject to all kinds of adversities.
The creative power may be misused, either willfully or because of ignorance. Now with the knowledge you are receiving you can reverse every negative condition by affirming the positive with the use of the creative word of love.

How is it the creative word of love?
Remember that My name is who "I AM," not just a name as it is usually understood but My Being. Therefore when you say and feel it the fire of My energy is released to manifest that which you call forth. Instead of acknowledging "I am not," "I cannot" or "I have not," you can replace the shadows by the light of "I AM what I desire to be". Know that when you say, think, or feel " I AM" followed by what you choose to manifest, God is ready to fulfill your demand.

Therefore, never accept anything less than who "I AM," always present and acting in, through, and for you.

If the individual is not receiving, accepting, or experiencing the good which "I AM," it means that there is an obstruction in his consciousness which causes him to repel it. He is preyed upon by destructive feelings or allows negative forces to dominate him; he is denying his Source of power or has forgotten it, and is using the creative Word wrongly and to a contrary effect.

I think that's what most people do as a matter of habit.
How unfortunate! They create their own unhappiness without knowing it.

Each human being is God individualized, and moves in a universe of consciousness and Law with the power to manifest anything he wants. But if he does not create according to the Law of the One, if he closes the door to the good I am offering all the time, whether it is love, peace, health, wealth, protection, or happiness, he separates himself from the very Source of everything he desires and is inevitably bound to the wheel of cause and effect.

I remember it:

> This vast universe is a wheel. Upon it are all creatures that are subject to birth, death, and rebirth. Round and round it turns, and never stops. It is the wheel of Brahman. As long as the individual thinks it is separated from Brahman, it revolves upon the wheel in bondage to the laws of birth, death, and rebirth. But when through the grace of Brahman it realizes its identity with him, it revolves upon the wheel no longer. It achieves immortality.[15]

It would be impossible to be free from one's Karma, and the necessity for re-embodiment, without the acceptance of My Presence as the "I AM" Self and the understanding of the Law of Love.

If the individual does not say "I AM" to what he wants or needs, how can he manifest or experience it? If you do not say or think, "I am going out," you will stay inside until you make the decision and expect to go out.

I created a universe of harmony, beauty, and perfection using the Word "I AM," and everyone can use his creative faculty, on his individual scale, by the self-same power latent within himself. But if he uses the creative Word followed by negative expressions, thereby misusing it, he will manifest and experience the opposite of what he really desires, and becomes limited and self-destructive.

Forgive me, but I am still not sure — and I know I should not say "I am not" — that I understand who you are and who I am. I mean, the nature of our relation.

I know that the truth is not recognized when it is first heard, and it is necessary to explain it several times before it is apprehended. I said that you have My immortal flame within your heart, the part of you which says "I AM," making you conscious of your self-identity and of your Source of life. You are clothed in bodies of substance of light, on a journey through this world with the overcoat of your flesh form. I am always present with you as your God Self, but not as an end-point of your ascent to Me, even though you and I become indissolubly and eternally One.

However, not as a formless and undifferentiated unity where love would be impossible because there is not interrelation and complementarity and not as a duality wherein each member would limit and oppose the other.

I am pleased to see that you begin to grasp the principle of polarity as two in one. But it can never become a living experience unless you realize both poles of the incommensurable nature of My love. "I AM" the presence always trying to expand My perfection through the individual.

From what I have learned from your explanation, the infinite Ground underlying all manifestation acknowledging itself becomes two, the polarity of spirit-matter, it multiplies itself, originating Divine Beings, each an individualized focus of consciousness as "I AM"-Self.

Yes, the primordial Ground is the ever-present starting point of manifestation, the foundation and principle of limitless potentiality.

Becoming actual through the individual by the affirmation of the Word "I AM."

687

The natural tendency of life, according to the cosmic scheme of creation is continuous and never-ending motion in spiral cycles in the creative ecstasy of expanding greater and greater love harmony, and beauty. Therefore, your destiny is mastery over all the energy of the universe by the fire of My love which will enable you to attain the victory of your ascension.

I will break down the walls of my self-created prison and finally, be free from all limitations.
No more enslaved and subject to the aberration and distortion of your personality.

But how can I be sure of it?
Once you make your decision to come home, your will is one with Mine, and I will lift you out of the web of cause and effect.

I will become a being of cause only, love, because I cannot fail to be what, in reality, "I AM."
Absolutely, the key to that glorious attainment is the awareness of My Presence and the feeling that I am acting in and through you, an extension of Myself, as the trinity of love, wisdom, and power.

"Like oil in sesame seeds, butter in cream, water in the river bed, fire in tinder, the Self dwells within the soul. Realize it through truthfulness and meditation."[16]
But it is not enough to listen to what I say or just read it. You must meditate on it, apply it, and feel its reality because then you become it, as I told you before. You live in a world created and sustained by the Word which was "with God," as the Scripture says, and "was God."[17]

It is by the Word that the Infinite reveals Itself from its latent state, and when It speaks as the God Self and says "I AM," becomes a creator by creating Itself, all beings, and the universe as interrelated individualities, forms and manifestations of the One existing in and through them.

The principle of polarity explains the seeming mystery of how Reality is One, and Beings and worlds not illusory and not separated.

"And God said" refers to the reality that He is no longer alone, that myriad worlds, beings, and presences are created. The hearer arises the moment He spoke; love, by its very nature, awakens its object, the existence of the beloved. "God-Love pours Himself out as a created world. 'God says,' and speaks the world; the Word and the World leave His mouth simultaneously."[18]

By its own power, a word implies someone that can hear and receive the word, the "you." "An image reflects its original: 'And God saw all that he had made, and it was very good'[19]; the initial relationship is pure transparency."[20]

God and everything that exists is the creative Word, "I AM": I, you and life itself. When you say "I AM," I say it with you, and as you, for the Infinite becomes conscious of itself as it individualizes through life-streams as Me and you.

"I AM" is the principle of consciousness and the individual's self-consciousness of life. That One consciousness appears as now waking, now sleeping in your body, or as giving up that physical form and taking up another. It never can conceive itself as beginning or ceasing to be. Bodies are seen being born and passing away; never an "I," the "I."[21] There is no "Another" consciousness, there is always and everywhere one "I" consciousness, and you relate to others not as "I – Thou" rather as "I – I."

I think that's what Shakespeare makes reference to as the foundation of the individual living in harmony and peace in a society.

> This above all: to thine own self be true,
> And it must follow as the night the day
> Thou canst not then be false to any man.[22]

Or woman.

This is the true meaning of relationship. One infinite " I AM" individualized in each being, whether human or divine. If we could realize it humanity and the Earth would be transformed!
You are right, one life and one consciousness animates and vivifies all that is, visible and invisible. In the Universe the levels and degrees of expression and manifestation are different, and although the variety and diversity of forms are infinite, there are not two alike. God does not repeat itself.

That is really amazing! Just to contemplate it, one is overwhelmed with a sense of wonder and awe.
Meditate on what I told you and above all practice it, and you will know yourself, God, and the universe because "I AM" and you are that I AM Self.

Is the use of affirmations with the words "I AM" related to prayer?

It is the fulfilled prayer, being the realization that you are or have already what you require and have asked. It is like the "Amen" of the Christians accepting the request.

Within My Name is the power to create or bring to you whatever you acknowledge and affirm. If you do not accept that which you demand, how can you receive it or become manifest? When you say "I AM," followed by what you require, know and feel that the life in you making the demand is the same life in Me that brings it forth.

Because life is one.
And since " I AM" life I cannot fail Myself.

Unless we obstruct the way by doubt. I know that the word "I AM" as God's name is present not only in the Bible. The Ormazd Yasht of the Zoroastrian religion declares:

> Then spoke Zarathushtra: Tell me thou, O pure Ahura –
> Mazda, the name which is the greatest, best, fairest and
> which is the most efficacious for prayer. Thus answered
> Ahura-Mazda: My first name is Ahmi (I AM) – and the last
> is Ahmi Yad Ahmi Marzdao (I am what I am)."

The Vedic Shatapatha Brahmana has the same significant words, "Yo ham asmi so-smi" (I am what I am); that is, "I am" ever the changeless One, ever the same Self, at the end as at the beginning.[23]

But might not repetition become hypnotic?
Speaking the Word is never hypnotic, for "I AM" is the essence and Reality of all that is in creation. When you use affirmations

with the Word "I AM," it is not the personality expressing its own concepts, for it cannot be the I AM Self.

Speaking and feeling the Word is to actualize that which lies quiescent in the womb of life and bring it forth as the perfect condition or thing required or desired.

In the "I AM" consciousness you are not dealing with the delusions of the personality; you are one with Me as the infinite Reality of life both manifest and unmanifest.

Moreover, it is not the repetition which causes the manifestation: its purpose is only to bring you into harmony or oneness with that which already IS and to enable you to feel it since it is the feeling of love that draws it to you and make you accept what you affirm.

What if the feeling doesn't arise?
If that happens it is because a negative feeling tries to interfere but it does not mean that the affirmation is ineffective. The way to overcome the hindrance completely is to build a momentum of positive-energy vibration by dynamic application to erase it, and then give thanks for what you are about to receive. It is a matter of opening up the consciousness to embrace and accept something that already exists at the inner level.

The Word enables the consciousness to actualize what otherwise would rest in a state of potentiality. The "I AM" affirmation must be used in order to express one's true nature, who one in reality is, instead of what one imagines himself to be.

Or not to be and not to have.
Correct. As you become aware of My Presence by remembering, loving, and being grateful for all you can receive, you increase the flow of My light in and around you.

Then, as your consciousness expands you will feel Me in your daily life as a living and tangible Presence taking care of you and fulfilling My plan of perfection. As one of your books suggested,

> Thus, I say, pray without ceasing. Your daily life is true prayer. By first knowing that this power does exist, then using it with absolute confidence, you soon become wholly conscious of it. You soon know that it is all inclusive in and through you. If you will but let it flow, it will rush to you in every instance. It flows to you as you let it flow from you ... This is God your Father in you, and you and your Father are one. Not servants but SONS, Sons of First Primal Cause. All that I AM has, is yours; for you are I AM.[24]

It is like turning on the light.

Calling to Me with My true Name and feeling My Presence as your true Self is the highest form of communion. It is as if someone calls you by your name, so that you can respond, and relate to him. Moreover, it is impossible for Me not to be conscious of your declaration because we are the poles of an inseparable identity. I AM is not only the fullness of existence, the "One Who Is," but also the "One Who Is Present," here, there, everywhere. I made you an extension of Myself on the physical plane, to express our mutual love.

Remember that a name is not merely a label by which a person is known or an appellation given to distinguish him from others. In its original meaning, as, for instance, in the Bible, a name not only is used to designate someone, it indicates the real nature of the individual, and it is who he or she is.

"The Lord is his name."[25]
Yes, "I AM" My name, therefore it is the key to all love and knowledge; it is spirit and matter, essence and existence, being and becoming. It is beyond comprehension yet reveals itself through the individual. It is the Source of everlasting life, endlessly flowing through self-conscious beings pervading and sustaining all creation You can never understand it unless you incarnate it by speaking and feeling who and what the Word is.

The "I AM" statement is Its complete fulfillment and realization, ever expanding to infinity. You may use its power, meditate and go deeper and deeper into it; and as you do, you will find that the more you enter it, and seek – the more you find.

Through the Word's self-generating and overabundant love, you will experience and taste the riches and delights that are in the bosom of the Father-Mother God. Since I love every individual with the same love with which I love Myself, you must love as you are loved, and you shall know yourself as you are known, lover and beloved as one.

As you reveal to me the meaning of your name, as deeply as I can grasp it, I see that it is essentially, the spring of love itself.
Yes, and the flow, as I said, of everlasting life.

It is life loving itself through the individual who is aware of his or her "I AM" Presence. And I begin to realize that all human love is a love of You unaware of itself, a participation in God's own love for Himself. What we seek is an act of love whereby we will love God as God loves Himself through us, each son or daughter.

When you seek nothing in love save love, and loving all in Myself, you receive all the joy that it brings. If you seek in love something other than My love, you lose love and joy together.

Studies have shown that "much hate and fear, and even many physical illnesses, are caused by a love which refuses to acknowledge itself as such, a love which has become ill because it fails to recognize its true nature and has lost sight of its [true] object ... Cruelty is misdirected love, and hate is frustrated love."[26]

I understand that love is the secret of the universe, the inexhaustible fountain of living water for which we all are thirsty. Help me to re-educate and re-order my love to its proper object, that I may say to you with the words of the poet:

> I love thee to the depth and breath and height
> My soul can reach, when feeling out of sight
> For the ends of Being and Ideal Grace ...
> I love thee with a love I seemed to loose
> With my lost saints – I love thee with the breath,
> Smiles, tears, of all my life! – and, if God choose,
> I shall but love thee better after death.[27]

You see how human beings have the capacity to love others, and it is good when the feeling comes from the heart. However, the love one shares with someone, unless it is anchored in Me, does not last and it is bound to lose its intensity. If the individual would send Me that same feeling of love, I will return it to an infinite degree. My love not only can never wane or change but it will increase and expand with every heart-beat for all eternity.

**I want to love you as you love yourself in and through me
and all there is. I ask you to enable me to rightly direct the
currents of love to bless also the world and expand it to embrace humanity and the rest of the universe.**

Love in its wide variety and forms is one as the feeling of life
qualified by individual choice, and is intensified by the acknowledgement of My "I AM" Presence.

All there is — and you may think of It as infinite being,
boundless space, eternal life, universal law, omnipotent consciousness, all-pervading divinity, all embracing love, cosmic
rhythm, ever-present creativeness, unlimited knowledge, and
so on ad infinitum — is contained and expressed in the Word
"I AM," the eternal polarity of the twin words "I" and "AM."

When you say and feel "I AM" it is like opening your
arms to enfold all that lives and experiencing the infinite within
you. It kindles and expands the upward leaping flame in the
depth of your heart in its ascent toward its Source.

Its very sound stands highest in the tonal scale of words,
it has the greatest intensity, the highest rate of vibration; therefore it is the supreme and most divine activity.

**I lost the consciousness of my I AM-ness and have fallen
under the domination of the personality and the outer
world. By believing "I am not" and "I have not" I came to
depend on that which is not my Source of life and accepted
the false appearances of lack and limitation.**

However, My love, wisdom, and power are always within you
for I AM closer than breathing, but they can only find expression by your use of them.

As Bacon said, knowledge becomes power through use.

Yes, that is how your capacity to love becomes greater and, accordingly also your aptitude of receiving.

I desire to love with all the intensity of my being because my finite passions are but the feeble images of the infinite one. And it is true that "The measure of love is to love without measure."

I hope you will decide to exert the authority and the privilege with which I endowed you in the beginning. You do not yet realize that who you are, your real being, is the "I AM," your God Self, and let me reiterate that there can be only one "I AM," not two. There is always and only the "single eye," or single "I AM," the One.

You remind me of the statement: "The eye is the light of the body, if your eye be single, your body will be full of light;"[28] but what does it mean to be "single"?

Do not divide your eye — your "I" — by giving power to something or someone else than My-Self, the "I AM" Presence within and above you.

As I did in the past by my many identifications. I now understand the meaning of that passage "The eye by which you see Me is the same as the eye by which I see you. Your eye and my eye are one and the same — one in seeing, one in knowing, and one in loving.[29]

Remember also that passage from *A Buddhist Bible,* "The mind has two doors from which issue its activities. One leads to a realization of the mind's Pure Essence, the other leads to the differentiations of appearing and disappearing, of life and death."

What is the "Pure Essence of the Mind?"

697

"It is the ultimate purity and unity, the all-embracing wholeness, the quintessence of Truth. Essence of Mind belongs to neither death not rebirth, it is uncreated and eternal."[30]

It reminds me of you.
Again I say, place Me first in your love. Keep your attention focused on Me as often as you can, for "I AM" the light of your life, and the shadows will not be able to exist in you or touch you. Affirm often, "I AM the protection of God! I AM the healing love of God! I AM the limitless supply of My Presence! I AM the success and the victory of God in all my endeavors! "Call to Me as your "beloved "I AM Presence" to fill you with the fire of My love, and you will be free from all your limitations of mind, body, and affairs! Demand to be charged with courage and strength to overcome all negative forces that try to enslave you. Feel that the I AM in you is greater than all the evil in the world. Learn to be still and feel that I AM your peace. And if thoughts disturb and torment you, command in My name, "You have no power!" and I will take care of them.

"The light shines in the darkness, and the darkness did not overcome it."[31]
Without your connection with Me you do not know what true love is and your existence becomes a delusion. It is by imagining that you are separated from Me that you forget who you are - your real identity and, above all, the Presence within and above you. Now I have revealed Myself to you and showed you the way. "I AM" is the only way and the goal of your final attainment of the ascension. No one has ever accomplished anything worthwhile unless, with determination and perseverance, he holds his objective before him.

And what can be more important than the recognition of the very fount of my life and how to drink from it?
I am giving you the key that opens the door to the limitless blessings I always try to pour to you, for all I AM and have is yours to use.

I remind you that the practice of affirmation with the Word "I AM" enables you to free yourself from your limitations and experience the happiness that is the divine plan for you. I am constantly giving you My pure and perfect energy, flowing into your mind and body. I exhort you, for your own sake, not to change and re-qualify it with discordant thoughts or negative expressions like irritation, criticism, worry, depression, self-pity which are self-destructive.

Again, I say to you, and I could never exhaust this subject, use My name as often as possible so that you release its creative power through you. When you pronounce the Word that, as you know, was in the beginning of creation, its energy frequency is the highest in the universe because it is the power of My love. Therefore you raise the rate of vibration of your body and expand the light in every atom of your being.

That's what Jesus did when he stated, "I AM the resurrection and the life."[32]
Yes, the vibratory action of that affirmation correlated and responded to the God Self with whom He was one and it was recorded in His body, and caused it to rise again. Even if you repeat one of His I AM statements only a few times you will never be the same because you will receive also His added assistance. Just try it and you cannot fail to experience the result because you are using the highest Principle of Life. You cannot comprehend all that "I AM" means, but do not listen to your

intellect, rather it should listen to the Word when you send it forth with positive force to repel doubt and confusion.

Now I realize that when I say "I AM" it is the universal life feeling itself through me. It becomes clear why God is love and Its (His, Her) name is "I AM." And the phrase I read somewhere, "Love is knowing "I AM" everything" makes perfect sense because " I AM" is all there is.

In one of your books there is a passage that you could not grasp when you first read it; I hope that now it is clear. "The true use of the " I AM" is to maintain man's original identity in and with his source, not allowing it to descend to include within his nature that which is not. Man is not his experiences, he is what he IS. Experiences with that which seems less than himself should never be admitted into his estimate of himself. I am always that which 'I AM IN SPIRIT,' not what I seem to be in experience, or what I have experienced in the world..."I" in the individual is the first movement of his nature, the central point of his identity. "AM" is that which embodies, or embraces within the "I" – individual identity – whatever it encircles.

The "I" is positive assertion, and the "AM" is the qualifying element. "I" is masculine and "AM" is the feminine principle. The "AM" brings forth into being whatever it embraces or conceives. The "AM" must become immaculate in its embracing power if man is to bring forth that which is in Spirit. "I" which is my identity in Spirit, "AM" that which embraces or embodies all that is in God, is the true use of these words, "I am THAT I am," which is the embodiment of God. I can never in reality be anything but THAT which is in Spirit. " I am THAT I am," and beside me there is no other."[33] (33)

It is very close to your explanation and I understand it.

Meditate on these glorious pair of words, "I" and "AM," because their loving union gives birth, nurtures and infuses life and love into all that is, from atoms to planets and countless universes. With this instruction under this new and final dispensation, whose keynote is forgiveness and mercy, mankind is given the possibility to gain their immortal freedom in the ascension by the purifying fire of divine love. The Earth must come into accord with the other planets of the system to which she belongs in their forward cyclic movement. The purification and the consuming of all destructive energy generated by mankind's misuse of their free will cannot be delayed any longer.

It is the demand of the cosmic Law that rules the universe embodied in Divine Beings, like the Seven Elohim, who are the creators of this system of worlds and sustain it by Their love. The cleansing will come harmoniously if humanity turn to the light and call for it. However, if they go on in their unbridled selfishness and defiance of the Law of Love, the forces of nature will take over and annihilate every record of human evil through cataclysmic activities. The knowledge of the I AM Presence as the God Self of every individual and the creative Word is given as the way and means to attain the freedom from the limitations and distress of the centuries.

It has been written that "In spite of the creed-bound thoughts of a portion of humanity, their traditional and idolized ideas of God, of Christ and man, of self, of life and death, all must go."[34]
The consuming fire of love must come to illumine humanity and purify the Earth, and the consequences for the individual will depend on its attitude toward it. If he draws it into himself with love to its God Self it will free and raise him into the ascension. Should he refuse and resist it, the purifying process is

accomplished by the fire of suffering which is still the action of unrecognized love. I proclaim to everyone of God's children from the love of My heart to theirs, the choice is before you between "I AM" and "I am not."

Between life and death, being or nothingness.
Choose life, and dare to become the God-Being you really are forever One as the I AM Self."

[1] *The Varieties of Religious Experience* (NY: The Modern Library, 1936), p. 498.

[2] Ibid., pp. 498-9.

[3] Quoted in, *The Varieties of Religious Experience,* p. 504.

[4] *Showings, The Long Text, The Fourteenth Revelation,* Ch. 59.

[5] John 1:1.

[6] John 1:3.

[7] Muqatta'at, 56, Das, p. 197.

[8] Indian folklore, traditional.

[9] Abhishiktananda Saccidananda (l SPCK, New Delhi, 1990), p. 40.

[10] Das, p. 76.

[11] John 17:26

[12] John 17:21-22

[13] Muqatta at, 35.

[14] John 14:10.

[15] The Svetasvatara Upanishad, in *The Upanishads: Breath of the Eternal,* transl. Swami Prabhavananda and Frederick Manchester (NY: New American Library, 1957), p. 118.

[16] The Svetasvatara Upanishad, in Walter T. Stace, *The Teachings of the Mystics* (NY: New American Library, 1960), p. 41.

[17] John 1:1.

[18] *Woman,* p. 140.

[19] Genesis 1:31.

[20] *Woman,* p. 10.

[21] Das, p. 122.

[22] William Shakespeare, *Hamlet,* Act 1, Scene 3, Lines 78-80.

[23] Das, p. 110.

[24] Baird T. Spalding, *Life and Teaching of the Master of the Far East,* Vol. III, (Santa Monica, Calif.: DeVorss & Co., 1962), p. 23.

[25] Exodus 15:3.

[26] From "Preface" by Thomas Merton to E. Cardinal, *Love,* p. 8.

[27] Elizabeth Barrett Browning, *Sonnets from the Portuguese*, 43.

[28] Matthew 6:22; Luke 12:34.

[29] Meister Eckhart, Blakney, op. cit., p. 206.

[30] Dwight Goddard, ed., *A Buddhist Bible*, (NY: E.P. Dutton Co., Inc., 1952), p. 362.

[31] John 1:5.

[32] John 11:25.

[33] *Life and Teaching of the Masters*, Vol. IV, pp. 30, 42.

[34] Ibid., p. 63.

CONCLUSION

Now I would like to conclude our dialogue, at least for the time being, and let us see if we can bring even a little light into a darkened world and illumine the path of your fellow human beings who desire to be free and are searching for Me.

Remember what I told you at the beginning of our conversation: intellectual explanations will never satisfy your hunger for the truth.

It is not enough to read the menu, one must eat the food.
I have given you enough knowledge to fulfill all your desires, but you must apply it.

It is not easy.
But it is worthy of every effort you are willing to make, and I am always ready to help you since you are one with My life.

I know that you are love, and love loves to serve.
My fervent hope is that you may join the enlightened ones and sing with them:

> Since we have learned the Alphabet of Love,
> None other text than this can we repeat:
> With the heart's eyes, wide-opened now, behold,
> Whatever we see is but a form of His/Her form!
> Since we have seen the Secret behind the Screen,
> With every breath the song springs to our lips:
> Whatever we see now with the heart's eyes,
> We know it is but a form of the Beloved.[1]

As a final word, whatever you do, try to do it in remembrance of Me so that My love keeps flowing through you uninterruptedly and without interference. Hold the harmony in your feeling, and I plead with you not to use My name in vain, do not follow the words "I AM" with negative words or expressions.

It is the Word that was in the beginning, the Word of love that created the universe. I offer you My infinite power by its use to bring into your life whatever you desire. Do not misuse it any more.

If you will keep My words and apply My teaching, your existence becomes a stream of ceaseless love, each day rich with precious meaning bringing you closer to Me, just as when in love your thoughts are filled with the loved one and the desire of her presence.

You have learned from your past experiences that what the world calls love is merely a counterfeited image, its fleeting pleasures, limited by senses, never fulfilling, and the happiness it seems to give is mixed with anxiety and accompanied by shadows.

I know that our earthly passions are consumed by their own flames and we are left with ashes. You have taught me that we must forgive and forget our mistakes, and I can only echo these words:

> My soul nor deigns nor dares complain,
> Though grief and passion there rebel:
> I only know we loved in vain;
> I only feel – Farewell! – Farewell![2]

Let your thirst for love rise on the wings of devotion and determination to Me, your exhaustless Source, so that you may drink from My heart the life-giving essence of liquid light filling you with its heavenly bliss. Let My love glorify you, come under its rays as Nature beneath the sun, expanding its radiance with each breath. Let it transfigure you until you are all aflame, all love, all joy, and at last, all Mine and I all thine!

Thou, Beloved One, who hast placed Thyself within our hearts to blossom there, who dost watch us and hear our slightest call and knows our every thought, giving of Thyself completely with every breath and heart-beat, seeking to make us your eternal happiness. Thou, who, like a mother, dost never weary and always smile, who dost not only forgive but revive us, elevate us, and make us all that Thou art! Glorify Thou me with Thine own Self, with all the glory which I had with Thee before the world was. Enable me to feel the same love for Thee that Thou feel for me. Possess my life and take me into the furnace of Thy heart, consume every mortal cloud, and transform my flesh by Thy sacred fire that I may die of love and be forever with Thee, in Thee, as Thee!

I will raise you by the power of your own divinity bestowed on you in the beginning. You will be clothed in the immortal garment of dazzling beauty, ascended and free in the light, a victorious God Being, brighter than the noon-day sun!

> I AM the Source of life constantly flowing
> with the light of love forever self-glowing.
>
> I AM the giver of blessing to all I see,
> mother earth, the sun, the sky, and the sea.
>
> I AM the One Self answering every call
> for happiness and mastery over all.
>
> I AM the soft grass, evr'y tree, fruit, and flower

that Nature grows and nurtures each passing hour.

I AM the glory of that I AM shining through
all that is beautiful, good, and true.

I AM countless angels and beings divine,
their joy in music and song is also mine.

I AM my twin flame and each heart of light,
ascended into my God Self's cosmic height.

[1] Sufi Writings, Muqiman Sa'di, in Das, p. 606.
[2] Lord Byron, "Farewell."

Selective Bibliography

o Abrams, M.H. *Natural Supernaturalism: Tradition and Revolution in Romantic Literature.* NY: W.W. Norton & Co., 1971.

o Armstrong, Karen. *Visions of God.* NY: Ballantine Books, 1994.

o Assagioli, Robert. *Psychosynthesis.* NY: Viking Press, 1965.

o Atwater, P.M.H. *Coming Back to Life.* NY: Dodd, Mead, 1988.

o Bailey, Alice. *A Treatise on Cosmic Fire.* NY: Lucis Publishing, 1973.

o Bailey, Alice. *Esoteric Healing.* NY: Lucis Publishing, 1953.

o Bailey, Alice. *Esoteric Psychology: A Treatise on the Seven Rays,* Vols. 1-11. NY: Lucis Publishing, 1979.

o Berendth, J.E. *Nada Brahma - The World is Sound: Music and the Landscape of Consciousness.* Rochester, VT: Destiny Books, 1987.

o Besant, Annie. *A Study in Consciousness.* Wheaton, IL: The Theosophical Publishing House, 1972.

o Besant, Annie. *The Riddle of Life.* Wheaton, IL: The Theosophical Publishing House, 1983.

o Bhagavan, Das. *The Essential Unity of All Religions.* Wheaton, IL: The Theosophical Publishing House, 1973.

o Blavatsky, H.P. *The Secret Doctrine.* London: The Theosophical Press, 1885.

o Bloom, Harold. *Where Shall Wisdom Be Found?* NY: Riverhead Books, 2004.

○ Bracken, Joseph A. *The Divine Matrix: Creativity as Link Between East and West.* Maryknoll, NY: Orbis Books, 1995.

○ Bucke, Richard M. *Cosmic Consciousness: A Study in the Evolution of the Human Mind.* Philadelphia, PA: Innes & Son, 1905.

○ Campbell, Don. *The Mozart Effect.* NY: Avon Books, 1997.

○ Capps, W.H. and W.M. Wright, eds. *Silent Fire: An Invitation to Western Mysticism.* San Francisco: Harper-Row, 1978.

○ Capra, Fritjof. *The Tao of Physics: An Exploration of the Parallels Between Physics and Eastern Mysticism.* Boston: Shambala Press, 2000.

○ Cardenal, Ernest. *Love.* NY: Crossroad, 1981.

○ Cerminara, Gina. *Many Mansions.* NY: Penguin Books, 1991.

○ Charles, C. Leslie. *Why Is Everyone So Cranky?* NY: Hyperion, 1999.

○ Chopra, Deepak. *The Path To Love.* NY: Three Rivers Press, 1997.

○ Cirlot, J.E. *A Dictionary of Symbols.* NY: Philosophical Library, 1962.

○ *Confessions.* St. Augustine.

○ Coomaraswamy, A.K. *Hinduism and Buddhism.* NY: Philosophical Library, 1943.

○ *Course in Miracles, A.* NY: Foundation for Inner Peace, Viking Foundation, 1975.

○ Crookall, Robert. *During Sleep.* London: Theosophical Publishing House, 1964.

o Cuthbert, Don Butler. *Western Mysticism.* Mineola, NY: Dover Publications, 2003.

o Deutsch, Eliot. *Advaita Vedanta: A Philosophical Reconstruction.* Honolulu, HI: East-West Center Press, The University Press of Hawaii, 1969.

o *Dhammapada, The.* Max Müller, trans. and ed. Mineola, NY: Dover Publications, 2000.

o Donoghue, Denis. *Speaking of Beauty.* New Haven & London: Yale University Press, 2003.

o Dossey, L., M.D. *Healing Words: The Power of Prayer and the Practice of Medicine.* NY: Harper-Collins, 1939.

o Dyer, W.W. *Wisdom of the Ages: 60 Days to Enlightenment.* NY: Harper-Collins, 1998.

o Ehrman, Burt D. *Lost Scriptures: Books That Did Not Make It Into the New Testament.* NY: Oxford University Press, 2003.

o Emoto, Masaru. *The Hidden Messages in Water.* Hillsboro, OR: Beyond Words Publishing, 2004.

o *Eros, Agape and Philia: Readings in the Philosophy of Love.* Alan Sobel, ed. NY: Paragon House, 1980.

o Evdokimov, Paul. *Woman and the Salvation of the World:A Christian Anthropology on the Charisms of Women,* trans. A.P. Gythiel. Crestwood, NY: St. Vladimir's Seminary Press, 1994.

o Ferrucci, Piero. *Inevitable Grace: Breakthroughs in the Lives of Great Men and Women — Guides to Your Self-Realization,* trans. D. Kennard. NY: Jeremy P. Tarcher, 1990.

o — *What We May Be.* Los Angeles, CA: Jeremy P. Tarcher, 1982.

o Franck, Adolphe. *The Kabbalah: The Religious Philosophy of the Hebrews.* NY: Bell Publishing, 1940.

o Fromm, Erich. *To Have Or To Be?* NY: Harper-Row, 1988.

o Gibran, Kahlil. *The Prophet.* NY: Alfred A. Knopf, 1995.

o Gilson, Etienne. *The Spirit of Mediaeval Philosophy,* trans. A.H.C. Downes. London: University of Notre Dame Press, 1991.

o Goethe, J.W. *Faust,* Part 1, trans. A. Swamwick. NY: Dover Publications, 1994.

o Govinda, Lama Anagarika. *Creative Meditation and Multi-dimensional Consciousness.* Wheaton, IL: The Theosophical Publishing House, 1976.

o — *Foundations of Tibetan Mysticism.* NY: Samuel Weisar, 1975.

o Graves, Robert. *The Greek Myths,* Vol. 2. London: The Folio Society, 1996.

o Hageneder, F. *The Meaning of Trees.* San Francisco, CA: Chronicle Books, 2005.

o Happold, F.C. *Mysticism: A Study and An Anthology.* NY: Penguin Books, 1971.

o Harpur, Tom. *The Uncommon Touch: An Investigation into Spiritual Healing.* Toronto: McClelland and Steward, 1994.

o Hazo, Robert G. *The Idea of Love.* NY: Frederick A. Praeger Publishers, Institute for Philosophical Research, 1967.

o Holmes, Ernest. *The Science of Mind.* NY: Dodd, Mead, and Co., 1938.

o *Holy Bible, The.* New Revised Standard Version. New York and London: Oxford University Press, 1989.

o Hunt, Valerie V. *Infinite Mind: Science of the Human Vibrations of Consciousness.* Malibu, CA: Malibu Publishing Co., 1996.

o Huntsman, B.W. *Wisdom Is One.* North Clarendon, VT: Tuttle Publishing, 1986.

o Huxley, Aldous. *The Perennial Philosophy.* NY: Harper-Row, 1945.

o Irvin, H.J. *An Introduction to Parapsychology.* Jefferson, NC: McFarland & Co. Publishers, 1989.

o Jaynes, Julian. *The Origin of Consciousness in the Breakdown of the Bicameral Mind.* NY: Houghton Mifflin, 1976.

o Julian of Norwich, *Showings.* NY: Paulist Press, 2001.

o *Koran, The.* J.M. Rodwell, trans. Mineola, NY: Dover Publications, 2005.

o Kundera, Milan. *The Unbearable Lightness of Being.* NY: Harper-Collins, 1995.

o Leadbeater, C.W. *The Hidden Side of Things.* Wheaton, IL: The Theosophical Publishing House, 1999.

o Levine, Barbara Hoberman. *Your Body Believes Every Word You Say.* Fairfield, CT: Aslan Publishing, 1937.

o *Life of St. Theresa of Avila by Herself, The.* J.M. Cohen, Trans. NY: Penguin, 1987.

o Lingerman, Hal A. *The Healing Energies of Music.* Wheaton, IL: The Theosophical Publishing House, 1983.

o Lorimer, David. *Whole in One.* NY: Penguin, 1990.

o Loy, David. *Nonduality: A Study in Comparative Philoso-phy*. Amherst, NY: Humanity Books, 1988.

o Marion, J.L. *The Erotic Phenomenon*, tr. S.E. Lewis. Chicago, IL: The University of Chicago Press, 2007.

o May, Rollo. *Love and Will*. NY: W.W. Norton & Co., 1969.

o *Meditaciones Sobre Cantares*. Madrid: Obras Completes, 1884.

o *Meister Eckhart, A Modern Translation*, tr. R.B. Blakney. NY: Harper-Row, 1941.

o Merton, Thomas. *Contemplation in a World of Action*. NY: Doubleday, 1973.

o — *New Seeds of Contemplation*. NY: New Directions Books, 1961.

o Milton, John. *Paradise Lost*.

o Mircea Eliade, Yoga. *Immortality and Freedom*. Princeton, NJ: Princeton University Oress, 1969.

o Morford, M. and R.J. Lenardon. *Classical Mythology*. NY: Longman, 1971.

o Moshe, Idel. *Kabbalah and Eros*. New Haven, CT: Yale University Press, 2005.

o Nicoll, M. *Psychological Commentaries on the Teaching of Gurdjieff and Ouspensky*. London: Watkins, 1980.

o Nietzsche, Freidrich. *Thus Spake Zarathustra*, trans. T. Common. Mineola, NY: Dover Publications, 1999.

o Norton, D.K and M.F. Kille, eds. Philosophies of Love. Totowa, NJ: Rowman & Littlefield Publishers, 1971.

o *Novum Organum*. Francis Bacon.

o *Other Bible, The.* Bernstone Willis, ed. San Francisco, CA: Harper-Row, 1984.

o Ouaknin, Marc-Alain. *Mysteries of the Kabbalah*, tr. Josephine Bacon. NY: Abbeville Press, 2000.

o Pagels, Elaine. *The Gnostic Gospels.* NY: Vintage Books, 1979.

o Paramahansa Yogananda. *Autobiography of a Yogi.* Los Angeles, CA: Self-Realization Fellowship, 1971.

o Pearce, J.C. *The Biology of Transcendence: A Blueprint of the Human Spirit.* Rochester, VT: Park Street Press, 2002.

o Pearson, E. Norman. *Space, Time and Self: Three Mysteries of the Universe.* Wheaton, IL: The Theosophical Publishing House, 1990.

o Peck, M. Scott. *The Road Less Traveled: A New Psychology of Love, Traditional Values and Spiritual Truth.* NY: Touchstone, 2003.

o Polkinghorne, John. *Belief in God in an Age of Science.* New Haven, CT: Yale University Press, 1998.

o Pope, Marvin. *Song of Songs.* Garden City, NJ: Doubleday, 1977.

o *Problem of Pure Consciousness: Mysticism and Philosophy, The.* Robert Forman, ed. NY: Oxford University Press, 1990.

o Pugh, J.C. *Entertaining the Triune Mystery.* Harrisburg, PA: Trinity Press International, 2003.

o Regis, Martin. *The Suffering of Love.* San Francisco: Ignatius Press, 2006.

o Retallack, Dorothy. *The Sound of Music and Plants.* Los Angeles, CA: Devorss & Co, 1978.

o   Ring, Ken. *Heading Toward Omega: In Search of the Meaning of the Near-Death Experience.* NY: William Morrow, 1984.

o   Schumaker, E.F. *A Guide For the Perplexed.* NY: Harper-Row, 1977.

o   *Sermons.* St. Augustine.

o   Shokek, Shimon. *Kabbalah and the Art of Being.* NY: Routledge, 2001.

o   Solomon, Robert. *Love, Emotion, Myth, Metaphor.* Buffalo, NY: Prometheus Books, 1990.

o   Spalding, Baird T. *Life and Teaching of the Masters of the Far East,* Vols. 1-5. Santa Monica, CA: : Devorss & Co, 1962.

o   St. Catherine of Siena, tr. Suzanne Noffke, O.P. *Dialogue.* NY: Paulist Press, 1980.

o   Stace, Walter T. *The Teachings of the Mystics.* NY: A Mentor Book, 1960.

o   *Synthesis: The Realization of the Self.* San Francisco, CA: Synthesis Press, 1978.

o   *Taoist Classics, The.* T. Cleary, trans. Boston, MA: Shambala Publications, 1996.

o   *Teachings of Rumi, The (The Masnavi).* E.W. Whinfield, trans. NY: E.P. Dutton, 1975.

o   Thompson, Bert and Brad Harrub. *The Origin of Consciousness.* Montgomery, AL: Apologetics Press, 2004.

o   *Treasury of Great Poems, A.* L. Antermeyer, ed. NY: Galahad Books, 1993.

o *Upanishads, The.* Max Müller, trans. NY: Dover Publications, 1962.

o Waite, A.E. *The Holy Kabbalah.* Mineola, NY: Dover Publications, 2003.

o Walsh, R.N., and F. Vaugh, eds. *Beyond Ego: Transpersonal Dimensions in Psychology.* Los Angeles, CA: J.P. Tarcher, 1980.

o Ward, Bobby J. *A Contemplation Upon Flowers: Garden Plants in Myth and Literature.* city: Portland, OR: Timber Press, 2005.

o Watts, A.W. *The Two Hands of God: The Myths of Polarity.* NY: Collier Books, 1969.

o Wei, Wei Wu. *Ask the Awakened: The Negative Way.* Boulder, CO: Sentient Publications, 2002.

o White, John. *The Meeting of Science and Spirit: Guidelines for a New Age.* NY: Paragon House, 1990.

o Wilber, Ken. *No Boundary: Eastern and Western Approaches to Personal Growth.* Boulder, CO: Shambala Publications, 1981.

o Wilber, Ken. *The Spectrum of Consciousness.* Wheaton, IL: The Theosophical Publishing House, 1977.

o Woodward, M.A. *Edgar Cayce's Story of Karma.* NY: Berkley Books, 1971.

INDEX

on self-identity, 100, 109, 111, 119
and Tribune God, 656–57
ecstasy, 667–68
education, self-identity and, 107
ego, self-love and, 453
Egyptians, ancient, 199
Einstein, Albert, 402, 412, 428
electricity, 384–85, 388, 595–96
elementals. *See* Fairies
Elijah, 49
Eliot, George, 422
Eliot, T. S., 361
elves. *See* Fairies
Emerson, Ralph Waldo, 431, 434, 436
emotions
 appetites of, 491
 and congestion, 630
Emoto, Dr., 487–88
energy, 75, 77, 169, 497–98
 and attention, 350
 and consciousness, 388
 Kabbalah, 658
 matter, basis of, 408
 re-qualifying as, 589
 universe as flow of, 576
"energy of life qualified," 130–31
enlightenment, consciousness and, 383
En-Sof (Kabbalah), 659, 664–65
entrapment, feeling of, 96–97
Erigena, John Scotus, 556
Eros, 530, 593–97
Esau, 40
Eternal Feminine, woman as, 480–83
"eternal life," meaning of, 230–31
eternity, 83, 278
etheric realm, 523–24
Eucharist Ceremony, 507
Evdokimov, Paul, 478
evil
 creation of, possibility of, 266–67
 cycle of, bringing to end, 70
 definition, 80
 existence, belief of, 43–44
 selfishness as root of all evil, 218, 629
 tendencies, those with after death, 352
evolution, 277
 and consciousness, 369–70, 373
 and self-love, 453–54

existence
 and consciousness, 367–68, 371–72
 purpose of, 501
 questions on, 4
Exodus, 677
Exodus, 25
expansion, cosmic principle of, 415
experience
 and polarity principle, 413–14
 visualization of, 442–43
eye, comparison of the "I" to, 166–67
eyes and ears as instruments, 142, 155, 180–81

F

faculties
 divine faculties possessed, 536–37
 relation with life events, 533
fairies
 appearance of, 493–94
 Fairy Queen, description of, 494–95
 and humans, differences, 496
 polarity differences, 496
 size of, 495
faith
 and love, 276
 and prayer, 215, 217, 220–23
"fallen angels," 503
falling in love, 478, 480
fall of man, 94, 327
false self, self-love and, 474
family, 532–33
fate and Karma, differences, 19–20
fear, 9–10
feelings
 colors of, 507
 and consciousness, 396–97
 creative nature of, 549
 as feminine site of nature, 535
 from heart, 561–62
 inability to feel, 592
 love as, 619–20
 love, different from, 455–58, 465, 467
 sense of union without, 461–62
festivals, fire, 343–44
final cycle, symbolism, 348–49
fire
 love as, 389–91

ABOUT THE AUTHOR

ALVARO BIZZICCARI received his Doctorate in Philosophy from the University of Rome in Italy before moving to the United States. He is a professor emeritus of humanistic studies at the University of Connecticut.

He is the author of several publications (in Italian), including a book on St. Theresa of Avila, and essays on Christian Mysticism from St. Augustine to St. Francis of Assisi, Dante, St. Catherine of Siena, and Michelangelo's poetry. He can be found online at *www.alvarobizziccari.com*

COSIMO is a specialty publisher of books and publications that inspire, inform, and engage readers. Our mission is to offer unique books to niche audiences around the world.

COSIMO BOOKS publishes books and publications for innovative authors, nonprofit organizations, and businesses.

COSIMO BOOKS specializes in bringing books back into print, publishing new books quickly and effectively, and making these publications available to readers around the world.

COSIMO CLASSICS offers a collection of distinctive titles by the great authors and thinkers throughout the ages.

At COSIMO CLASSICS timeless works find new life as affordable books, covering a variety of subjects including: Business, Economics, History, Personal Development, Philosophy, Religion & Spirituality, and much more!

COSIMO REPORTS publishes public reports that affect your world, from global trends to the economy, and from health to geopolitics.

FOR MORE INFORMATION CONTACT US AT
INFO@COSIMOBOOKS.COM

- ➤ if you are a book lover interested in our current catalog of books

- ➤ if you represent a bookstore, book club, or anyone else interested in special discounts for bulk purchases

- ➤ if you are an author who wants to get published

- ➤ if you represent an organization or business seeking to publish books and other publications for your members, donors, or customers.

COSIMO BOOKS ARE ALWAYS
AVAILABLE AT ONLINE BOOKSTORES

VISIT COSIMOBOOKS.COM
BE INSPIRED, BE INFORMED

CPSIA information can be obtained at www.ICGtesting.com
Printed in the USA
BVOW07s0055100913

330698BV00003B/13/P

9 781616 407407